101 SEA STORIES

Those Tales Marines, Sailors and Others Love to Tell

101 SEA STORIES

Those Tales
Marines, Sailors and Others
Love to Tell

Donald F. Myers

Almar Books
United States of America

Semper Fi to my fellow
Marine Mike Perrone –
Donald F. Myers
10 Nov 2002

Staff Sergeant Donald F. Myers,
U.S. Marine Corps Retired

Two Silver Star Medals	Two National Defense Service Medals
Two Bronze Star Medals V	Korean Service Nedal 1 *
Five Purple Heart Medals	Vietnam Service Medal 7 *
Navy Commendation Medal V	Cross of Gallantry With Palm
Combat Action Ribbon	Medal of Military Merit
Two Navy Presidential Unit Citations	Korean Presidential Unit Citation
Army Presidential Unit Citation	Vietnam Presidential Unit Citation
Two Navy Unit Commendations	Gallantry Cross Unit Citation
Three Meritorious Unit Commendations	Civil Action Unit Citation
Four Good Conduct Medals	Vietnam Campaign Medal

The characters and events in this book are not intended to be fictitious

101 Sea Stories

Those tales Marines, Sailors and Others Love to Tell

Published by ALMAR Books
5342 Elmwood Avenue — Suite G
Indianapolis, Indiana 46203
United States of America

ISBN 1-57197-187-4

Library of Congress Catalog Card Number 01-74221

First Edition
2001
10 9 8 7 6 5 4 3 2 1

Printed in Hong Kong by: Man's Co.
www.pcprinted.com

101 SEA STORIES

Those Tales Marines, Sailors and Others Love To Tell

DEDICATION

To the United States Marine Corps and United States Navy of course.
And to all of those veterans that made this book possible by sharing their "Sea Stories."

OTHER BOOKS BY DONALD F. MYERS

Your War - My War, A Marine In Vietnam
Award winning narrative of a platoon sergeant

Tell It To The Marines
A historical collection of poems and songs for Marines and others

Never Kiss An Angel
Classic novel of a young Marines' first year of service in the early 1950's

Marines Remember World War II
Concise history with emphases on Pacific Island Campaigns
coupled with personal experience stories of men who fought in the war - photos

Custer's Gatling Guns
Novel of what may have happened if Custer would have taken his machine guns to
the Little Big Horn

INTRODUCTION

I've had a writing bug in me since the 4th grade. Nothing wrong with that of course except I didn't do anything about it until retiring from the U. S. Marine Corps on permanent disability in 1973 as a result of combat wounds from the Vietnam War. The Corps was good enough to let me make my 20 years, which I wanted to do even though my fifth Purple Heart left me blind in my left eye and serious right leg damage. It also froze me in rank. For years it had been a desire of mine to write a book and I got started on my Vietnam War memories shortly after my retirement. Boy! I had no idea what I was getting into. I learned the craft of writing the hard way by having people I trusted and admired rip my manuscript to shreds with a blue editing pencil time and time again. It took twelve years to produce a reasonable correct manuscript that my better-educated pals accepted and another six years to find a publisher willing to put my war story in book form. But instead of being fed up of what I'd went through the opposite happened and I can be found most days tap, tapping away on my PC.

The brain-storm of writing a few of my sea stories and invite others to share theirs as well was planted in my mind during the early 1960's while stationed at Camp Lejeune, North Carolina. I love to hear and tell sea stories. Camp Lejeune abounded with guys that not only told their tales over a few beers but also created a few on the spot at the same time. I even managed to create several sea stories in my own right with some of my not so mature antics. Anyway, I thought back then wouldn't it be a great idea to collect some of those tales under one cover to share with the world. It took almost 50 years but I finally got around to doing it. You will not only read my favorite sea stories about myself that Marines are so famous at telling, you are also going to read a goodly share from Marines and sailors around the country that thought well enough of this idea to contribute their own. In addition, you will read a few from members of the other branches of service who reminded me we Jarheads and Swabs don't corner the market on Sea Stories. I have taken author's privilege by getting mine in first but don't despair, there's enough to go around for all hands to get a chuckle or two, or to be amazed at, or to take with a grain of salt.

I sincerely hope you enjoy reading all of these sea stories as much as I did. I had a blast writing mine and working with the other Marines, sailors, etc., to get them on paper the way they wanted them told.

Semper Fidelis

Donald F. Myers

Indianapolis, Indiana

10 November 2001

FOREWORD

By
Rear Admiral Jeremiah A. Denton, Jr., U. S. Navy Retired
Former U. S. Senator, Former POW, Founder National Forum Foundation

In the naval service "Sea Stories" is a way of life. So, just what is a "Sea Story?" A sea story comes in varied forms from the ridiculous to the sublime. Many of them grow in stature with each telling and are told so many times that they become legend.

Truth or fiction? All sea stories have at least a grain of truth in them, especially those about unusual experiences. These are much closer to the truth than many listeners, or in this case, readers, might believe.

The primary categories of which most sea stories evolve have to do with the following: Something you got away with or a stunt or joke pulled on a military superior, fellow sailor or Marine and sometimes civilians. A seemingly outrageously humorous situation, at least it appeared so at the time considering the grim or gallows humor military men acquire. An extraordinary, unusual (at least different) combat event and of course the poignant, sometimes heart rending experiences of war.

There are other areas for sea stories I'm sure, but those mentioned all have the key ingredients.

I greatly admire Marine Don Myers, not only for what he accomplished on the battlefield, but also his foresight by compiling these sea stories that should have been done years ago. How someone else missed the boat by not putting a series of "Sea Stories" together under one cover is a disservice to the naval service and military as a whole.

Jeremiah A. Denton, Jr. Was born and raised in Mobile, Alabama. A graduate of the United States Naval Academy his naval career spanned 34-years.

In 1964, Denton was shot down and capture by the North Vietnamese. He spent the next seven years as a prisoner of war. During a television interview by the North Vietnamese in 1966, he repeatedly blinked his eyes spelling out in Morse code, "TORTURE."

Upon his release as a POW in 1973 and arrival in the Philippines, speaking as the senior officer of his group of fellow POW's, his remarks received international attention. "We are honored to have had the opportunity to serve our country under difficult circumstances. We are profoundly grateful to our Commander-in-Chief and to our nation this day. God bless America."

Among his military decorations, are: The Navy Cross, Distinguished Service Medal, Distinguished Flying Cross, Three Silver Stars, Five Bronze Stars and Two Purple Hearts.

Denton served in the U. S. Senate for six years. He is the author of When Hell Was In Session.

Of course, Don has only brought us 101 of those famous tales. We will just have to wait until his next book, 102 Sea Stories comes out. "Well done Marine!"

Read and enjoy my friend, I certainly did.

FOREWORD

By
Andy Jacobs Jr.
Retired Congressman and Attorney At Law

Don Myers is a Marine's Marine. He has literally "walked through the shadow of the valley of death," and survived. He brought back from combat a sterling record laced with silver and bronze stars, purple hearts and wealth of "sea stories."

Every organization has its legendary tales, some tall, some short and even some that are about the size of truth. "No story," my father said, "ever loses anything in the telling." For example, I don't believe I ever met a Marine in the Korean War who wasn't a champion athlete in his hometown. Immediate verification was not available.

Andy Jacobs:-A native of Indianapolis, Indiana, served in the Korean War as a teenage Marine Corps combat infantryman. Andy served fifteen terms as a member of the US House of Representative between 1965 and 1997. The retired former US Congressman currently teaches courses on American politics. He is also a columnist for the Indianapolis Business Journal and has written three books. In addition, he is a practicing attorney in Indianapolis.

Marine sea stories are the spice of otherwise terrifying, agonizing and painful action against an enemy, the moments of calm and comic or inspirational relief that make it possible to carry on and be depended to do one's duty. They are also capable of making boring peacetime garrison duty more interesting and livable.

One might suppose that Marine or Navy sea stores have a great deal in common with fish stories, somewhat exaggerated, but often scintillating delights to hear, or in this case read.

Sea stories are about the humor of "putting one over on a superior," or about a heart-rending tragedy such as seeing a strong, agile friend suddenly, instantly, become a lifeless and bloody mass of torn flesh and viscera because of a mortar shell that somehow missed you.

Every Marine and sailor has heard and told sea stories, but hardly any could write them as superbly as Don Myers has.

I admire no Marine more greatly that I admire Don Myers. Read on--and know that you are in for a treat.

•

1

GUARD DUTY AT NAVAL MINE DEPOT
Staff Sergeant Donald F. Myers, USMC(Ret.)

My first duty station after boot camp at Parris Island, South Carolina, was the Naval Mine Depot, Yorktown, Virginia during early 1952. I was 17 years old, a big strapping lad of six foot and 175 pounds. Biding my time doing boring guard duty in the pine forest of eastern Virginia along with other young teenage Marines my age didn't set well with me, but I did my best to take it in stride.

All of the 17 year old Marine's at the depot had been told by our barracks gunny, Tech Sergeant Emeilo Charlo that we were being "aged," to that magic day when we turned 18. The importance of our 18th birthday was not lost on us because Gunny Charlo made it a point to tell every youngster to expect orders to the Land of the Morning Calm, better known as Korea, after blowing out those 18 candles.

The four on and eight off, every other day guard duty was enough to drive any teenager up the wall, let alone 17-year old Marines that knew all they had to look forward to was the uncertainty of combat. Being glorified night watchmen was the pits that we all felt was totally useless. Weekends were the worst when the depot was closed up tight with most civilians and military personnel gone. All that remained were those unlucky teenager watch-standees doing their around-the-clock four-on eight-off shifts.

I usually did some stunt to while away the hours to entertain myself in an effort to keep from going bonkers. One of the stunts I enjoyed doing had to do with Post #14. Post #14 was smack dab in the middle of the boonies and consisted of a 200 yard long warehouse which boasted both rail and truck docks along the length of either side of the huge building. All kind of gadgets that went into naval mines and torpedoes were housed in the building. A sentry's job was simple; walk along the perimeter road around the building and report in on a call box every half-hour.

The one thing I liked about Post #14 was the fact the navy left a pickup truck at one of the loading docks. I had found out that the truck did not require keys in the ignition to start it up. Many military vehicles had toggle switches on and off, in lieu of keys. At first I'd only drive the truck in short stretches as I feared having the Officer of the Day or the Commander of the Guard catching me with my pants down some night. But as time went by I got bolder and it wasn't long before I was driving during 80% of my tour of duty. This was one of those little secrets I didn't share with my bunk mates because even ass-hole buddies have a tendency to spread high-jinx going on and I didn't want the wrong ears to hear about me and Post #14.

So it came to pass that I got the twelve-to-four watch on Post #14 during the week-end, which meant both A.M. and P.M., Friday night through Monday morning. Driving the Navy pickup truck during the entire weekend made my miserable tour of duty a lot easier.

After morning chow Monday, my weekend duty over with, Gunny Charlo passed the word he wanted to see the three watch standees that were on the guard roster for Post #14 that weekend. When the three of us reported to the barracks gunny he informed us the Marine Barracks commanding officer, Lieutenant Colonel Lipot wanted to have a chat with us. I'm sure the other two guys who'd shared duty with me on Post #14 during the weekend felt as apprehensive as I did as we were ushered into the CO's office.

Lieutenant Colonel Lipot was a rather short man with dark skin that told of his French heritage. To add to his French Foreign Legion appearance he wore a hairline mustache. After the barracks first sergeant marched us three watch standees in front of the colonel's desk and reported to the CO our commander left us at attention for better than two minutes as he gave each one of us a flinty eyed appraisal. His mustache twitched in distaste when he at last said "Stand at ease."

He then proceeded to have his little chat with the three of us that left me weak kneed.

"It has been brought to my attention that for some time now the Navy has suspected someone has been tampering with one of their vehicles on Post Fourteen. The vehicle in question is a Navy pickup truck, which is kept parked at bay twenty at the warehouse complex. My first question I have, are the three of you aware of the pickup truck I'm referring to?" He looked directly at me because I suppose I was the first Marine to his right. "Private Myers?"

Answering my CO in a voice I hardly recognized as my own I squeaked out, "Yes sir, I know the truck you're talking about."

The colonel went through the same routine with the other two sentries who offered similar replies.

Then he asked us as a group, and awaited our answers one by one, if any of us had seen anything suspicious during our tours of duty at Post #14 and to our knowledge had the pickup truck been there the entire time. All three of us answered that yes we had seen the truck parked all weekend and no, nothing out of the ordinary had taken place.

The Marine lieutenant colonel did a drum roll tattoo on his desk with his fingers, then dropped his bombshell on us. "What the three of you are telling me is highly unusual. The Navy says they wrote down the pickup trucks mileage on Friday afternoon when they closed up shop for the weekend and checked it again this morning. They report that five-hundred and seventy miles was put on that truck from 1600 Friday to 0800 this Monday." He paused for a moment to give the three of us an evil, mustache-twitching stare. "Now I realize you young Marines do some immature things occasionally out there on guard duty for the simple reason you don't have a full appreciation of the importance of your mission. I have stressed time and time again I will not tolerate any goofing off while standing duty as a guard under my command and if this report from the Navy wasn't so far fetched I'd have all three of you standing by for courts-martial. There is no doubt in my mind that one of you has been driving that Navy truck. This I am convinced of! However, I cannot punish all three of you for what one of you has obviously done. I did some rough calculations before I had the three of you come into my office. To put five hundred and seventy miles on that truck each one of you would have had to driven it during your entire tour of weekend duty. That is totally implausible and that's exactly what I'm going to tell the Navy. But let me give you this warning. I don't want to hear of any more reports coming from Post Fourteen. DISMISSED!"

The three of us left the commanding officer's office and after being told by the first sergeant we were being allowed a late start on the normal Monday morning liberty for weekend watch standees, we headed for our squad bay to get out of our dirty uniforms. The three of us had the communal shower room all to ourselves as we got rid of the weekend crud before hitting the liberty gate.

While showering, Dale Edwards, a farm boy from South Carolina, was the first to say something about what we'd just went through. "Ah got to apologize to ya'all fellows, cause I'm the one that was fuck'en 'round with that pickup this weekend. A'hm sorry I got ya'alls tit in the wringer fer my do'ens."

Harry "The Horse" Sneed, a young cowboy from Montana, let out with a guff-haw. "Sheet...you weren't the only one. I drove that some-bitch the whole time I was out there."

The two of them looked over to where I was staring at them dumbfounded. With a sheepish grin, I said. "Yep—me too."

Our outburst of laughter was so loud the charge-of-quarters NCO came into the head wanting to know what was going on that was so funny.

2

PICKING UP TOP SECRET MATERIAL
Staff Sergeant Donald F. Myers, USMC(Ret.)

One of the best stories of my youth while stationed at the Naval Mine Depot, Yorktown, Virginia, took place during the spring of 1952. Being guard company Marines we all knew that some of the weaponry housed at the depot was highly classified with nuclear capabilities. This was all hush-hush of course and as Marines we took it in stride that some of the buildings we guarded or train cars we were responsible for, may have had atomic bomb components in them. No big deal. Except, we did enjoy getting to ride on top of boxcars occasionally as a break from our normal duty routine of walking around some complex out in the middle of the Virginia pine forest.

Corporal John Xavier Williams, was a tough little Irishman that did his job well and expected those under him and over him to do the same. He was a no nonsense Korean combat veteran that was one hundred percent pure Marine. His bantam rooster cocky attitude went well with his flaming red hair and snapping green eyes; but this is not to say he wasn't professional to his roots, just that he was the type of NCO that refused to take much crap from any rank that he thought was unnecessary. My respect for him held no bounds. I was a happy camper when Corporal Williams informed me that I was to be a part of a four-man detail, with him in charge, to go to Fort Eustis, Virginia, to pick up three Army boxcars and bring them back to the Mine Depot. The Army camp was located 25 miles southeast from the depot situated in its own pine forest..

Corporal Williams, two other PFC's and me were all armed with our normal weaponry, which consisted of .45 caliber pistols and 12 gauge, sawed off, shotguns that were called trench-guns. The four of us stood on the narrow steel meshed platform running along the engine compartment on one of the depot's pint-sized diesel switch engines. We held a tight grip on the guardrail for balance as the stubby little engine hummed along toward Fort Eustis. We thought nothing about our light armament since the nearby pickup was considered a routine milk run.

You can imagine our surprise when we neared the siding the three Army boxcars were on and got a gander at a full platoon of soldiers armed to the teeth.

"Jesus! Would ya look at them assholes," Corporal Williams remarked. "What do they think they're guarding, a gold shipment from Fort Knox?"

It was true the Army platoon of about 40 men was loaded for bear. In addition to three light machine guns with crews on top of the box cars in sand bagged emplacements, there were 20 men with M-1 rifles, five with Thompson sub-machine guns, a three man 3.5 rocket team the Army called bazookas. Hand grenades hung from web suspenders and extra cloth bandoleers of ammunition was draped Mexican bandit style across most of the soldiers chest.

With a laugh, I said, "Who do you suppose they think is gonna attack them, a Chinese hoard?"

With a snort, Corporal William quipped. "Shit! I've seen less firepower than that hold off a Chinese hoard."

As we soon found out, our presence wasn't a laughing matter for the Army Military Police captain commanding the detail.

While the depot shuttle engine maneuvered into position to link up with the three boxcars, an angry voice from the tall, skinny Army captain yelled out. "Who's in command there?"

Corporal Williams raised one hand, then climbed down off the engine with the three of us peons right behind him. The Army Captain was wearing a helmet with tankers goggles strapped across the front and field glasses looped around his neck. Taking to no one in particular, Williams muttered. "Who in the hell does this character think he is, General Patton or some such shit?"

True to his professionalism, Corporal William stopped three paces in front of the officer and executed a precise military hand salute. "Sir, Corporal Williams, Marine Security Detail, Naval Mine Depot, Yorktown, reporting to assume responsibility for three Army type boxcars, one each and material thereunto. Sir!"

Appearing dismayed, the tall, skinny wannabe General Patton returned the corporals salute with a cupped hand version of his own like he'd knocked a fly off his eye brow. The officer muttered a quick string of jumbled words. "Captain Fielding hundred-thirty-third-Military-Security-Police-Battalion-Baker-Company-Detachment-Fort-Eustis." He paused for a moment and looking over Corporal Williams shoulder, spoke again, in a firmer tone of voice. "Dija say corporal? Where's your officer?"

"I'm the senior man in charge of the detail sir." Williams answered.

"Well where is your detail then? The pickup time distinctly reads sixteen-thirty hours precisely and there's nothing in my orders regarding meeting up with an advance party."

"This is the Marine security detail sir and I hereby relieve you of the consignment. Do you wish for me to sign a release endorsement on your orders sir?" Corporal Williams said tersely.

"You've got to be kidding! Why do you have any idea what's inside those box....." The Army officer caught himself and took a different tact. "There is no way I will entrust this shipment to four raggedy ass looking Marines!"

That's all it took.

Corporal Williams took a long moment to digest what the officer had said to him, his eyes all but squinted shut. With a minute shake of his head, he said. "With all due respect sir, I ain't got time to fuck around with you and your hundred and thirty-third mess kit repair battalion or whatever....so if ya don't want me to sign an endorsement, me and my men will be going now."

With a stunned look, the Army officer exploded. "Why I just told you I'm not letting you take this shipment anywhere!"

Ignoring the officer's comment the corporal looked up at the switch engine engineer and yelled out. "Willis are you hooked up and ready to roll?"

The old ex-Navy vet sitting high up in the cab of the diesel, and having seen and heard the short exchange down below him, went through a slow ritual before answering. He adjusted his blue and white stripped railroaders cap, wiped his face with a big red and blue patterned bandanna handkerchief, then let fly a large squirt of tobacco juice. Some of the brown juice splattered driblets on the highly polished boots of the Army officer, which seemed to please the engineer because he offered a toothless smile before drawling slowly. "Red...dee ta roll when yew are Johnny me boy."

The Army captain listened to this short exchange totally confused, as he no doubt was not used to being ignored by mere corporals.

The mere corporal in this instance turned to me. "Myers, you on the engine, one man each for the first two cars up on top. I'll take the last car."

I, along with the other two PFC's hopped to it as Willis released the brake handle with a grinding squeak.

A hysterical shout came from the Army captain. "I'm ordering you to stop right this second! I'll have my men to stop you forcefully if I must!"

Corporal Williams eyed the finely uniformed group of well-armed soldiers that were now huddled like a mob behind their leader. The corporal talked loud enough for everyone to hear. "Well, the odds are about right. A fire team of Marines against a platoon of can't hold their line doggies like up at the frozen Chosin. But it's still unfair being only ten to one so I'll tell ya what I'll do, I'll set it out and let you have a go at my three Marines." Williams paused and looked up at the engine and three boxcars.. "Lock and load! And make sure you shoot this sonofabitch wearing railroad tracks first if anyone makes a move toward the train or their weapons."

The three of us on the train casually followed the traditional order to prepare to fire our weapons by cranking shells into the shotguns that made unmistakable metallic sniggering clicks. Then we all three aimed our shotguns at the officer wearing the twin silver bars of a captain.

Willis and his fireman let out a big horse laugh with Willis shouting, "Board...next stop Yorktown!" And he sounded the diesels horn with one sharp blast.

Corporal Williams walked away from the Army captain who was staring at us three Marines aiming our shotguns at him with his mouth agape. The corporal moved up the embankment to the last boxcar that was moving slowly.

The Army officer shot his last salvo off at the departing back of Corporal Williams. "This is gross impertinence and disrespect!"

John caught hold of the boxcars ladder rung and swung aboard. Looking back at the Army captain, he offered a salty salute, saying. "You got that right sir!"

It was a happily manned, laughing little choo-choo train that puffed its way back to the Naval Mine Depot.

It didn't take long for a morale building legend to sweep through the mine depot when word got out how four Marines shanghaied the Army's top-secret load of material right from under the watchful eyes of a platoon of dogfaces. Under normal circumstances higher Marine authority would have taken a dim view of a NCO being sarcastic to a senior officer, regardless of what branch of the service was involved. In this instance however, when the full story came out about how skittish and overbearing the Army captain had been, an exception was made. It was said that the Army was notified to tell their captain that in the future he should handle "Raggy ass Marines," with better leadership. Especially one that was the recipient of the Navy Cross earned at the Chosin Reservoir in Korea who felt the Eighth Army's panicked retreat in November 1950, had caused his unit to be surrounded by thousands of Chinese. Two weeks after this incident, jut jawed, ruggedly handsome John Xavier Williams was meritoriously promoted to sergeant.

3

PLAYING AT BEING A SEABEE
Staff Sergeant Donald F. Myers, USMC(Ret.)

Despite the rigors of Marine Corps Boot Camp the average 17 year old Marine doesn't have the sense God gave a deranged goose. I admit I was in this category and being in a Marine guard company waiting my 18th birthday so I could be sent to Korea only added to my lack of maturity. Walking around out in the middle of the pine forest prevalent around Yorktown, Virginia's Naval Mine Depot was so boring that it was not unusual for teenage Marines to do some odd things.

At a little past 4 A.M., Friday, the 24th of July 1952, I sleepily stumbled from the rear door of the 1947 Dodge panel truck the Navy seemed so fond of.

PFC Gaston, the sentry I was relieving had begun his challenging routine when our Corporal-of-the-Guard Corporal Dan Masters, yelled at him. "You can knock off that challenging bullshit Gaston. Lets get the show on the road if you want to get relieved!"

Gaston was happy to comply and stood in front of me to go through the rest of the silly routine by reporting his post, which was demanded of all sentries before turning over his duty to another guard. "Post twenty-nine is all secure.........."

As the squat, heavy-set teenager droned on I looked over his shoulder at a big yellow earth grader sitting off the road alongside the large warehouse I would soon be walking around. Interrupting Gaston's droning dialogue, I asked. "What's the scoop with the grader?"

The swarthy, rumpled looking PFC turned his head around as it to see what grader I was talking about, and seeing only one, was apparently satisfied that another one had not miraculously appeared. "Some civilian contractors have been fucking around out here for over a week, so I've been told. They're supposed to be lengthening the road around the end of the warehouse that's been enlarged down at the far end. If'n you'ens ask me they've been fuck'en off mostly. A platoon of gyrenes could have done as much as work as they've done with picks and shovels."

Corporal Masters was tired of hearing the crap. "Okay you two...you can stop shooting the shit anytime now——this ain't the fuck'en white house yer guarding!"

I smiled at the dumpy PFC. "Okay Gaston you're relieved."

The fading rear lights of the Dodge panel truck no sooner disappeared back down the long single lane that had brought me to my guard post than I headed for the grader. Like most boys I'd always been fascinated by heavy construction equipment. Now I had one up close and like a kid at Christmas with a new toy to play with I was up in the metal bucket seat sitting on a dirty pillow, looking at all the levers and stuff. After a couple of minutes I pictured myself as John Wayne in the Fighting Sea Bee's and acted like the grader was the bulldozer the Duke drove into the gas storage tanks, heroically saving all his buddies and wiping out the enemy. Growing tired of this vicarious theme I started fiddling around with the buttons and switches on the panel of the mammoth machine. The third switch turned on two large lights attached to the open framed motor mounting. A bright beam of white light stabbed out into the surrounding forest. Luckily it shined directly past the end of the warehouse where my Detex key station was located. I jumped off the grader and made a beeline to the key station to punch in my Detex clock, thus proving I had walked past this part of my post. I glanced at my Detex clock and noted I was ten minutes late, but it wasn't the first time. I had to chuckle to myself as I headed back to the road grader with it twin lights shining. "The damn thing looks like giant bug eyes." I told the surrounding forest.

Once again in the high seat I pushed more buttons. Other than an electrical hum that came from underneath the seat nothing interesting happened. But when I pushed a large black button on the front panel the motor tried to turn over. I kept pushing and the whine of the starter button grew shrill but the motor wouldn't catch. Then I spotted a throttle knob on the panel under the big steering wheel and pulling it out slowly the engine coughed a couple of times, then roared to life. The grader began lurching and jerked ahead a few feet. But the engine died and the huge machine shuttered to a stand still. Looking around some more I saw under the steering column several metal pedals sticking up out of the rippled patterned steel floor of the cab. It came to me in a flash the pedals must be the clutch, brake and accelerator, just like on a car or truck.

A minute later I felt very smug as I tooled slowly down the graveled road alongside the warehouse. Even at slow speed I was bouncing up and down in the tractor like seat and having a little trouble steering the big rear tired monster with its two smaller wheels in front. Being the smart ass I was, I couldn't leave well enough alone and pulled at one of the levers on the metal bar that went across the steering wheel at eye level. The long curved blade on the undercarriage beneath me dug deep into the newly built roadway the civilian construction workers had been laboring on. The grader began to vibrate and jerk badly as it dug into the ground and I over reacted and began pulling the other levers to lift the blade. All I did was to make things worse. The blade underneath me went up and down, left to right and all the time digging a trench like furrow in the road. And I wasn't paying good attention to my driving and was driving over large piles of gravel and dirt; and in general plowing up what work the civilians had done plus pock marking the old road as well. Finally, I got the grader blade under control and the transmission in neutral. Looking behind me to survey the damage that I could clearly see from the illumination of a full moon, I realized I was up to my neck in trouble. A vision of me being imprisoned at the Portsmouth, New Hampshire, Naval Disciplinary Barracks for the next several years crossed my mind as I pondered on what in the hell I was going to do.

After thinking it over I came to the conclusion that my only chance was to try and repair the terrible damage I'd created. But before I could do that I had to learn how to properly operate the road grader. I got the grader behind the back end of the warehouse out of sight of the main road leading to the storage area, and got to work. I took out my notebook and ripped one of the small perforated pages off the coiled wire and printed the letter A on it with my pencil stub. Using my flashlight I pointed it at the row of levers and with a nervous hand pulled down the one furthermost to my left. When I saw what the blade did from this action I printed another letter A in my notebook and jotted down next to the letter what I'd seen the lever do. Then I tagged the lever by placing a small strand of electrically wire I'd found on the deck of the cab and placed it through the notebook paper I'd printed an A on and twisted it around the lever. Gingerly testing the next lever I saw that this one tilted the blade to the left and the more I pulled it down, the sharper the tilt. I tagged this lever B and as before jotted down my finding under B in my notebook. I did the same thing to all the other levers and buttons until I knew roughly what each function they performed. It took me awhile to do all of this and when I glanced at my Detex clock I saw I was late again on keying in the thing and rushed to the next key station on foot to make the report. I no sooner got back to the grader and had it revved up when I saw headlights in the distance bouncing up and down at the far end of the access road to the warehouse. I was already a nervous wreck but had sense enough to know I couldn't let whom ever it was drive along the side of the warehouse looking for me. I turned off the machine and took off at a run toward the front of the building where the access road teed into the warehouse parking area.

I got there just in time as the glare of the headlights swept over me and I saw it was one of the pickup trucks we used at the guard company. I got my shotgun off my shoulder and at port arms with one hand and put the brass pea whistle in my mouth and blew it as hard as I could. Then shouting at the top of my lungs, "HALT——WHO GOES THERE?"

The truck immediately braked to a stop and a voice came from the open window. "Commander of the guard!"

Continuing the standard military procedure for challenging, I shouted, "Commander of the Guard, dismount from you vehicle and advance in front of your vehicle headlights to be recognized."

Expecting these instructions, a short, bordering of obese staff sergeant got out of the pickup truck and walked in front of the headlights.

I knew the commander of the guard for the night was Staff Sergeant Thompson, the overweight chief clerk in charge of the barracks administrative office. "Commander of the Guard recognized." I approached the staff sergeant and stopping the required three paces in front of him, stood at attention with my shotgun at the port and barked out the final part of the required ritual. "Commander of the Guard, PFC Myers reports that post twenty-nine is all secure with no unusual activity!"

The round-faced staff sergeant responded in a soft tone of voice. "At ease Myers. So how's it going out here? Pretty dull huh?"

"You got that right staff sergeant." I replied, aware of fact Staff Sergeant Thompson had the reputation of detesting his four times a month extra duty of having to be the Commander of the Guard.

Nodding his head in a sympathetic way the staff sergeant spoke to me not only in a friendly manner but in a conspiratorial tone as well. "I don't have much to pass on, 'cept Cap' tin White the OD has already checked out to quarters with no piss call made, so the odds are you won't be visited by him tonight."

Normally, I would have enjoyed the visit by the Officer of the Day and guard commander, as it broke up the monotony of standing watch. But not this night.

Staff Sergeant Thompson spoke up again, this time in a jovial tone of voice. "Say, I've got a thermos of coffee here'n the front seat 'long with some paper cups if you'd like a cup."

"That's real nice of you staff sergeant, I wouldn't mind a cup. It'll taste pretty good about right now."

Smiling broadly, the squat NCO said. "That's why I always bring it along. I know this shit sucks out here for you guys and I kind'a figure it'll cheer ya up a little."

While Thompson filled my cup with black coffee, he remarked. "I best be taking off as soon as you get yer java: got six more post to visit before I can call it a night."

I couldn't see any harm of buttering him up a little, so I said. "Well the coffee is sure appreciated. Not many Commander of the Guards look out for the troopies like this."

My BS had him smiling from ear to ear. "Hey———I used to be a peon once myself. The way I look at it, you look out for your troops and they'll look out for you in the long run. That's one of the reasons you don't see me try'en to sneak up on any sentries out here. I come out here, get my job done and that's it! Hang loose Myers, I'll see ya later."

He turned his pickup truck around in the big gravel parking area and waved at me as he drove past, heading back down the long access road. I stayed planted where I was at, sipping the luke-warm coffee, waiting for the taillights to disappear. When they were out of sight I continued to stand there for a couple of minutes. Regardless what he had said, I couldn't take the chance he would double back like some of the commander of the guards did with their headlights off in an attempt of catch you doing something you shouldn't be doing. The dilemma I was faced with already showed I'd done something I shouldn't have done.

With less than three hours to try and straighten up the mess I made. I finally headed back to the road grader to get to work.

By the time I heard the distant rumble of the Dodge panel truck stopping at various guard post that Saturday morning, I had finished the job I'd set out to do. Once I got the hang on how to operate the grader by reading my notebook directions and working the alphabetized levers, I'd worked my tail off. I only stopped long enough to punch in my Detex clock and make the once an hour call in from the telephone call box. All the ditches, furrows and various holes were filled with dirt and gravel and smoothed out. The only worry I now had was I may have done too much. I know there were several piles of dirt and gravel the civilians had piled up around the new construction that wasn't there now, and in my haste, I must have smoothed them in the roadway as well. Oh well! Hopefully, no one would ever be the wiser.

(I was dead wrong about no one knowing what I'd done. After Monday morning roll call, the nine sentries that had the duty Friday night through early Monday morning were summoned to the barracks commanding officers office. Lieutenant Colonel Lipot had a long chat with the nine of us wanting to know if anyone had seen any work being done on Post #29. It seemed the straw boss of the civilian road builders was accusing the Navy of using Seabees to finish up the work they'd started. The Navy naturally said no and go talk to the Marines. I liked to shit my pants when Colonel Lipot held up a grimy, torn page of a note pad that had a rough letter D printed with pencil on it. It had been found on the floorboard of the road grader. Did any of us know how this piece of paper got in the road grader and what it signified? The colonel looked at us all with an icy stare when one by one we denied knowledge of the torn piece of note pad paper with the bit of wire dangling from it. No more was said about this situation until October 1952, when I got my orders to report to the staging regiment at Camp Pendleton, California as an overseas replacement to the 1st Marine Division. The barracks sergeant major bid me farewell and the last thing he said to me was, "And don't go building any roads over there——hear Myers!" How the senior NCO knew about my escapade is still a mystery to me to this day since I didn't tell anyone.)

4

A MORTAR ROUND IN KOREA
Staff Sergeant Donald F. Myers, USMC(Ret.)

I was a heavy machine gunner, the old water-cooled .30 caliber, that February of 1953 when talks of peace spread throughout the allied units in Korea.

By this stage of the war all Marine outfits were firmly dug into defensive positions above the 38th parallel. Weapons Company of 1st Battalion, 1st Marines, 1st Marine Division, was no exception and we hunkered down in fairly roomy sandbagged bunkers when not standing watch.

Even though I was only 18 years old I had read enough about history to have the feeling what we were going through was much like what the Dough Boys of World War I had experienced. The war of big movement had long since passed by, by the time I got to Korea and living in bunkers and fighting from trenches was a way of life that we endured as best we could. I joked with my fellow teenage Marines that it seemed only apt that the date on my weapon was 1917. My machine gun section of two guns was attached to Abel Company 1/1. The infantry boys had to go out on daily patrols down around no-mans land in front of our Main Line of Resistance (MLR). Since the heavy machine guns were dug into bunkered pits with fixed fields of fire along probable enemy approaches, we didn't have to go on these daily patrols. Besides, each rifle company had their own weapons platoon of which .30 caliber air-cooled machine guns were a part of in the event heavier firepower was needed.

Sometimes a rifle squad or platoon (depending on the size of the patrol) would bring back a captured Chinese soldier. In a way I felt kind of sorry for these Chinese because their quilted uniforms and tennis shoe style foot wear was just no good for the freezing weather and snowy conditions we were living with. Occasionally, one of our patrols would stumble upon an enemy patrol and a hard, sharp firefight would result. Other than these forays life was fairly peaceful along our sector of the war.

At least it was until the CCF (Peoples Chinese Army we called Communist Chinese Forces) high command decided to start pelting our lines with 82mm mortar fire. Hundreds of enemy mortar rounds would rain down upon us in a heavy barrage, which would last for a couple hours, then all of a sudden they would stop firing. Then what they'd do was pick out one section of our defensive line and try and zero in on that position with a single mortar tube by walking rounds all over the area in an attempt to knock out whatever particular target their forward observer had selected for the day. In doing this the Chinese sort of got into a rut. What I mean by this is they'd tear hell out of one portion of the trench line and the following day it would be a location practically next door to what they'd aimed for the day before. This selectivity of hitting our lines with this one tube gave us a good idea what position was going to catch hell the next day. It didn't take much smarts for our infantry captain company commander to figure out to move all his people from the sector that appeared to be the next target for the Chinese mortar.

At about o-eight early on the 23rd of February a runner from the CP informed me the skipper wanted to see me at his bunker. I put my A-gunner in charge of our machine gun and traversed the muddy trench line to reach the command post bunker. The captain was terse and to the point on what he had to say. He told me my heavy machine gun bunker was the likely target for the Chinese mortar that day and he assigned his company gunny to go with me to help select a temporary position for my gun to be placed out of harms way.

The wiry, short gunny and I threaded our way through the long narrow trench which was dug into the military crest, which is to say the downward slope of the large mountain like hill we was on. Before reaching my machine gun pit that was bunkered with sand bags with a log top, the gunny paused and stared up the snowy slope behind our trench. "Lets climb up there," he said, pointing a gloved hand toward the top of the snow covered hill. "We'll be better able to find you a new location from up there so your heavy will still have a good field of fire." We had to practically go up the slope on our hands and knees since the snow was so deep it made walking through it almost impossible. Once on top however, it was not so deep due to the wind blowing the snow in drifts we'd just went through. It was colder than all get out though and the gunny laid down in the snow with just his head looking over the crest so he could scope out the trench line below. I got down next to him with about five feet separating the two of us. The guns knew his business because the wind wasn't as piercing lying down like this. We had no sooner begun scanning the area below us when the hollow pop of a mortar leaving its tube alerted us that incoming was on its way. With a minced oath the gunny said, "Shit! They're starting early today."

The banshee wail of the arching mortar round grew shrill but I wasn't overly concerned, figuring it was meant for the trenches below. But when the gunny yelled out loudly "OH SHIT!" it dawned on me we might be in trouble. The trouble came quickly as the screeching Chinese 82mm mortar round hit between us with a resounding PLOP. I know I must have looked as wide eyes as the gunny did and like a couple of idiots we stared at the tail fin of the mortar round sticking up in the snow between us for a couple of seconds before delayed reaction in our brain-housing caused each of us to roll away from the small bomb. Anyway you look at it our reaction was a waste of time for even with a delayed fuse the thing would have got us before we could have gotten out of the kill zone. The gunny shouted, "Fuck this shit," and dived over the crest to the snowdrifts below, rolling down hill like a runaway train. I was right behind him!

A thousand to one mortar shot that turned out to be a dud! Must have really pissed off the Chinese FO (forward observer.)

5

YOU CAN STILL GET INTO TROUBLE FOLLOWING ORDERS
Staff Sergeant Donald F. Myers, USMC(Ret.)

Upon my return to the United States in January 1955, after having served in Korea and Japan and a visit off the shores of Indo China, I was given orders to report to the Marine Barracks, Naval Ordnance Plant, Indianapolis, Indiana, to await discharge after a 30 day overseas returnee leave. The Marine Corps wasn't aware of the fact that I'd decided to sign on for another hitch.

Boy, was I happy! Here I was stationed right in my hometown and would more than likely stay here for a couple of years after I shipped over for six. And good duty it was in so far as military creature comforts was concerned. The Marine security detail only consisted of around 45 personnel and our barracks squad bay looked more like a large bedroom with partitions than gloomy sleeping quarters. Each Marine even had his own dresser drawer in addition to his wall locker and footlocker. Plus single racks to sleep on and outstanding chow. The mess hall was actually a small building directly across the street from the office and living area at the main gate of the plant. We ate off real china and of all things we had a waitress. This was unheard off as for as I was concerned and it never failed to amaze me when I gave my chow order to the lady who waited on us. The duty wasn't that bad either. Besides the main gate guard post there was a morning and evening post called the Arlington Avenue Gate. This was only manned when the civilian and Navy people came to work and left for home. There was also an inside gate before going into the large building that was the primary plant which dealt with all kinds of naval weaponry. This same plant had developed and manufactured the Norton bomb-sight during World War II. During the afternoon when the civilian work shift was over Marines had to man the main building and scan open lunch boxes and any packages as the workers left for home. The only really disagreeable duty was the nightly perimeter fence patrol that armed enlisted Marines had to walk. The entire complex was four city blocks by four Blocks Square so that made for a pretty long trek at night, especially in the winter with the cold wind blowing and snow drifting against the fence.

I guess I didn't make a good first impression with my new first sergeant and he saw to it I was kept busy and it seemed I spent a lot more time walking the perimeter fence line than some of my peers. In some respects I could understand my first sergeant's displeasure with me since I more than likely appeared to him as being too salty for my own good. I was rather cocky and after more than three years service was a private, having got busted several times along the way. Among my five Korean War ribbons there was one award that was conspicuously missing: the Marine Corps Good Conduct ribbon. Plus, no doubt the first shirt had taken a gander at my punishment page in my service record book. I wasn't really a bad Marine, just a mischievous one and still immature. What barely kept my head above water with my superiors; was the fact I worked as hard as I played and didn't bitch about any duty given me regardless of how bad a shit detail it was.

All the same this particular senior NCO was constantly on my back and reminding me to follow orders to the tee. He'd already chewed out my ass real good for one incident that had taken place since I'd reported aboard and even though I thought that situation was stupid. I was trying to be very careful of my duty and I felt he gigged me for no good reason. What had happened to bring down the first sergeants wraith on me took place during a blinding blizzard. I had fence line patrol and the snowy wind had caused three to four foot piles of snow to form along the wire mesh fence. The snow drifts came out eight feet or so from the high, barb-wired topped protective barrier.. So using my 20-year-old logic, with what I thought was common sense, I walked a path on the outside of the drifting snow. It just so happened that the first sergeant had Commander of the Guard duty this night and when he traced my path to check up on me, he let me know in no uncertain terms that when I was told to walk the fence line it meant just that, not ten feet from the fence. I damn near came down with pneumonia slogging through three-foot drifts for four hours.

A few days later the first shirt calls for me to come to his office before 0730. I'm still pissed about the snowdrift chewing out and wasn't in the mood for anymore of his chicken-shit but braced myself for whatever ram he had in store for me. It wasn't as bad as I thought it would be. He told me since the Navy Doc (enlisted corpsman) said I was on the sick list, (bad cold caused by the fence line tour) he was taking me off perimeter fence duty and reassigning me to the Arlington Avenue Gate the following morning and other light duty until I got to feeling better. It wasn't that he was being benevolent and he managed to get his zinger in on me by saying: "You will insure your gate is secured at oh-eight hundred. Now Myers, that doesn't mean at oh-seven fifty-nine or oh-eight oh-one. You read me? Oh-eight hundred on the nose!"

Early the next morning the first sergeant was standing by at the barracks as I was leaving for the Arlington Avenue Gate. First he gave me the once over and evidently satisfied that my freshly pressed green uniform with white barracks cover and military police accouterments was ship shape, he reminded me again what he'd told me about closing the gate at 0800 on the dot. He even went so far as to check my watch to make sure it was on Naval Ordnance Plant time.

Arlington Avenue ran north and south and the gate I was to man was on the west side of the Naval Ordnance Plant not far from the south end of the complex. Directly on the other side of the south fence was a military housing area for senior officers. The Navy Captain who was the senior officer at the plant lived there with his family as did my commanding officer a lieutenant colonel. Other Navy and Marine brass lived there also in the six very nice looking one and two story brick homes.

By the time I arrived at the gate at 0600, after walking from the Marine barracks, early bird plant employees were already lining up along Arlington Avenue waiting for me to open the gate. I actually didn't have much to do other than wave cars into the plant and stop southbound traffic on Arlington to let the people coming from the north to cut across the street over through the gate. As it neared 0800 I walked from the middle of

Arlington Avenue back inside the government property in preparation of locking the gate and heading back to the barracks. I positioned myself behind the gate and was looking at my watch on my left wrist while my other hand was on the gate, ready to slam it shut. As the second hand on my watch swept up to the 0759 mark I heard the loud bang of a door being slammed shut that came from over in officers country which was about 200 yards away. I didn't even glance up and continued to gaze at my timepiece. Then I heard the sound of a car door being shut loudly that was followed immediately by an automobile engine being started and the rev of the motor as someone steeped on the gas, with tires screeching. My second hand was nearing twelve along with the upright minute hand when the car roared around the corner less than a block away and sped up Arlington Avenue toward my gate. Brakes squealed as the new looking car did a screeching right turn into the gate entranceway at about the same time as I slammed the gate shut with a resounding THUNK-CLICK. As I put the padlock in place on the gate the door of the car opened and out stepped a Navy four-stripper, a full captain, the equivalent rank as a Marine bird colonel. I glanced at the Navy officer as I started to turn away to walk back to the barracks and he in turned yelled at me. "You—there—Marine stop—open the gate!"

I stopped and turned around. "Sir, my orders are to close this gate at oh-eight hundred and I was given those orders on the threat of a court-martial."

The uniformed Navy captain sputtered for a couple of seconds, then said, "I'm the commanding officer of the Naval Ordnance Plant and I'm ordering you to open this gate!"

For half a second I was tempted to do as the man had ordered. But they weren't about to get me in that trick-bag! I'd never seen the Navy CO of the place before and far as I knew this could be an elaborate set-up concocted by my first sergeant to test me. So, without saying anything further to the astonished officer, I turned on my heel and walked toward the Marine barracks.

Guess who was waiting for me when I arrived? Standing next to my commanding officer and first sergeant was the Navy captain whom I'd just denied access to the Arlington Avenue gate. (The naval officer had driven on around to the main gate.) To put it mildly my CO wasn't in a happy frame of mind. When he got done chewing on me I blurted out my orders from the first sergeant and how he'd threatened me with disciplinary action if I didn't shut the gate at exactly 0800.

After giving his first sergeant a baleful stare, the lieutenant colonel turned back to me. "Private Myers, there are some orders you are supposed to use common sense with...don't you have any sense of logic?"

CAMP ELMORE'S NEWSPAPER
Staff Sergeant Donald F. Myers, USMC(Ret.)

I didn't last a year at the Naval Ordnance Plant, Indianapolis. I don't know who was more surprised when I re-enlisted, my first sergeant or my commanding officer. Anyway, as it turned out, it must have been determined that I wasn't suitable for such prestigious guard duty and I got transfer orders to Norfolk, Virginia, with a reporting date of 15 January 1956.

My new duty station, Camp Elmore, was a little known top-secret communications complex located between Headquarters, Fleet Marine Force Atlantic and the Norfolk Naval Air Station near Camp Allen, the Tidewater Naval disciplinary barracks (brig.)

I had no idea what in the Sam hill I was supposed to be assigned to do at Camp Elmore. My orders were somewhat vague in that they stated "Report to the Command-ing Officer, Headquarters, Camp Elmore, Norfolk, Virginia, for duty." I had absolutely no skills or training in military electronic communications, nor did I have an MOS (mili-tary occupational specialty). For whatever reason, Marine Barracks, Indy had taken away my machine gunners MOS and reverted me to a 9999, Basic Marine. I was a hash mark private boot!

This fact was not lost on my new first sergeant when I reported in to Headquarters, Camp Elmore.

Master Sergeant Timothy O'Connor took one look at my orders and then at me. He slammed his big hand down on his desk. "And just what in the hell am I supposed to do with you?"

Standing at rigid attention in front of the first sergeants desk I sure as hell didn't know what he was supposed to do with me, so I kept my mouth shut.

Glancing at my red and green hash mark on my battle jacket, then at my two rows of ribbons and weapons expert badges, my new first shirt shook his graying sandy haired-head sadly. Then, as if almost talking to himself, he said, "Don't have a secret clearance let alone a top secret clearance, and a page twelve (punishment page in Marine service record book) that looks like the Sunday comic strip, so that means security duty is out of the question. Someone in personnel at Headquarters, Marine Corps is really pulling a fast one on me." He drummed his fingers on his desk in a loud tattoo for more than several seconds, staring at me with his squinty blue eyes the whole time. Again the palm of his huge hand hit his desk with a resounding slap! "Okay Myers, here's what we're going to do. You see that little table back there?" He turned slightly in his chair and pointed to a small table with a coffee urn on it with cream, sugar, several white mugs and spoons that was behind his desk. "You're going to be in charge of the coffee mess! Go across the hall and getcha-self one of those folding chairs and put it next to the table. Your job is to make sure there is fresh coffee, cream, etcetera, on that table at all times. You will also keep the area policed up and when the colonel calls for a cuppa' coffee you will immediately get him one. Do you have any questions?"

"I don't know where I'm supposed to live first sergeant."

The six foot six craggy faced master sergeant gave me a pained look and muttered, "Why me Lord, why me?"

I ended up sharing a room with a young Navy Chaplain's assistance that wore thick eyeglasses and looked like he was going to burst out in tears at any moment. Actually, my new living quarters was pretty fancy living for a private as I was used to a dormitory squad bay. And with no weekend duty and liberty every afternoon beginning at 1630, I felt I'd fell into a nice little barrel. I didn't find being in charge of the coffee mess as demeaning and other than being bored out of my mind the first few weeks was most satisfied with being aboard the high wired compound that was half the size of Naval Ordnance Plant with wall to wall buildings. I'd pulled liberty in Norfolk when stationed at Yorktown Naval Mine Deport so knew the places to stay away from and where to go to have a good time.

It wasn't long before the first sergeant had me running errands for him in addition to the coffee mess and I sort of became his unofficial go-fer. A lot of paper work crossed his desk and he was always pecking away at his manual typewriter. He was a two-finger typist who preferred to do a lot of his own administrative work than trusting it to the clerk-typist section down the hall from his office. He came rushing into his office one day with a stack full of papers and talking to no one as he often did, said, "I haven't got time for this shit! No one reads the damn thing anyway!" Then he eyed me. "Myers, do you know how to type?"

"I failed typing in high school first sergeant," I answered.

"Oh..that's just great. Why does that not come as a surprise to me? Well, you're going to bone up on your failed skills. The colonel is raising hell that we haven't published the camp newsletter in two months since our public relations winnie got transferred out and he's ordered me to take care of it. Here's all the stuff the PR guy left behind. Look through it and come up with something to put on a stencil. I don't suppose you know how to run a stencil copier do you?"

"No, but I can learn." I said, taking the package of papers from the first sergeant.

"Fine. Go down to the clerks office and tell the admin chief I sent you to learn how to operate the mimeograph machine. You can use that empty office directly across the hallway and I guess for the time being you can forget about the coffee mess. This months edition of the stupid newsletter is already late so hop to it and get something typed out and distributed." He paused for a moment like he was trying to think of something he'd forgot to say. Then, shaking his head, he muttered to me. "Okay, that's it; get the damn thing done and distributed. Oh...that's what I wanted to say. Even though nobody reads the damn newsletter except the colonel you've still got to print up three-hundred of 'em and see to it that about twenty-five each is given to every section leader in the camp. You can put 'em in their pigeon holes out in the admin office when yer done."

I fell in love with my new assignment immediately. Me a newspaper editor! Wait a second: not only was I the editor I was also the publisher, the reporter, the whole kick and caboodle. Visions of Clark Kent and Lois Lane, The Daily Planet and Super-Marine all flooded my brain housing. When I was a kid of around 11 or 12 I'd gotten one of those tin toy printing presses where you set the rubber type and run a piece of paper through it. I must have had visions of literary glory even back then because I remember enlisting the help of my best pal Larry Bickley and we toiled for hours putting out a four by six sheet I titled The Harlan Street Press.

After reading over all the material the first sergeant had given me from the former newspaper Marine, the first thing I felt was needed was a more profound mast head title. CAMP ELMORE NEWS just didn't have a ring to it, which was what the old newsletter was titled. I pondered on that for a while until finally deciding that THE ELMORE LEATHERNECK had a much better ring. After reading about a dozen of the old news-letters my predecessor had published I saw why the first shirt had said that nobody read the damn thing. There was nothing personal written about anyone or anything taking place inside the camp. About the only news in it was the monthly schedule the Marine reserves would be aboard for their weekly drills. The rest of the two page, front and back sheet offered cut out items from the two Marine magazines, Leatherneck and Gazette. I knew I had my work cut out.

After renaming the newsletter I sharpened my pencils so to speak and went out on a tour of Camp Elmore in my new role of roving reporter. I took all sort of notes of various observations I made inside the aging compound that I thought would fit nicely into a monthly column I was toying with. Sort of an expose' thing to fill up space in the news-letter; like the rusty fire escape I came across on one of the radio relay buildings. I mean what would happen if the place caught on fire and all those people topside came rushing out onto the fire escape and it collapsed on them? And who did the MP's think they were speeding all over the place when they ticketed everyone else rigidly? And why could officers and staff NCOs go into the mess hall anytime they wanted to for a cup of coffee and snack? You get the picture of what my expose' column was going to be. Something to really spice up the old newsletter with interest items the enlisted men could relate to. I also hit the PX, the mess hall, slop chute and chapel and got some spicy info for fill in items from these places too. My wimpy roommate who worked at the chapel turned out to have a wealth of knowledge concerning all kinds of juicy tid-bits on going on that I could hardly wait to get into print. The short-statured sailor was the ultimate gossiper. I also decided to have a "Meet The Trooper" article each month, which would give the peons like me a chance to see their name in print. I topped off my investigative reporting by interviewing a second lieutenant at the ultra-top secret radio decoding facility located inside Camp Elmore. This was the most secure place in the camp, a box like one story brick structure enclosed with barbed wire and sally port gate. It had tall antennas stick-ing up all around it and the inside walls were reinforced with steel plating that I didn't know about until talking to the lieutenant. I had a bitch of a time even getting inside the damn place and only managed to reach the front foyer by my insistence that First Ser-geant O'Connor had sent me over to talk to any officer for an article in the camp newsletter. The second lieutenant was pretty nice about my mission and we talked for 20 minutes. I thought I'd also mention the steel plating inside the place. Probably a lot of people didn't know about that.

All in all, I figured I'd done real good, and once back at the headquarters building I begun to rough out The Elmore Leatherneck in the small office that was now mine. I wrote out in long hand a dozen or so articles that would go into this first issue of the upgraded newsletter. Then I typed everything I'd written on bond paper to get an idea what the thing was going to look like. Since I wanted the thing to look like a newspaper, headline and all, I quickly found out that I had enough material for a four-page edition. I must have went through a half dozen legal size blue stencils before getting the hang of it how to use a stylist to print the mast head and head line. The typing came much easier, although very slow since I hadn't used a typewriter since high school. Typing a stencil is a lot different than typing on paper and at first, with my heavy hand on the keys, I must have used a half bottle of blue correction fluid to repair ruined letters. The first sergeant wasn't helping me any either as he kept popping in wanting to know how I was doing and when did I expect to get the paper done. I finally told him I'd work all damn night if necessary to get the newsletter completed. He seemed very pleased with my dedication.

As it turned out, I was almost a man of my word. It was past normal working hours and I was still on the typewriter. Around 1900 I was finally ready to go to press. I took my completed stencils to the repro room next to the deserted admin office to try out my newly learned skills at running a mimeograph machine. After getting ink on me and about everything else in the small room I turned on the machine and stared at it dumbfounded as it began spitting out ink wet paper all over the place at a tremendous rate of speed. I fumbled around until I was able to stop the thing but it was to late for the front-page stencil I'd cut. It was ripped right down the middle and would have to be re-typed. A little late, I discovered the mimeograph machine had various speed settings and it was obvious it had been on full tilt when I turned it on. An hour later I was again back in the repro room with a freshly typed front page. Putting the mimeograph on slow speed I smiled as sheet after sheet of legal paper begun to fill the tray under the big rotating drum. By midnight I had scrubbed most of the ink off my hands and face and was in my rack feeling pretty good about myself.. The Elmore Leatherneck was folded neatly and in the proper pigeonholes for distribution in the morning. I could hardly wait for the reaction of my readers once they took a gander at what a base newsletter was supposed to look like.

The reaction didn't come until the day following the initial distribution.

After returning to the headquarters building from noon chow, the first sergeant walked into my newspaper office and said the colonel wanted to see the two of us right away. My grin was a mile wide that was in stark contrast to the first sergeants dour expression. But then, he wasn't going to get all the praise for a job well done like our commanding officer was going to bestow upon me.

Colonel Farmer was a handsome man with blond short-cropped hair and a ruddy complexion. The rather tall, slim officer could have been a prototype for a Marine Corps recruiting poster. He put the first sergeant and me at ease right after we reported to him. His icy blue eyes looked directly at me with an expression of appraisal and he said, in a soft tone of voice. "So you're Private Myers?"

I answered "Yes sir."

He sort of shook his head a couple of times, then said. "Well Private Myers, let me tell you a couple of things. During my two years as commanding officer at this camp the one thing that was constant was the lack of enthusiasm for our camp newsletter. I'll even go so far as to say the monthly newsletter was the lowest priority on our administrative totem poll, and as First Sergeant O'Connor would so succinctly put it, nobody read the damn thing in the first place. Perhaps, no one did take an interest in the newsletter but since it is regulations that we put one out, it is one of those items of business I had to insure was done." He paused for a second, I suppose to make sure I was listening to him, which of course I was. Then he continued. "But you have seemed to have changed all of that overnight. My telephone has been ringing off the hook since yesterday. Not only has every officer in charge of the various sections on camp been calling me, which is to say, includes, the PX officer, guard officer and mess officer, I even received a call this morning from FMFLANT, the generals office, his adjutant. Your effort has been far reaching. It seems everyone is now reading Camp Elmore's newsletter. What is it you've renamed it? Oh yes, The Elmore Leatherneck———anyway people everywhere are now talking about the newsletter with great enthusiasm. Your headline and lead story about the fire escape even brought in a telephone call from Norfolk's own Virginia Pilot who wanted to send a reporter out for a follow up article about the decaying conditions here. And I don't suppose you were aware that Private Morison, who was your trooper of the month, has just been released from Camp Allen and is awaiting a bad conduct discharge!"

By now my legs were getting rubbery and a quick glance at the first sergeant found him rolling his eyes upward.

"And in the future you really shouldn't put in anything that deals with the sensitive mission we conduct on this post. For all I know the Russians and Chinese have read your newsletter, and while they probably already know about the existence of this communications facility and what we do here, I would imagine they're snickering that a junior officer had so much to say to a lowly private. And that the inside of the facility was so vividly described, up to and including the steel walled construction. That particular article is why FMFLANT gave me a call"

He did say "future." Did that mean I had a future?

"I will mention, that while you do have a certain style, there are a few minor things you must deal with in the future.

There...he said it again - "future."

You have a lot of trouble with spelling; you can't punctuate and evidently don't know a noun from a verb." The colonel paused again. And I'll swear, with half a smile and a twinkle in his eyes, he resumed talking. "But you have done something that no one else has accomplished with the newsletter the two years that I've been here and that is to have people take an interest in it." He turned his head from me and looked at his first sergeant. "Myers will continue putting out the newsletter. However, you will personally review each story he writes before it gets printed and as long as his articles are not as radically inclined as what he did this month, you may feel free to give him reasonable lee-way. I'm holding you accountable for this first sergeant. Also, I want the Admin Chief to go over each of his articles for proper spelling and punctuation before he puts them on stencils."

The first sergeant came to attention when he said a terse, "Aye, aye sir, I'll see to it sir!"

The colonel did smile at me this time. "That's all I have, you're dismissed."

I snapped to attention, said, "Yessir!" took one step backward and did an about face.

As I was stiffly walking out of the colonel's office along with the first sergeant, Colonel Farmer stopped us. "Oh, by the way first sergeant. Have promotion papers typed up for Myers, making him a PFC."

Outside in the first shirts office, he said one thing to me before letting me go. "Thanks a lot Myers, I really enjoyed that little session with the colonel. Do me a favor and don't do me any favors in the future!"

How about that, I had a future!

7

MAKE ME ONE OF THEM LANCE CORPORALS!
Staff Sergeant Donald F. Myers, USMC(Ret.)

Early in 1957 the U.S. Marine Corps adopted a new rank structure along with the other branches of the armed services. Prior to this change the Corps had used a limited enlisted rank structure for a dozen years with several honorary titles thrown in to make do with the job at hand and also to perpetuate tradition. Most of the old timers said the Army created the mess with their specialist this and specialist that and their E-3 this and E-4 that. This change caused a lot of confusion at first, for both officer and enlisted. I'll admit I was confused because I was accustomed to the simple seven grades: Private, Private First Class, Corporal, Sergeant, Staff Sergeant, Technical Sergeant and Master Sergeant. Our Company Gunnies were actually the most senior tech sergeant aboard, as were master sergeants called first sergeants and sergeant majors when the billets called for those slots. Now we had to deal with a nine grade rank structure with eleven titles.

Master Sergeant Timothy O'Connor was the first Marine on Camp Elmore to get promoted under the new system. We had a big formation for him with Colonel Farmer reading the promotion warrant and telling all hands how much Top O'Connor merited being promoted to his new rank and handing him his new stripes. After we was dismissed from the promotion formation I made it a point to be one of the first to congratulate my first shirt. Not that I was brown nosing but rather I too felt he deserved the honor since I greatly admired him. In his typical false, gruff fashion he thanked me then said, "I've been in grade as a first sergeant for fifteen years now and what do I get when they promote me? First sergeant!"

What he said was true but now his actually rank was that of First Sergeant (E-8), not Master Sergeant, and he was going to get a raise in base pay to go along with it. And he wasn't fooling me anyway as I saw him fondly looking at his new set of first sergeant stripes with the three up and three rockers down with a large diamond centered in the middle. Before, all he had was the title with no diamond. Now he was really a first sergeant. The Corps continued a master sergeant rank and it was thrown in with the E-8 structuring. This particular rank was reserved for those senior enlisted people with more technical skills than an administrative or combat arms background. The same was true of the new E-9 ranks of Sergeant Major (with a star in the middle of four up and five rockers down) and Master Gunnery Sergeant, which had a bursting bomb in lieu of the star in the middle of the eight stripes. The actual pay grade of Gunnery Sergeant was brought back and the term Technical Sergeant erased from regulations. For those getting promoted to Gunnery Sergeant with three stripes up and two rockers down, they got crossed rifles in the middle field as did all the other new ranks except PFC.

There was a transition period in place whereas all the old ranks would continue on for a certain time frame. Say for instance the case of an old three-stripe buck sergeant.

His new official rank title was Acting Sergeant (E-4). If the Marine didn't get promoted to Sergeant (E-5) within the given time frame, he would be reverted to Corporal (E-4). Like I said, it was pretty confusing, just like when they brought back the old squad drill.

I had kept my nose clean for the past year and was still doing the camp newsletter. It had been decided to give me a 01 MOS, that of a basic administrative man, and I was also breaking into doing some work in the headquarters office. I got along fairly well with the Staff Sergeant (now Acting SSgt (E-5) but soon to be promoted to SSgt (E-6)) Admin Chief. When First Sergeant O'Connor had told the Admin Chief to make me a basic 01 I bitched and moaned about having lost my machine gunners MOS so much and that I was really an infantryman at heart, that the good natured chief clerk put into my Service Record Book as a secondary MOS, 0311 Rifleman. It made sense to me since I'd been preached to for years that every Marine, regardless of his current job, was really a rifleman. (That reminds me of the old story about the Marine pilot in the 1st Marine Air Wing in Korea. As the legend goes, Mgen. Robert H. Pepper paid a surprise visit to a Marine forward airfield that had recently been defended from an enemy ground attack by the wing wipers. The general was nosing around unannounced when he came across this grimy character in a flight suit. He stops the fellow and asks: "What is it you do around here son?" "Well sir," the guys says. "I'm a rifleman temporarily flying an F4U Corsair!") Sorry about the digression but that story cracks me up every time I think about it. Anyway, I was doing a decent enough job and was somewhat surprised when I got a summons to report to the First Sergeants office a couple of months after his promotion. I wondered what I'd done this time.

I knocked on the first shirts door and was advised to enter at my own risk. "You wanted to see me First Sergeant?"

"Oh, Myers, yeah I do. Look...we've got a minor problem and I want your input on the mater since it concerns you. Whether you know it or not Colonel Farmer is pretty impressed with the initiative you've showed since reporting aboard last year. Maybe he liked the way you used to serve him his morning cuppa coffee but whatever it is he had you slated for promotion to corporal prior to all this bullshit change that's taken place. So here's the problem. He's still willing to promote you to Acting Corporal E-3 since the warrant has been on his desk for better than a month or if you want, he'll make you a Lance Corporal which means you won't have to sweat making Corporal E-4 for the next year or so. So what do you think—you want to be an acting Corporal or a Lance Corporal?"

I did some fast thinking since it was obvious I had to make a decision right now. The first thing I thought about was a corporal was a corporal anyway you look at it. I didn't cotton to the idea of being an "Acting" Corporal and besides the old fashion two stripes wasn't in the same class at the new Lance Corps stripes that boasted a single stripe with a red (or khaki) rocker that had crossed rifles on it. Plus the fact the title "Lance" Corporal had a certain ring about it that I rather fancied. I could almost picture me out there in the boondocks surrounded by red coats or whatever, throwing spears and shit at them and yelling Gunga Din. Yeah..Lance Corporal had a diffident sound about it. So I give the first shirt the eye and says, "Make me one of them Lance Corporals!"

(One of the biggest mistakes of judgment I made in the Marine Corps. The first thing I did after getting promoted was take my dress blue trousers to the tailor shop and have red NCO blood stripes sewn down the outside of both pant legs. This was how I found out I wasn't an NCO at all, not even an "acting" one. The first time I wore the blues I was told to get the blood stripes off the trousers. Not only was I a glorified PFC., it took me damn near two years to make Corporal (E-4). Then, because of rank freezing, I spent 52 months in grade as a Corporal before making Sergeant E-5). I would have been a lot better off had I taken the Acting Corporal two stripes when it was offered.)

8

INSTANT JUSTICE DOESN'T WORK ALL THE TIME
Staff Sergeant Donald F. Myers, USMC(Ret.)

During the summer of 1961 I received orders for Temporary Additional Duty (TAD), to assist training reserves at Camp Lejeune, North Carolina. To be more specific, I was assigned duty at a sub-camp at Lejeune, Montford Point. This was a former camp where Negro Marines had went through boot camp because of segregation before President Harry Truman put a stop to it. After just one week on Montford Point I had a lot more respect for black Marines. The Corps should have called the place Camp Swampy because that is exactly what it is, a swamp! A snake populated, mosquito breeding, cockroach crawling, pine forest jungle with humidity so bad you were soaked with sweat just driving up to the gate. There was a field cook and baker school located on the place and that was it, other than a torture chamber for Marine reserves who stayed in one story, cement block barracks for their summer camp. Someone of higher authority must have had a diabolic sense of humor or a real hate for reserves.

By now I was a salty corporal with nine years of service and I was so used to doing things the Marine Corps way that it came as a great shock to me to see the casual attitude within the lower ranks of the reserve Marines. I mean it was a battle royal to get the reserve privates or PFC's to perform the simplest task. Such items of making their racks properly, policing up their squad bay, carrying out trash to a dumpster, you name it, it was a constant clash of wills.. I cringed any time a reserve NCO ordered one of his lower ranks to sweep or swab or do the simplest task, then have to listen to the sass and more likely than not, the NCO was told to do it himself if he wanted it done. My job was to "assist" a reserve sergeant (E-5) with his 40-man platoon that was housed at the very tip of Montford Point where a tidal channel lapped around the jut of land. Tall pine trees hovered over the barracks area like moist umbrellas and since our barracks was the last one on the company street, we were but a matter of a few yards from the surrounding jungle leading down to the tidal flats.

I was a product of the old Corps way of handling sassy, talk back young Marines, having learned my own personal lesson years ago at Naval Mine Depot, Yorktown, Virginia. A Master Sergeant twice my age beat the living shit out of me down in a gully, behind the cleaning shop away from the Marine Barracks. You had best believe I didn't want to go back for seconds, which the old six stripper was willing to do and I learned not to back talk, sass or question an NCO in the performance of his duty.

As it was, I had already invited three of the reserve malcontents out behind the barracks, across a ditch to a level area in the trees. All three had declined and I made it a point to tell them that the next time I saw them giving their barracks sergeant a bad time, I would insist they deal with me behind the barracks. It had more than likely got their attention when I'd sucker-punched them in the gut when I'd made my initial invitation. While it was strictly forbidden for an NCO to strike an enlisted man, the reserve sergeant was grateful for my intervention and at least those three characters got the message and started doing what they were told to do without bitching or back talking.

This was not the case with Private Herzog. Herzog was a burly lad a little younger than me but about my height of six foot. We both weighed around 185. I guess it was the summer heat but with his longer than regulation pure black hair coupled with extremely dark features and a pox marked face, he was greasy looking. His summer cotton khaki uniform was the worst looking of all the reserves, and that was saying something. With the intense heat I changed my starched khaki's three times a day but Herzog's khaki's didn't know what starch was or for that matter an iron. I have to admit I really didn't like the fellow and while that statement shows some lack of objectivity, his surly attitude and sloppy appearance rankled me even more.

After the first week of this particular reserves unit's summer two-week camp, I had had it with Private Herzog. I was standing next to the reserve sergeant at the barracks screen door when noon chow call was sounded by the field music on this particular day. The reserve Marines began filing out of the barracks and naturally Herzog was one of them. He had just lit a cigarette while coming out of the hatch and no doubt it was the last one in the pack as he tossed the wadded pack on the deck next to the sergeant's feet. I immediately said, "Private, pick up that cigarette pack you just tossed on the deck and dispose it in a GI can."

He didn't even break his stride and continued on walking toward the mess hall.

I ran and caught up with him. "You didn't hear me? I told you to pick up that cigarette pack you threw on the deck back there."

His reply stunned me for a moment. "Fuck you...you want it picked up, pick it up yourself!"

Private Herzog had just crossed the line. And I wasn't about to run to the company office and put him on report. This was between him and me!

"Okay Herzog...you go ahead and eat chow. But I'll be waiting for you when you get back and when you get back, you and I will take a little stroll out behind the barracks."

He actually gave me a sneer when he turned on his heel and headed for the mess hall.

The reserves got an hour and a half noon chow break but I stayed near the barracks I was assigned to during the entire time. I was so boiling mad I could hardly think straight. This character wasn't some boot teenage Marine who didn't know what the score was. No, he was just a complete ass hole that needed to be taught a lesson of what the real Corps is all about. I could hardly wait for the chow period to end.

Around 1300 I saw him casually strolling up the company street by himself toward the barracks. I was standing just inside the door and was watching him through the screen. When he opened the screen door I was waiting for him. I yanked him inside the barracks and slammed him against a wall locker. "Okay smart ass...you like to mouth off. Well I'm going to give you a good chance to see just how much mouth you've got when it comes to seeing if you've got any balls. Personally I think you're all mouth and a fuck'en coward that can't back it up." I was right in his face when I was saying this and he recovered enough to shove me away a little. When he did that I took him by his arm and swung him toward the screen door. "Okay big man, lets get behind the barracks and see what kind of a hot-shot you really are." And I pushed him out the door.

He looked to be a little crest fallen with his shoulders slumped but when I prodded him toward the end of the barracks he went along with me. In back of the barracks I crossed the five-foot deep drainage ditch and got up on the other side to the level area in the trees. Herzog was right behind me. We faced off and I told him to take off his sunglasses. He no sooner laid the glasses down than I smacked him with a round house right to his jaw. The blow staggered him but he didn't go down. I followed up with two more jabs to the head and he grabbed me around the waist and we wrestled for a minute. He was stronger than an ox but I finally got away from his bear hug and landed another right to his head. This shot seemed to daze him and he shook his head back and forth, then like a charging bull he came at me with both arms swinging. I quickly realized this guy had been in fights before and his powerful swings had me bobbing and ducking. He got me a good one to my right temple, which was followed with a left to my mid section. It was me this time that grabbed him around his waist to stop those deadly punches. I was using all of my body strength like a football tackler to push him back, waiting for the right second to break free and tag him on his jaw again. The next thing I knew the both of us tumbled into the drainage ditch headfirst. I was slow getting up and he pounded my head with four blows that had me trying to duck away from the punches. With one arm I grabbed him around his neck and bending him down rapped him hard with a serious of short power punches to his face. His nose started bleeding but he wasn't done yet. Herzog threw me away from him and pinned me against the slimy clay wall of the ditch while going at my head again. By this time my head was buzzing and my ears felt like they were on fire. It came to me that I may have bitten off more than I could chew! It took about all of my remaining strength to get him off me and with the both of us slipping and sliding in the muddy ditch. We faced off again but our flaying swings were not connecting as good as they had before.

As if by mutual consent we rested for a moment each still with our fist at the ready. We were both out of breath and gasping for air. Out of swollen lips I said, "Have you had enough?"

"I don't know. If I look half as bad as you do corporal I might. Have you had enough?"

Not quite, but I didn't tell him that. Instead, I tried a sucker punch to his gut that was only half successful, then followed it with an uppercut under his jaw, which did connect and rocked him back on his feet. Damn, if I didn't piss him off with my sneak attack, just as we were getting friendly and talking. He came at me again with all cylinders and I warded off the blows as best I could. I saw he was going to throw a power hammer shot directly at my head and I lowered my skull just in time and his fist hit solid bone with a resounding blow. That hit brought me to my knees and I knew the fight was all over as my head exploded with pain that brought flashing lights to my eyes. Through an echo chamber of sound I heard Herzog yelling. "Sonofabitch, I think I broke it!"

When the haze of my vision cleared enough for me to focus my eyes I looked up at Herzog and he was grimacing in pain while cradling his right hand with his left one. His hand looked like it had grown twice in size and had a sickly reddish, blue tint about it. Then I saw the white bone of a knuckle exposed. In my dazed condition I dumbly asked him: "Have you had enough now?"

Herzog could barely talk, he was in so much pain, but he said, "I think I broke my hand...it hurts like hell."

"Here, let me take a look at it."

"Don't touch it," he admonished me.

There was no doubt in my mind, Herzog had one hell'uva broken hand. I turned to try and get out of the ditch to get some help as I didn't think Herzog could get out of the ditch by himself. The reserve sergeant was standing there looking down upon the two of us. I guess he just had to see me in action. Boy, did he get an eye full! Anyway, I muttered for him to get an ambulance and had no sooner got that request out of my mouth than a tremendous dizzy spell came over me and I fell flat on my face in the mud at the bottom of the ditch. For what seemed to be forever I went in and out of being awake and I couldn't make myself sit up. I seem to remember seeing Herzog sitting in the mud with his back against the clay wall, holding his right hand and grimacing. I do remember the distant wail of a siren but have no memory of the fifteen-mile ride to the Navy hospital located on Camp Lejeune proper.

I was admitted to the Camp Lejeune Naval hospital with a severe concussion in addition to the scraps, cuts and bruised skin suffered from Herzog pounding on me. In the bed next to me was my pugilistic nemesis with the same diagnosis plus his busted up right hand that was now encased in a plaster cast. Both of us sported black eyes and split lips. The slightest move caused severe pain and the two of us laid very still staring at the overhead.

We didn't have much to say to one another for the simple reason, what would we talk about? We'd beat the shit out of each other and that was about it.

During the early morning of our second day of hospitalization, a Marine captain walked into the room and identified himself as Captain Roberts. He informed us he had been assigned duty as the investigative officer to make a report regarding the circumstances why the two of us were hospitalized. An icy chill went up my spine as it hadn't occurred to me that I could be in a whole hell of a lot of trouble. The same thought must have hit Herzog too because he glanced over at me with an expression of panic on his face that was asking me a question I did not have an answer for.

Captain Roberts first question was, "What happened?"

The pregnant silence that followed lasted for better than 30 seconds until the captain looked directly at me, and said. "Okay Corporal Myers, we'll start with you. I must warn you that there are several witnesses to the..ah..incident, but I want to hear your version of what took place to put into my report. It will be best for you to be straightforward and to tell me what happened. So consider this an order, tell me now what took place yesterday that caused you and Private Herzog to end up in here?"

My mind raced in high gear as I tried to conjure up something to say to the officer. At my wits end I finally said, "Well sir, Herzog and me were grab-assing out behind the barracks after noon chow, sort of wrestling around with each other, when we both fell into this ditch. There was some rocks in the ditch and I guess we both hit our heads on the rocks when we fell.."

Captain Roberts gave me a long stare before saying, "I see. And that's your statement, you two fell into this ditch?"

"Yes sir." I replied.

"How do you account for Private Herzog's hand being so severely broken?"

I had to think that one over for a couple of seconds. "Ah...well sir, if I remember right, I think I fell on top of Herzog when we hit the bottom of the ditch and his hand must have been underneath him and I suppose that's how it came to get broken............." I trailed off lamely.

Turning to Herzog, Captain Roberts, said. "What's your version Private. Did you fall into the ditch like Corporal Myers told me?"

I have to give Herzog credit. Even though he hesitated before answering, he backed me up. "Yes sir........just like Corporal Myers said, that's exactly what happened."

Our bullshit story didn't make any difference because unbeknown to Herzog and me about a half-dozen reservist had followed the two of us to the back of the barracks. They had stayed on the barracks side of the ditch but had a clear view of the little forest clearing where Herzog and I first went at it. The reserve sergeant tried his best to stand up for me but the other reserves ratted me out by making statements I'd thrown the first punch.

It was an interesting Summery Courts-martial. The one officer court, Captain Robert Book, knew he had me cold, but just the same advised me that I could plead not guilty and that I could offer extenuation and mitigation evidence in my own behalf. I'd already decided I would go down fighting and came to the late afternoon courts-martial prepared to offer my version of extenuating circumstances as a rational of why I had done what I'd done.

Captain Book was a fine looking officer with sandy hair, steely blue eyes and a square chin. He was older than me but in such great shape physically that he looked to be my age which was 26. Going through the traditional ritual of a deck court the thing moved along fast to the point Captain Book told me it was time for me to offer any plea of mitigation and/or extenuation before he made his decision on my trail. I'll never forget the look on his face when I picked up a large ditty bag I'd brought with me, unzipped it, and dumped the contents on the table that was being used for my courts-martial. I know he had been curious when I had first arrived carrying the ditty bag and now his mouth hung open in astonishment as he looked at the array of 40 books that had spilled out of my bag. Every one of the books had to do with military history with most of them pertaining to the U.S. Marine Corps. The captain looked from the pile of books across to me. "What's all this for Corporal Myers?"

"Sir, I realize this is a little dramatic but I wanted to show you my sincerity of being a Marine and an NCO. I've read every one of these books and gained a lot on what military leadership, discipline and principals is all about. If you will bear with me I've marked several passages in the various books that I'd like to read which may give you some insight on my personality and my beliefs as a Marine."

Having been granted permission to proceed I began reading from the various books which I had marked with paper page markers. Every thing I read had to do with the rough and tumble life of NCOs down through the ages and how non-commissioned officers were the backbone of any military organization. Many of the passages I read pinpointed the accepted practice of corporals and sergeants using brute force to keep their men in line. I ended my defense with what I thought to be the crowning glory of making the point I was trying to make. Picking up Lieutenant General Lewis B. "Chesty" Puller's book titled MARINE, I flipped through the pages of the life story of the Corps greatest hero and most decorated Marine until finding the page I had marked. Looking directly at Captain Book, I said. "Sir, I won't read this entire page but I will read what Chesty Puller told one of his corporal's who was having a bad time dealing with one of his men on the march from the Chosin Reservoir. "Son—why don't you just pull that sonofabitch out of ranks and bust him in the mouth!"

What I did was a good try but solid evidence was stacked against me and Captain Book spent no time at all in deliberation. I was found guilty on several counts, the most serious; striking an enlisted man of lower grade. My sentence was reduction to private, 30 days restriction to camp and a fine of two-thirds of my base pay for one month. It was a good thing I was a Marine or I might have burst out in tears.

One of the saddest things I've ever done in my life was removing my corporal stripes off the sleeves of my uniform shirts, blouses and battle jackets. I was also placed in a casual status awaiting transfer orders back to Norfolk since I was no longer allowed to be an instructor for the reserves. After waiting ten days for the termination of my TAD I was beginning to wonder what in the Sam hill was going on. But since I was feeling pretty low at being a two hash mark private, I wasn't about to ask anyone what the delay was all about. At day twelve after my courts-martial I was ordered to the office of the training command First Sergeant. He informed me that reviewing authority in the chain of command regarding my courts-martial had determined that the punishment was too harsh and that my restriction was lifted and that my bust was rescinded to a Private First Class. The kindly old timer also told me I'd more than likely remain on station until a complete review of my case was completed and it might take a month for that to be done.

Another week went by and I was still twiddling my thumbs in the transit barracks going a little bonkers with little to do except an occasional police detail of cleaning something up the building and grounds NCO put me on. Once again a summons from the training command first shirt had me in his office. This time he informed me that I could sew Lance Corporal stripes back onto my uniforms and the fine had been rescinded completely. I casually asked the first sergeant if he had any idea what was going on. Like I said, he was a pretty nice guy for a first shirt and he offered me his opinion. "Well Myers, I'll have to admit that all this crap going on with you seems a little odd. There's only a couple of things that's had to have taken place as far as I'm concerned. Either the courts-martial officer screwed up his handling of your deck court or you've got some friends in high places......and/or a combination of both."

Now, I was well aware that the Corps sometimes worked in strange and mysterious ways and most odd things that took place never surprised me. But this situation was beginning to baffle me. At least I had plenty of time on my hands to remove stripes and sew different ones back on.

A full month went by and this time when I was summoned to see the first sergeant he said that I was to report to the base sergeant major ASAP and to make sure I wore a good uniform. I opted to wear a set of my tropical worstered with field scarf, ribbons and piss-cutter. The rough nap on the summer dress uniform had worn off years ago but the heavy fabric was still itchy as all get out in the hot climate but I wanted to look my best. My shoes were spit-shined to a sheen that looked like patient leather and my brass sparkled in the bright sun light.. I took the base bus the fifteen miles to main-side and reported to the office of the Sergeant Major, Marine Corps Base. After cooling my heels in his outer office for better than 20 minutes his staff sergeant administrative aide fetched me and advised me to formally report to the sergeant major.

I marched into the sergeant major's office and executed a loud German heel snap when I came to rigid attention in front of the sergeant major's desk. "Lance Corporal Myers reporting as ordered Sergeant Major!"

The grizzled, sharp nosed, pigeon-cheasted man sitting at the desk had to have been sixty years old if he was a day. But damn if he wasn't 100% Marine from the tip of his short cropped haired head to the soles of his spit-shined size 12 shoes. His weather beaten face had a dark ruddy cast and the webbing at the side of his milk blue eyes told of the hundreds of field watches he had stood. His eyes actually sparkled with a glint of humor when he looked at me and when he spoke I could tell it was a false gruffness he was using. "Myers, you look pretty sharp in those trops for a Marine that's out of uniform."

His remark stunned me and I blurted out, "Sir how am I out of uniform?"

"You've been around long enough to know better than to call me sir but I'm going to let that slide since I know you're trying to be respectful. To answer your question lad a corporal of Marines is not supposed to be running around base headquarters wearing lance corporal stripes. I have your orders releasing you from TAD and five days delay in route is on them. The Base Legal section has over turned your court martial convection due to procedural error and you have until 1300 today to clear this camp. Have I made myself clear?"

"The courts-martial has been over turned. Does that mean I'm still a corporal sergeant major?"

"Didn't I tell you, you were out of uniform? You better have those two stripes on when you leave this base Corporal Myers."

(In 1969 I had the pleasure to serve in the outfit Colonel Robert M. Book commanded. He remembered me from the Montford Point court-martial and we became good friends, considering the gap between a staff NCO and full colonel. I retired before he did and was given the honor of being a participant at a Mess Night Roast when he retired. I guess Colonel Book created a minor legend when he related the story over the years about the crazy corporal who had dumped a suitcase full of military books on his desk during the corporal's court-martial and using Chesty Puller as a defense witness. Though I had asked a few times if he had had anything to do with me getting reinstated to corporal, he'd just smile and never gave me a straight answer. The night of his retirement party he said it was time for me to know the truth. "Don, you have no idea what a dilemma you created with that little fiasco of yours at Camp Lejeune. Every senior NCO at Montford Point went to bat for you and called in every ticket owed to them from every officer on the base that they'd previously saved their ass in one way or the other. And that list had some pretty high-ranking officers on it. What you did was one of those situations where you was wrong as hell and right as rain at the same time. Your biggest sin was getting caught in the act that forced the issue. You wouldn't believe the man-hours that went into the sessions we conducted behind closed doors on how we were going to get you off the hook. I'm telling you that quite a few officers, up to and including a general officer, burned some midnight oil trying to come up with a reasonable way to solve your problem and at the same time go by the book. Your deck court was so riddled with errors that a PFC legal clerk could have overturned it. So now you know."

Now I ask you. Does that make a man feel humble or what?

One last tid-bit about this story. After I retired from the Marine Corps in 1973, I was sitting in this very nice pub one evening with one of my brother-in-laws, Harvey Renforth. And who walked into the place but Private Herzog. Almost 18 years had passed but we both recognized one another instantly. He came directly over to where I was sitting and began pumping my hand and slapping me on the back like a long lost buddy. After inviting Herzog to join us he and I relived our adventure over several beers about what had brought us together at Montford Point, much to the amazed disbelief of my brother-in-law).

9

PROMOTION PARTY
Staff Sergeant Donald F. Myers, USMC(Ret.)

On June 28, 1964, my closest buddy, Pete DeConinck got promoted to sergeant while we were stationed at Camp Geiger, North Carolina, which is a part of the Camp Lejeune, Marine Corps Base complex. We were both troop handlers at the Infantry Training Regiment and when our first sergeant told Pete he could have the day off to celebrate his promotion I did some fast talking and asked the first-shirt to let me have the day off also. After all, I told the senior sergeant, my pal couldn't be expected to cruise around Jacksonville all by himself. (J-ville was outside the gate at main-side Lejeune.) Old Zebra arm gave me a pained stare, then shaking his head in a resigned manner gave his blessing and said I too could have the day off.

My short, swarthy complicated pal of Belgium and Irish ancestry and I hurriedly went to our squad-bay and changed into civvies for our day on the town. Neither one of us had every been to Jacksonville's famous or infamous (depending on how you look at it) Court Street during daylight hours except on a weekend when it was as wide open as all get out. We sped the seven miles from Geiger to downtown Jacksonville in Pete's '55 Chevy and parked the rust-bucket near the railroad tracks that was the starting point for the four-block stripe that catered to Marines.

It was just a little past 0900 when the two of us started walking down the sidewalk along Court Street. The entire four blocks was made up of bars, greasy spoons and gyp-joint shops. Naturally, what we were looking for was a beer to celebrate Pete's three stripes. We soon became dismayed as I tried door after door and found the joints were locked tight. We looked at each other with realization that we weren't going to find any of the beer bars opened this early in the morning because Court Street was a liberty night environment.

Undaunted, I kept trying the doors for a couple of more blocks until coming abreast to one of our favorite watering holes, The Palomino. Figuring, "What the hell." I gave the doorknob a twist and low and behold the door swung open. Smiling at one another I pushed my 200 pound, six foot frame through the door into the dark confines of the large beer bar and walked to the long bar. The fact that the only light in the dump came from the bright neon signs boarding the mirror behind the bar didn't phase us as most of the joints we hung out in were dimly lighted. We did note that we were the only customers as we waited patiently at the bar for the bartender to appear to take our order.

After about five minutes waiting Pete said, "I wonder what the hell the bartender is doing?"

We'd already yelled out a couple of times that business was awaiting at the bar: but got no response.

"You think maybe something's happened to him?" I ventured.

So Pete and I made search of the place thinking perhaps the barkeep had a stroke or whatever. Even though it was darker than hell in the place we still looked in every nook and cranny and finally ended up back at the bar without having seen any signs of life.

We stood there at the bar for a couple of minutes staring at our reflections in the big mirror then we turned at looked at each other. "Maybe he stepped out for awhile," Pete mused.

I took my money clip out of my trousers and peeled off five one dollar bills and laid them on the bar. "Well, if that's the case, then we'll just have to be our own bartenders." After using my Indiana, Marine type logic I strode around to the end of the bar and opened various coolers until I found one that was stacked with Budweiser. After opening four bottles I returned to my side of the bar and lifting one of the brews toasted Pete on his promotion.

Three hours later Pete and I were still toasting his three stripes and feeling no pain. The top of the bar was littered with empty Budweiser bottles and a small stack of bills which totaled twenty some odd dollars, the extent of our before payday loot. We had resorted to making an IOU after having gone broke by making lines on a piece of paper we kept on top of our pile of money.

Who knows what beer we were on when the front door opened sometime around noon. Bright daylight streamed into our little private party. We turned to see who was joining us when a loud booming voice yelled, "What in the hell are you guys doing in here and how in the hell did you get in?"

Without waiting for us to try and offer an answer the big hulk of a guy rushed to the bar and getting behind it made a bee-line to the cash register which he immediately opened with a ringing ding of the NO-SALE button.

Pete, in his particular New York City accent, said in a serious tone. "It's all there...we checked that out more than an hour ago. I think I counted two hundred and forty bucks, plus some change."

The big guy looked up from the cash register and with an incredulous expression said, "How long you guys been here?"

When we told him he shook his head, then asked, "How did you get in?"

I answered his question. "Well, the front door was open and we took it for granted the place was open for business." Pointing to our pile of money and IOU slip I then said, "There's our bar tab, we paid as we went along....huh..but we do owe you for a few. See, here's our IOU we were keeping."

The guy shook his head again as if he couldn't believe what he was hearing. "You mean you've been in here all this time by yourselves and you left my money alone and was keeping a tab?"

Newly promoted Marine sergeant Pete DeConnick fielded that question with a haughty dignity. "We weren't after your money, we wanted a beer!"

(This may have been one of the very rare times that a bar owner in Jacksonville, North Carolina tore up a beer tab IOU, gave two sot Marines their money back and gave them a free night in his joint later on.) P.S. The night bartender had forgot to lock the front door.

10

FLYING ACES
Staff Sergeant Donald F. Myers, USMC(Ret.)

My buddy Pete DeConinck was really proud of his 1955 Chevrolet sedan. Even though it was a piece of junk he took pretty good care of it and was always farting around trying to make it look better. Behind Camp Geiger, where we were stationed with the 1st Infantry Training Regiment, is the Marine Corps Air Station, Jacksonville. Somehow Pete had conned one of the wing-wipers into giving him a gallon of corsair blue aircraft paint and he hand painted his Chevy with the bright glossy dark blue paint. He even went so far as to trim the lower body panels with a cloud-light blue which the Corps uses for the underside of airplane wings. Old Pete thought his handy work looked pretty nifty while I thought it looked like a conspicuous bomber without wings that the good-old-boy sheriff's in the surrounding counties would just love to pull over.

On many of our off duty weekends during the early sixties, the two of us would cruise the countryside, enjoying the scenery, going through small towns and hamlets, stopping once in awhile to chat with the locals and maybe have a beer or two in some out of the way little tavern. We found most Tar Heels to be a pretty nice people and I think we fascinated them as much as they did us. With Pete's New York City brogue and my Hoosier twang, the North Carolinians pegged us right off as being Yankee's but we got along with them real good.

The only problems we encountered riding Pete's blue bomber out in the sticks was the narrow, sharp turning roads. A couple of times we'd go through an ess curve next to a farm house or barn and before Pete could stop the car he'd already hit a chicken and one time he got a slow kitten. I knew these killings were accidental as Pete was not the type of guy that had a cruel streak, especially when it came to dumb animals. But he did possess a diabolical sense of humor.

This one Sunday found us over 100 miles from Camp Lejeune on some back road someplace. Even though I was supposed to be the navigator I seldom knew where in the hell we were at except for a rough idea. Anyway, just as we passed this group of farmer's gathered in their pickups and small bed trucks at a cross road I'll be damn if an old sow and five or six piglets didn't amble out right in front of us on the road. We weren't going fast at all but before Pete could brake his car he hit one of the piglets, killing it. Pete and I got out of the car and was staring down at the small creature when several of the farmers walked up. Feeling contrite Pete said he didn't mean to hit the pig and he'd pay whom-ever it belonged to. One of the redneck farmers drawled it belonged to some fellow up the hill away, pointing to a small white farm house about three hundred yards distance. Being good Marines we drove up the gravel path and told the farmer what had happened. After thinking it over the thin, chiseled face farmer "reckoned" that $20. would be "about fair" for his dead pig. We paid the man and went on our way, all but broke since the $20 was about all the money we had between the two of us.

Later that evening after being forced to return to Camp Geiger for a Sunday supper at the mess hall since we didn't have enough money to eat off base, I noticed Pete out in the parking area near our barracks. He was messing around near the driver's door of his Chevy. Being nosy I strolled out to where he was farting around and saw he had an artist paintbrush in one hand and a small can of yellow paint in the other.

"What in the Sam hill are you doing?" I inquired.

Glancing up from his handy work Pete offered me one of his famous lop sided sly grins, and replied. "That pig I got today made me an ace. And since I had to pay for it I figured I may as well take credit for my kill."

Looking closer to what he had been painting it dawned on me what the silhouettes of the five little forms represented. Three chickens, one cat and a pig were clearly identifiable on the hoods rear panel near the door.

11

REFEREEING A FREE FOR ALL
Staff Sergeant Donald F. Myers, USMC(Ret.)

Moorhead City, North Carolina, is located about 25 miles north by northeast from Camp Lejeune. The small southern burg boasts deep-water port facilities which gives it an important function for the amphibious combat mission of the Marine Corps. The Second Marine Division stationed at Camp Lejeune utilizes Moorhead City as its port of debarkation for its assault troop transports better known as APA's and AKA's. Although the city fathers are not overly pleased about the idea the town also functions as a liberty area for Marines stationed at the nearby Cherry Point Marine Corps Air Station located at Beaufort and for Camp Lejeune Marines bored with Jacksonville.

Like any service town that caters to the military Moorhead City has its share of sleazy bars and gyp joints. And like most service towns the local population barely tolerated the influx of young uniformed men invading their sanctuary looking for a little action. I suppose this was understandable since the average mentality of a single Marine on liberty had a limited focus: beer and broads. As usual, beer was plentiful and woman or girls not. About the only female companionship readily available was B-girls that frequented the beer joints. These gals had one thing in mind and that was to separate a Marine from his money without giving of any virtue they may have had left. Prostitution was all but non-existent in this part of North Carolina, but you better believe Marines of all ages were constantly on the prowl trying to find a lady of the night.

I won't go into the moral issue when it comes to individual Marines seeking the pleasure of a fallen dove; because like any soldier away from home and feeling lonely among 20,000 other men, the beckoning light of the worlds oldest profession had its merits.

After having offered that excuse, I admit, that I was among those thousand faces that occasionally sought that particular degree of female companionship beyond the B-girl variety.

My best pal at Camp Geiger, which is a part of Camp Lejeune, was Sergeant Pete DeConinck. The dark featured, short. slim New Yorker possessed one of the highest IQ's within the enlisted ranks of the Corps. His GCT, the Marines version of a IQ test was an incredible 178. You had to have a 130 GCT to be accepted for officer's candidate school. Several times Pete was encouraged by higher authority to apply for a limited duty officer position but he always declined. However, one of the new breed of warrant officers the Corps had in the 1960's, Chief Warrant Officer One Daubenspeck, our adjutant, would not take no for an answer since he was convinced Pete would make an outstanding officer. Now, while Pete was highly intelligence, he had absolutely no common sense. I mean I would have to literally drag him in out of the rain. But his lack of common sense did get CWO-1 Daubenspeck off his back about applying for OCS. The adjutant had Pete cornered, all but demanding that Pete put in for a direct commission to second lieutenant. Pete stopped the adjutant in his tracks and was never bothered by him again, when he said. "How possibly could I fuck over you officers, if I were one of you?"

As it was, Pete and I were inseparable. Where you saw one, you saw the other. My six foot height contrasted sharply to Pete's five feet, five inches, and many of equal rank or higher, including our sergeant major, called us Mutt and Jeff.. This September of 1965 found us both buck sergeants facing a long liberty weekend in honor of Labor Day. We hashed over what we should do and I casually mentioned I'd heard some scuttlebutt (rumor) that a taxi cab driver in Moorhead City was working a couple of girls. Pete found that news interesting but we finally decided to start our liberty at the joints on the Second Front, and work our way through J'ville, and maybe later hit Moorhead City. The Second Front by the way, was an area directly across from the front fence line of Camp Geiger and consisted of seven of the roughest, toughest, tumble-down bars found on the eastern seaboard. More bar fights took place on the Second Front than in Madison Square Garden.

Even though Pete and I were well known in the dumps that made up the Second Front, and our reputation was that of good humored sots not looking for any trouble, I still carried a sheathed carbine bayonet down the crack below my back. The weapon wasn't intended for fellow Marines but rather to get the attention of young red necks who always seemed to be looking for trouble. The few times I had been forced to pull out my bayonet had abruptly ended those conflicts I had been faced with. The local toughs loved to gang up on unsuspecting Marines but they had a respectful fear for anyone who pulled a blade out in defense. Plus the fact they thought all Marines were crazy and bloodthirsty anyway.

We didn't make it to Moorhead City until after dark Sunday night. After spending an entire evening at the Second Front we spent about all day and night Saturday drinking pitchers of beer at our favorite spot in Jacksonville, the "V" Bar. I had been trying to put the make on Donna, the well-stacked barmaid for better than three months and she in turn kept the game going by flirting with me, giving me a sense of hope. Charlie Grimes, the owner of the "V" Bar was a nice dude and when we'd get overly tired (A quaint expression meaning close to passing out) he'd let his better-known customers sack out for a while in the back supply room. This was one of the reasons Pete and I particularly liked the "V" Bar. Plus the fact it was off the beaten path and few Court Street liberty hounds ventured this far north in J'ville. While not sucking down pitchers of beer there was pool games to be played and more than a few card games going on. In other words it was a decent liberty bar for older NCOs such as Pete and me.

That Sunday we had a beer breakfast after Charlie woke us up from where we'd sacked out in the back room, and after getting a taste of the hair of the dog that bit us, we started in on another day of fun and games. Pretty Donna came in at noon and I renewed my effort at trying to convince her what a great guy I was regardless of what she may have heard about me. I guess flirting with Donna got my hormones fired up because late that afternoon I suggested to Pete we go to Moorhead City to see if we could find the taxi cab driver who knew how to get in touch with the type of female I felt the need for.

Pete was agreeable to my idea although he cautioned me to ease up on the sauce as I wasn't in the best of shape. With that admonishment, I only bought a six-pack to take with us instead of two six-packs.

After arriving at Moorhead City we drove to the taxi stand which was actually a four by four shed located on a parking lot that was used as a dispatchers office. The little white shed was packed solid with local rednecks with an overflow standing outside. Getting out of Pete's 55' Chevy we looked at one another and Pete said, "What the hell they doing, having a cab drivers convention."

In my half inebriated condition Pete's remark cracked me up and I countered with a zinger of my own. "Yeah its probably a state convention of redneck safe drivers, all twelve of 'em."

Pete was a little dubious of approaching the shed after seeing the group of men on the outside passing around a mason jar that no doubt contained white lightning. "You sure you want to do this Myers? Those guys don't look very friendly."

"Aw, what the hell," I replied, "business is business and one of 'em is bound to know which cabby is running the girls."

So I walk on up to the shed and stick my nose in the front door. "Say, do any of you fellows know who the cabby is that's got a couple of gals on the string?"

For a couple of seconds there issued a deathly quite then this kid of around seventeen who was on crutches bellowed out. "Who you Yankee sons'abitches think you are com'en in heah a'try'en ta buy our women-folk!"

This outburst was quickly followed by most the other men throwing epitaphs of their own at me, using language that showed they were not in a happy mood. The kid on crutches screamed again over the din he'd created. "Let's show the Marine bastart what wean'ens think 'bout him want''en to mess with our women. Let's strip 'em and send him on his way naked as a jay bird afta beating the tar outta him." And he took a swing at me with one of his crutches that didn't connect with me but did hit one of his companions.

The quick outburst had stunned me I suppose, because for a few seconds I was frozen in place. I clearly remember the Keystone Kop scene of those eight or nine guys packed in the dispatchers shed all trying to get out the door at me at once.

When Pete yelled, "Myers! Watch your back!" I quickly saw that those on the outside were drawing a circle around me. The crippled kid on crutches made it out of the door first for the simple reason he was pushed from behind and came stumbling out where he fell flat on his face. With the rest of the mob coming at me I reached behind my back and pulled out my bayonet unsheathing it and brandishing the thing for all to see. It stopped the hoard in their tracks. But only for a moment. Clumsy ass that I am, I dropped the stupid bayonet on the cinder covered parking lot!

The rednecks renewed their charge with a fury.

Then out of nowhere, Captain Midnight of the Marine Corps, in the guise of Sergeant Pete DeConinck, jumps into the middle of the circle of men just as the group was closing in on me. He held out both hands with fingers splayed like a traffic cop and in a loud voice yells, "STOP!" And damn if everyone didn't halt in their tracks staring at Pete. Pete casually looks at me and says. "Pick up the bayonet."

Like a robot I bend over and retrieve the bayonet and once Pete saw I've got it firmly in my grasp again, he shouts. "OKAY—GO!" Drops his hands in a sweeping motion and steps out of the circle.

I looked at him dumbfounded for a second thinking, that's it? That's his effort to get me out of this mess——acting as referee, making sure fair play and all that crap was being followed? And then of all things he turns his back on me and heads back to his car.

In the meantime, the group of rednecks, recovering from the initial confusion created by Pete was once again closing the circle tighter around me, but being wary of the fact that I now held the bayonet in a tight grip. The cripple kid was on his feet again shouting encouragement to his pals from the edge of the circle. I was growing a little weary of his intimidation and snarled at him that I may end up dead but I sure as hell was going to gut him before I went down.

A few seconds later a blasting horn got everyone's attention. We automatically tuned to face bright headlights coming right at the group. Captain Midnight strikes again! The passenger door swung open as the Chevy braked, throwing cinders on everybody and Pete yells, "Get in dumb ass!"

I dove into the front seat and we sped off leaving a dozen rednecks reduced to throwing cinders at the blue bomber. On the way back to Camp Geiger I thanked Pete for bailing me out.

He glanced at me as I sucked on a bottle of Bud, then said. "Oh no problem. I figured you were just being your normal, loud mouth, drunken, obnoxious self, having a little fun, but when you told that kid on crutches you'd gut him I could just see tomorrow's headlines: Marine Kills Cripple. So I decided it was time to get you away from there."

This is one of the reasons I love this guy. No common sense at all!

12

SAW HORSE BARRICADE
Staff Sergeant Donald F. Myers, USMC(Ret.)

Returning from overnight liberty we pulled on the Second Front, Sergeant Pete DeConinck and I weaved our way along the sidewalk leading to our barracks from the parking lot for privately owned vehicles at Camp Geiger.

The 3:00 A.M. stillness of the sleeping camp was made darker that early morning by a cloud covered October moon. The two of us were in good spirits and had spent the evening celebrating the fact we were both on draft orders to Southeast Asia with a reporting date of January 1966. Our mutual thoughts were, if it took a war to get us transferred out of the First Infantry Training Regiment, then thank God for the Viet Cong. Teaching raw recruits the basics of infantry tactics got a little long in the tooth after two plus years.

Anyway, like I said, we were in good spirits and maybe just a wee bit tipsy from enjoying watching all the action that usually took place on the Second Front. It was more than likely our semi-inebriated condition that made the two of us come to a screeching halt in front of a huge hole dug right in the middle of the sidewalk next to one of the troops outdoor heads and shower room. The deep hole was barricaded with six sawhorses with flashing amber lights blinking on each horse. I think it was the blinking lights that held our fascination. We must have stood there for a good three minutes without saying anything, just staring at those blazing lights twinkling on and off, casting eerie streaks of yellow off our rapt faces and surrounding buildings.

Finally, I made a remark. "There must be something we could do with one of them."

Pete nodded his head. "That's what I was thinking too."

"We could put one up on the roof of the head." I ventured.

"Naw——that's too childish, we've got to be more creative." My pal countered.

Not giving up, I said. "Okay then, how about we place one in front of the main hatch of the headquarters building. That should blow a few minds in the morning."

"It's already morning dumb ass," Pete said sarcastically, "but that's a pretty neat idea, lets do it!"

We practically ran the two blocks to reach our low slung, one story headquarters building. Each of us had one end of a long sawhorse which boasted two blinking warning lights. We placed the warning barricade maker directly on the large cement stoop that acted as a step to the main door of the building.

Satisfied with our handy work we walked back down the walkway to our barracks with smug expressions. After taking our traditional dose of aspirins to ward off hang over headaches we hit the sack to get four hours of shuteye prior to reveille.

On our way to the headquarters building at 0700 to pickup the morning report, Pete and I had completely forgot about the escapade with the sawhorse we'd pulled off earlier. You can imagine our surprise when we turned the corner of the building to reach the front hatch and confronted a throng of other troop handlers and admin types milling around the front stoop. There in all its splendid, blinking glory, was our sawhorse, merrily winking its dual yellow eyes at the assembled Marines. Before Pete or I had a chance to guffaw the double doors swung open and standing behind the screen doors to the outside was our regimental sergeant major, Sergeant Major Edgar Huff. The giant black sergeant major who was a legend in the Corps scowled at the group of Marines in front of the blinking sawhorse. In his resonant, bellowing voice, he addressed the Marines. "I don't know what the hell it's doing here, but its gotta be there for a reason, so you clowns can just walk around to the back of the headquarters and use the rear hatch!"

(The sawhorse stayed in place for a full week until Pete and I returned from another liberty and I tossed it on top of one of the outside heads.)

13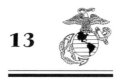

DISNEY LAND
Staff Sergeant Donald F. Myers, USMC(Ret.)

During a routine physical prior to leaving Camp Geiger on transfer orders to the Fleet Marine Force Vietnam it was discovered I had a cyst on my heart sac. Therefore, after surgery at the Portsmouth, Virginia Naval Hospital, and resulting convalesce it was November 1965 before I reached Camp Pendleton, California. Because of my recent surgery Headquarters, Marine Corps selected me for a billet within my 0141 MOS instead of my 0369 Infantry Unit Leader MOS, and I found myself working my tail off as the Battalion Administrative Chief for the newly formed First Military Police Battalion. I came by this position almost by accident since fate, or whatever, pulled a Murphy's Law on me. I was the second man to report for duty to the 1stMPBn. After going nuts trying to find out where I was supposed to report to since nobody on Camp Pendleton seemed to know what an MP battalion was I finally found the battalion headquarters building sitting up high on a hill near the Corporal and Sergeants Club. I recognized the building instantly on my climb up-hill since it had been used as a prop for the movie Battle Cry. Colonel Sam Huxley, portrayed by Van Heflin had a scene with his officers on the wrap-around covered porch of the one story, white painted wood building. The place was deserted and all doors locked and I had no idea what I was supposed to do now. While staring through one of the windows at the empty office space I noticed a human form looking into a window on the other side of the porch. The person must have spotted me too because we did a little comic routine of going around the porch and I ended up where he had been and visa versa. We did it again until a booming voice shouted, "STAY WHERE YOU'RE AT!"

One of the oldest and skinniest sergeant majors I'd ever seen approached me and asked, "Who are you and what's your MOS?"

When I told the tall, thin sergeant major with a beak nose, he promptly said, "You're my new battalion Admin Chief, go find a clip board, pencil and paper, and the two of us will get to work."

Sergeant Major Bill Thompson was right about that comment because work we did. For the first week it was just he and I aboard the new outfit and I followed him around like a puppy jotting notes he'd throw at me concerning things that needed to be done. It was the first time I was ever involved in creating a new unit from scratch and before it was over with I was working around the clock, taking cat naps when I could find time in the newly furnished battalion headquarters. While this is not a part of the sea story I want to tell about, I do have to relate this one incident that took place at base headquarters that is a sea story in its own right. Sergeant Major Thompson and I spent much time at the sprawling base headquarters building that had been built during World War II. The low ceiling,, one story white wooden building was a maze of narrow hallways that criss-crossed throughout the place. The two of us were going down one of the main corridors at the full steam ahead purposeful stride my long legged sergeant major walked at; when I spotted coming at us from the other direction the most beautiful Woman Marine I had ever seen. I mean this gal was absolutely gorgeous! Blond hair, tanned skin, ruby lips, a figure most Marines would die for. The young female sergeant was the epitome of love-liness. My entire focus was zeroed in on her and I wasn't paying one bit of attention on what was going on around me. It so happened that I started across a hallway intersection at the same time the commanding general of Marine Corps Base, Camp Pendleton, Lieu-tenant General Robert E. Cushman, Jr., walked in front of me, coming from my right. I knocked the three-star general on his ass. As people in the crowded corridor rushed to pick up General Cushman, Sergeant Major Thompson was beating me on my head and shoulders with his clipboard, screaming what a dumb ass I was. The wraith of my ser-geant major barely penetrated my senses as I stared wide-eyed at General Cushman, who was now on his feet and brushing himself off. A vision of me holding onto black steal dungeon bars soared through my brain housing. The general shook off the do-gooders who had been helping him brush off his full dress green uniform and he told Sergeant Major Thompson to stop beating on me. With a humorous glint in his eyes he waved off my stuttering apology and putting one arm around my shoulder led me to a corner a couple of feet away and with a wink, said a few whispered words "She's my personal secretary. Can damn well be a distraction sometimes." He patted me on the back, then told everyone milling around to get back to work, the fun was over, and cautioned Ser-geant Major Thompson to forget the incident. (I was never able to figure out how he knew I had been ogling the WM————but then, he is a general and obviously a pretty smart one since he ended up as Commandant of the Marine Corps.)

Several situations came up while putting the 1stMPBn together that I won't go into but it appeared I'd done a good job for the combat MP's. The reason I say this was the disappointment I felt when told I wasn't going to ship overseas with them. Maybe I'd done to good of a job as a desk jockey because shortly after the MP battalion debarked for Vietnam, I was assigned temporary duty as the Marine Corps Base Assistant Legal Chief. I moved my gear to base Support Company. I could write an entire book about the several months I spent with Support Company because it was the strangest outfit I'd ever served with. The Marine Corps has this imaginary line which splits the United States into two distinct areas. East of the Mississippi River and West of the Mississippi River. All problems the Corps had of a serious disciplinary nature ended up at Camp Lejeune on the east coast or Camp Pendleton on the west coast. The increasing involve-ment of the Corps in the Vietnam War brought on an unusual change in policy, in that, all legal problem Marines would be sent to Camp Pendleton for dispossession. That is to say, that civilian jails across the United States that had Marines in them for offenses less than murder, was unloaded on Camp Pendleton. To be more clear on this, the Corps' problem children were assigned administratively to Support Company, Marine Corps Base, Camp Pendleton Most of these people were placed in the Camp Pendleton brig until their situation could be sorted out but a goodly number also resided in the Support Company barracks where I lived and worked. The legal section had the mission of salvaging what we could from the steady flow of Marines' in trouble and to get rid of the rest through the three types of less than honorable discharges. Once those disciplinary cases that could be salvaged had been taken care of and after punishment was given they were sent to the Fleet Marine Force Pacific for duty in Vietnam. Believe me when I say, this is a very general overview of what we did. Never before or since, did I weld so much administrative authority. We had production line office hours (unit punishment-Article 15) along with production line courts martial and undesirable discharge boards. A part of my job was to clue in the First Sergeant of Support Company each morning as to our legal section recommendations on the 20 or 30 office hours that were waiting outside in the hallway to see the commanding officer, Major Bugler. I'd go over each case with the first shirt and say such things as, "Refer this for special court, this one a summery, this fellow you can fine him and bust him and send him on his way." I remember one case, that of a buck sergeant that the FBI had tracked down after being a deserter for two years. By the time the former deserter got to us he'd spent a year in a civilian jail awaiting for the Marines to get around to him. I interviewed every prisoner we got. This sergeant was a nice enough guy and contrite about what he'd done. His story was an old one, personal problems at home with a wife, which didn't get solved since she divorced him anyway. Then, after that slam-dunk he was scared to turn himself in for being AWOL. When I asked him if he was looking for a dishonorable discharge he practically cried and kept saying how sorry he was for having messed up and that he'd been a good Marine and was there any chance that he could stay in the Corps. His service records prior to the offense had been outstanding and my recommendation in his case was a special courts martial with a sentence of time served, bust to private, three months two-third pay fine, and ship him to Vietnam. That's exactly what took place. I've often wondered what ever happened to that fellow after he got to the Nam.

But not all was doom and gloom at Support Company. I developed a good buddy relationship with one of the Marine Corps' top combat photographers, SSgt John G. "Mac" McCullough. Mac was just back from Vietnam and lived topside with me in the NCO section of the barracks since the base Photo Section was a part of Support Company.

We became liberty hound twosomes even if it was only the Acy-ducy club near the base naval hospital we were going to for the evening or out on the town. Our favorite watering hole was Ethel's in St. Luis Ray just outside the rear gate. We became such a fixture at Ethel's that even the local B-girls would buy us a drink or two before payday and if we were really hard up the owner, Pop Jenkins, a retired Marine, even let us run a tab which was all but unheard of in the Oceanside area. Due to our constant bragging what a great joint Ethel's was, several other guys at Support Company made it their hang out also. Old Pop Jenkins was real happy with the sudden popularity of his out of the way, run down dump even though some of the characters from Support Company were real odd balls. This had more to do with the job all of us was doing as a part of the base support company since you had to be somewhat weird with a line of BS to get anything accomplished considering the mission at hand. Anyway, Ethel's became an unofficial clubhouse for our outfit.

This one Saturday I'd went to Ethel's with a foursome of "club members" from Support Company. Mac hadn't come with us since he'd got an early morning frost call to report to the photo lab as something special had come up that required his expertise. I told my tall, lanky pal from Fort Worth, Texas, to try and make it on out after whatever it was he had to do got taken care of.

It may have been an omen of fate that for some reason all five of us had opted to wear our tropical summer uniforms with field scarves (neck ties), and piss-cutters (fore and aft caps). The reason I mention this is because Mac comes bouncing into Ethel's about an hour later and he's in a pissed off frame of mind. I was nursing a cold one, watching three of my fellow Marines play cut throat on the pool table when Mac sidled up to me at the bar with a cold one of his own.

The Alabaman turned Texan shook his head with disgust and said to me. "You won't believe what them some-bitches at the photo lab dreamed up for me. My weekend off and they're sending me to Disney Land to shoot pictures of all the brass and civvies mucky, mucks at some sort of a reception they're having to kick off Marine night at Disney Land. Ain't that a crock?"

I sympathized with my buddy and bought him a beer to drown his sorrow. As a matter of fact, since Mac didn't have to report to Disney Land's fancy banquet center until just before evening, we had several beers together. The other four Marines from our company was just as sympathetic as I had been in consoling Mac about having got the famous shaft which all of us at one time or the other had experienced.

Then "Pappy" Joe Allen, a short statured Marine and Bronze Star winner from Vietnam combat, came up with an idea. The tough little bantamweight who'd lost his upper front teeth in a brawl, said. "Why don't we all go with him. We can have a couple on the way and who knows, we may even get lucky since there's got to be a lot of single gals floating around over there."

It didn't take long for everyone to agree that this was a swell idea.

The only minor flaw was that Mac had been assigned to drive the photo sections small bed pick up truck, but what the hell, Marines were used to being herded around in the back of one type of truck or the other.

We stowed a case of beer in the back of Mac's Marine green pick up and off we went with me riding shotgun up front with Mac. The 90 miles to Disney Land was an adventure in its own right with people honking their horns at the happy group of Jarheads and occasionally toasting us with beers of their own. We even stopped three times to pick up hitch hiking Marines who thought it pretty neat to be handed a beer when they climbed aboard.

When we arrived at Disney Land and Mac got his truck parked in a VIP slot, the original six of us mulled over how we were going to handle the evening without getting lost from Mac. Then I came up with a brainstorm. "Why don't we be your helpers? I mean the brass won't know the difference and we can carry your gear and act like we know what we're doing."

Just the thought of pulling a stunt like that over the brass appealed to Mac and he began telling us how we could pull it off. Although Mac wasn't planning to use his movie camera he had one of the guys to carry the black wood box it was housed in. Another fellow he gave his ditty bag to which held film, different lens and other assorted camera gear. Sergeant Pappy Allen and Sergeant Miguel Gomez were each given a clipboard with several sheets of paper attached. This was a simple logic as no one ever questioned an NCO with a pencil and clipboard. Mac told the two-buck sergeants just to walk around and look important once we got inside the banquet hall. Then, with his typical sense of humor, Mac turned to me. "Myers, you're gonna be my personal assistant. When I start taking shots of the generals and what not, you tell 'em how to pose."

Now, I don't want to imply that the Marine Corps has a special school that teaches its personnel how to be bull shit artist, but after you've been around for awhile and wearing the stripes of a non-commissioned officer, a Marine has reached that point in his career where he thinks he can do anything without hesitation! And that's just what we did. We pulled off our little charade without a hitch, even considering after walking into the huge room the five of us espied about six bars set up around the perimeter where free drinks were being served. Mac, as always, was serious and professional in his work, but he had this big, shit eating grin on his face the entire time like he was going to bust out laughing at any moment. If any one thought it strange that it took six Marines to take an hours worth of photos we never got wind of it. Pappy Allen summed up his feelings on what we pulled off with his Irish wit. "We were just like the Polish Marine Corps where it takes six guys to screw in a light bulb."

The five of us stood on the large front porch pavilion in front of the reception center mulling over what to do next. Staring at the mob of Marines and their families flooding into the theme park we nixed the thought of touring the facility. Off in the distance was the Disney Land Hotel with its round, futuristic looking space age bar sticking up in the air. We decided to take the overhead monorail train to the hotel and have a couple of drinks.

I was about ready to bust my bladder since I had to take a leak so bad: so once inside the bar I told Mac to order me a brew and I'd be right back as I had to go to the head.

There was a long carpeted hallway outside the bar and I noted several private parties going on inside various banquet rooms as I made my way to the head. I was about to enter the men's room when a well stacked blond with short cropped hair, with a drink in her hand got my attention by saying, "Oh——a Marine! How you doing hon?

I smiled at the young woman and said I was doing just fine except I had to go so bad I might explode. She giggled and came up to me. "Well...do you need someone to hold your hand to make sure you don't explode?"

Oh boy!

It didn't take any smarts on my part to realize this good looking little package of joy with her short, page boy cut hair style was just a teensy-weensy tipsy. Make that plastered.

She took hold of my field scarf and tugged it a couple of times. "You want ta have a drink with me hon?"

I placed both my hands on her shoulders and backed her against the wall next to the bathroom door. "I want you to promise me you won't move from this spot until I get back. You promise?"

With a giggle she pouted those wonderful ruby lips, then said, "Don't be long."

I liked to pissed all over myself trying to get back out of that head post-haste.

Sure enough, when I got back in the hallway the girl was gone. I looked around frantically and spotted her weaving down the far end of the hall past the door to the Disney Land space bar. At double-quick march I caught up with her. "I thought you wanted to have a drink with me." I said, all but out of breath.

"Oh—it's you. Hi again Marine. That's where I'm going, to get another drink." And she held up her empty glass. "You want to come along?"

"You betcha!"

The main hallway made a right turn and dead-ended at a banquet room several yards down a short hallway. She led me into the room and I came to a knee jerking halt with mouth agape. There must have been 200 females milling around in that large room with what I could see, only a small contingent of males, scattered here and there. A large red and black on white banner hung on one wall. WELCOME TWA STEWS - WE'RE PROUD OF YOU.

A sort of squealing titter hit my ears as a dozen or so women came at me standing just inside the door. My little blond instantly grabbed me by an arm and held on to me in a possessive manner.

"Where did you find him?' A female voice asked from the crowd.

"He's all mine, so you just don't worry about it," came the reply from the blond holding onto me tightly.

Another female voice asked a question which was directed at me. "Hey Marine! Are there anymore of you around out there?"

Ignoring the question I asked one of my own. "What is this? What's going on?"

A somewhat older woman with red hair answered my question with a smile. "Why we're having a party for TWA stewardess. You want to join us?"

Before I could answer the redhead another voice quipped. "You never did answer my question. Are there any more Marines here?"

Noting this time a tall brunette with high cheekbones who looked as if she could have been a movie star, I dumbly replied. "Yeah, I've got five buddies sitting in the bar."

"Well, just don't stand there, go get them!" The movie star look alike all but shouted.

I went to the back door of the space bar on the double and didn't even take the time to walk the 50 feet or so to where my fellow Marines were sitting. I waved my hand but didn't get their attention so I gave a shrill whistle that made everyone in the bar look up. Mac, sitting next to my full glass of untouched beer, cocked his head as I frantically waved my arms in a come to me motion. I resorted to Marine Corps arm and hand field signals by pointing to the group of Jarheads, then pointing to myself and then pumping my right hand up and down which translated to: You-come to me fast. It worked as all five left their glasses of beer and made a beeline to me.

Pappy Allen asked. "What's going on, somebody giving you a bad time?"

I had a big shitting grin on my kisser and shook my head no. "Boys, as old Al Jolson used to say, ya ain't gonna believe this cause ya ain't seen nothing yet!"

The crowning glory of this little story is the next morning when Mac came tapping on the door of the Disney Land hotel room I was in. When I cracked the door open an inch and saw who it was I said, "Wait a second" and jumped back into bed leaving the door unlocked. "Okay, you can come in now." Mac strolled into the room to find me with arms draped around the little blond on my left and the tall brunette on the right.

Shaking his head with a wide grin, old Mac says, "And I end up with the red head chief-stew."

(I ran into both Pete and Mac again in Vietnam which I wrote about in my book titled YOUR WAR - MY WAR, A Marine In Vietnam.)

14

SAM AT GIO LINH
Staff Sergeant Donald F. Myers, USMC(Ret.)

The unusual seemed to be the norm at times in Vietnam. I'd had my share of strange things happen to me in this war but November 7, 1967 marked one of the damnedest and most harrowing situations I ever experienced.

Drizzling rain coupled with low, dark clouds covered the hill I was on like an ill omen all day. Yet from our northern perimeter the view looking across the valley down below toward the DMZ found clear skies with a brightly shining sun. It was almost like setting in the rear of a cave or tunnel seeing the light through the entrance at the other end.

Our artillery position was located on the highest ground in the surrounding area and called Gio Lihn (pronounced Jewel Lynn) hill. Marines have permanently manned this hill for the past two years and various caliber artillery units formed what was termed the First Combined Artillery Battalion. The North Vietnamese Army couldn't make a move within a five-mile radius without us knowing about it and we guarded the approaches to the Dong Ha Combat Base, 10 miles to our rear. My job for the past three months has been that of convoy commander for our re-supply trucks and the NCO in charge of stretcher-bearers while on the hill.

Just before dusk on 7 November, Marine Phantom Jets armed with 500-pound bombs and napalm streaked into the valley below Gio Linh and pounded enemy positions between our hill and the DMZ. I was walking the trench line heading back to my underground bunker after having been at the CP bunker to pick up tomorrow's supply order when the jets commenced their run. From my box camera like perch from the open trench line I paused to watch the sleek jets do their thing down in the valley.

After ten minutes or so I noticed the jets were no longer bombing but had taken up strafing with cannon and machine gun fire. I figured they must have unloaded all their heavy ordnance and were making final passes before heading for home.

Evidently the North Vietnamese Army commander in the sector the jets were working over thought the same thing as I had. Because when the last two Phantom's made a strafing run, almost wing tip to wing tip, four little puffs of smoke appeared at ground level as surface to air missiles were fired at the aircraft.

Tell tale white clouded contrails followed the SAMS from their launching pads as they sought out the jets. The heat seeking missiles rapidly approached the American warplanes from the rear and homed in for the kill. I stood transfixed, staring hypnotically, hardly believing what I was seeing.

Abruptly, both jets took violent evasive action. They peeled away from one another in a wild air show of twisting maneuvers as they initiated tactics to throw off their would be killers.

One pilot headed his airplane toward the coastline less than five miles to the east. He was soon lost from sight as he poured on the coals to out-race his deadly pursuer. The other pilot jerked his Phantom around and flew straight at Gio Linh hill with a SAM locked on his tail.

Within seconds, the Marine jet roared through and under our cloud cover and streaking low overhead did a screeching right turn. The airplane appeared to be less than 500 feet directly above me when the pilot did his banking maneuver. He must have pushed his throttle to the firewall because the throbbing whine of the jet engine suddenly took on a more throaty roar, and with a loud "boom" the plane sizzled away out of sight in a flash, heading south toward Dong Ha.

This was not the case of the SAM that had been following him.

The SAM broke the cloud cover over my head not less than three seconds behind the vanishing jet. All of a sudden, I got the feeling as if everything was transpiring in slow motion. So help me God the SAM appeared like it was confused!

It was like watching a movie cartoon where Deputy Dog or whom-ever, would shoot off his gun at another character who would run around the corner of a building, and the bullet would stop, sniff around, then pursue the character again in the new direction.

The SAM actually seemed to pause over my head. It may have been less than a second, but as it hovered overhead, pulsating and hissing, my legs gave away and I was on my knees looking upwards and saying, "No God.....no God.......PLEASE NO!"

It seemed as if it took a great effort for the missile to make a turn in the general direction the jet had taken. All the while, it was spitting and making rumbling noises, like it was ready to fall apart. Then laboriously it lurched awkwardly toward the southern perimeter wire of the encampment.

As I watched the SAM stagger away, my stomach churned and I felt a cramp in my gut. The large silo long missile traveled less than 200 meters when a tremendous explosion momentarily flashed an orange-white brilliance over the darkened hill. A loud thundering echo followed the initial explosion and rolled down into the valley, re-echoing the boom as it went. A large mushroom of black smoke boiled in the sky where the SAM had self-destructed. The drifting ball of smoke spiraled upward to join the cloud cover like a dark blemish on a satin sheet.

Shakily, I got to my feet and wobbled a few steps in the direction of my bunker. A lightheaded dizziness flooded over me from the sheer relief of still being alive. Once again my stomach churned and the sourness coupled with the brassy bile taste in my mouth caused me to gag. I retched in the misery of dry heaves.

A wide-eyed private stumbled into me while he was running along the trench line. His thoughts were obviously concentrated on the spectacle he had just witnessed as he did not even note my own shaky condition. We untangled ourselves and he looked at me with a wide-eyed stare. "Didja see that somebitch? What was it? What the hell was it?" He yelled at me.

Regaining a measure of composure I explained to the young private that the SAM was not meant for us.....it was a mistake.......it was meant for aircraft, not ground troops....that the pilot of the jet had been trying to get away from the thing and he just happened to fly over our position in the process of doing so.

The teenage Marine snorted in frustration as he turned and walked away toward his bunker. "Mistake!" He observed out loud as he walked. After a few more steps he stopped and looked back at me. Then in a low voice, he said. "Sarge...that fucking pilot almost got us killed! It scared the shit outta me sarge."

I told the Marine it had scared the shit out of me too.

As I threaded my way through the trench to my own bunker I wondered to myself if the jet jockey would ever have any idea of the havoc he caused on this outpost. Then I reflected that he was probably so worried about saving his own ass that he didn't have time to think about how he went about doing it. Anything to save your ass.

Even though I'd left my dignity in the puddle of bile my dry heaves had brought up, I smiled a grim smile. I understood self-preservation. Somehow this made me feel better about the entire incident as far as the pilot's actions were concerned. One thing about it.......that unknown pilot was the catalyst of an event that will be imbedded in a few hundred Marines' minds until the day they die.

The thought of death, coupled with my grim sense of humor, made me smile again as I walked down into my bunker. A ground-pounder almost getting zapped by a Russian surface to air missile. That would have definitely been an expensive over-kill.

Parts of this sea story was taken from Sergeant Myers' book titled YOUR WAR - MY WAR, A Marine In Vietnam.

15

BEER RUN IN VIETNAM
Staff Sergeant Donald F. Myers, USMC(Ret.)

The Marine Corps supply system in Vietnam was strained to its limit of capability. This was mostly due because the primary mission function of the Corps is not to engage in sustained combat operations such as the fighting in The Nam.. The actual mission of the Marine Corps is short termed amphibious operations with the entire logistics concept geared toward supplying combat units for a duration of 90 days or less. As the Marine Corps neared its third year of a full-scale land war, the supply system was defiantly in a hurt.

What this boiled down to in simple language is that it took a lot of individual effort of a special nature when a unit found itself on the short end of the stick at the lower end of the supply echelon chain. And what I'm driving at has nothing to do with legal requisition forms, or priorities, or anything else found within the "system."

What I am getting at is the true fact of life in the Corps that I've yet to hear of a Marine outfit in Vietnam that didn't have at least one "scrounger," whose job was to come up with the needed material that his unit leaders felt necessary to fully accomplish its mission. And for whatever reason, the particular material desired could not be obtained through normal supply channels. The commanding officer of a unit would never want to know how the job was done, just so long as it was accomplished to his satisfaction.

In the case of the First Composite Artillery Battalion, it seemed the only necessary supplies the Third Marine Division Supply Section (better known as G-4) felt was required was the double B's: Bullets and Beans. Our red headed battalion commander of 1stCAB, Major John Campbell, feels differently about the four-shop's assessment of his supply requirements, so among my "other duties," is that of his very unofficial scrounger.

At least once a week I report to Major Campbell and he hands me Gio Linh hills shopping list. The green eyed, stocky major with a booming voice goes over the list with me in minute detail to see what I think of our chances of obtaining certain items or possible substitutions in some cases. He would usually give me items of captured enemy gear to add to my souvenir collection which was used for barter if necessary. On the whole Major Campbell relied upon my ingenuity to procure whatever was on the shopping list.

It's a wonder I don't have an ulcer from the close calls I've had, coupled with the constant nervous strain of wheeling and dealing. On the other hand, my own brazen gall even amazes me at times. I never realized I possessed this kind of talent and sometimes daydream I missed out on my true profession. I should have been an actor or at the very least, a con man.

The division supply center forward is located at the Dong Ha Combat Base. The combat base is an extremely large military complex of over 1,000 spread out acres. Since my assignment as Convoy Commander (and scrounger), I have cultivated many friendships from different unit personnel located on the base. For the most part my bullshit sad story with my hands always sticking out wanting something, have been met with good humored understanding, and I'd end up with a completed shopping list before a day was over. This was not always the case when dealing with a couple of Army Supply Depots located on the combat base and I had to come up with a special talent to confuse the dog-faces enough to convince them to let me have whatever it was I was looking for at the time.

This special talent revolved around a half pad of Army supply requisition forms I'd got my hands on. I've doctored the forms up pretty good with rubber stamps I "borrowed" from the 12th Marines CP, also located on the combat base. The stamps are titled: SPECIAL, APPROVED, SECRET, INITIAL HERE. I figured with enough purple ink on the damn things they would look so official that the average Army supply type would hesitate to question my "Inter-Service Supply Request." (That term, also my brainchild.) I would fill in the blanks necessary to complete the requisition form, including the military unit which naturally I invented. My favorite fictitious organization was: Special Combined Forces Intelligence Company (Detached), Army/Marine Corps, RVN. On the requisition form I'd print a typical military acronym: SPLFORRECONBN - AUS/ MC - RVN. I once had an Army captain whisper to me after having arranged for my supplies: "CIA. Right?" I just gave him a tight-lipped stare and he grinned at me sheepishly and suddenly found something else to do.

The authorizing officer for my requisitions was a full bird Army colonel I invented by the name of E. J. Goddard. I thought it had a nice ring to it and felt making him an Army colonel was brilliant. This was especially true since among my bag of tricks was I presented myself to the Army supply depots as a Marine first lieutenant. Between Colonel Goddard and First Lieutenant Roger L. Brewster, USMC (nee Myers), for some reason I always-got priority treatment. One time when a snotty Army second lieutenant asked his major about my unit, the major looked over my requisition and seeing the printed name of the authorizing officer below the signature, knew Colonel Goddard, having served with him. (Beats the hell out of me but I chatted with the major as he reminisced about the good colonel while his second lieutenant supervised the loading of my supplies.)

The first lieutenant roll which I created for the benefit of the Army was simplicity to the nth degree. The entire disguise consisted of a small piece of cardboard cut from a C-ration box which was wrapped with silver tinfoil from a stick of C-ration chewing gum. A wad of the chewed gum placed on the back of the little bar acted as a fastener which held it securely in place on the front-center of my utility cap. "Ta-da!" Instant first lieutenant.

The "Silver Bar" had opened several doors for me and occasionally in ways I never dreamed of.

On December 11, 1967, my truck driver, Corporal Leroy Wiggins and I departed an

Army supply depot around noon after First Lieutenant Brewster had signed for six galvanized, 30-gallon trashcans. (I had no idea what in the hell they were going to do with six trash can on Gio Linh hill, but they were a bitch to find.) John and I headed to our last stop of the day which was the 3rd Marine Division forward supply drop point. In many ways this was considered the most important supply pickup of the month, Gio Linh's PX issue, free beer allotment.

I prepared myself for an argument as it never failed yet that the supply gunny sergeant could not find the 1st Composite Artillery Battalion voucher on his table of organization roster. In a way I could understand the gunnies problem because 1stCAB is sort of a bastard outfit made up from different batteries around the division and working independently at the Gio Linh outpost as a separate artillery battalion. Empathy or not, it was always a hassle to convince the gunnery sergeant that we were under the administrative control of the 12th Marines and that we deserved our two cans of beer per man just like everyone else in the division did. Naturally, the Marine gunny didn't remember my previous visits and I think he just liked to fuck with me. Even after I would finally convince him that my outfit was for real, I still had another battle to fight. How many cases of beer did 1stCAB have coming? With tongue in cheek I would argue that 1stCAB's total strength was 825 officers and men, (We were actually nearer to 375.) It was just a greedy streak in me wanting to get a little more beer than we really rated. Anyway, it never worked out that John and I would load 68 or 69 cases of beer. The gunny would bitch and moan, then make a begrudging compromise of 45 or 50 cases, which meant we were still making out and I'd leave the place feeling pleased with myself.

I girded myself for the coming confrontation as John pulled up to the large Butler building warehouse that contained stacked cases of beer 20 feet high along both walls for 50 feet.

Stepping down from the cab of the six-by-two and one half-ton truck. the first thing I noticed was no gunny standing at the cavernous doorway with his hands behind his back, rocking back and forth on his heels with a pencil behind his ear, guarding his sanctuary with his clip-board weapon. Instead, a tall, thin faced young corporal wearing thick framed, black horned rimmed eye glasses greeted me with a snappy salute, and a, "Good afternoon sir."

My first reaction was to gape at the corporal open-mouthed. Then, I thought to myself, "Oh shit! I'm still wearing the phony silver bar." My damn disguise was never intended to fool Marines. I knew I could fake out a doggie, but never a Marine. I finally got my right hand up and returned the corporals salute with a half-ass brush across my cap. John looked like he was going to have a baby on the spot. His damn face got so red from his puffed up cheeks that he had to walk to the rear of the truck before he busted his gut. I stared at the young corporal for what seemed to be minutes but was probably only a few seconds, while my mind churned and told me I was committed to being a first lieutenant. "Where's the gunny?" I asked in a squeaky voice.

"He's at a meeting up at the airstrip sir, but that's okay sir, I've been left in charge." He paused for a second or so, then quickly added, "You here for the beer sir?"

I relaxed a little and answered him in all honesty that, "Yes, I'm here for the beer."

The corporal looked over my shoulder at the lone truck parked behind me, then looking back at me, he asked, "Where's your other trucks sir?"

"What other trucks?" I responded dumbly.

"Sir....you are from Twelfth Marines to pick up the regiment's beer supply aren't you?" He asked me with some hesitation in his voice.

"Yeah. Sure." I replied automatically as my brain started clicking into high gear. ("Oh dear God," I thought to myself. "If I can pull off what I think I'm going to try and pull off........it's going to be the coup of the century!") Speaking out loud, I said, "Ah...I came over early to see........ah...to see.........ah how many trucks you think I'd need."

Though I hardly knew what in the hell I'd just said, the corporal seemed pleased that I needed his help, and he also seemed relieved that I knew what he was talking about regarding the regimental beer supply. He took his time calculating my question, but at last gave me an answer:

"Well sir, you're talking about eight-hundred cases of beer. You figure to make an even load distribution, I'd say you'd need at least four trucks."

I stared at the corporal for a moment in amazement because I only had a total of seven trucks and except for John's truck, the others were all loaded by now. Trying to pull myself together a little, I said, "That's about what I figured. I......ah....I just wanted to make sure.........yeah...to make sure." I croaked out in a voice I didn't even recognize. Then, continuing to stammer, I acted like I'd just got off the boat by remarking, "Well.....okay now........let me...........ah.........get my vehicles here........Okay?"

"Yes sir," he answered with a perplexed look. He must have thought I was the most stupid lieutenant he'd ever seen.

I turned and walked to John at the rear of the truck. His face was still red, but no longer from wanting to bust his gut laughing, but rather, from a serious sweat that was pouring off his brow.

"Do you believe this shit sarge?" He asked in a low whisper.

Ignoring his question I spoke to him rapidly in a low voice. "I want you to high tail it to the staging area and get me three empty trucks. I don't care if they have to dump their loads on the fucking ground, I just want them up here fast. You understand?"

For once my slow thinking corporal didn't have to mull my question over in his mind.

"Hell yes! I'll have the other three trucks to load up as much as they can from the off-load. What you want me to do about the trash cans we got?"

"Get rid of them. I don't give a shit how!" I told him tersely, hardly believing he could ask such a dumb question at a time like this.

John, not even catching the sarcastic bite of my answer, smiled at me, jumped into the cab of his truck and had it cranked up and gone in a flash.

I played the buddy-buddy bit with the young corporal while John fetched the trucks.

I told him war stories up the ass and said it was a shame he was stuck doing this kind of work since I figured as squared away as he was, I knew he would make an outstanding field Marine if given the chance. But, on the other hand, he must be pretty well qualified in supply to be doing the job of a gunny sergeant. And I had a few war souvenirs I'd be glad to give him when my trucks got back and would he mind if some of his men helped my men load the beer on the trucks? I may have out-done myself during the 15 minutes John was gone to get our trucks. For it appeared I had created my own "pet person", devoted to me and loyal without question.

When the four 1stCAB trucks pulled into the warehouse the corporal had all 10 of "his men" turn to and help load the 800 cases of beer. Actually, 801 cases were loaded as the corporal placed a case in the cab of John's truck with a sly wink and sheepish grin. His gesture made me feel bad about myself, but that was just tough shit and I'd learn to live with it. I helped with the loading myself which rather amazed the supply troops seeing an officer dirtying his hands at menial labor. I told them I was a mustang (former enlisted man) and the sort of officer that worked right along beside his men.

We were loaded and moving within the most hectic 25 minutes of my life. I kept waiting for the gunny to show up or better yet, the real 12th Marine convoy looking to get their beer.

The supply corporal gave me a parting salute while he held in his left hand his new NVA battle flag, NVA canteen, NVA pith helmet and a SKS rifle. (A twinge of guilty conscience over-did the souvenir bit.) I smartly returned his salute and as we passed by on the road leading away from the supply compound, I smiled and waved at him and gave him a thumbs up. I was probably going to be the last officer or staff NCO that was going to be nice to him for a long time.

As we tooled down the road toward the main gate, we passed our other vehicles which had been waiting at the 12th Marine's convoy staging area. Telling John not to slow down, I got out on the running board and pumped my arm up and down then pointed toward the direction we were traveling in the military manner of arm and hand signals that indicated I wanted the waiting trucks to follow me on the double.

The drivers of the heavy-laden trucks started their engines immediately and were soon following us. The trucks looked like they were part of a Gypsy circus with gear of all description piled up and hanging over the side and tail gates, including six 30 gallon galvanized trash cans tied by their handles to the wooden side-rails of one truck.

When I saw the trashcans I looked over at John and smiled which he returned with a broad grin when I mentioned having seen them.

"You know sarge....nobody is gonna believe this," John said.

I replied I sure as hell hoped that nobody, but a chosen few, would ever hear about it as I didn't relish the thought what the 12th Marines commanding officer would do if the beer ever got traced to Gio Linh hill via this convoy.

John thought about that for a moment then in a subdued voice replied, "Yeah...I see what you mean."

We made it to the hill without any problems, but once there I was faced with a major problem. Where in the hell was I going to hide 800 cases of beer?

I went down into the Battalion Aid Station bunker and told my good buddy, since coming to the hill, Chief Navy corpsman Bert Hensley I had a little problem I needed his help with. Chief Hensley's usual low eyelid, silted stare all at once became an attentive, wide-eyed glare as he listened to my story. I swear the Chief's beer belly started quivering in anticipation as he heard me out.

Two hours later found Gio Linh's Battalion Aid Station redecorated with wall-to-wall cases of beer. You could hardly make a move in the BAS without coming into contact with a case of beer.

All the bed space was stacked with cases of beer as was the medical supply bunker. In the middle of the aid bunker stood a new treatment table made out of cases of beer. All the home made tables, chairs, the desk and two door frames were made out of cases of beer. (The previous wooden versions now laying outside the tunnel entrance in a jumbled heap.)

By midnight we were able to reclaim most of the bunk bed space as distribution of the suds to every outfit on the hill had depleted the supply somewhat. Even after issuing triple the amount the outfits normally received, we still had almost 500 cases stowed away. However, no one was complaining.

By the wee hours of the morning I was sitting glassy-eyed with my glassy-eyed comrades, listening to profound words of wisdom from our glass-eyed commander.

In not so simple logic, Major Campbell solved a perplexing question regarding the possibility of facing a disciplinary situation of misconduct. This question had seemingly been puzzling him since the convoy returned to the hill with the abundant cargo of fermented malted barley and hops.

"If there is no evidence, then there is no crime. Therefore, since I don't know about any of this in the first place, I can't do anything if it's brought to my attention by higher authority and I can't find any evidence. So....the way I look at it, is this: If there did happen to be any evidence laying around, then it better be disposed of as soon as possible!" With a satisfied look on his face he emitted a tremendous belch and reached for another can of evidence after having tossed his empty one in a brand new, 30-gallon galvanized trash can.

Parts of this sea story was taken from Sergeant Myers' book titled YOUR WAR - MY WAR, A Marine In Vietnam.

16

LISTENING POST DUTY
Staff Sergeant Donald F. Myers, USMC(Ret.)

Serving as a platoon sergeant of the 3rd Platoon, Charlie Company, 1st Battalion, 9th Marines, in Vietnam while on Operation Dewey Canyon during February 1969, I had one of those opportunities to practice what I preached.

I prided myself of never ordering one of my men to do something I wasn't willing to do myself, and no doubt my 45 troopers got tired of hearing me tell them just that. All the same I had a great platoon of young Marines who did what I told them to do (most of the time) and I like to think that they all thought well of me. In heavy combat you cannot help but to have causalities which include members of my platoon killed in action. But my guys knew I was fiercely devoted to them and was careful not to do anything stupid to put them unnecessarily in harms way. I lead by example and did not hesitate to get in the thick of things myself when the situation called for it. Like I said before, my guys knew this and in their own way had a respect for me as their platoon sergeant.

One of the things I did that was not by the book I did routinely. With 16 years of service behind me there were times I made the "book" up as I went along. The thing I'm talking about is a green trooper in the platoon going out on listening post duty for the first time. Anytime this happened, I would go out with the trooper. A platoon sergeant wasn't supposed to ever do this since his safety and life was supposed to be more important than taking such a risk. Well, platoon sergeants weren't supposed to carry rifles or fight with them either; rather direct their platoon fire: but I never met a platoon sergeant in the Nam that followed that book rule. Not only did I carry an M-16 rifle in addition to my TO weapon, a .45 caliber automatic pistol, I also carried a sawed off 12 gauge shotgun and enough M-26 hand grenades that I could have probably blew up a tall building..

Now listening post duty is one of those really extra scary jobs in combat but one that is essential for unit security. Each night when we would circle the wagons and set up a nightly perimeter, a two man team from every platoon in the company would be sent out anywhere from 50 to 75 meters in front of the platoon where they would spend the night. The obvious intent of listening post duty was to be an early warning system of enemy activity coming against your line. Each two-man team carried a radio with them and we had a code system in place when they couldn't verbally communicate because they might give their position away. This simple code system consisted of pushing the rubber toggle switch that you had to press down to send a message verbally. The static squelch it created could be used to answer yes or no whispered questions from whomever was on radio watch. "Do you hear movement?" could be a question. One squelch for yes, two squelch's for no. Those young Marines on listening post duty would only use there M-16 rifles as a last resort.

An interesting aspect of life in a jungle, especially at night, is that an individual on watch can hear things and see things that are not there. Your judgment of distance is very hampered and it's a truism that sound carriers in the jungle. There have been times I would have sworn I'd seen enemy soldiers coming at me, but the light of dawn proved my "soldiers" to be bushes or small trees. The same goes for hearing things. I've heard everything from vehicle engines to men marching in cadence across a wood bridge. As I said, it can get real spooky on night watch.

Near dusk on 11 February, Corporal Duke Heller, squad leader of our platoons third squad informed me his squad had listening post duty that night. Duke went on to say that PFC William "Billy" Caitlin, a new replacement on his first combat operation had drawn the short straw and was I going to take him out as I normally did with a FNG. (Fuck'en New Guy.) I told Duke I'd take the kid out.

This was our second night in the A Shau Valley, a location the North Vietnamese Army thought they owned. Caitlin, as to be expected, was scared out of his mind, but was doing his best to keep up a brave front. He was medium built lad with rosy cheeks and a tad on the thin side. Before we left our perimeter I talked to the 18 year old Marine in an attempt to reassure him he would do just fine. I further explained to him that when his squad was clearing brush for clear fields of fire down hill when we'd first sit up during daylight that his squad leader had selected a recess in the ground about fifty feet in front of a rain shed gully and I knew the location.

The jungle gets dark fast and during February the sun sets before 8:30 P.M. Shortly after sun set the two of us crawled out away from our perimeter being as quite as we possible could. I had carried the radio as I didn't want Caitlin banging it around, making unnecessary noise. I followed the water shed downhill like Duke told me to do for approximately 50 feet, then veered off to my right until spotting a big rock sticking up he'd told me about. At a 45 degree angle from the large white rock I slithered another 20 feet or so until finding the natural grass covered bowl scooped out on the gently sloping, tree covered hill. Castling and I got down in the three foot dip and I pushed the toggle switch on the hand set three times to let the radio watch back at our CP know we had made it. My report was answered by a quick squelch. We settled down as best we could and I told Caitlin I'd take the first two hour watch and for him to try and get some shut eye. He whispered back he didn't think he could sleep. I told him to try anyway.

I actually extended my watch but by 2300 was starting to feel tired and told the still awake young man the watch was his as I was going to get some shut-eye and wake me up at 0100.

It seemed I had no sooner closed my eyes that Caitlin was nudging me. In a panicked whisper he said. "Sergeant Myers, I hear something out there."

Instantly alert I joined Caitlin on the lip of our little hole and listened intently with my M-16 at the ready. After five minutes without noticing anything out of the ordinary I whispered to my watch standee that he'd done the right thing but I didn't hear anything to be worried about.

This time Caitlin gave me 15 minutes before he was nudging me again and as before the frantic whisper that he heard something in front of us. And, as before, I waited and listened without hearing anything.

Twice more the scared witless teenager pleaded with me he heard footsteps coming up hill toward us. By his last cry wolf I was at the end of my patience and I got right in his ear and whispered in a low, yet harsh tone of voice. "I'm telling you there ain't nothing out th......."

An enemy soldier tripped, and fell right in our hole!

With all the training Caitlin had received at Boot Camp, the Infantry Training Regiment and Staging Battalion, he had but one thought in mind. He stood up and screamed at the top of his lungs....."AUGGGGGGAUGGGGG!" And takes off toward our lines like a bat out of hell, screaming as loud as he could muster, "THEY'RE COMING! THEY'RE COMING!"

The enemy soldier staggers to his feet, takes one look at me, eyeball to eyeball and screams, 'AUGGGAUGGGGE!" And takes off back the way he'd came, jabbering in Vietnamese at the top of his lungs!

In the meantime, Caitlin must have found the ravine the watershed led to because I distinctly remember hearing his last frenzied cry. "THEY"RE COmmmmmmmminnnnng." He must have ran right off the damn cliff.

For a few seconds there was a stunned silence, then suddenly, all hell broke loose. Our side opened up like they were firing the final protective line and orange-red tracers arched over my head. Then the NVA opened up with a fury of automatic fire with their green tracers bouncing all over the place. It was like being in the middle of World War II.

And so what was I doing while all this shit was going on? I'm laying flat on my back in the narrow hole laughing my ass off! I couldn't fucking believe it! Every time the picture came to my mind of Caitlin screaming and shagging ass, followed by the NVA soldier doing the same damn thing, I cracked up. My belly hurt I laughed so much. But after a couple of minutes my own predicament sobered me and I decided to try and stomach crawl back to friendly lines before the NVA made an all out frontal assault.

It seemed like it took forever but finally I got to a position where the outgoing fire from my platoon was going directly over my head 20 feet away. I wasn't sure what to do next and while I pondered on that I heard a loud voice yell over the din of rifle and machine gun fire:

"There's one over there————get the sonofabitch!"

I recognized the voice of Corporal Gary Chastine, Squad Leader of my second squad but there wasn't much I could do as it seemed the entire platoon refocused their fire to where I was on my belly trying to dig a hole to crawl in with my nose. To the best of my ability, since I wasn't about to raise my head an inch, I started screaming as loud as I could in a muffled scream: "CEASE FIRE.....CEASE FIRE....CEASE FIRE YOU DUMB BASTARDS........IT'S SERGEANT MYERS.. CHASTAIN YOU SONOFABITCH, IF YOU SHOOT ME, I'LL KILL YOU!"

Chastain heard my frantic shouting and offered a dumbfounded, "Cease Fire...Cease Fire...Its Sergeant Myers." Then, in a somewhat lower voice he yells down at me. "What the fuck you doing down there Sergeant Myers?"

After getting inside the Marine perimeter, for a brief moment I had the urge to kill Caitlin for leaving me out there like that. But after thinking it over, he had been right, hadn't he?

17

R&R IN SYDNY AUSTRAILIA
Staff Sergeant Donald F. Myers, USMC(Ret.)

As a reward for leading a raid on a North Vietnamese Army radio relay station which my platoon destroyed, Brigadier General Frank Garretson, commander of Task Force Hotel in northern I Corps, awarded me an R & R of my choice. I choose Sydney, Australia, which would be my third trip to that wonderful country.

As the bus took the group of Marines and soldiers from the Sydney Airport to the R & R Reception Center in downtown Sydney that 27th day of December 1968, I felt very smug. It was like old home week for me and I knew a beautiful girl and her wonderful family was waiting for my arrival with a sincere welcome mat laid out.

Denise Kingsley was a red haired, green eyed, shapely young woman I had met on my first R & R to Sydney. We had been writing to one another for better than a year since that first visit. Her mother and father insisted I stay at their home and better hospitality could not be found anywhere in the world.

To celebrate New Years Eve, Denise invited one of her co-workers from the electrical apparatus wholesale firm where they both worked as secretaries to join us with a date. The girls name was Audrey which fit her perfectly with her horse face look. Audrey brought along her mousy looking boyfriend Robert (Not Bob, but rather Rob-Bert.) He was a bookkeeper, or something like that, and he looked the part. Anyway, it was mutually decided that the four of us would go to one of Sydney's more popular nightclubs, named Chequers.

The Everly brothers, Don and Phil, held top billing for the evening's entertainment and we were all looking forward to seeing and hearing the popular American singing duo perform.

After three or four rounds of drinks at our table that was pretty far away from the stage, Robert asked me in his prissy, correct English accent, if I had ever seen the Everly Brothers perform before? I suppose I'm the typical Yankee bullshit artist who loves to hook 'em and reel 'em in. Or as P. T. Barium was to have said, "There's a sucker born every minute." Anyway, I laid it on thick. I knew Don and Phil had gone through six-months Marine Corps reserve training and had spent time at Camp Pendleton, California during the late fifties. So naturally I just had to tell Rob-Bert that I was practically a personal friend of the Everly Brothers, having been their instructor when they were in the Marines. To say the least the two girls were duly impressed and even Robert managed an, "Oh, I say—that's smashing."

Ah.....but the tangled webs we weave! I excused myself after the Everly brothers has completed their first show of the evening so I could make a head call. When I returned and set back down at the table I noticed my three companions were all smiling at me with looks of excited anticipation of their faces. For a second I thought maybe I'd left my fly undone, but then Denise squealed:

"I've got such grand news. While you were away Audrey and I talked with the club manager and after we explained about you being acquainted with the Everly brothers and having been their sergeant and all when they were in the Marines, he arranged for all of us to visit with them in their dressing room. Isn't that just wonderful?"

I thought to myself, "Yeah...that's just great!"

Denise's beautiful green eyes were actually sparkling like a neon sign, while my eyes I feel sure were rolled back in my head, a very dull as in dead, white luster.

Sure enough, a few moments later, before I had time to regain my composure, or to get instantly drunk and pass out, we were being led down a dimly lit corridor, following the club manager to the stars dressing room..

A hundred thoughts raced through my fuzzy brain housing, but all I could think of was, "boy you've had it now," and "if you've ever faked it before, you better fake it good this time."

I guess the one thing I didn't count on was the fact we were dealing with professional performers and even more than that, for my part anyway, fellow countrymen. For when the four of us were ushered into the spacious dressing room with me last in line, Don and Phil charged past Robert and the two girls and started shaking my hand and hugging me, pounding me on the back like a long lost brother and saying things like, "Damn Sergeant Myers, it's great to see you again" and "It's been a long time old buddy."

Everybody had wide grins including the club manager. The Everly brothers chatted with us for a while and told stories of all the fun things the three of us had supposed to have done together. Hell, after 10 minutes I was starting to believe it myself. Both girls looked like they were going to faint when Don and Phil kissed them and good old Robert was starting to sound like Porky Pig with his "ba-dap, ba-dap" trying to spit something out intelligent. Don and Phil asked if we were going to stay for their next show and we all said we wouldn't miss it for anything. After autographed pictures and good-byes the four of us were once again led down the corridor toward our table. This time I was thinking, "There ain't nobody in Nam that's going to believe this!"

However, the thrill of the event was not over yet. For as we returned to our table, the club manager told us not to sit down and invited us to a VIP table reserved for friends of the Everly brothers that was almost next to the stage. In addition, as we sat down at our new table, a waiter quickly brought up an iced, silver wine bucket with a jeroboam of champagne in it and prepared the large bottle for pouring. The headwaiter, who was dressed in a black tux, was instructed by the manager to, "Keep the wine fresh." (That means to keep it coming in Marine talk.) The manager bowed to us and said, "Sergeant Myers, compliments of the Everly brothers and your prior receipts (check) and the remainder of the evening, compliments of Chequers."

I have fallen in a lot of barrel of shit before in my life and have occasionally come out smelling like a rose, but I could not recall anything like this.

When Don and Phil came on for their last show of the evening, they dedicated their songs, "To our good friend Sergeant Don Myers of the United States Marine Corps, whom we served with when we were in the Marines." Then, they made me stand up and wave at the crowd. Denise couldn't have been happier had I been a four star general and as far as I was concerned that's all I wanted anyway, to make her as happy as I could in the short time allotted to us.

Latter, after dancing had started, I spotted Phil Everly leaning against a pillar in the shadows near the corridor going to the dressing rooms. I casually walked over to where he was standing. He was apparently watching the crowded dance floor, but when he noticed me he smiled and asked how everything had worked out? I thanked him with sincere praise and told him how he and his brother had really gotten me out of a tight spot because of my big mouth. He grinned at me, shaking his head back and forth as I told my story of trying to bullshit Robert. He said he admired my audacity and typical jarhead brass balls.

There was one thing I was curious about and I decided to go ahead and ask him what was on my mind. "Since we're not allowed to wear our uniforms here, how did you know I was the Marine sergeant when we walked into your dressing room?"

He looked at me for a second with an obvious expression of disbelief, then laughed out loud. "Hell sarge...you stand out like a sore thumb. You're probably the only guy in the whole joint with a sunburned face, crew cut hair and a suit a half-size to small. Besides, you were the only one with a sick looking smile on your face."

I laughed with him and was curious no more. We talked for several minutes and Phil mentioned he and his brother Don were not about to let a fellow Marine down and besides, with all the instructors they'd had, I could have been one of them for real. After answering several questions he had about Vietnam, which he had a sincere interest about in so far as troop moral, how we were taking the protesters, the attitude in our country, etc., I said my good-byes and returned to my party.

The remainder of New Year's Eve was spent in joyful harmony and I got to feeling so good that I even started liking Robert. He really wasn't such a bad dude once he let his hair down. You'd thought I'd pinned a medal on him when at midnight I shook his hand and toasted him as "My good ole ass-hole buddy Rob-Bert!" I also gave Audrey a New Year's Eve kiss and after she came back for seconds with gushing enthusiasm, I was thinking perhaps I also deserved a medal for above and beyond the call of duty.

Parts of this sea story was taken from Sergeant Myers' book titled YOUR WAR - MY WAR, A Marine In Vietnam.

18

MOM WITH AN AK-47
Staff Sergeant Donald F. Myers, USMC(Ret.)

I extended my tour in Vietnam for a third time and was looking forward to my free 30 days special leave home that October of 1968. The reason for a part of my eagerness was a smug satisfaction I had pulled off a fast one on the military brass. Taking home war souvenirs was authorized except for automatic weapons. Even though I was aware of this, in the course of several months I had mailed home to my folks in Indianapolis, Indiana, parts of an AK-47 sub-machine gun which I had detailed stripped to the smallest parts possible. Being a typical Marine, I felt I rated the AK as a souvenir since my men had given it to me after a North Vietnamese soldier hand tried to kill me with it. I'm not the gun-nut type and considered the weapon only as a trophy. More or less sort of like being presented the game ball after sitting up the winning touchdown. I could hardly wait to reassemble the automatic rifle so I could show it off to my friends.

As it turned out I spent many hours of my leave trying to put the thing back together correctly without success. Finally throwing up my hands in frustration I bundled the weapon up and took it downtown Indianapolis to Emrose Sporting Goods where I knew they had a gunsmith. The old gunsmith of German decent was rather fascinated by my war souvenir and said he'd play around with it at no charge in his spare time. The only problem was he couldn't work on getting it back together properly on the time I had remaining on my leave. So I enlisted the help of my 70-year-old mother to fetch the AK when the gunsmith called her it was ready.

Back in Vietnam just before Christmas, I received a letter from my mom, that painted a hilarious picture of her adventure picking up my souvenir.

The German gunsmith had wrapped old newspaper around the AK-47 and held the package together with a couple of rubber bands. My mother put it under her arm and strolled down Indy's main drag to catch a bus back home on the corner of Washington and Meridian streets, the cities hub. It was a cold, blustery day with the wind whipping down Meridian Street from the north. When mom got to the busy intersection filled with a multitude of holiday shoppers someone jostled her knocking the package out of her hand. It landed with a resounding metallic bang on the sidewalk which caused the rubber bands to snap. The strong wind quickly ripped off the newspaper which flew away in all directions. My mother bends over and calmly picks up the AK-47 and holding it with both hands, stands up waving it around a little to steady herself.

Complete bedlam broke out as shoppers scrambled to get away from the crazy old lady with a sub-machine gun. People shouted, some hit the deck, while others ran like mad. Discarded Christmas packages littered the street.

When a police cruiser pulled up, mom was standing all- alone on the northeast corner of Washington and Meridian. As could be expected the cops weren't too happy about this old woman carrying an ugly looking military sub-machine gun. But when she explained the story, the two cops cracked up in laughter.

Maybe it was because it was Christmas time, or perhaps it was because it just happened one of the cops was a Korean War veteran of the Marine Corps, but whatever it was, my mother got a ride home that day (along with my AK-47), compliments of the Indianapolis Police Department.

19

TAKE ME OUT TO THE BALL GAME
Staff Sergeant Donald F. Myers, USMC(Ret.)

While recovering from wounds at the Great Lakes Naval Hospital, Illinois, I was informed both my mother and father had been hospitalized in my hometown of Indianapolis, Indiana, each suffering from different ailments. Since I was in a convalesce status I was granted 30 days emergency leave so I could be near my folks.

I arrived home in May 1969 and spent most of my leave time going from one hospital to another as my folks were in two different hospitals. Near the end of my 30 days emergency leave my mother was released from the hospital. But with dad still in the hospital I went to the local Marine Corps Inspector-Instructor who was in charge of a 16 man staff of regulars that trained Marine reserves, and requested temporary duty. This was granted and eventually Headquarters, Marine Corps ordered a permanent change of station for me to this location for humanitarian reasons.

I had lost the vision in my left eye from an enemy mortar shell in Vietnam and also had a banged up right knee cap and leg. This, plus the fact the reserve unit was a communications outfit, meant of course the I-I Staff had no use for my 0369 MOS (Infantry Unit Leader), but fortunately I still carried the 0141 MOS of an administrative man, so I was put behind a desk and told to go to work. I soon found out that being on independent duty, regardless of your MOS, called for much ceremonial work. Two or three times a week members of the small active duty contingent was sent out on burial details, color guards and other various duties which called for Marines in dress blues.

Every member of the I-I Staff was a combat Marine, many of them with combat awards for valor and Purple Heart ribbons for having been wounded. The eight sergeants that did most of the ceremonial color guard jobs were all a great bunch of guys with a great sense of professionalism. We looked sharp in our dress blues and did our ceremonial work with precision. And we also knew that if someone did flub a movement or whatever else that may happen, not to stop but to keep right on going with whatever it was we were doing. This recovery aspect was ingrained since we all knew the average citizen, nine times out of ten, wouldn't notice the difference if we screwed up anyway. Sometimes though, it did take presence of mind to keep on trucking after a foul up. Like the time I hit a low slung chandelier in a banquet hall with the American flag I was carrying, which resulted in a few crystal doo-dads in a dignitaries soup bowl. The only other flaw in an otherwise outstanding team of Marines was we were all a little bit goosey by being recent returnees from Vietnam combat and had the tendency to twitch occasionally at sudden loud noises.

Indianapolis is a very patriotic city and for July the 4th, 1969, the city fathers planned a gala event at the local Minor League baseball field. A double-header game was scheduled between the Indianapolis Indians and the Louisville Sluggers. plus fire works, a free carnival, hot dogs, peanuts, the works. Indiana Governor Ed Wiccombe and Mayor of Indy Dick Lugar would be in attendance along with a host of other dignitaries, including a lot of military brass from nearby Fort Harrison. Officers from the other services would be there in full uniform also. Among the Marine officers to be aboard was our own Inspector-Instructor Major Al Nichols and the Assistant Inspector-Instructor Captain Ron Love.

To set the right atmosphere to get things going for the evening, the Mayor's office had requested a Marine Corps Color Guard to present colors during the playing of the National Anthem. I was placed in charge of this detail and would carry the American flag. The sergeant in charge of our motor pool, Sergeant Bob Gabbard would handle the Marine Corps colors and Sergeants Larry Stikeleather and Don Evans would tote M-14 rifles.

As we always did we got to Victory Field early to check the lay of the land and consult with the people in charge to make sure there were no hitches involving our portion of the program. From the home team dugout this official explained what was expected of us and how we should go about doing it. He pointed toward left center field and asked if we all saw the large cement teepee near the far wall on the other side of the foul line. You couldn't miss the thing since it was an oversize version of what an Indian teepee was supposed to look like. Then he pointed out a small green door in the ivy covered brick wall by the teepee and told us we would enter by this door and stage in back of the tee pee, out of sight. What he wanted the flag detail to do was march from behind the teepee toward center field, then do a right wheel and head for the pitchers mound. He said our cue for this movement would be an announcement on the loud speaker about our Marine Corps Color Guard presenting the colors for the evening. Once we were in position we'd stand fast and the person on the loud speaker would invite everyone to stand for the playing of the National Anthem. Our cue for presenting the colors would be the organist doing a lead in to the playing of the Star Spangled Banner for the vocalist.

At dusk we were in position behind the teepee and as soon as we heard the announcer start his remarks about the Marine Corps Color Guard we marched out from behind the teepee and made our way from center field to the pitchers mound where I halted the detail. I waited for the announcers next remark in preparation to ordering Present Colors which meant Sgt. Gabbard would lower the Marine Corps standard and both riflemen would give the rifle salute of present arms. The announcers booming voice came over the loud speaker and I gave an audible command without moving my lips, "Stand By." awaiting the organist to play the lead in to the National Anthem.

What the official had neglected to tell the four of us at the dug-out when he outlined our mission, was that the cue for the organist to start playing the Star Spangled Banner was a tremendously loud cannon shot being fired out of the teepee behind us, to be immediately followed by an array of fire works rockets shooting up in the air over the pitchers mound.

When that unexpected BOOM went off behind our backs the Marine Corps lost its first color guard at a ceremony as we self-destructed in front of God and 30,000 people.

The array of rockets popping over our heads only lent to the total chaos.

I was holding onto the American flag with both hands like I was supposed to and when the cannon went off I tossed the flag by its staff straight up in the air. It must have traveled ten feet up before stopping and coming directly back down in the same trajectory. I don't know if I was moving around or not as all my focus was to try and catch the flag when it came down. It slid through my hands with the bottom end planting itself in the ground. I quickly jerked it up and placed it back into the cup socket on my carrying harness.

Sergeant Gabbard did somewhat better than me, in that he didn't throw the Marine flag up in the air. He was contented in waving it back and forth furiously while he tried to duck as rockets streaked over his head.

Stikeleather and Evans said they tossed both their rifles in the air, flipping them right off their shoulders which made them spin upward like batons and both had to move around to catch them when they fell back down. Somehow, they had sense enough to get their weapons back to present arms before the National Anthem ended.

I was a nervous wreck and shaking from the experience which no doubt made the flag flutter above me like a leaf on a tree. In addition to everything else that had happened unexpectedly, we had not been informed our detail would be bathed in a bright spot light. I don't think I'd ever been so embarrassed in my life but when the last note of the singer who sang the anthem died out, my training and sense of duty got the detail to Carry Colors and we marched straight ahead as we'd been told to do until coming abreast of the dug-out where I was to dismiss the detail. The first I realized that something was radically wrong with the spectators thinking was when we approached the dug out and the entire Indian team was on their feet clapping and cheering, plus the crowd was roaring and clapping also.

Major Nicholas told me later he saw his career flash in front of his eyes when my detail dissolved and he just walked away until stopped by an army colonel who wanted to know what special training it took to perform such a marvelous color guard.

Everybody but Marines......thought it was a put on act!

If I was asked once I was asked a half dozen times how I made the American flag to shimmer like that while holding it and how long had I practiced to get it down pat to make the flag stick in the ground between my feet like I'd done. And they thought both riflemen had performed an extra fancy Queen Anne salute and could not believe they'd tossed the rifles so high without dropping them. The governor and mayor both congratulated the entire detail in Major Nicholas presents, who by now, was going along with the charade. Ballpark officials insisted we Marines stay for the games in box seats along the first base line.

And several much needed beers were provided free of charge.

20

BURIAL DETAILS
Staff Sergeant Donald F. Myers, USMC(Ret.)

When telling a good sea story the Marine relating his tale is always supposed to start off his narrative by saying, "Now this is a straight-scoop no shitter," or other such colorful claimer that tells the listeners what they are about to hear is nothing but the absolute gospel. Now any Marine worth his salt knows that somewhere along the line a sea story has got to be embellished, at least just a tad. Therefore, I must put forth this sworn statement that what I'm about to relate regarding several burial details I was on during the late 1960's may sound a little fishy, but are absolutely accurate down to the last word. No shit-straight scoop!

I've already related how the Marines I served with on the Indianapolis Inspector-Instructor staff were all combat Marines and to a man, including myself, we worker bees that went out on details, were all a little gun shy, goosey if you will. You can call it battle fatigue, or thousand-yard stare or Post Traumatic Stress Disorder, or anything else you might want to put a label on it, but it is a fact that a man fresh off the battlefield has certain little quirks that he learns to live with. Now sometimes these quirks come to an individual quite by surprise as he didn't realize he would act in a certain way under certain conditions, until it actually happens.

One incident comes to mind that I was not a part of but does offer an illustration of what I'm talking about. A funeral detail left the training center in the carryall and made it seven blocks when a clap of thunder so startled the driver that he drove the Marine vehicle into a ditch, jumped out and got under it. He later told us the only thing that hit his brain housing was incoming artillery.

I have offered this rather lengthily observation to set the stage so to speak when telling the story about my first military burial detail I was a part of upon my return from the Nam.

A retired World War II sailor was the deceased veteran our seven man detail along with an Army bugler was assigned duty to pay graveside honors for.

The sailor's funeral and burial was to be held in Shelbyville, Indiana, which is about 25 miles southeast from Indianapolis on the way toward Cincinnati, Ohio from Indianapolis. It was a clear summer day and the ride in the Marine International carryall was pleasant enough and we had no problem finding the cemetery on the outskirts of the small farm community. As a matter of habit most Marine burial details arrive at their location at least an hour before hand to get a look-see at the lay of the land and how best to position the firing squad and place the bugler. Master Sergeant Larry Lane was the NCO in charge of our detail and he'd already told me I was to be on the flag, which meant the flag draped casket when it arrived. My job was to stand at one end of the grave with my counterpart Sergeant Fogle at the other end. We would fold the American flag in the traditional tri-angle fold. Since this was my first burial detail, Sergeant Fogle would present the flag to the next of kin after the musket salute and taps, and offer the widow words of condolence from the President of the United States and a grateful nation.

Our detail was at the ready when the hearse and long line of automobiles threaded their way through the small cemetery to the tent awning gravesite. I was a little nervous and the warmth of the summer sun caused the high color of my dress blue uniform to chaff at my neck. Just the same I remained at rigid attention and made the proper salute when the flag draped casket was placed on the lowering device. My spit shined shoes were just inches from the long, deep hole at my feet and I was conscious of a trickle of loose soil that fell into the grave when the casket was put on the heavy straps. I think my mind may have flashed to the many men I had seen killed during my recent combat service as I remember feeling very sober.

The way our detail handled the formality of a military burial was when the minister gave Fogle a nod that he was finished Fogle would give me the eye and we would slowly lower our white gloved hands to the edge of the American flag and gently lift it up waist high where we held it taut. This was the cue for Master Sergeant Lane to order the firing squad, which was behind us to fire three volleys which would then be followed by the playing of Taps. Upon the completion of Taps, Fogle and I would step aside from the grave and then fold the American flag.

To this day I do not recollect the minister giving his cue but when I saw Fogle's hands reach for the hem of the flag I automatically did the same thing and clearly remember holding the large burial flag out flat with a tight grip.

When the loud crash of the first volley of the rifle salute fired. I tossed my end of the American flag up in the air and made a scrambling dive into the grave. Fortunately or unfortunately, depending on how you want to look at it, the space between the lowering device and the grave itself was so small I couldn't squeeze myself all the way down in the deep hole as the other two volleys of shot rang in my ears. But I certainly got a worms eyes view down into that grave.

The Army bugler was playing Taps when Master Sergeant Lane came to the grave and dragged me out. If looks could kill I would have been buried with the old sailor. While he was apologizing to all the mourners I regained enough composure to shakily assist Fogle in folding the flag, I mean I was really trembling. As it turned out the widow shooed some of her relatives off the folding chairs next to her and she ended up consoling me, demanding that I sit down with her. I was damn near in tears but like a mother hen she put her arms around my neck and shushed me when I tried to tell her how sorry I was I messed up her husbands funeral.

More than likely, what saved me this time from the wraith of my first sergeant was a hastily written note by the widow saying she would write headquarters, Marine Corps if she heard one word that disciplinary action had been brought again me.

As it were, First Sergeant Bill Mains was pretty understanding about the entire disaster. After Top Lane told the first sergeant what had happened and let him read the widows note, First Sergeant Mains glanced at me with a shake of his head then said to Top Lane, "Put Myers on the firing squad in the future. Make damn sure he knows damn good and well when they're going to fire!"

Gunnery Sergeant Lloyd Beatty twice had interesting rolls in burial details I was assigned to. The NCO in charge of firing details carries a sword. When ordering commands the sword is at the carry, which is to say in the crook of your right arm. When the order Present Arms is given the bottom hilt of the sword is swiftly brought up between the eyes with the blade standing straight up, then quickly lowered in a sweeping motion until the sword is pointing at a 45 degree angle to the side and the wrist is then turned sharply to complete the maneuver.

During this one military burial Gunny Beatty was doing just fine until he made the sweeping motion with his sword and lost his grip on it during the downward stroke. The blade flew from his hand and with a resounding twang stuck upright in the ground fifteen feet from where we were standing. It waved to and fro with the bright sunlight bouncing off the mirrored stainless steel casting eerie flashes on the group of mourners who stared at it in fascination while it swayed back and forth.

But the gunnies classic goof came the day he ordered present arms, came up to the sword salute and cold cocked himself with the hilt right between the eyes. The three man firing detail stared in awe as the guns went out straight forward and face down at the position of attention. Sergeant Gabbard muttered under his breath, "What should we do?" I whispered back, "We'll pick him up after Taps is finished, hell he's at attention ain't he?"

The saddest burial detail I ever served on was the one the young Vietnam war widow beat me with the folded American flag I'd just presented her. I just stood there at attention taking it, letting her get rid of some of her grief the only way she knew how, until family members took her away.

On the other side of the coin is the burial of a Polish descendent Marine officer that was killed in Vietnam. For years Indianapolis Marine reserves related the story of the Lost Detail.

Since the deceased Marine was an officer, by tradition, an officer will attend the burial ceremonies and present the folded American flag to the next of kin. The Assistant Inspector-Instructor, Captain Ron Love, along with Master Sergeant Lane, drove down to the little country village on the Ohio River in the Marine sedan we had. The rest of the detail, with Staff Sergeant Gene Cummings in charge, drove the 135 miles in the carryall. Because the deceased Marine had been a first lieutenant we provided him with a four man firing detail. Besides me, Sergeants Gabbard, Fogle, and Evans, made up the honor guard.

It was a long trip due to the fact the nearest big city was Evansville, Indiana, and even getting there wasn't easy because of a two lane highway all the way from Indianapolis. Then we threaded our way on a narrow country road with hills and curves for another 30 miles to reach the small hamlet where the burial was to take place.

The ceremony went off without a hitch and our detail had done an exceptionally well performance for the surprisingly large group of mourners that flooded the small cemetery. As we loaded the carryall with our weapons and prepared to leave the cemetery the five of us all noticed Captain Love and Top Lane conversing with several civilian mourners at the grave site. Although, somewhat unusual, we really didn't think much about this, other than perhaps the dozen or so men were offering thanks and congratulations of the fine job we'd done.

Then Top Lane broke away from the group and walked over to the carryall. "Okay you guys, listen up. They've got some kind of a lunch prepared at this meeting hall down the road and are insisting we all join them and have a bite to eat. The skipper says for you to follow us since we don't want to do anything to hurt their feelings. I expect you guys to conduct yourself in a correct, yet friendly manner, so getcha-selves something to eat and then we'll bug out."

The place turned out to be a huge white painted wood one-story building which was somewhat reminiscent of some World War II built chow halls that I'd been in at Camp Lejeune and Camp Pendleton. We were treated as royalty and each Marine had an escort to lead him into the large hall. Black dressed women fussed around us making sure we had table sittings and asked what we wanted to drink. A Catholic priest came over to our table and told us what a grand job we'd done and sat down and chatted with us for a few minutes. I'd never eaten ethnic Polish food before but found it delicious. The mother-hen ladies kept piling up portions of food on our plates until I thought I was going to bust.

Naturally we all felt a little out of place, especially since a majority of the civilians kept asking us if we'd known the deceased lieutenant or wanting to know what our military ribbons were for and other questions about Vietnam. After half an hour Staff Sergeant Cummings said, "Okay guys, lets see if we can get out of here gracefully."

We all stood up and started toward the door. Captain Love and Master Sergeant Lane was sitting at sort of a head table at the far end of the hall and Cummings gave them a high sign we were leaving. At least we thought we were.

All five of us was trying to get out of the door with about a dozen people protesting our leaving when Captain Love came scurrying up to our group. The young captain takes Cummings aside and whispers in his ear.

Staff Sergeant Cummings comes back to us shaking his head. "They've got some kind of a wake planned and Love says we've got to go to it as it would be an insult if we didn't. There's this little burg down the road about ten miles and we're supposed to go there and find the American Legion Post. The captain says it's okay if we have a couple of drinks with 'em."

By midnight I wasn't exactly sure where I was at. And I don't think my four comrades in arms did either or really cared. We weren't at the American Legion Post anymore, where we had been plied with drink after drink to make toast after toast to the fallen Marine lieutenant. Boy, Polish folks certainly know how to put on a wake! But like Captain Love had said, we sure didn't want to insult anybody. I don't think we did, especially after the first half-dozen toast where we'd learned the quaint custom of tossing your beer glass into a brick fireplace. That American Legion Post must buy beer glasses by the double gross and pay overtime for the custodian to clean up the mess in the fire place that looked to be three feet high and spilling out onto the dance floor as I remember. I have a vague memory of Staff Sergeant Cummings saying something along the line that it appeared the men folk at the wake had this stupid idea they could drink us Marines under the table and for the sake and honor of the Corps we couldn't allow that to happen. I'm not sure which side won that battle. I also don't remember how Captain Love and Top Lane got away from us. Maybe they wimped out by sneaking out the back door. Anyway, when I asked where in the hell we were at, none of my fellow Marines seemed to know, other than we were no longer in the same burg where we'd started at. We were obviously the hit of the joint we were in as our table was stacked with beer bottles and laughing women surrounded us along with jolly men who kept slapping us on our backs.

After the bar closed at 0300 the five of us wondered around the small town like lost sheep trying to find our carryall. It took awhile, but we finally discovered the carryall in a back alley. There was only one minor problem. None of us was in any shape to drive. Within minutes that became a mute point as one by one each of us fell asleep, a quaint term for passing out. The morning sun found us still in the back alley and when we all came to our senses we found we had another problem. We really didn't know where in the hell we was at.

The old farmer on the town square whom we asked directions from is probably still laughing about the five sad-sack Marines who didn't know where they were at.

We made it back to the reserve-training center before 0800 and was met at the rear garage area by First Sergeant Jim Mains. I won't relate what he had to say to us but suffice to say it wasn't pleasant. He did inform us that the Indiana State Police was conducting a search of the entire southern half of the state trying to find the Lost Detail. Major Nichols, our I-I didn't find our situation amusing either. Naturally Captain Love was the epitome of innocence and Master Sergeant Lane was nowhere to be found. Staff Sergeant Cummings, to his credit, tried to take the rap for being the NCOIC in charge of the Lost Detail, but to no avail. All five of us ended up in hack for 30 days restriction, confined to the training center, except for outside details.

There was times on the many burial details the Inspector-Instructor Marines in Indianapolis conducted during the late 1960's and early 1970's that one of our M-14 ceremonial rifles would fail to fire during the traditional salute. We never could figure out what caused this: Bad blank ammunition perhaps or something haywire with the blank adapter? Sometimes the weapon would fire but sounded like a fizzled fart going off. While those of us performing firing details always knew when our own weapon or someone else's had miss-fired, like the good Marines we were, we kept right on going as if nothing amiss had taken place. We'd joke about these screw-ups later, especially if one of the rifles let go with that particular Pffffeeetttttttt sound like a squeezed out fart. It was just one of those unfortunate facets of duty that you learned to live with.

On August 19, 1970, which happened to be my 36th birthday, I, along with my fellow Marines were standing at the ready in a small cemetery outside the small town of Pendleton, Indiana. I was the middleman of our three man firing party, with Sergeant Don Evans to my right and Sergeant Tom Fogle to my left. Staff Sergeant Gene Cummings was in charge of the firing detail and stood in front of us with his sword at the carry.

Sergeant's Gabbard and Allen was at the grave to fold the American flag.

When Staff Sergeant Cummings got the cue from Sergeant Allen, he did a right face and marched several paces, then did a right flank until coming almost abreast to the right end of the three man firing party. Doing another right face he stood at rigid attention and commenced to give the detail its orders. "With three rounds, lock and load!"

From our previous position of facing the grave, the three of us did a half right face, brought our rifles to port arms, unlocked our safeties and spread our legs in a firing stance.

Continuing with the sequence of commands, Staff Sergeant Cummings, said, "Ready——Aim————FIRE!"

Squeezing the trigger on my M-14 rifle, I got a "click" in response. A miss-fire.

Nothing sounded from Gabbard's rifle and a Pffffeeetttttttt fart issued from Evan's M-14.

The three of us automatically brought our rifles back to port arms and like we always did with a miss-fire the three of us manually pulled back on the firing lever to eject the dud round which inserted a new round into the firing chamber. This was done in a second because once Staff Sergeant Cummings started giving his commands, there was no turning back.

Dismayed, but being professional, Staff Sergeant Cummings ordered, "Ready......FIRE!"

The three of us brought our rifles up to our shoulders and squeezed the triggers. All that was heard was three clicks.

Again, we brought our weapons to port arms and cleared them for the next volley, or as it were, a lack there of.

By now Cummings was red in the face and I'm sure his shaken composure reflected our own in the firing party. "Ready————FIRE!"

When I brought up my rifle this time I offered a silent prayer. God was obviously in a playful mood, because as before, the only sound heard was three dreadful "clicks."

To this day I don't think any of the three of us know who did it first, and it had to have been caused by embarrassment and total frustration, but talk about Marines thinking alike! No sooner had the rifles miss-fired the third time, when three loud voices sounded off, not quite together. "BANG!" "BANG!" "BANG!"

Not missing a step, Staff Sergeant Cummings ordered, "Present ARMS!"

And the three of us, like robots, did our half left face and came to present arms.

The family was very understanding and even amused about what had happened when it was explained to them. And so was the Navy Chaplain who had conducted the services. I never could figure out if his parting remark to us was sincere or sarcasm. "That was a nice touch boys, going bang, bang, bang!"

21

THE SAGA OF PRIVATE BOBBY DOG
Staff Sergeant Donald F. Myers, USMC(Ret.)

Little thought has ever been given on what the Marine Corps did with its rejected war dog recruits that failed kennel boot camp. Canine recruits accepted for training automatically lost their civilian status rights and could never be returned to their former owners. In other words the dogs became government property and for those animals that got USMC stamped on their breeding papers, they belonged to the Marine Corps, lock, stock and barrel. Anyone knowing an iota about the Corps will tell you Marines loathe to waste anything; even war dog rejects.

As it turned out, a lot of dogs that couldn't pass muster for duty in Vietnam, ended up in Marine guard companies in the U. S. of A and found themselves walking fence patrol along with a young sentry. A few of these failed canines got issued to Marine Corps Reserve Training Centers for duty. The reason for this had to do with the climate of the times. The 1960's and early 70's saw several National Guard and reserve armories broken in to by militant radical groups who's aim was to steal all the automatic weapons they could lay their hands on. To prevent this happening at Marine Corps Reserve Training Centers, the powers to be in Washington, D.C. Marine headquarters, ordered around the clock armed personnel aboard all training centers. Headquarters, Marine Corps also ordered training centers to be manned with "Guard Dogs," the new title for War Dog rejects.

The first time I met Private Bobby Dog he impressed me right off the bat. It was a drill weekend for the Indianapolis Marine reservist when I reported aboard for duty that Saturday in 1969. I had just entered the building through the front hatch and noted all the uniformed Marines walking here and there when all of a sudden the hustle-bustle came to an abrupt halt. Marine reserves froze in their tracks, many plastered themselves against walls like statues.

I looked around, thinking maybe an officer was coming down the passageway of the long, narrow hall that ran the length of the building, and the enlisted men were 'making a hole' for him so he didn't have to push his way through the peons. Not seeing any brass I stepped over to a lance corporal who was standing stiff as a board, and asked, "What the hell's going on?"

The chalky white-faced young Marine reserve gave me a fearful look, his eyes darting wildly left and right. With a low hiss, he muttered, "Bobby's loose."

I was about ready to ask the young reservist who or what in the hell a bobby was when I heard a throaty low growl coming from behind me. Turning around I looked into the most evil pair of yellowish brown eyes that belonged to the biggest, meanest looking German shepherd I'd ever seen. The low growl turned into a snarl with bared teeth and with little warning the animal sprung at me. By pure reflex I flung my arm up across my face and it's a good thing I did for I think the 130 pound sleek-haired monster was going for my throat. I was knocked to the deck by the German shepherd's leap. He had my right arm I'd protected my face with in his mouth, shaking his head back and forth like he was trying to rip the limb off my body. I was hitting the big dog with my left fist that didn't seem to bother it at all, other than make it growl louder. And I was yelling at the reservist to get the damn thing off me. During the 30 or 40 seconds I thrashed around on the deck, the kid didn't make a move; just stood there wide-eyed, watching me getting ate alive.

A red faced husky sergeant dressed in utilities suddenly materialized and yelled at the dog. "Damnit Bobby! Let him go! How'n the hell did you get outta the day room anyway?" The Marine then grabbed the German shepherd by its large collar and dragged the animal off me who reluctantly released the death grip it had on my arm. Without saying anything else, the husky, florid faced Marine dragged the stiff legged dog by its collar down the hall way past frightened looking reserves while I got to my feet. Right before the sergeant turned left down another passageway, he looked back to where I was examining my right arm. "Better let the doc take a look at yer arm—looks like Bobby broke the skin."

When I walked into the sickbay holding my bloody right arm, the chief Navy corpsman took one look and said. "Bobby....right?"

While the chief doc cleaned and stitched my lacerated arm and gave me a tetanus shot, he told me about my assailant. "Bobby's gun-shy, can't stand the sound of a weapon being fired. That's the reason he flunked out of War Dog school down in Alabama. He'll take off like a bat out of hell if he hears a car back-fire but since he'd already completed most of his training before that flaw was discovered, they figured he'd make a good watch dog and that's how Bobby ended up here."

"Geez....how'n the hell do you control him?" I asked.

"Well, in a way that's another problem because the dumb shit has got so many masters he sometimes gets excited and tries to bite everybody. But for the most part, once he gets to know you he's like a big, overgrown puppy. If you're gonna be on the staff you'll see what I mean. Just stand still around him until he gets to know you."

"Who was that big red headed dude that pulled him off me and told me to come see you to get fixed up?"

"Oh..that was Tom Fogle. He's a regular like you. He stopped by for a second on the way to returning Bobby to the day room and told me you'd probably be by. Fogle's a buck sergeant like you and he's got the duty today."

I shook my head at the friendly chief corpsman and offered a grin. "I sure as hell hope that's not the norm around here. How'd the dumb ass dog get loose in the first place?"

Returning my smile, the rather handsome former Fleet Marine Force combat doc, said. "They keep Bobby locked up in the day room which is really the duty NCOs bunk room but occasionally he gets out. During the evenings when there's no reservist around the guys let him roam the place as he see fit but during normal working hours they keep him under lock and key, or at least try to. The reservist have learned that if you stand completely still Bobby won't bother you, but make a move and he'll attack in a heartbeat."

I thanked the doc for patching me up and went to the first sergeant's office to formally report in.

In the months that followed I got settled into a duty routine and came to know Private Bobby Dog a lot better. The doc was right, Bobby was just a 130-pound pup that liked to horse around like any young dog does. I eventually got to like the big overgrown mutt that had a killer instinct along with his loud noise complex. Other than roaming the hall ways in the evenings Bobby got his outdoor exercise during the hours of darkness also. It was part of the duty NCOs job to walk the dog on a leash around the entire perimeter of the training center that was located on the fringe of a huge public park. Matter of fact, the three big Butler Quonset buildings with the wood and cement office facade belonged to the Indianapolis Park Department and was leased to the Marine Corps at a dollar a year.

There was also a 75-foot cable tether line we could hook Bobby up to in the back of the training center which allowed the animal to stay outside longer if the duty NCO decided to do so.

The active duty Marine administrative personnel even kept an official Marine Corps Service Record Book on Bobby, the same as they would for any Marine. The record book showed his enlistment contract and date of enlistment, along with Bobby's picture and his inked paw print for a signature. The National Defense Service Medal was listed on Bobby's award page and on special occasions we'd put his dress blue dog jacket on him along with the medal on it. His promotion and reduction page in the service record book showed he had made Private First Class five times but always managed to get busted back to private. One time he even got to lance corporal but that didn't last long. It was Bobby's Page 12, the offensive and punishment section of his record book that explained why he kept loosing his stripes. Bobby had a bad habit of biting officers and every time he did so he was hauled in front of Major Alton Nichols, the Inspector-Instructor, for company punishment, which is called an Article 15, but better known as Office Hours. Poor old Bobby would never get the Marine Corps Good Conduct Medal which from an enlisted man's point of view was a little unfair, since we didn't see that much wrong with him chewing on an officer once in awhile.

My most memorial experience with Bobby took place during the middle of July 1972. I was patrolling around the outside of the training center with the German shepherd on a leash around 2100. Attached to one of the rear garages a shrill bell was hooked up to the telephone system that was activated when duty NCO was on the outside. The bell went off and I hooked Bobby up to the tether line, then jogged through the open garage bay to answer the telephone. As the call came to an end I heard a series of loud explosions come from the baseball diamond area that was directly in back of our garages. I had to smile at the audacity of a neighborhood kid or kids, that lived nearby that had the daring to snoop and poop and set off a string of left over forth of July firecrackers to scare the Marine watch-stander.

When I returned to the outside through the garage bay the first thing I noticed was the tether line was bare except for a dangling leash with a split in two dog collar at the end of it. Bobby Dog was gone!

I could just see my hard earned staff sergeant stripes disappearing when Major Nichols showed up in the morning and found out his four-legged, furry, barking bit of government property had vanished while in my care. I searched far and wide for over an hour, leaving the training center unattended. I walked through the park and nearby neighborhood yelling at the top of my lungs, over and over. "BOBBYEEeee, BOBBYEEee!"

My effort was to no avail and I was really at a loss of what I should do. I even thought about calling some of the I-I enlisted staff members to come in and help me look for the missing German shepherd. I did call the Navy duty NCO at the Naval Armory a block away at the 30th Street bridge that crossed Fall Creek. The Navy dude said he'd look around his area and let me know if he spotted anything. Since we Marines were pals with the Indianapolis Police Department; they used our parking lot for sector mustering and meeting area, I gave the cops a call too. Every local sector cop in our area knew Bobby from them visiting the training center. (We always had the coffee pot on and usually a doughnut or roll laying around.) The dispatcher listened to my tale of woe and said he'd pass the word to be on the lookout for a scared German shepherd.

Another hour went by and I was again standing out in back of the garages staring at the large expanse of park that Bobby must have ran off in. The shrill rattle of the outside hook up to the telephone went off and I rushed back to the duty room and grabbed the phone. "Marine Corps Reserve Training Center, Staff Sergeant Myers speaking sir!"

A voice on the other end of the line snapped back. "Hey Myers, this is Second Class Dietz from across the street. Don't know if this means anything or not but every once in awhile I swear I hear a dog whining close to the river by the bridge when I'm outside."

"Okay Dietz...thanks; I'll be right over." I grabbed a flashlight from one of the trucks in the garage and once again leaving the training center unattended, raced the long block to the Naval Armory. I went in the side gate off of 30th Street and Dietz was waiting for me in the parking lot that led down to the slow moving river.

The swab pointed out the area where he thought he'd heard the whining coming from and I aimed the flashlight in the direction he indicated. The illumination was too faint to be effective at that distance and I decided to get closer. I climbed over the floodwall and carefully made my way down the backside of the twelve-foot wall to the bank of the river like creek. The water was down due to the summer lack of rain and I had about three feet to play with from the floodwall and the edge of the creek. I walked out on a sand spit under the bridge and got my dress shoes wet by doing so. Flashing my light under the bridge I called out "Bobby, Bobby!" I'll be damned if I wasn't answered with a whimper. Focusing my flashlight where I thought I'd heard the sound the light gleamed off the lower center support pillar of the bridge. The entire bottom of the pillar was piled high with driftwood. I shifted the light around a little and the beam reflected on a pair of red eyes, and there was Bobby clinging to some driftwood. I yelled up to the Navy petty officer that it was Bobby, then stepped closer to the water and tried to coax the dog to come to me. I must have pleaded with Bobby for fifteen minutes but to no avail. By this time I had stepped into the water far enough that it covered my dress shoes and the bottom of my khaki trousers were soaked. Through my constant urging Bobby finally got brave enough to swim the 20 feet to where I was standing in ankle deep water. I'll never understand why but the dumb ass got to about five feet from me and wouldn't come any further. It didn't make any difference how much I pleaded the dog wouldn't budge. So what the hell: in for a penny, in for a pound; and I wade out a little more, talking gently to Bobby who looked like a drowned rat. Bobby just whimpered but my coaxing didn't do any good as he wouldn't come any closer. So I wade out a little more. The water is now above my knees. I manage to get a hand on Bobby's wet mane and with a handful of hair I pull the dog to me. He seemed real pleased to be in shallower water and broke from my grip and beats me back to the creek bank. As I wade out old Bobby gives me a friendly shower, shaking the water off him.

Even with Bobby ashore, I now had another problem to face. I had the dog on dry land but how was I going to get him up the twelve feet of the floodwall? Second Class Dietz thought he had the answer. "Don't let 'em go Myers. I'll get a ladder from the armory."

The sailor was back within minutes lowering a 20-foot wooden extension ladder over the side of the floodwall. I got the thing anchored in the damp soil and tested my weight on it. It was steady enough so I got hold of Bobby and commenced to work the German shepherd up the rungs. Let me tell you something. Have you ever tried to walk a dog up a ladder? I struggled with Bobby for 10 minutes, inching him up that ladder one rung at a time. I had to be directly behind the dog, using one hand to get his paws up and my other hand to steady myself. Slowly, rung-by-rung, I made it to the top edge of the wall.

Now, another minor snag confronted me. The ladder extended a few feet above the floodwall and I couldn't figure out how to get the 130-pound German shepherd around the ladder and up on top of the wall. Being the nice guy he was, Dietz comes to my rescue again. He told me to shift Bobby around to the side of the ladder and he would grab hold of the dog and pull him over the wall. To do this I had to use both my hands and try to balance myself with Bobby sandwiched between me, the ladder and the out-stretched hands of the petty officer. Can you guess what happened?

It suddenly occurred to Bobby he doesn't know this person grabbing at him and all his killer instincts learned at the War Dog school come rushing back to him. With a throaty growling roar Bobby lets loose with his fearsome attack bark and thrashes madly in his quest to level mayhem on this stranger in blue dungarees.

Bobby's snarling bared teeth coupled with his loud barking right in his face, obviously startled Dietz. The sailor couldn't be faulted for wanting no part of the German shepherd but his instantaneous reaction did me no favors. I suppose all Dietz could think about was to push the dog away from him and the ladder was a handy thing to push on. It really didn't make much difference anyway because I'd already lost my balance and was starting to fall. All Dietz's action did was to further propel me, the ladder, and Bobby out at a different angle. I splashed into the creek on my back with the ladder on top of me. Evidently Bobby fell straight down because he did not hit the water. The dog watched me curiously as I fought to get the ladder off me before I drowned. When I made it back to the creek bank I was so flaming mad that a momentary flash blazed through my head to drown the dog there and now. But how could you drown anything that stood there with its tail between its legs, head cocked to one side, staring at you with open fascination, asking the silent question, "What are we going to do next?" So saneness prevailed and I only slapped Bobby across his snout and yelled "Dumb Ass!"

I retrieved the ladder and put it back up against the floodwall. Then I yelled up to Dietz to back away. My uniform was already in complete ruin so a little more destruction to it wouldn't hurt any at this stage of the game. I grabbed Bobby and put him over my shoulder like a wiggly sack of potatoes and went up the ladder. This in itself wasn't an easy task but I managed to get up and over the floodwall where I dumped Bobby on the ground, ordering him to stay. After thanking Dietz from a distance Bobby calmly strolled at my side as we made our way back to the training center.

As I was taking a hot shower to get all the river muck off me I surmised that when the firecrackers went off Bobby broke free from the tether and ran hell bent for leather straight across the park. He must not have even slowed down when he came to the creek and went right in. That must have been a sight to have seen. But what amazed me was the fact Bobby had to swim upstream better than 300 yards to reach the bridge. If he'd went with the current I may have never found him as Fall Creek emptied into the much larger White River about a mile down stream.

The rescue, or whatever you want to call it, did have an effect on Bobby Dog. It was a little quirk I noticed that had to have its origin from the incident by the way the dog acted around me from then on. I was definitely his buddy now and he'd do anything I'd tell him to do without having to say it twice or more. Sometimes I would be at my desk and Bobby would come up and nuzzle me for no particular reason, other than to say, "Thanks again pal."

When I retired from the Corps in 1972, Bobby was still at the training center doing his job that sometimes included terrifying Marine reservist. In the spring of 1974 an active duty pal at the training center called me saying that Bobby was dead and he figured I'd want to know. When Sergeant Wing told me what had happened it sounded so typically Bobby Dog that I couldn't bring myself to be overly sad. Bobby left this earth the way he would have wanted to if given a choice. He attacked a moving school bus and was doing a pretty good job of chewing up the left front tire until he fell beneath it. Private Bobby Dog had a military funeral.

22

WHAT'YA MEAN FILL SANDBAGS?
Former Corporal John G. McCullough, USMC

During early 1967, while stationed at Camp Pendleton as a staff sergeant Marine Corps photographer, I got a job offer from General Dynamics which is located in my hometown of Fort Worth, Texas. It was too good of a deal to pass up, I'd already served a full tour in Vietnam (1965-66) that earned me an Air Medal, which is not to shaggy for a combat photographer. I left the Corps with regret but a clear conscience. I reckon the previous ten years I'd spent in the Corps had me in a mind set on doing my work the Marine way. I soon found out, my demand for excellence and leadership style didn't quite mesh with the laid back civilian way of doing things at General Dynamics. I got tired of the constant clash of wills, and feel sure my superiors and those working under me at General Dynamics felt the same way. After nine months I decided to return to an outfit where professionalism was appreciated and where my work would be respected. So, I went to the local Marine Corps recruiter in Fort Worth and said I wanted to "re-up." That was no problem, except for one minor snag. To get back in the Corps I would have to reenlist as a corporal. So what the hey! Welcome back Corporal Mac!

Naturally it didn't take long before I was again on orders to the Fleet Marine Corps Pacific, more specifically the 3d Marine Division Photographic Services. , Vietnam. It was now March 1968. I was immediately assigned duty to the forward photographic unit just sitting up at Phu Bai. This military complex, to put it mildly, was very crude and located out in the middle of nowhere, so to speak. It looked to me as if Marine engineers and Navy Seabees had just scraped off the topsoil with their bulldozers on a rolling plateau a half-mile long and declared the campsite complete. The red-yellow clay was like walking on mush that clung to your boots and every step was a labor. I guess I'd got spoiled during my first tour with the 1st Marine Air Wing at Da Nang in '65, where photo lab, offices and living facilities were all located in an old French provisional stockade constructed with building blocks and cement in the French colonial style. Boy! What a shocker it was for me when I first saw the two hastily built A-frame structures constructed with plywood and two-by-fours that was to be my working home when not out in the bush on assignment.

Upon entering the primitive hooch that had a crude OFFICE sign printed on it, I was met with an old acquaintance I'd served with before. First Lieutenant Joe Heard was a mustang, meaning he'd came up from the enlisted ranks. He had been the officer-in-charge at West Coast Motion Picture Unit, Camp Pendleton when I'd been in that unit as a still and movie cameraman.

Seeing my six foot, three inch, lean frame walk in, he said. "Welcome aboard Mac, you're just in time to help us build a bunker between our two hooch's!"

Another old buddy of mine who was in charge of the still section of our outfit, Master Sergeant "Top" Butch Arnold, smiled at me from behind Joe Heard, and said. "Ain't that a pisser Mac, your first day here and you get to fill sandbags!"

I blurted out, "What'ya mean fill sandbags! I'm still a frigging NCO!"

Sergeant John Smith, who was in charge of the motion picture section, let out with a horselaugh. "Yeah ace, so are we, and guess who else is gonna be helping you fill the sandbags?"

The urgency of needing a bunker was due to the high degree of shelling Phu Bai had attracted by the North Vietnamese Army and Viet Cong since the build up of the semi-permanent Marine cantonment had begun to be constructed. Surrounding units had already sustained several causalities and the word was to "dig in!"

And dig in we did. Ten of us from the 3dMarDiv Photography Section busted or buns for three days working on our bunker that was located between the 40 feet separating the two wooden A-frame hooch's. I still couldn't believe I had left a "cushy" job back in the states so I could come back to Vietnam and fill sand bags. The only moral boost was a steady supply of hot Black Label beer which we consumed at the rate of about one can per ten sandbags filled.

By the third day, our future, hopefully bombproof shelter was waist high with many hundred sandbags. We had heavy timber and steel runway matting lying near by to place on top of the thing eventually which we would then cover with four layers of sandbags.

It must have been around 1300 when all ten of us froze in our tracks for a brief moment after hearing the familiar "whoomph", "whoomph", "whoomph," of NVA 82mm mortars leaving their tubes. By the time we all dived into our half built bunker the deeper sharp-crack sound of enemy artillery was also heard. We automatically formed a circle inside the large pit, hugging the sandbagged walls as we cringed from the steady explosions of enemy incoming.

After fifteen minutes of listening to the shrill whine of shells whistling overhead, the clown of our little group, Lance Corporal Jim Lamont, says. "Screw this shit!" And jumps out of the pit. A few seconds later, he dives back in with a case of Black Label. We all laughed or assess off as we popped the tabs so we could drink the warm beer. I was taking a swig of my beer a few moments later when all of a sudden there was a loud thud followed by a spray of sand that splattered everyone. The first thing that came to my mind was Jim Lamont was trying to be cute by kicking sand up, trying to scare us. It pissed me off because I'd gotten a mouthful of it with my beer. I was just getting ready to chew ass when I saw this odd object standing upright in the middle of our bunker pit, that hadn't been there a couple of seconds ago. The damn thing had fins on it and was so close to my outstretched legs I could have reached out and touched it. My first reaction was one of confusion, not fear. I started to reach out and touch it when Top Arnold said. "Don't mess with it Mac, it's a damn mortar!" That's when I pissed my pants.

We all sat there quietly for what seemed to be several minutes, just staring at this menacing sight until Jim Lamont gave off with his trademark low moaning wail. "Ooooooeeee shitttttttt!" This broke the tension and everybody cracked up, but still stared at the dud mortar. With no place else to hide we had no choice but to wait for the enemy barrage to cease.

The end of this little tale has a bit of Marine humor in it also. After the attack was over and EOD disposed the dud 82mm mortar for us, you never saw ten Gyrenes work so hard in your life to complete a bunker. Not only did we do more than we had done the previous two days, we even placed a layer of six sandbags thickness on top of the timber and matting instead of the originally planed four layers. I mean everybody pitched in filling and stacking sandbags before the thought of getting any sleep that night even entered our minds.

I've often wondered what the odds are of a mortar round hitting right in the middle of a sandbagged pit with ten Marines in it without going off?

23

DEAR JOHN IN KOREA
Former Sergeant Bernard R. Loechel, USMC

I'd be willing to bet anyone wanting to put up the money that nobody can match the particular circumstances of how or why I ended up getting two Dear John letters while I was with the 7th Marines in Korea during the winter of 1951.

I enlisted in the U. S. Marine Corps in 1949. My hometown is Cincinnati, Ohio, but I joined the Corps in Chicago, Illinois. Now I live in Plainfield, Indiana. The only thing Plainfield has to boast about is it's the birthplace and hometown of the now deceased actor Forest Tucker.

I was a big strapping lad of 19 when I enlisted, full of piss and vinegar. With my six-foot, five-inch height, wavy hair and ready smile, I was more or less considered a good-looking kid. After Boot Camp at MCRD, San Diego I was assigned duty at Marine Corps Base, Camp Pendleton, Oceanside, California. In the next two years I developed an earned reputation as a liberty hound and skirt chaser, spending a lot of time in Los Angles. Like I said, I was full of myself and took the image of being a "ladies man" with a dose of pride.

When the Korean War broke out, in June of 1950, I like thousands of other Marines and Marine reserves, eventually ended up in Staging Regiment, Camp Joseph H. Pendleton. Anyone who has ever been through staging knows that your liberty hours are damn well restricted. The "keep 'em busy" regime, effectively cut my previous off base liberty activities to practically being non-existent, especially to LA. Trudging the streets of Oceanside didn't appeal to me which meant I was restricted to practicing my charm and persuasion on the fairer sex aboard Camp Pendleton. That in itself limited my activities with not a sufficient number of Women Marines being stationed there. With 12,000 male Marines cramming into the camp, with more coming in every day, it was not an easy task to strike up a relationship with a WM since they had their choice of men to choose from.

As it turned out I was one of the lucky or fortunate ones and was soon dating a good looking WM, who worked at the PX, by the name of Carol. We were both corporals so that worked out for us as a mixing of ranks between male Marines and female Marines was strongly frowned upon. I was honestly smitten by Carol and spent every spare minute I could find to be with her. In turn, Carol was strongly attracted to me. As it were we only had a couple of months together before she got transfer order to MCRD, San Diego. At the time, we both felt we had fallen into a sort of love with one another.

I promised Carol that I'd get to Diego to see her before I left for overseas and she said that somehow she would get back to see me too. We exchanged photos of each other and bid a sad farewell.

I moped around for several days missing Carol and feeling heartsick. To get out of my doldrums I took in a movie one evening at the camp theater. I have no remembrance of the movie shown that night but I do have a clear remembrance of the pretty, petite blond that sat next to me. Her name was Judy and she helped me tremendously in getting over the heartache of not having Carol around. Naturally I didn't tell Judy anything about Carol, nor did I let on that there was any other girl in my life. For the few weeks I had remaining at Pendleton, Judy and I were an item. She too was a Woman Marine but her duties was at the base headquarters where she worked as a clerk. It may have been a matter of conscience but I'll admit I felt like a heel when it came to Carol. She'd written me several letters already and had called me at my barracks a couple of times. Carol was very disappointed when I told her I didn't think I could make it to San Diego, but she was understanding about it. After all, she was a Marine.

It came to pass that the draft I was on finally boarded APA's at the San Diego Navy pier and I was on my way to Korea.

Several months went by and both Carol and Judy were very faithful in writing me nice letters which included both of them professing their love for me. Boy, was I confused! I mean I really liked both girls and couldn't make up my mind which one I liked the best. So I kept up my correspondence with both of them and when Judy asked for a picture of me, naturally I sent her one as I already had one of her she'd given me plus I had the one of Carol.

My outfit was up around the Punchbowl sector that winter of 1951 and went through some tremendous fighting with the Chinese. With the war raging around me I certainly didn't have time to worry or to think about my love life or the dilemma I'd created by trying to keep up with two girl at the same time.

After my battalion got put in reserve to re-fit and rest up a little, our mail finally caught up with us. I was pleased to see I had several letters waiting for me from both Carol and Judy. I separated the letters by the postmarks so I would be reading the oldest one first. Taking the three letter from Carol first I read the first two then started on the third. It was a Dear John letter. On top of that it was not a very nice Dear John letter as she was rather pointed on what she thought of me in an unflattering way, plus writing she never wanted to hear from me, or see me again. Stung and dismayed, I began reading Judy's letters, hoping hers would erase the bad taste in my mouth after having read Carol's. By the time I read the first sentence in Judy's last letter I know my face was burning red. It too was a Dear John and in no uncertain words she blasted me out of the water with both barrels, letting me know what a drip I was. To be honest, my feelings were really hurt and my morale plummeted as low as whale shit in the bottom of the ocean. But after re-reading the final letters of the two girls I began to see the humor in it and had to agree with them that I was an asshole.

As Paul Harvey, the radio commentator would say......and now for the rest of the story. Carol was settled into to her new job at MCRD, San Diego when Judy also got transfer orders, and guess where? To MCRD, San Diego! Not only that, they shared the same barracks with their bunks almost next to one another. Can you imagine Carol's surprise when Judy opened up the letter from "her" boyfriend, who was in Korea, and proudly showed Carol the picture I'd sent her?

Like I said at the beginning, if anyone can match those odds, I'd sure as hell like to know about it.

Bernie Loechel was severely wounded in Korea and spent three years in naval and VA hospitals to repair a damaged leg. In addition to his Purple Heart he holds the Silver Star Medal for conspicuous gallantry. He is a retired railroader who lives with his wife in Plainfield, Indiana. He is active in the Marine Corps League and currently serves as Commandant of the Indianapolis Detachment.

24

"SCATTER!"
Commander Charles R. Clarke, USCGR(Ret.) - Former Corporal USMC

After the Koran War broke out in June 1950, and President Harry S. Truman made his executive decision that U. S. forces would be committed, my Marine reserve outfit, the 16th Infantry Battalion, was one of the first to be activated.

We left Indianapolis, Indiana on a troop train the 21st day of August with crying wives and sweethearts waving their handkerchiefs at us from the union station platform.

The five-day trip across country is a sea story in its own right but I'll let somebody else relate that one of these days.

I had a childhood pal I was raised with by the name of Jack Smith. Jack was about as salty as they come. He'd been wounded twice on Saipan in World War II with the 2d Marine Division, and the short, dark curly headed bantam rooster, could not have been any more cockier than when he used to charge cave emplacements as a BAR man. Jack was a corporal and had been assigned duty with the advance party that had preceded our reserve outfit to Camp Pendleton, California. During the two weeks he'd spent awaiting for the 16th Infantry Battalion's arrival, Jack had already established himself as a wheeler-dealer with the regulars, and as was his nature, pretty well did as he pleased.

When our troop train finally came to a steam-hissing stop at Oceanside's small train depot, who else but Corporal Jack Smith, was waiting next to a jeep to welcome the new arrivals. A long row of Marine six-by trucks were staged out in front of the depot to transport the hot, sweaty Marine reserves to Camp Pendleton.

I'd spotted Jack as soon as I'd gotten off the old Pullman car to form up with the rest of the peons while our officers milled around on the train platform letting the sergeants do the drudgework. He raised his eyebrow at me and offered a smirky smile. I nudged Andy Jacobs who stood next to me and whispered under my breath. "Didja see Jack over there by that jeep and trailer?"

My old buddy Andy, who would one day become a long-term congressman from Indiana, muttered back. "Yeah, I see him."

As over 500 Marine reserves stood at ease awaiting the order to board the trucks I noticed Jack casually stroll over to the command group of officers and after saluting our colonel, looked at a clip board he was carrying and conversed with our CO.

A couple of minutes later my platoon sergeant, Sergeant Leroy Callahan, a tough Indy cop in civilian life, approached to where I was standing. Looking at his own clip-board, he said. "Okay, Clarke, Jacobs, Curtis and Ashley. Fall out and go over to that jeep there. You're being assigned to Corporal Smith for a work party."

I couldn't help but to smile as I approached the jeep and trailer but with a stern look and slight shake of his head, Jack muttered lowly. "Knock it of Charlie till we get away from here."

I rode shotgun and the other three squeezed in the back seat of the jeep. As we pulled away from the depot with our outfit now starting to board the trucks, I turned to Jack, and asked. "What kind of working party you got for us?"

Glancing over at me with another smirk, Jack says. "What working party?"

Andy Jacobs, who had listened to my question then asked one of his own. "Then what the hell are we doing?"

"Just wait a minute and I'll show ya." Jack answered.

It actually took more than a minute but after being waved through the front gate of Camp Pendleton by a white helmeted Marine MP we tooled down Basilone Boulevard until reaching Sixteen Area. Jack drove up one of the many hills abounding at Camp Pendleton and passing a row of white painted, two story wooden barracks, went down a little trail in back of the barracks until coming to this sort of grassy bowl. He braked the jeep, saying. "This looks like a good spot, pretty well hidden from view."

The four of us he'd picked up looked at one another in confusion, shrugging our shoulders.

"What are we doing here?" Joe Curtis wanted to know.

"C'mon 'round back to the trailer, and I'll show ya." Jack replied with a shit-eating grin.

We gathered around the tarp covered jeep trailer and noticed for the first time water dripping from the tailgate. With a flourish, Jack pulls back the tarp he'd untied and there in the back of the trailer was at least five cases of iced down beer. His grin grew wider as he saw our awed expressions. "You didn't think I was a' going to forget about my buddies Didja?" And he produced a church key and began popping cold cans of beer.

"Where did you get it?" Ashley asked.

"Don't ask. Lets just say I knew what a bummer of a trip you guys went through on that hot sonofabitching train and figured you'd all like a little cooling down."

Happily sucking down the cold beer we shook our heads in amazement at the audacity of our fellow Marine.

Not being able to let well enough alone, future congressman Andy Jacobs just had to ask. "Where'd ya get the jeep and trailer?"

Offering his pal a pained look, Jack answered tersely. "I borrowed it!"

By taps, none of us were curious or concerned about much of anything, let alone what barracks we were supposed to be in or whether or not anyone was wondering what had happened to the working party that had left the train depot at 1900. As a matter of fact, we were enjoying ourselves so much that we'd became what can be best described as somewhat boisterous. A pile of empty beer cans clanked at our feet as each new one was opened and like many Marines before us we serenaded the bright moon above.

Our singing and other loud activities finally got a response from Camp Pendleton's military police. Two MP jeeps with spotlights stopped on the knoll above our little bowl. Of course we didn't know at first the jeeps had spotlights, but when the dual stabs of bright white lights hit our little group, it froze us in place for a long moment like frightened deer's on a highway. When a gruff voice hollered out. "Okay you guys, stay right where you're at!" It effectively broke up our party.

Jack yelled in a loud voice. "SCATTER!"

Yeah, we scattered okay. Like five ducks in a row stumbling up from the grassy bowl, all going in the same direction, right behind one another, heading toward the row of barracks we'd passed much earlier in the day.

Jack was leading the pack as we ran toward one barracks. To this day, I don't know what in the Sam Hill he had in mind, but with the MP's hot on our tail, we all followed him into the barracks. We crashed through the front hatch and milled about in the front passageway in total confusion for a few seconds, then Jack heads to one of the squad bays. The first rack he sees he yanks the sleeping Marine out of it from the top bunk and jumps in the rack and covers himself with the blanket. Hearing the pounding footsteps of the MP's entering the barracks, three of us, follows Jack's stunt and toss Marines from their racks and crawl in. Ashley ran into the shower room. By the time the four MP's got into the squad bay they find four pissed off Marines in their skivvies cussing, and yelling, trying to figure out what had just happened.

It was with a touch of genius when Jack yelled out. "Sonofabitch, get them fuck'en drunks outta here. Bastards running in here taking their clothes off and raising hell."

In muffled tones the other three culprits of this little fiasco offered similar pleas to let us get back to sleep.

Naturally the four guys in their skivvies are raising an uproar but the no nonsense Marine MP's weren't in the mood to take any shit from them and roughly push them to the outside passageway.

I have no idea what took place in the passageway with the four yelling Marines and four yelling MP's, but the distraction gave four sot Marine reservist the time to get out the fire escape door, and get the hell away. In the meantime, Ashley had been hiding on top of the large shower stall like a big bird and he told us later that one of the MP's had even came into the head and looked around but didn't look up. Ashley said he stayed put until he heard the commotion fade to the front of the barracks by the main door, then he ran through the squad bay we'd been in and also made it out the fire escape hatch.

I'll admit that over the years I've often wondered what ever happened to those four Marines we tossed out of their sacks. Even at this late date, I hope they don't read this yarn.

Charlie Clarke has an interesting military background. He enlisted in the U. S. Army Air Corps in World War II and had finished Air Cadet Training when the Army found out he was married, a no, no, in those days. So the Army discharged him and he ended up in the Marine Corps. He finally got his military wings through the Coast Guard Reserve where he flew rescue helicopters and other aircraft for twenty years. This time, his childhood sweetheart and wife of 55 years, Shirley, was able to be a part of his military life, and she obtained the rank of full lieutenant in the Coast Guard Auxiliary. Clarke is a retired railroad engineer and resides in Indianapolis, Indiana.

25

SANDS OF IWO JIMA
Former Private First Class Sam L. Queen, Jr., USMC

By the time the 5th Marine Division laid off Iwo Jima we had been at sea for six weeks. Our long voyage from Hawaii's Camp Tarawa, located on the famous Parker Ranch, was due so all the ships that eventually became a full-fledged armada could rendezvous. As it were, the brass miscalculated how long we'd be aboard ship and our less than great chow, got down to 900 calories a day.

The APA (Attack Troop Transport ship) I was on held 2,500 Marines of the reinforced 5th Engineer Battalion of which I was a part of. We also had 500 naval personnel aboard whose responsibility it was to land us. At one time the 5th Engineers was a part of the 16th Marine Regiment, but now we were an independent battalion for the division.

On D-Day, February 19, 1945, I was awoke at 0345 by a sergeant-of-the-guard who put me on guard duty at the topside hatch leading up from my unit's compartment. I was ordered not to let anyone out of below decks until told by higher authority to do so.

At exactly 0600 all hell broke loose. More than 500 ships surrounding the seven and half square mile, pork chop shaped island, opened up with their big guns. The Marines down in the compartment below deck scampered up the ladder to get a look-see at what was going on. I held them at bay at the hatch per my orders.

A short time later, with the all but deafening din of crashing naval guns still firing, the sergeant that had put my on guard duty came by again. This time he issued me live ammunition for my M-1 rifle and told me to stand at the railing and shoot anything I saw floating. The Japanese were known to send out suicide swimmers to set off explosives on troop ships.

Since the hatchways were no longer under guard it didn't take long for a thousand Marines to be standing topside watching the pre-invasion bombardment. Airplanes from 14 aircraft carriers added their weight to the explosive onslaught with their bombs and rockets. Most all the Marines watching this spectacle agreed that not many Japs on the island could still be alive. How wrong we all were.

The Navy finally fed us a good breakfast at 0800; the traditional steak and eggs. This meal which would be the last one many Marines ever ate was at least a far cry from the diet of boiled beans and potatoes we'd eaten for the past three weeks.

I landed on Iwo Jima dragging a bunch of blankets ashore I'd been ordered by my sergeant to carry, along with several other fellows. I also carried four pints of whole blood in a water-sealed .30 caliber ammo box. It was a bitch getting those water logged blankets up the sloping black sand beach and we immediately discovered there were a lot of Japs left alive. Withering small arms fire raked our beach area, along with artillery and mortars. After depositing the blankets at a hastily set up aid station 50 yards from the water, I looked around my new surrounding. The first thing I noticed was the Higgins boat that had brought us in had got stuck. The two sailors manning the landing craft tried to back it off but it turned sideways where a wave caught it, rolling it over. One sailor jumped clear but the other one was trapped by the boat and crushed into the sand. Several fellows ran down to help the guy but when they reached him they just shook their heads and walked away.

My outfit was told to dig in along the beach as our mission for the night was to be perimeter defense for the BAS (battalion aid station.) It was to be a night I'll never forget and the primary reason I'm telling this story.

You didn't "dig in" on the black sand of Iwo's beach. What you did was fill sandbags and place them around the shallow pit you scooped out in order to keep the coarse volcanic sand from filling your hole back up. Four of us labored for better than an hour putting together a reasonable sized foxhole.

We were just getting settled into our nights accommodation when our sergeant came by with orders that word had been passed that there would be two men per hole with one awake at all times. He further told us that the man standing watch was to keep his mouth shut regardless what took place and not to shoot at anything unless it fell into your position.

So what the four of us did was to put up a partition of sandbags across our hole to halve it. As it grew dark we all chuckled at the way we'd outfoxed the brass and had still complied to the spirit of the order of two men per hole. Nobody said the holes couldn't be right next to each other.

Very late that night Jap mortar shells began walking the beach. I was on the watch and could hardly believe my buddy I shared the hole with could sleep through such a terrifying ordeal. Explosions continued to erupt nearby as I cringed in my hole. Suddenly, the partition part of our dual foxhole blew apart right in my face. I gagged getting the sand out of my mouth, and had to do the same for my eyes and ears since I was covered with the stuff. Scared out of my mind I followed my sergeant's orders and kept my mouth shut and went on with my watch.

At daybreak I sneaked a peek on the other side of the caved in sandbag partition. Both Marines were laying in a mangled heap, dead. A Japanese mortar round had scored a direct hit on there half of the hole.

26

SHOT ONCE - 56 BULLET WOUNDS
Corporal Charles J. Hutson, USMC(Ret.)

For those Marines that may read this, it will come as no surprise when I say that after having trained as, and given the MOS 0351-Anit Tank Assault Man, that upon my arrival at Camp Pendleton, California, in mid-1968, I was immediately sent to language school.

The sometimes strange and mysterious ways of the Corps had me undergoing a 20-week course in Vietnamese at the Defense Language Institute, Presidio of Monterey.

In all fairness to the paper shuffling, billet filler types who works on TO's (Table of Organization), I suspect the reason I was sent to Monterey for a crash course in Vietnamese was because I scored high on that part of the GCT (General Subject Test) taken at MCRD San Diego that pertains to language proficiency.

The female Vietnamese instructors at the school must have done a good job teaching me as 30 years later I can still order rice and beer in any Vietnamese restaurant.

Anyway, upon my successful graduation from the language course I received my orders to Viet Nam.

After a late April 1969 arrival at Dong Ha Air Base I was told to report to the 1st Battalion, 7th Marines, 1st Marine Division. The adjutant of 1/7 hastily scanned by Service Record Book and noted my recent completion of the Vietnamese language course. The balding, red headed adjutant warrant officer was quick to point out to me that 1/7 had no need for Anti Tank Marines but could use some scouts for their Kit Carson volunteers. He ordered me to further report to the S-1 shop for assignment.

As any person with a military background knows, S-1 is the combat intelligence gathering section of a battalion. A first lieutenant who gave me the scoop of what was expected of a Marine Intelligence Scout greeted me warmly. He also explained the Kit Carson Scout program to me which I had absolutely no knowledge of prior to him telling me.

The program was named after the famous western frontiersman and soldier, Colonel Christopher "Kit" Carson. Kit Carson, who helped open the west in the early-mid 1800's, used captured hostile Indian's to do his scouting for him. Although there is no record of what he used as an incentive, other than fair treatment, historical records are also silent that once converted the turncoat Indian's were ever disloyal to Carson.

Someone in the Marine Corps hierarch of command came up with the brilliant idea to do as Colonel Carson had done and thus, the birth of the Kit Carson Scouts. Only this time, instead of Indian's, these scouts were recruited from prisoner-of-war compounds holding captured North Vietnamese Army soldiers.

The Kit Carson Scout I got was named Nguyen Ai. Ai was married with 13 kids and had been captured in 1968 during the Tet Offensive. He told me the last time he's seen his family was six years ago when he had bid them good-bye at the end of his last military home leave prior to heading south with his regiment. The thin, short statured and wiry Vietnamese, at age 28 was a lot older than my 19 years, plus he had at one time out-ranked my corporal stripes, having been a senior sergeant, the equivalent to American platoon sergeants. In addition, he had a hell'uva lot more military experience behind him than my less than two years. It was a good thing I was a cocky Marine who thought I could do anything because other than not completely trusting Ai at first, I never felt intimidated by him. He also told me he figured his family still lived in the small hamlet 25 miles west of Hanoi but was resigned to the fact he would probably never see them again. His reasoning was simple. How could he ever go back home since he felt certain his defection to the American Marines would be found out? I thought it very sad that his matter of fact attitude left no room in his mind to ever make the attempt.

The two of us got along good together and Nguyen proved to be an asset on the patrol operations we were assigned to. In reality my function was to keep an eye on Nguyen while at the same time protect him from my fellow Marines, many who did not understand or appreciate a former enemy soldier in there midst. And I also had to act as a buffer between what my orders were from Battalion S-1 and what many times company or platoon commanders thought my two man team should be doing. Nguyen and I were "farmed out" to the different letter companies of the battalion on a mission-by-mission assignment. The only time we remained with Battalion Headquarters in the field was when it was a Battalion Op.

It was a constant battle for me to try and convince the company commanders that my mission was not to walk point, which they always wanted me and Ai to do. Time and time again I explained that Ai's primary job was to advise and to examine anything the rifle companies came across. My stout refusal to waste Ai on point, where sooner or later he was bound to be a causality, came damn close to insubordination. I know the officers thought of me as a snot nose, six foot, two inch, 200 pound, wise ass kid and I was threatened with disciplinary action more than once. When this happened I used my last ditch argument by requesting they check with our battalion commander, Lieutenant Colonel John A. Dowd, before running me up with morning colors. Evidently they took me at my word and did just that. Colonel Dowd knew Ai was more valuable in explaining various signs of the NVA we came across such as comm wire, probable ambush sites, interrogating captured enemy soldiers, etc. Therefore he backed me to the hilt.

In time things got better for me and Ai and we were mostly left alone to do what we was supposed to do. But we weren't very popular with the officers. We did however gain a measure of begrudging respect from most of the NCOs and grunts. Ai proved effective in setting up ambushes, finding booby traps and more than once warning us we were about ready to get hit. It was also noticed he did not hesitate to fire his weapon at his former comrades in arms. In addition we would occasionally team up with a two-man sniper team and conduct little foray patrols of our own in enemy territory. On one of these patrols we discovered a company of NVA taking a bath break in a deep stream and called in artillery on them. After adjusting the arty fire we shagged ass and did not see the final results since we were too close to the impact area. Even though we'd done good this particular company commander was still pissed off at us because we didn't confirm a body count. Viet Nam was indeed a strange war.

In early August 1969, 1/7 got into a brawl with regular hard-core NVA. This took place in the Que Son valley which the Marines called the Arizona Territory. The valley is located several miles south of Da Nang and our area of operations was not far from a large ville Hiep Duc.

On August 13, Ai and I was humping with the battalion CP group in back of the rifle companies which were line abreast going across dried up rice paddy acreage toward a not to distance jungle tree line. Because of Ai's examination of enemy dead Colonel Dowd knew his battalion was fighting the 90th NVA Infantry Regiment, 2d North Vietnamese Division. For two days it had been a toe-to-toe battle royal with no holds bared and neither side giving an inch without it being contested to the utmost. Colonel Dowd had one thing in mind and that was to destroy the 90th NVA Infantry Regiment or to hurt it so bad they would have to retreat. Since I was a part of S-1 I was aware we'd already killed over 200 of the enemy and now, finally the NVA was giving ground and pulling back. Colonel Dowd's orders to his rifle companies was straightforward: closely pursue the NVA into the jungle forest and eliminate them.

At a little past 1200 the enemy regiment showed 1/7 it still had a lot of fight left in their ranks. We were roughly two football fields away from the tree line with a river to our left when all hell broke loose. Enemy rockets, mortars, machine guns, AK automatic rifles and SKS rifle fire raked our entire front with a vengeance. Colonel Dowd and the entire command post group rushed forward on the run to join the fray from the front lines. A heavy volume of fire hit the command group and I was not more than fifteen feet away when I saw Colonel Dowd get violently punched to the ground. He had taken a machine gun burst to his upper body which killed him instantly. I ran toward a little mound of earth and dived behind it with bullets chewing up the dirt all around me. Our Marine Air Liaison Officer made a headlong dive and landed right beside me and the two of us huddled together behind the not so high mound of earth. All of a sudden it seemed that every NVA RPG man (Rocket Propelled Grenades) was focused on the small mound I was cringing behind. Explosion after explosion hit on or around the mound sending up clods of soil in every direction. I couldn't figure out what in the hell was going on until I happened to see the big whip antenna sticking up from the air officer's radio he was carrying. The frigging NVA thought they had the battalion commander located. I screamed at the air officer to pull the antenna down but before he could react a sizzling hunk of an RPG round did it for him, cutting it right in two leaving about a foot sticking up. At this time I noticed two Marines in a ditch approximately 20 feet from where I was at. Neither one was moving and I figured they were either wounded or dead. I thought to myself if they were wounded they needed help and without thinking raised myself to a crouch and crabbed my way to them as fast as I could move with bullets whizzing by me. When I dove into the ditch the two Marines jerked back in fright, like I was the devil himself paying a visit I asked them why in the hell they weren't firing back at the NVA and they sheepishly answered they weren't going to raise their heads above the rim of the ditch to aim. Instead of chewing them out I tried to calm them down and showed them how to stick their 16's over the berm and fire at the tree line without exposing themselves. After seeing me fire my M-16 in this manner they both followed suit and begin laying down a field of fire. I stayed with them a couple of more minutes until satisfied they'd licked their fear and was acting like the well trained Marines they were.

I knew I had to find Ai as he was my responsibility. I belly crawled to the end of the ditch and decided to make a run for it toward the last area I'd seen Nguyen at. I didn't make it more than a dozen yards when an enemy bullet must of hit my upper right chest. My flak jacket evidently deflected the round from penetrating my body but as it were it didn't make much difference anyway. I was carrying a bandoleer of ammunition Mexican bandit style across my chest. The NVA bullet hit my bandoleer and my own ammo started cooking off before the entire bandoleer exploded with one big bang. Naturally it stunned me but I swear I don't remember feeling any pain. I sat down on my ass right there in the open cradling my right arm with my left one. Somehow I'd lost my helmet with my soft cover in it and I looked around for it while NVA bullets chewed up the dirt all around me. It must have been a bunch of Maggie drawers no quals firing at me since I wasn't hit again from this action. (Red Maggie drawers is a firing range signal of having missed the target. No quals means you didn't qualify as a rifle marksman or higher.). The two Marines in the ditch evidently saw what had happened to me as they were blasting away with aimed fire at the tree line where they thought the enemy fire was coming from. A gunnery sergeant began yelling at me to come his way but I just continued to sit there wondering where in the hell my cap was at. The gunny obviously knew I was in shock and he ran over to me and tried to drag me away. I yelled at him I wasn't going anywhere without my damn cap. I'll be damn if he didn't say "Okay," and with all that shit hitting the fan around us he calmly stalks the ground until he finds my soft cover and gives it to me.

So there it is: a Marine getting shot once and ending up with a total of 56 bullet wounds, counting the ones that exploded.

I had a brief moment's good-bye with Nguyen Ai before the med-evac helicopter took me and other wounded to a field hospital. I wished him luck and chided him to break his habit of dangling his legs over the side of personnel carriers as a mine would get him one day. Over the years I've often wondered what may have happened to him.

Chuck Hutson underwent numerous operations because of his serious wounds. Although his right arm is semi-paralyzed he did not lose it. He is married, the father of four children, a grandfather and attorney in Raleigh, North Carolina where he lives with his wife Susan.

27

HANG ON TO YER HAT——WE'LL GET THERE!
Private First Class Herbert R. "Lefty" Luster, USMC(Ret.)

I was born in Heaane, Texas which is in Robertson County on June 21, 1931. At age 17 in August 1948 I enlisted into the United States Marine Corps at Little Rock, Arkansas. Saw the ocean for the first time when I took the train to MCRD, San Diego. I was the "baby" of Platoon 83; only weighed 125 pounds and at five foot, ten inches tall was a skinny kid. Just the same I was a feisty young'en and I'd been the wrestling champ of my weight division in high school. My wrestling ability probably helped me to hold my own with the other fellows in boot camp. The Corps put a few pounds on me and I ended up as the high expert rifleman of our series on the Camp Matthews range. I made PFC out of boot camp.

When the Soviet backed North Korean Army invaded South Korea with eight divisions led by Russian-made T-34 tanks on June 25, 1950, my outfit, the 5th Marine Regiment had just returned from Guam and was busy getting settled in at Camp Joseph H. Pendleton, outside of Oceanside, California.

After President Harry S. Truman made his famous decision to help stop the communist treachery by committing U.S. forces, Commandant of the Marine Corps General Clifton B. Cates immediately placed the Corps on a war footing. That war footing hit our under-strengthed regiment right between the eyes when orders came down that we were to be made into a brigade. What this boiled down to was that we would be a small combat division with supporting arms that was on par with the U.S. Army's regimental combat team. The 5th Marines was so under-manned that a call went out to all Marine post across the United States to ship us as many bodies to us as they could. Marine Barracks and other security details were stripped of their personnel. The 2d Marine Division in Camp Lejeune, North Carolina, was also ordered to send what they could. Even with all the new men that flooded into Camp Pendleton; when the provisional brigade built around the 5th Marines was called ready for duty, on July 7, 1950, the three rifle battalions only had two companies apiece.

This did not stop our commanding general Brigadier General Edward A. Craig, a slim, white-haired Connecticut Yankee, from issuing the order to mount out on July 14, just seven days after being activated. And if things had not been interesting enough all ready with the hussle-bussle of putting our brigade together, we soon found ourselves facing strange problems trying to get into the war, which is the real gist of this little story.

Arriving in San Diego to board the APA Henrico, the long truck convoy of Marines was greeted at the entrance to the Navy shipyard by a large crowd of pickets. They were all young men and were blocking the gate to the pier where our troop ship was waiting. For whatever reason they were all dressed the same: blue jeans and white T-shirts. And they all looked about the same with their long greasy hair and holding various signs of protest of an anti-war nature.

I was at the front part of the convoy and my sergeant was in the lead truck. He dismounted from his six-by and walked down the line of trucks that held his company. He paused at each truck and talked a couple of minutes. When he got to the truck I was in he gave us his words of wisdom. "We ain't gonna start fighting this fuck'en war on the streets of Diego but if these clowns try ta start any shit with ya, ya know what to do. My truck is going through the gate and I ain't planning on having it to stop, so follow my lead and remember you're Marines!"

When the sergeants truck moved forward toward the idiots waving their signs I guess they realized the truth of the situation as they all stepped aside with big grins on their faces.

Commandant Cates was at the dock to wish us a bon voyage and told us to get the job done and get our asses safely back in a hurry.

On the second day out, even dumb Marines who didn't know diddlysquat about ships knew our tub was sick. The ships engines were making weird rumbling noises and we got the word it was caused by obvious sabotage. We limped our way in for repairs at the Frisco-Oakland docks. To keep us in shape we went through daily calisthenics on the dock along with a few military subject classes thrown in.

It took five days to repair the ship but we finally went under the Golden Gate bridge and once again headed out to open sea unescorted. It seemed we'd no more got out of sight of land than those top-side noticed the ship was making a wide, sweeping turn, heading back east. The U.S.S. Henrico, APA 45, returned to the Frisco-Oakland docks, Someone was obviously delaying the ready to fight U.S. Marines as much as possible since the ship was messed up again.

After anti-war protesters and two delays for repair the Henrico was at last nearing Japan. A Red sub jammed the APA's radar and damn if the skipper of the Henrico didn't turn his ship to try and ram the commie sub; causing more delays as we chased the submarine.

So what happens when we at last have Pusan, Korea in sight? The tide is going nuts and we spend the day offshore and didn't land until the night of August 2, 1950.

Then, after all the crap I went through just to get to Korea, I last 15 days as a BAR man with A-1-5 before getting zapped by a Russian burp-gun that destroyed my BAR and mangled my right arm. This happened on No-Name Ridge and I was taken out to the USS Consolation AH 15, a hospital ship, where the arm had to be amputated.

"Lefty" Luster was medically retired from the Corps on May 8, 1951. He says his most prideful accomplishment in the Corps was being an instructor for Colonel L. B. "Chesty" Puller at Marine Barracks, Pearl Harbor. This amazing Marine's retirement is a great story in its own right that has been previously published in newspapers. He immediately used the GI Bill to go to Ouachita College in Arkadelphia, Arkansas, where he met and married his wife Romaine on December 2, 1951. He and his wife raised five sons and two daughters and he wrote they are now enjoying being out of the "kid business." His two brothers and one son followed him into the Marine Corps. He taught school, coached track, pastor of a small church and received special permission from President Kennedy in 1963 to join the Texas National Guard. He served as a non-pay member of the 49th Armored Division as an instructor during the Cuban crises. He and his wife of 45 years Romaine, who he calls "Billie" reside in Big Springs, Texas.

28

IT WAS A PLEASURE T' MEETCHA
By former Private First Class Webb "Mac" McKelvey, USMC

In the Fall o' forty-four I spent some time as a patient in the Long Beach Naval Hospital. I had 'bout healed up from wounds got at Saipan while a rifleman with Baker Company, 25th Marines, 4th Marine Division. After the Japanese bullet with my name on it found me it had been first-aid on a combat ship, th' Hospital Ship Relief, a field hospital on Kwajalein, a flight to Oahu, Oak Knoll Navy Hospital and then to Long Beach.

By th' time I got to Long Beach I was able to get around pretty well a' driven my crutches. An' when I heered they was a'letting patients go on special semi-supervised liberty to places that wanted ta entertain th' "troops," I put my name down 'cause sure 'nough I was a "troop" that needed som' entertaining.

I was spruced up in my Dress Greens and ready for one of them passes when this lady civilian volunteer aide suggested I join them for a trip to Hollywood-Park racetrack. It seemed like a great way to spend th' day to me, especially since it would give me the first opportunity in quite a spell to have anything to do with horses, which I dearly loved.

Edward Arnold-Born in New York City in 1890, Arnold began his movie career in 1916. A burly man with a commanding style and superb baritone voice he appeared in over 150 films before his death in 1956. He was the star in the film classic Diamond Jim Brady.

All us guys that signed up for the race track was driven there in private cars that delivered us right to the club house. We were told we had the run of the place with complete permission to go anywhere we liked and for us to relax, have a good time and enjoy ourselves. I was already enjoying myself jus' being there 'cause it was sure a great change of th' pace and routine I'd a'been going through, believe you me.

Unless you've been a combat wounded vet not too far removed from th' battlefield you can't imagine what a change of atmosphere it was like being at that racetrack. I mean heer I was, fresh from combat, to hospital after hospital, an' now I'm in th' middle of all this luxury and elegance of that clubhouse. An' surrounded by well-dressed folks who didn't seem to even be aware that there was a war going on! To tell the truth, it was a little overwhelming.

I chose a table near th' windows where I could see th' action out on th' track, and also gave me the chance to watch the people around me. There were many familiar faces of movie stars. I was the only guy in uniform in this part of the club house I'd decided to park and these movie stars and other well ta do's would nod their heads and smile at me in warm recognition. It jus' made my mind spin with so many thoughts going through it. This was truly th' end of the rainbow. I was back among happy human beings, whose primary function as far as I could tell was to be happy. Nobody was makin' a fuss, everyone was a'laughen an' hav'en a good time. Th' talk was of horses and wagers and inane gossip.

I was leaning back, enjoying my drink, my mind in a swim of bullets an' bodies, perfume an' furs. Stylish haircuts and helments..Jack Daniels in a glass n' soft carpets...th' screams of dying men. Yeah...I'd made it back........if only there were Paul n' Mitch, n' Stony n' Joe...n' Luke, Fred and on and on........ I quietly raised my glass in a silent salute and took a long pull. For half a second they were all there. God dam th' war! I never felt more alone in my life as I did this moment, sittin' there in th' midst of tinkling ice n' female giggles. Damit anyway! Those fellows paid for all this...damn how they paid, n' there I was, th' survivor..th' lucky one.

How I wanted one o' them guys to come mozyin' in like they always did n' say, "Hi ya Mac...it's all a mistake! We made it too!"

My glazed over eyes focused on my surroundings and standing across th' room from my table a familiar face caught my attention. A large, well dressed man with twinkling eyes and known world wide for his spontaneous laugh was talking to a couple of folks. Our eyes met from clear across the room and he walked away from th' people he'd been talking to and strode directly over to me and stuck out his hand. He uttered his famous laugh, then said: "I'm so glad to see you, I'm Edward Arnold." After the famous movie actor shook my hand he asked me if he could sit down and chat for a while. We talked for quiet a bit and he went on to say a lot of nice things as if we'd known each other all our lives. What impressed me about him was he wasn't play-acting, he was being for real. We drank our bourbon and talked, n' I suppose he thought he was bein' nice, to one Marine kid. I didn't say nuthin' 'bout them other guys I'd been think'en 'bout. It wasn't th' time or th' place. Besides, I was th' one that was play-actin'. Edward Arnold didn't know it....but we was actually drinkin' to Third Platoon, Dog Company, 25th Marines......Hell! ALL "Dog Company AND "Baker Company, Twenty-Fifth.

Not many o' them made it.

That was th' day at th' Hollywood-Park race track that Texas Sand Man won th' Stakes and I had 'em on th' NOSE.

29

MARINES USE SHIPS GUN ON LAND TO DOWN JAP AIRPLANE
Former Corpsman PHM2/C Ernest J. "Doc" Irvin, USN

In the Fall of 1941, those of us stationed in the Philippines knew damn good and well that the Imperial Japanese Army and Navy would be com'en a'call'en before to long.

I was a Pharmacist's Mate Second Class attached to the 4th Marines stationed at Cavite. For the uninformed, my job was that of a Fleet Marine Force Navy corpsman. Like most FMF corpsman the Marines called me "Doc."

It must have been sometime in October or early November when the Marine commander issued orders he wanted his anti-aircraft batteries increased two-fold. Under normal circumstances that would have been a reasonable order by making requisition requests through regular supply channels and maybe asking Headquarters, Marine Corps to approve a new organizational manning level doubling AA guns and personnel. As it stood the Marines didn't think they had time for such niceties. Using the time honored system of the Corps to make do with what they could find the Marines went to work complying with their commanding officer's desire with typical enthusiasm.

The Cavite, P.I. Navy Yard scrap heap of discarded ships material proved invaluable for the scrounging Marines. Their biggest find was four Three Inch Guns which had been taken off the Navy cruiser U.S.S. Houston. No doubt the 4th Marines C.O., Col. Samuel L. Howard, felt very proud of his men since it hadn't taken long for him to get his additional Ack-Ack batteries.

Along with the new batteries came a new job for me. I was assigned to C Battery, 1st Separate Marine Battalion, commanded by Lt.Col. John P. Adams. Colonel Adam's battalion provided antiaircraft defense for the Navy bases. C Battery boasted one of the refurbished Three Inch Guns off the Houston. The first thing they did with my new battery was to put it out in the boonies. And I do mean boonies. We were sent across the bay from Cavite to the mouth of the Imus River which emptied into the bay. This was a heavily jungled peninsula near a little village of bamboo huts fishermen and their families lived in. The ville was called Binakayan and C Battery guns were set up in an abandoned turnip patch across Bacoor Bay, which was little more than tidal mud flats.

Once a week I'd walk a mile through the jungle to a dirt road that went to Manila. There, I'd flag down one of the small Philippine buses that traveled the countryside and eventually made my way to Cavite where I picked up supplies and medicines. Then, loaded down with a huge brown bag I would board a bus heading to Manila with liberty-bound sailors. It was a bumpy ride on the packed bus as we traveled along the road that cut through the thick jungle. Out in the middle of nowhere I would stand up and ring the bell to signal the driver I wanted off. Of course, it was the long mile walk back to the battery. This ritual got to be such a habit that some of the liberty-bound sailors recognized me and got curious what I was up to. Finally, one of them asked me about my girl friend I had stashed out in the jungle forest. When I explained where my outfit was at and what I was doing they all cracked up laughing. All the sailors thought I was shacked up in the boonies and had gone native.

The war came to the Philippines on December 8, 1941.

Although we did not get an early warning about the first Japanese bomber formations coming at us we were all prepared just the same since we knew about the sneak attack on Pearl Harbor. When the first wave of Jap bombers flying in a V formation came over out position they got a warm welcome from every AA outfit we had. In addition, Army P-40 fighter planes from Nichols Field went up to meet them. I have to give those Army pilots credit because they flew right through all the stuff we were throwing up in the air as they pressed their attacks on the Jap formation. One of the P-40's crashed landed in the surf near C Battery and we waded out and got the pilot who was shaken up but otherwise unhurt.

There was just to many Japanese airplanes for us to stop and they dropped their bomb loads on various naval installations that did a lot of damage. We could look across the bay and see the flames and black, oily smoke rising in an ever-growing pyre.

The attacks from the sky continued on unabated. The enemy did learn one lesson we taught them. On 10 December a Jap V formation came in very low which gave our machine guns and smaller caliber AA guns on the ground the chance to hit them pretty hard. I was standing close by our Three Inch Gun in the event medical help was needed by the gun-crew when a flight of six twin engine Japanese bombers came in low over our position. The C Battery Marines worked like well-oiled machinery throwing up a steady barrage of three-inch shells at the enemy aircraft. Suddenly, a bomber in the middle on one side of the V burst into flames at an engine mount and dropped out of the formation. A long trail of black smoke followed the falling aircraft as it made a shallow dive toward the bay. I stared hypnotically at the enemy airplane as did the entire gun-crew until it crashed into the black-green waters of the bay, throwing up a big white spout of spray. All of us let out with a big cheer which faded quickly when the gun-crew captain growled at his men there was plenty more Jap planes to shoot at other than the one they had just downed.

I'll always remember that day when a group of raggedy-assed Marines using an AA gun salvaged off a Navy ship of war shot down a Jap airplane with it from dry land. For some, this may not sound like much of a sea story, but for me this event sustained my moral for the next three years, four months and six days I spent as a POW, most of it at Kobe, Japan.

Ernie "Doc" Irvin received the Silver Star medal by orders of Lieutenant General Jonathan M. Wainwright, who took command of the Allied forces in the Philippines after General Douglas Macarthur was evacuated. Doc Irvin was cited for gallantry in action on Bataan when he braved enemy fire to get a wounded Marine of C Battery out of harms way, then administered first aid which saved the Marines life. His capture by the Japanese took place on Corregidor with the remainder of the 4th Marines. He was also awarded the Bronze Star medal for his meritorious service as a corpsman while a Prisoner of War. He had been previously awarded two other Bronze Stars with Combat V's for heroic achievement on Bataan and Corregidor. The U. S. Army credited C Battery with a total of 19 Japanese airplanes shot down with two probables. C Battery personnel received the Army Presidential Unit Citation. In addition, Doc Irvin holds the Purple Heart medal. He lives in Jensen Beach, Florida and is active in the "Battling Bastards of Bataan" association as well as the American Defenders of Bataan & Corregidor.

30

SAVED BY A SONG
Former Corporal Lee Scarborough, USMC

Most Marines know what a "ten-percenter" is. Every outfit has one. The guy that doesn't get the word, who always mixed things up when told to pass the word and usually screwed up any order given him.

In my outfit, the 7th Marines, our ten-percenter was Private Winstead. Winstead was a friendly enough fellow, and it was just an unfortunate fact that he couldn't get anything right. I mean he was a real eight ball. His constant screw up's earned him the name "Bumstead" after the Sunday comic stripe Dagwood and Blondie. He was also the butt of a lot of practical jokes and it wasn't that any of us was trying to be really cruel to him; it was just that he was so gullible that he fell for anything, hook. line and sinker. You may remember the old shipboard joke about sending a greenhorn to fetch a bucket of steam. Bumstead never did understand the sailors were pulling a fast one on him and went from one ships division to another on our APA trying to get his bucket of steam.

It was also a sad truth that Bumstead could never remember the password for the night no matter how simple we made it or tried to pound into his head. This character flaw almost got him killed by his fellow Marines.

It happened one night on the 1st Marine Division front around Panmunjom, Korea in October 1952.

Our company had got some new replacements and most of them hadn't been subject yet to Private Winstead and his unusual Sad Sack ways. This particular dark night several of the new guys were standing perimeter guard.

For some unknown reason Winstead was out and about in the inky midnight blackness and was heard stumbling around near one of our Listening Post manned by our fresh replacements.

One of the young Marines on LP duty made a challenge: "Halt! Who goes there?"

Private Winstead answers: "It's me Winstead."

The LP Marine then says: "What's the password?"

A couple of silent seconds pass, and a small voice is heard: I don't know it." Then in a louder tone of voice. Aw—come on guys, its old Bumstead."

Now it's the LP turn to be quiet for a few seconds until the other Marine on duty pipes up: "We don't know any Bumstead. If you're a Marine, sing the first bars of the National Anthem."

An indigent Winstead blurts out: "What? Come on you guys quit screwing around!"

There then issued the unmistakable CLICK, CLICK sound of safeties being snapped off M-1 rifles.

Winstead, now in a panicky tone of voice quickly yells out: "Wait a second fellows........okay here goes; Oh beautiful......for spacious skies.....for amber waves of grain..."

God bless Winstead, he made it out of Korea alive.

The two new guys later said they'd been scared out of their heads but anyone dumb enough to substitute America the Beautiful for the National Anthem had to be a stupid Marine.

Lee Scarborough is a life member of the First Marine Division Association.

31

FRIENDLY FIRE
Master Gunnery Sergeant Peter deConnick, USMC(Ret.)

On my second combat tour in Vietnam in 1968 I was assigned to the 1st Marine Division's G-2.

I more or less ended up in this military intelligence section at division headquarters by the process of elimination. The reason I say this is because my military occupational specialty was that of an ABC NCO. ABC stands for Atomic, Biological, Chemical warfare. This MOS field, although a required one in the Corps, was also a very limited field. I don't think during the Vietnam War there were over 1,000 ABC Marines in the entire Corps.

Most of the jobs I'd held since becoming an ABC Marine in the mid 1950's always found me in a regimental or battalion headquarters, usually in the S-3 shop as an instructor. The one exception regarding my previous assignments was a two and one-half year hitch as a Troop Handler at Camp Lejeune's Camp Geiger's Infantry Training Regiment.

I believe this experience as a half-ass drill instructor helped me get my staff sergeant stripes but wearing the rocker caused some minor problems when I reported in to the 1stMarDiv Personnel Assignment Section. There were no billets calling for an ABC MOS staff sergeant in Vietnam. If I'd been a buck sergeant they could have shipped me off to one of the battalions and left it to them to find me a billet. So this is what it really boiled down to since personnel didn't know what to do with me, and therefore I ended up in combat intelligence.

As it turned out the people in G-1 didn't know exactly what to do with me either. Major Blaylock, who was the assistant G-1 noted my ITR background in my Service Record Book and after mulling it over for a while he finally invented a slot for me. He told me I was going to be the Intelligence Scout Section liaison NCO for the division. When I asked him what my duties were to be, he answered me rather tersely, "You work it out."

My new position was an enlisted mans dream. I could do almost anything I wanted to do!

Using the name power of Colonel Davis, the G-1, along with a billet duty chit I typed and had Major Blaylock sign, I didn't have any problems obtaining a nook and a field desk in the Kit Carson Scout's hooch down at the bottom of the hill from the division CP. I was even assigned an assistant. Hoa Cuu Thi was an ARVN staff sergeant who'd been assigned by the district commander of the Republic of Vietnam Army to be a liaison NCO with the 1st Marine Division headquarters. I suspected Hoa was pawned off on me by the Two-shop to get him out of their hair the same they'd done with me.

As it were, Hoa Thi and I hit it off from our first meeting. We were both wirily built on the thin side and about the same height of five foot seven. Because of my Belgium, Greek and Irish ancestry, my short-cropped hair was as black as Hoa's and our dark skin color was also similar. Even my high-pitched Queens New York City accent matched Hoa's equally reedy singsong tone of voice. Fortunately, his English was a lot better than my all but non-existent Vietnamese. This meant we didn't suffer big problems in verbal communication.

The two of us got down to work and we quickly went about brainstorming what we thought our mission should entail. Hoa had family in nearby Da Nang and quite a few of our brain-storming talks took place in the cool confines of his relatives old French colonial villa over cold Tiger beer. Like I said; my new job was an enlisted mans dream.

What Hoa and I came up with concerning our dual rolls of liaison NCOs, was to put together an agenda whereas we would visit all the infantry battalions within the division while they were employed in field combat operations. Our rational was that this would give us the opportunity to personally check out how Marine Intelligence Scouts, along with their counter-parts, the Kit Carson Scouts. were doing their job. We'd be kind of like field supervisors with Hoa dealing with the Kit Carson Scouts who were all former NVA soldiers, and I would deal with the Marine scouts. Then I would write up a report of our observations and submit the report to the G-1.

Major Baylock thought it a splendid idea, saying something along the line that we'd be acting as on the scene eyes and ears for the One-shop. After giving us his blessing he said to "get cracking!"

My next move was to come up with a set of orders that outlined our mission on a perpetual bases and giving us blanket travel authorization. When Major Baylock got Colonel Davis to sign off on our orders, Hoa and I went to work.

The Headquarters, 1st Marine Division travel and mission document got the desired results I was looking for. No one hassled me or Hoa and we were treated with professional courtesy at all the battalion CP's.

It didn't take me long to realize the two of us were performing a needed job even if it had been invented at the onset. Hoa and I would spend several days with each battalion, going out on patrols with the Marine Intelligence Scouts and their Kit Carson Scouts. With the power of the division commanding general through the G-1 section backing me, I was able to square away what minor problems or obstacles the young Marine corporals and sergeants who were scouts ran into. My reports to the Two-shop were well received and Hoa and I even got a "Well done," from Colonel Davis.

Now what I've related here so far is a sea story in its own right how I created my own billet on my second tour. But the gist of this entire tale is the conclusion which I feel is the biggest sea story of them all.

In September 1968 Hoa and I visited the 1st Battalion, 7th Marines. The battalion was on a sweep through "Indian County" between Da Nang and Chu Lai. (Chu Lia is 57 miles south of Da Nang.) We joined Bravo Company which was out in the Que Son Valley west of the town Hoi An. Before dusk on the third day out with Bravo we stopped to circle the wagons like we always did by sitting up a full 360-degree defensive perimeter. Hoa and me had no sooner dug us a nice two man fighting hole when the company commander, a young first lieutenant approached us. He looked directly at me as he spoke. (The following is pretty close to what he had to say:)

"I want to send out five ambush parties tonight but I've got a problem. I'm short of experienced NCOs and was wondering if you would volunteer to lead one of the ambush squads?"

He may have been a young officer but he sure as hell knew how to get what he wanted from a professional Marine. There was only one answer to his question and I gave it to him. "I'd be happy to help out sir."

I then asked if it would be okay for Hoa to accompany me and could I also take both scouts along. He was a little hesitant about the Kit Carson Scout but said if that's what I wanted it was okay by him.

So Hoa and me, along with the two scouts and a depleted squad of seven Marines led by a corporal, made our way out into the jungle gloom to set up a L shape ambush site. Both the Vietnamese took advantage of the natural foliage by covering their helmets and flack jackets with bits and pieces of greenery and we Marines seeing what a smart idea this was did the same. What kept us on the alert, other than being on ambush, was the occasional eruption of gunfire. Some of the gunfire seemed to come from outside our perimeter and I surmised that the other ambush teams must have opened up on enemy soldiers that walked into their trap. However, most of the weapons firing probably came from trigger happy Marines on the line. It was a long sleepless night at our location without any sign of enemy movement.

When the light of a false dawn got bright enough to see our surroundings I whispered the order to saddle up and follow me back to our perimeter. Hoa and the Kit Carson Scout was directly behind me with the Marine scout right behind them. The squad leader corporal and his men followed closely in our trace as we cautiously made our way the several hundred meters back to where we'd left the perimeter.

I guess we couldn't have been more than fifty yards from our lines when my group emerged from the heavy tree line into a high grassy area. All of a sudden and without warning the Marine perimeter opened up on us. I got stitched across my arms and chest with M-60 machine gun fire that punched me to the ground like someone with a sledgehammer had hit me. Hoa and the Kit Carson Scout landed next to me with bullet wounds of their own. Hoa was also hit bad and the Kit Carson Scout had taken some bullets to the face and he was dead. The Marine scout started yelling but got cut down also as more perimeter weapons focused in on my group. The squad ran back into the trees and I can still clearly hear them cussing and screaming at their fellow Marines that they were members of the second platoon. The shooting ended as abruptly as it had started.

As we waited for a medevac helicopter to take me, Hoa, the Marine scout and the dead Kit Carson Scout to the field hospital at Da Nang, the young first lieutenant company commander was near tears as he attempted to explain what had happened and to voice how sorry he was. The M-60 man that had initiated the friendly fire swore he thought Hoa, the Kit Carson Scout and me were NVA. I guess my dark complexion, short stature, Vietnamese style camouflage, along with my two Vietnamese companions walking up front with me, did in fact bite me on my ass.

Pete deConnick spent four months in Navy hospitals recovering from his wounds. Although he did take four bullets to his chest his flack jacket deflected the rounds enough that they weren't fatal. He also got hit in both upper arms. Hoa Cuu Thi also survived the friendly fire incident as did the Marine scout. In his letter telling of his experience deConnick said that at least he left Vietnam with the feeling he'd accomplished something. His idea of maintaining close contact with Marine scouts out in the battalions while on operations became a permanent billet in the G-1 TO (Table of Organization.) The retired Master Gunnery Sergeant now lives in Romoland, California with his wife of 32 years. They have two daughters and a son. Pete deConnick is employed with the United States Post Office.

32

THE PAUSE THAT REFRESHES
Former Staff Sergeant Christopher E. "Chris" Sarno, USMC

I enlisted into the United States Marine Corps from Medford, Massachusetts at age 18 on December 20, 1950. Spending Christmas at Parris Island, South Carolina as a raw boot recruit isn't the worse thing I ever suffered through in life, but it sure comes close.

By the spring of 1951 I'd enjoyed the delights of Camp Tent #1 and the Del Mar Tankers School, both at Camp Pendleton, California. I arrived in Korea in July of 1951, and joined my new outfit Abel Company, 1st Tanks.

My tale is about three cruddy and intolerant tank Marines with a story that unfolded on the Western Front in the Korean Marine Corps' sector near the MLR (Main Line of Resistance). Abel Company tanks were assigned to the Korean Marine Corps to support their forays into No Mans Land.

Any combat Marine who served in Korea, knows how hot it is just prior to the monsoon rainy season. It was desert hot, compounded by a baked on humidity and the inside of our steel coffins was like being in an oven. We had to stay buttoned up when offering supporting fire on the line because the gook's counter-battery fire was always seeking us out and their rounds would splash all around us. Fortunately for us, they were lousy shots, at least most of the time.

After one sultry morning's direct fire mission for the Korean Marines was success-fully completed, my driver Cpl. Woods, assistant driver PFC Lindstrom and loader, PFC Jones along with yours truly, pulled off the line in our beast and made our way back to our staging area. This was an isolated area below the mountain we used as a firing platform and other than Korean Marines we were virtually alone, being the only Ameri-cans at this location. We went through the normal routine of cleaning up all weapons and doing preventative maintenance on the tracks and turret of our M-26 (Pershing) tank. The enveloping blanket of smothering humidity and the relentless searing of an after-noon sun bleached us out to dirt clad, sweaty lumps that left us drained after our arduous task of taking care of the tank.

In an effort to get any kind of relief from the intense sun the four of us tried to crap out in the shadow of our sandbagged bunker's entrance. This did little good but it's all we had. Lazily, I was keeping an eye (through binoculars) on a group of Korean Marines thrashing grain with long poles and leather straps about 200 yards distance. I made a wiseass remark to my companions about our allies having to work for their chow by tending a garden. Cpl. Woods took the field glasses from me and scoped the Marine farmers out for a couple of minutes. Then he came up with the bright idea for us to go check them out to see what they were up to. Leaving PFC Lindstrom on watch, the three of us left our tank and ambled over towards the KMC's.

We stood at the edge of the small field the Korean's were working and silently watched them do their thing. Neither group could converse without sign language or pidgin English. The few words of gook talk we knew wasn't conducive to long talks so after a short spell of shit-eating grins and listening to the KMC's offer "You numba ones." we decided to depart.

The heat and humidity was really knocking us down and you couldn't take a step without kicking up powdery dust. Even the brush along the path we were walking on was heavily coated with a choking silt and the three of us was covered with a film of sweat-streaked dust. None of us had had a bath in weeks and we all smelled like goats. What little water we had on the tank in jerry cans was for drinking only and no word had been passed when the motor transport pogues would come by with the water trailer. As we trudged along we all sucked on a small pebble to keep some semblance of saliva in our mouths.

Our route back to the tank was a different one than we'd taken to reach the KMC's. The path we were on took a bend which was out of sight from the Koreans working in the field. Damn if we didn't stumble upon a water well in a secluded little area just off the path. The top of the well was only inches above the surface of the deck and was covered with a mating of twigs and branches. Little bugs zigzagged to an fro-on top of the water, seemingly enjoying themselves immensely. Cpl. Woods, Johns and I stood there staring at that wide pool of cool water for what seemed to be five minutes. Without saying a word Cpl. Woods reached into his first-aid pouch and held up a small bar of soap. Johns and me immediately knew what our corporal had just said without saying a word.

While two Marine cruds stood watch, quick as a flash Cpl. Woods dropped all his web gear and weapon, stripped to his skivvies, and was taking a bath in the inviting water well. Then it was our turn as Johns and I slipped down into the well to bathe one at a time. Maybe you would have had to have been there to fully understand this, but that quick bath was the biggest moral boost I ever got in my years in the Corps. Within a short time span all three of us were 35 degrees cooler and totally refreshed.

As I was putting my gear back on Cpl, Woods gave the alarm that three Korean Marines carrying jerry cans were coming down the trail towards us. Quickly, Johns and I brushed away the soapsuds in and around the rim of the well.

I don't know if the smiling KMC's noticed how cool looking and clean we appeared to be but whatever the case one of them got down on his knees to dip a jerry-can into the well after splashing aside the bugs, while the other two bummed smokes off Cpl. Woods. One thing for sure: we weren't about to tell them we had just polluted their hidden water well. We watched them fill their three jerry cans and as we turned to leave offered a friendly salute in bidding them a fond farewell. Then we shuffled down the dirty, dusty trail to our steel chariot.

If a certain KMC grunt outfit ever suffered stomach cramps, or worse, it was because of three skuzzy, mean and filthy USMC tankers who were in dire need of the pause that refreshes. Sayonara.

Chris Sarno was later wounded in the Punchbowl area of Korea. After a stateside tour he was promoted to staff sergeant and at his request volunteered reassignment back to Korea. He returned to the 1st Marine Division in September 1953, this time as tank commander Antitank Company, 7th Marines. He was honorably discharged from the Marine Corps on January 22, 1955. Chris served 23 years as a Medford, Massachusetts's policeman. He received the FBI's Medal of Valor for foiling a bank holdup in progress that resulted in a shootout with one gunman wounded, another one killed. Now retired he writes stories about the Corps and breeds famed "Tennessee" racers greyhounds.

33

MESS CALL
Former Corporal Howard E. Stout, USMC

The way I ended up in the Marine Corps during World War II is a sea story by itself before I even knew what a sea story was.

In January 1944, at age 17, I enlisted into the Merchant Marines from my hometown of Crawfordsville, Indiana. I was fresh out of high school and I guess I figured at the time that because of my slight build; 128 pounds soaking wet and a lanky five foot eleven frame, that the military wouldn't take me. The Merchant Marines did. I had a reporting date of 1 March 1944 to be at the Chicago Maritime office to be assigned a ship for my on-the-job-training stint.

One afternoon in early February I was goofing off at the local pool hall when this pal of mine, a big, strapping fellow of six foot two, 210 pounds, started bugging me to come along with him to Indianapolis to enlist in the Marine Corps. I told him I thought I was to skinny to be accepted by the military but he kept after me until I finally consented to go give it a try. I'll be damn if the Marines didn't take me but rejected my buddy, the former high school football player. I never did get back in touch with the Merchant Marines and to this day I still wonder if they carry me on their rolls as being AWOL.

So, when I was supposed to have been learning how to be a deck hand I found myself undergoing the quaint learning experience of being transferred from a puke civilian to a United States Marine at MCRD, San Diego, California. My advanced training took place at Camp Pendleton where I obtained dual MOS's as both a light (air-cooled) and heavy (water-cooled) machine gunner, 30 caliber.

My baptism of combat came during the horrendous Okinawa campaign, April 1 to June 21, 1945. My outfit was Fox Company, 2nd Battalion, 1st Marines, 1st Marine Division.

F-2-1 remained on Okinawa for the mop up that continued on until late July 1945. Then we commenced a training and replacement phase in preparing for the invasion of mainland Japan. Of course the A bomb droppings in August negated the 1st Marine Division having to make a combat landing on Kyushu island, Japan.

It didn't take the Marine Corps high command very long to come up with another mission for the 1st Marine Division and by September of 1945, I along with the rest of F-2-1, found ourselves as occupation troops in Tientsin, China.

We were billeted at Maki School, a former Japanese girls school which was built in 1939 during the Japanese occupation of Tientsin. Like most public buildings in the sprawling Chinese city Maki School was located in a high walled compound. It was a well-constructed two story brick building shaped in an L with a high gabled red tile roof. The eaves stuck out to form a porch cover over a wide veranda that ran the length of the front of the building which had a wood railing on the top deck. The short L portion of the one time school was for the officers and our Headquarters section. The remainder of the big building's classrooms was used as barracks. I lived topside in about the middle room of the ex-plural's school. The grassy compound in front of the school was our parade ground and on the fringe of this parade ground, near the fence line, were several large general-purpose tents. Two of the big tents was our chow hall and cook tent.

The Chinese New Year was going to start the first of March 1946, and me and a buddy of mine, Pvt. Dale Bigger, decided we would help the local citizens celebrate their holiday. On one of my liberties to downtown Tientsin, I purchased a considerable amount of fireworks just before the Chinese New Year celebration from a vendor in the "Bazaar." I'm sure that all Tientsin Marines remember the "Bazaar"; you could purchase anything there and I do mean anything. A quick side story about this is if anyone who wanted to rent a hotel room in Tientsin they had to accept the fact that all hotel rooms came automatically with a girl. It didn't make any difference if you wanted a girl or not, if you got a hotel room you got one anyway. After buying my fireworks I returned to the barracks.

The next morning I told Dale Bigger we should test some of the rockets or Roman Candles to make sure they worked. What we did was place one on an open window ledge of our room on the second deck and lit the fuse. Well, it sure enough worked okay. With a sputtering hiss it shot out across the school yard/parade field with a trail of white smoke and went directly into the mess tent opening about 150 feet away where it exploded with a huge bang and a spectacular color display. Needless to say Bigger and I quickly disappeared.

We later learned that the mess sergeant had just finished getting his mess tent in shipshape for inspection and wasn't at all amused at the debris left as a result of the explosion. Plus, no doubt what it had done to his nerves. In fact, word was passed that if the culprit was found, that regardless of his rank, he would be on "pot-walloping" and "potato peeling" for the remainder of his stay in North China. Since my battalion colonel didn't like me that much anyway, thinking I was to cocky for my own good; I knew he'd just love to take my two stripes before sending me to the mess sergeant. So this is one sea story that Bigger's and I kept to ourselves until now.

Okay mess sergeant, if you're still around, now you know who did the "dastardly deed." We really didn't intend to hit your doorway, but we failed to check our "elevation" and "windage" before firing. Sorry about that.

===

Howard Stout is a widower who retired in 1982 as a Construction Manager for Indiana Bell telephone company. He is active in the China Marines Association, the 1st Marine Division Association and the Marine Corps League. Howard resides in Indianapolis, Indiana.

34

YA WANT TA SHOW US THAT AGAIN LIEUTENANT
Former Sergeant Michael L. Deaton, USMC

In May of 1967 I was a platoon sergeant in Bravo Company, 1st Battalion, 1st Marines. I'd extended my tour in Nam for six months more or less out of loyalty to the young troopers I led. I'm not trying to pat myself on the back but the young "old timers" in my platoon were convinced I was a lucky omen of some sort after having taken over as platoon sergeant as a corporal. The reason I had to step up to platoon sergeant will be obvious to any combat Marine who reads this since after our staff sergeant was KIA I was the oldest and most seasoned corporal in the platoon. The other thing about being a lucky omen was pure superstition that seemed to grow bigger as the teenage Marines in the platoon told the myth time and time again. I have no logical thought to offer why it happened but after I took over the platoon it is true that in four operations I didn't lose a man KIA. Had my fair share of WIA's but the troopies overlooked that fact and was convinced I had some kind of supernatural vibes for the combat environment that kept them alive.

Most everyone in the company called me Big Mike, including our skipper and other platoon commanders. With my 200 pound, six foot one inch frame, ruddy complexion and balding sandy hair, I guess I did stand out in a crowd. I also have a gravely voice and even though I was only 21 years old at the time, I looked and talked like an older Marine. If there's any credence about being lucky, I think it had more to do with the way I looked, the way I talked and my attitude of not taking too much shit off of anyone. I looked out for my people but I expected them to damn well do what I told them to do without thinking it over, especially while on combat operations. In a nutshell I suppose you can say I was rather intimidating and for what it's worth, that suited me just fine.

But it came to pass that I got a brand-new second lieutenant fresh out of OCS Quantico who thought he knew it all. For the sake of this tale I'll call him Lieutenant Butterbar. Well it didn't take long for Lieutenant Butterbar to developed a reputation among the enlisted men of being a dumb ass who wouldn't listen to any advice from his more experienced troops which naturally included me as his platoon sergeant. I did my best to get the green off him but the young lieutenant, who was younger than me by a year, took his shiny gold bar to heart. He tried to run the platoon strictly by the book; from proper squad tactics, using arm and hand signals to keeping the overnight bivouac area looking neat for inspection. It's just one of those facets of life that has not changed in over 200 years of American military history. Second lieutenants are second lieutenants, and there is no changing them. That is of course, until they have learned on their own that the "book" is a guide to survival, not a bible chiseled in stone.

A month went by with Lieutenant Butterbar doing his thing which meant I had to be extra alert at damage control. Then we got orders that our platoon was going to be a blocking force. Our assignment was to set up defensive positions at this small ville after securing it and act as a blocking force against the NVA that the remainder of our company would try to push our way. Intelligence reports said the little hamlet which was north of Da Nang in an area called "Happy Valley" was deserted but we were to check it out just the same before setting up our ambush.

We approached the hamlet cautiously and got to within 100 meters when Lieutenant Butterbar went through the totally unnecessary routine of giving arm and hand signals to deploy the three squads side by side on line. There was nothing wrong with this standard maneuver but at our distance from the ville he could have just gave a verbal order to fan out and the squads would have automatically got into position without all the arm waving which could attract more attention than just spitting it out.

What he did next surprised me and I told him he had no business doing it. We always sent a point fire-team in first to make an initial inspection while the remainder of the platoon halted outside the perimeter. Against my advice Lieutenant Butterbar joined the point fire-team.

The rest of the platoon watched from a hasty defense as the fire-time cautiously neared the first bamboo and grass built hut. Everything was quiet when suddenly, without warning, the lieutenant broke from the fire-team and ran to the doorway of the grass-thatched hut. The fire-team froze in stunned silence as did the rest of the platoon, as they watched their leader perform a textbook example of house-to-house combat, right out of the training course of Quantico's Officer Candidate School.

The lieutenant flattened himself next to the doorway holding a hand grenade. He pulled the pin, opened his hand slightly to allow the spoon to fly loose, thus arming the little bomb: waited a couple of seconds, then reached around the open door and with a flip of his hand tossed the grenade inside the grassed walled hut. He immediately flattened himself again with his back against the wall of the bamboo-framed structure, and yelled. "Fire in the hole!"

When the grenade exploded, Lieutenant Butterbar just stood there for a few seconds with a startled expression on his face. Then he fell face down in a crumpled heap.

Platoon members ran forward to check on their fallen leader. Our "Doc" (Navy corpsman) turned the now groaning officer over on his side. Even with his flak jacket on the lieutenant was splattered with tiny fragments from his neck to his ankles. Although the wounds were no doubt painful they were not fatal because the thick walled hut did absorb a lot of the force from the blast. Second Lieutenant Butterbar would live to tell his grandchildren about his combat experiences and how he led a platoon of Marines in Vietnam.

As we waited a medi-evac chopper to haul the wounded lieutenant away to a field hospital the remainder of Bravo Company came to the hamlet, finishing their sweep as planned without encountering any enemy.

My company commander wanted to know what had happened.

I had to compose myself to keep a straight face and the rest of my platoon wasn't helping any with their twitching facial expressions which the skipper took in. What the hell, I told him the truth as I saw it. "Sir, the lieutenant showed us how not to throw a hand grenade into a grass-walled hooch."

Captain Thoubiz stared at me intently for a long moment, then he sort of shook his head just a tad, and said. "Okay Big Mike, you're now the acting platoon leader."

===

Mike Deaton served 10 years in the Corps and then tried a hitch in the Navy. He is currently a retired federally sponsored veterans employment counselor for the State of Indiana and lives in Indianapolis. He cooks as a hobby and is a life member of the Marine Corps League.

35

SAVING FACE
Former Sergeant Michael L. Deaton, USMC

As a reward for capturing five NVA soldiers and in general for kicking ass and taking names on a combat operation in late August 1967, my platoon, along with the rest of Bravo Company, 1st Battalion, 1st Marines, was given four days in-country R&R at China Beach.

Let me say something here at the onset. Every once in a while Marine Corps brass do come up with some great ideas. And China Beach was damn sure one of them. Giving an outfit of grunts a few days of normalcy from the rigors and horror of combat because they did something good is a whole hell of a lot better than awarding them some kind of unit citation so they can have a pretty floss gong to wear on their chest.

The R&R center at China Beach was located a few miles east of Da Nang, Republic of Vietnam right smack dab on the South China Sea. This eight-mile oceanfront was bounded by 2,000-foot high Monkey Mountain to the north and Marble Mountain to the south. American Seabees and Marine engineers had done a suburb job in constructing a class-act resort area.

An individual could almost forget he was in a war zone while lazing on the white-yellow sandy beach staring up at the azure sky or looking at the gentle surf roll in.

There was plenty of cold beer, hot dogs, burgers and fries and while the so called cabanas we stayed in were plywood constructed they were a whole hell of a lot better than a muddy fighting hole or canvas tent.

Like Marine platoons tend to do my second platoon guys stuck together during the R&R and where you found one, you found the other thirty. (We were under strength which was normal in rifle companies.) This facet was much more than just being clannish, we were family and very proud of that fact. And as a family of brothers who looked out for one another, I suppose it can be said that my roll was that of the older brother or the father image.

I was content to watch the guys frolic on the beach and flirt with the few Red Cross and USO girls that helped run the place. They played volleyball and tackle football on the part of the beach they'd staked a claim to or horse-played in the ocean. Occasionally they would badger me until I joined them in one of their games but for the most part I was happy sucking on a cold can of Bud and soaking up the rays to help cure my jungle rot.

On the third day about two-dozen Korean Marines invaded the domain the platoon called their own. The KMC's just plopped themselves right in the middle of our play area and made themselves at home. From my viewpoint the Koreans were an arrogant bunch and much to cocky for there own good. They must have believed in all the publicity being generated about them through the media on what fierce fighters bad assess they were supposed to be. I wasn't impressed.

My dad was a former World War II and Korean War Naval aviator who flew fighter planes. His rank at discharge was that of a full commander and among his military decorations was the Distinguished Flying Cross. When I was a kid I'd hear him tell stories about what a useless bunch of turd's the ROK soldiers and Korean Marines were during the Korean War. I guess what he had to say about the Korean soldiers and Marines and their lack of aggressiveness on the battlefield made an impression on me.

As it were, my lads and the Korean Marines soon got together after the KMC's indicated through sign language they wanted to play volleyball with them. They must have played ten sets and my guys got clobbered every game much to the amusement of the Koreans. Then the KMC's showed my boys one of their games. A circle was drawn in the sand with a piece of driftwood by one of the Korean's which was roughly ten foot across. Then two guys would stand in the middle of the circle and left and right ankles were tied together about three feet apart with a length of cloth. The object of the game was when the referee, or whatever in the hell the dude was supposed to be, when his hand went down, the opposing players would try and get his opposite out of the circle by any means.

The Koreans were very agile and quick on their feet, plus the fact it was their game and they knew what in the hell they were doing. It was more of a balancing style wrestling game something along the line of Japanese Sumo wrestling, using hands and feet where you tripped up the other guy and dragged him over the line. One by one, my guys got tossed from the circle. The more I watched the more pissed I got because I knew my Marines were better soldiers than the Koreans and the lop-sided contest was getting to me as a matter of honor. I finally got my fill of watching the smiling little bastards having their fun and stood up pointing to myself indicating that I wanted play.

The Koreans were not intimidated by my six foot, one inch, 200 pounds and selected one of their biggest Marines to face off with me. This dude was big for a Korean and stood about five foot ten and was also husky like me. Grinning and bowing he pointed to himself while we got tied together and said, "Me Kim." I returned the introduction by growling I was called Big Mike.

We got ourselves braced in the middle of the circle like two Sumo wrestlers awaiting the referee to drop his up raised hand. When the hand went down I quickly brought my right fist up in an uppercut and tagged my opponent hard on his chin. His knees buckled and he sagged like a sack of potatoes. I grabbed him under his shoulders and dragged him over the line and dumped him on the deck in front of his comrades. As my men started cheering I offered a grim smile and said to the stunned Koreans: "That's one for the United States Marine Corps!"

36

THE YELLOW ROSE OF SAIPAN
Former Corporal Jack W. Smith, USMC

Sometimes being a cocky little feather-merchant has its drawbacks. After enlisting into the Marine Corps on October 12, 1943, at age 17 and getting through San Diego Boot Camp, I went to 81mm mortar school at Camp Pendleton. I don't know if it was because of my shortness (5' 8") or what but I have to admit I was cocky and didn't put up with very much crap that anybody tried to give me.

When I joined the 8th Marines as a replacement on Guadalcanal the 2nd Marine Division was still recuperating from the hellish battle of Tarawa. One of the first men I met in K Company, 3rd Battalion was the company gunny Gunnery Sergeant Samuel Cipparone. Gunny Sam was a big hulking giant who growled instead of talked and for whatever reason he took an instant dislike for me. The first words out of his mouth was that my blond hair was to long and for me to get a haircut. And naturally, since I was a mortar man he just had to make me an assistance BAR man in one of the rifle platoons. I didn't endear myself with him when I voiced my opinion that humping 30 caliber ammo for a Browning Automatic Rifle wasn't really my idea of fighting the Japanese.

By the time we got through fighting on Saipan and Tinian it didn't make much difference anyway since I took over the BAR on Saipan after the gunner was killed and ended up as a Forward Observer for the 81mm mortars on Tinian. The fact that I was attached to Headquarters Company as an FO hadn't stopped Gunny Cipparone from being on my case constantly like stink on poop however.

One stunt I'd pulled was in celebration of my 18th birthday on July 26, 1944, the day after the 2nd Marine Division landed on Tinian. At the time I was still carrying the BAR and when my platoon got pinned down in front of a cave complex full of Jap defenders I decided to light my birthday candles. I crept up close to the cave entrance and let go with two full clips of tracer rounds. Naturally, I burnt up the barrel and Gunny Sam didn't see the humor in my stunt. Sure scared hell out of the enemy though and my buddies thought it was funnier than hell.

After Tinian was secured the division was shipped back across the three-mile channel to Saipan. We were to refit and get some rest and relaxation prior to staging for our next campaign which would be Okinawa. To amuse myself I pulled off another one of my cocky little stunts. A Navy cargo ship crammed with cases of beer was unloaded and distributed to the various battalions. When the 3rd Battalion six-by trucks brought hundreds of cases of beer to our area and working parties started unloading the beer and putting them into big supply tents I had my own working party at the rear of one of the tents taking the cases out as fast as they were being stacked. Gunny Sam never did know for sure if it was me that was behind the beer heist but he made me pay anyway by having me dig slit trenches to be used as outdoor heads.

There's no doubt that I was a snot nose kid and my level of immaturity got me to the point I was fed up with the Gunny Cipparone picking on me all the time Reflecting back, I probably deserved his attention but I didn't think so at the time. The older career Marine from South Philadelphia seemed like he had one thing in mind and that was to make my life miserable. I just couldn't understand it, especially since I'd been wounded on Saipan and was now an acting sergeant FO. So I made up my mind I was going to pay him back for the way he was treating me. But how?

Sometime in November of 1944 I noticed Gunny Sam outside his tent washing his cloths in a cut in two 30-gallon drum. Actually, he had a fire lit under the drum and was boiling his cloths which was a good way to get rid of the lice and other little creepy things that burrowed in your uniforms. The idea of how to get to him came to me in a flash.

It took me a couple of weeks to come up with some atebrine tablets which were quinine based the Navy corpsmen gave us in the chow line to ward off malaria. The Doc's were so contentious they would stand there at the chow tent and watch you take the big yellow pill before letting you eat. It took some sleight of hand on my part to palm four of the pills for my little plan of revenge. The damn pills were so potent that over half the Marines that took them had a yellowish tint to their eyes and some of them their skin even took on a yellow pallor. I figured they sure should make a good dye.

The next time I saw Gunny Cipparone boiling his clothes I waited for him to step away from his wash drum and just happened to stroll by and drop in the four atebrine tablets which I'd mashed up into a fine powder. The steaming water quickly dissolved the yellow powder.

The success of my revenge was beyond my wildest dreams. Half the battalion made it a point to walk by Gunny Sam's clothesline when the word got around about his newly colored wardrobe. His khakis were such a bright yellow that he could have passed for a Shell Oil filling station man which was the color of their uniforms in those days. And his once green utilities now had a yellow cast about them that they almost looked like Japanese mustard colored uniforms. I was one happy Marine, very pleased with myself.

That is until the gunny, who was not at all amused at his new wardrobe, called out the troops to stand in formation. At first, I couldn't figure out what he was up to as he walked past each man in the company and asked to look at their hands. But it came to me real fast when I stuck out my hands for him to inspect and saw how yellow they were. Not only did I dye the gunny's uniforms, but horsing around with the atebrine tablets I managed to dye my hands also. He took one look at my hands then looked directly at my eyes. "It was you, wasn't it Smith?"

I held his stare and said. "I ain't got anything to say one way or the other."

He nodded his head slightly a couple of times while towering over me. "Very well Smith, if that's the way you want to deal with it, let's just say I'm finding you guilty by your silence. You report to the mess tent right now and tell the Mess Sergeant you're his new pot walloper for the next thirty days by my orders."

I whistled a happy tune all the way to the mess tent.

==

Jack Smith was discharged from the Marine Corps on January 25, 1946 after occupation duty in Japan. He was recalled to active duty during the Korean War. Now retired I asked him what I should say he was retired from. He said "Lets tell them I was a transportation operative eminence; that has a lot nicer ring to it than semi-truck driver." He is the father of five sons and a daughter. One of his sons was among the 179 Marines that assaulted Koh Tang Island to retake the container ship U.S.S. Mayaguez which was seized by a Cambodian gunboat. Smith lives in Franklin, Indiana. Jack said that years later he talked with retired Master Sergeant Sam Cipparone, by telephone, who was living in New Jersey. They reminisced about old times and Jack finally confessed it was him that had made Top Sam the Yellow Rose of Saipan. Jack is also a life member of the Marine Corps League and 2nd Marine Division Association.

37

A REAL, GENUINE VIETNAMESE JUNGLE WILDCAT
Former Sergeant Rod Hinsch, U.S. Army Special Forces

In the summer of 1967, I was in Vietnam, stationed at a Special Forces base camp near the Cambodian border. Our primary mission was special reconnaissance and intelligence gathering "across the fence" inside Cambodia. Of course this was all hush, hush, Top Secret at the time. A part of this job was for our Camp Commander to submit a weekly-classified report to the Special Operations Group Commander at headquarters in Saigon. This report always had to be hand-carried to headquarters and the armed courier and his armed bodyguard had to be the rank of sergeant or above.

This Classified Information Courier duty was considered a plum assignment. Not only did the courier and his sidekick get to wear clean clothes; yeah, they were camouflaged jungle fatigues but clean just the same, they also got some free time in Saigon until a return pouch of orders and information for our commander was prepared. Good fortune smiled upon me and my buddy Sergeant Raferty as the luck of the draw selected the two of us for courier duty.

A special armed helicopter provided by Air America to Saigon, where a jeep was assigned to us for our stay, flew us. Our immediate duty and responsibility was to deliver the classified documents which we carried to headquarters. After completing this duty we were told to report back early the next morning.

On our own for fifteen hours. Unbelievable! So many things to do and so little time. First things first.........our stomachs. With the food we had been eating, anything would have tasted great, but we hunted up one of Saigon's best restaurants and proceeded to order and eat almost everything on the menu.

After our adventure in gluttony, we decided to leave our jeep and see some sights on foot. It wasn't long before we found ourselves down by the Saigon Zoo. A virtual mob of Vietnamese surrounded us trying their best to sell us things we didn't need or want. It took some time but we were finally successful in ridding ourselves of the all the street salesmen except for two little kids around 10 or 11 that just wouldn't go away.

The two boys kept badgering us, picking at our sleeves and chattering away in broken English. "Hey G.I. you buy special present, yes? Numba one present, you like very much G.I.."

Raferty and I finally gave in and asked the boys to show us whatever it was they wanted us to buy.

One of the kids disappeared, then returned within a couple of minutes holding a small bamboo cage. With dismay, I stared at the object that had orange fur and black spots.

Raferty took one look, then whispered out of the side of his mouth at me. "This is really gonna be good." He glanced at the young boy holding the cage, and asked. "What the hell is it kid?"

The kid answered, "Hey G.I this real genuine Vietnamese Jungle Wildcat, very valuable, very rare........you very, very lucky you buy. I give good price, you buy okay G.I.?"

It didn't take a rocket scientist to realize just what the two boys were trying to sell. It was a poor little malnourished house cat that someone, more than likely these kids, had spray-painted a bright orange and dabbed on black spots. To top it off the cat's body was shaved in an attempt to give it a more ferocious look. The cat's head, tail and paws boasted splotchy orange hair.

The kids probably thought they did a wonderful job creating this real genuine Vietnamese Jungle Wildcat because Raferty and I ended up chipping in five bucks in MPC to buy it. The truth was that the poor little creature was about the most pathetic living thing either one of us had ever seen. and we felt sorry for it.

After talking it over Raferty and I decided to name the little guy Killer and take him back to our base camp with us.

Back in camp we took Killer to our sandbagged plywood hooch, otherwise known as living quarters. Letting Killer out of his cage I placed the small animal on my cot. Raferty thought our new bunky should have something to play with, so I picked up a tiny roll of C ration toilet paper an tossed it on the cot next to Killer. Maybe there was a bit of wildcat in him after all, because he immediately stalked and attacked the roll of toilet paper.

Just about the time Killer was really getting into his vicious final phase of completely destroying the C ration accommodation, our C.I.A. Field Operations Officer walked through the door. In an instant he spotted our new team member and asked, "What the hell is that thing?"

I was a little slow on the uptake and Raferty beat me to the punch. Looking the agency man straight in the eye he said in all seriousness. "Sir, this is a real genuine Vietnamese Jungle Wildcat, very valuable, very rare, very lucky for us he is a team member."

I was literally biting my tongue trying hard not to laugh. The C.I.A. man glanced at me, then back at Raferty and finally at Killer. who had finished tearing the toilet paper to tiny bits and was now eating it. Turning on his heels, the C.I.A, rep moved quickly back out the door.

Once he was outside we clearly heard him mumble to himself aloud. "God, I hate working with the Special Forces, they're all nuts!"

And he went on down the hill from our hooch continuing to use colorful language about what he thought about his assignment.

And what became of Killer? Well, he went on to become a great team member and the nemesis of all V.C. (Viet Cong) mice or rats who dared attack our camp.

Rod's tale proves the point that Marines and sailors do not have exclusive rights on Sea Stories. He is the manager of an apartment complex and resides near Beech Grove, Indiana.

38

8" HOWITZER-SELF PROPELLED PLAYS AT BEING A SUBMARINE
Author's Name Withheld By Request

I was a driver and cannon cocker on the old style eight-inch self-propelled howitzer during my tour in Vietnam from May 1966 until June 1967. Our howitzers were constructed with large steel turrets, not unlike the main batteries of Fletcher class World War II destroyers. As far as I'm concerned this type of eight-inch howitzer was far superior than the present day models where the cannoneers and loaders are completely exposed during fire-missions. I'm aware of the fact that artillery is supposed to be behind the lines and out of harms way when it comes to frontal attacks, but that wasn't always the case when fighting in Vietnam. All to many times the North Vietnamese Army would sling counter-battery right into our batteries position and I liked the idea that we could "button up" inside our steel cocoon. World War II, Korean and early Vietnam vets will remember that the eight-inch howitzer turrets were placed on a base frame with caterpillar treads similar to a tank. As a matter of fact we drove the eight-inches in the same way you would a tank. The driver and assistant driver had seats and controls up front when on road marches and just like tanks had hatch covers which could be closed down if need be. There was also a hatch on top of the turret where the howitzer commander could ride in the same manner as a tank commander and there was enough room inside the turret for the remainder of the seven-man crew.

My outfit, the First Eight Inch Howitzer Battery was spread out all over hells half-acre. During my tour our main encampment was located in the sand dunes south of Da Nang near what was called "the old French Bridge" which was about five miles north of Red Beech. We maintained a couple of howitzers at this location and the other three were farmed out to infantry battalions. One of our eight-inches was located at an out-post off Highway One not to far from the ville of An Hoa. The An Hoa firebase was the pits and no one ever volunteered to go there. Besides the extreme primitive living conditions, An Hoa was also "Indian" country where the VC and NVA conducted constant assaults on the firebase.

In late October of 1966, our headquarters section located at the sand dune cantonment below Da Nang, got word over the land line that the howitzer at An Hoa was disabled and in need of in shop repair. Something was wrong with the firing mechanism and a replacement eight-inch was needed ASAP. You won't even have to guess who's howitzer was available to travel the 50 miles to An Hoa.

Our Gun Captain Staff Sergeant Purdue told us it would take a couple of days to make the trip and for us to load down our howitzer with extra ammo since he didn't know how much ammo was left with the broken down eight-inch we were replacing. By the time we got done stacking rations, and other creature comforts in and on our howitzer, it looked like a gypsy wagon. It was so damn hot, over 100 degrees, that the rest of the crew rode on top of the gun in folding beach chairs they'd got at the Marble Mountain PX. Lance Corporal Simmons and I weren't so lucky as we had to drive the steel beast.

U.S. Marine Corps 8" Howitzer (Self Propelled) being pulled from river.

Driving the narrow roads of Vietnam and all the problems we encountered along the way would probably make a good Sea Story of its own and sufficient to say I was all but a nervous wreck by the time we came to the river blocking our passage as we neared An Hoa. I can't remember the name of this river but it was very wide and had a rather large island in the middle of it near the river crossing. Directly across the river was Hill 55 which was manned by Marines and guarded the approach to An Hoa. Allied forces couldn't keep a bridge in place at the crossing and every time the Seabees built one, the VC or NVA would blow it up. We just happened to arrive at the river crossing when the bridge was down. But this wasn't a problem since the Navy had a LCV (World War II era Landing Craft Vehicle) they were using as a ferry.

It was a tight squeeze but I managed to maneuver the huge eight-inch howitzer onto the fairly small boat without mishap.

Staff Sergeant Perdue elected to stand in his turret for the crossing and the rest of the gun-crew stood on top. With a chugging cough the Navy coxswain edged his craft out into the rough waters of the river.

What happened then when we got to the middle of the river either shows the NVA had a diabolical sense of humor or they were one hell'uva lot smarter than we gave them credit for. From the small island to our right commenced the hollow popping sounds of 82mm mortars leaving their tubes. One mortar dropped a shell alongside one side of the LCV while the other mortar hit in the water on the other side. The gook gunners were slamming shells into their tubes as fast as they could and exploding water drenched all hands aboard the LCV. All of the rounds were hitting on either side of the boat, either my accident or design.

Someone yelled. "They got us bracketed!"

"Bracketed HELL!" Staff Sergeant Perdue screamed back. "Those sonsofbitch's know exactly what they're doing."

By now the small landing craft was rocking from side to side from the churning water caused by the exploding enemy mortars. like it was a baby's cradle. From my perch inside the open drivers compartment I could feel the heavy eight-inch howitzer shifting. The odd thing was that it was inching backward and not sideways. Before I could shout a warning the gun began a backward slide that couldn't be stopped. It crashed through the rear of the LCV into the river. A 25-ton eight-inch howitzer does not float.

Those crewmembers who had been standing on top of the turret were fortunately thrown clear as the howitzer sunk to the bottom of the river. Simmons and I barely made it out of the two front hatches before the gun plunged to the bottom. The amazing part of this Sea Story is Staff Sergeant Perdue. He didn't have time to make it out of the top hatch and went down with his gun. His presence of mind is what makes U. S, Marines what they are. Afterwards, Staff Sergeant Perdue, said, "The damn gun slid off so fast that I didn't have a chance to bail out. When the water started rushing into the hatch it tried to suck me down inside the turret but I knew damn good and well if it did it would be Adios Amigo for me. It took every ounce of strength I have in my arms to brace myself against the rush of water pouring in the hatch but I just held my breath until the turret got filled up and once the water equalized, I just floated to the surface."

It was either by design or dumb luck that the North Vietnamese Army made a submarine out of an eight-inch howitzer.

===

Although I promised the Marine in question here that I'd abide by his request of anonymity for personal reasons, he did say I could go ahead and add a short ending to his story. The 8" howitzer (SP) was eventually pulled from the river and placed back into action after a thorough cleaning. No one was injured in the guns sinking though SSgt Perdue's arms were so sore he had to be placed on light duty for several days. The two NVA mortar teams was caught by Marine air as they attempted to leave the island by canoe like boats and eliminated.

39

CALIFORNIA DREAMING
Authors Name Withheld By Request

An Hoa, South Vietnam, had to be one of the worst Marine encampments in Southeast Asia. During the monsoon season the small airstrip at An Hoa became a quagmire that you couldn't even walk across. If you think I'm kidding, let me relate a quick story before telling my Sea Story. We had a six-by truck try and cross the muddy airstrip and even with its four-wheel drive it got stuck fast. So the brass sent out a tank to retrieve the truck. The tank got mired down so bad that it took a tank-retriever with its long cable to get the tank un-stuck and back to a semblance of firm earth. The six-by was left on the airstrip and by the time the monsoon rains ended it had sunk up to its cab with the hood all but underground. It had to be eventually bulldozed out. And naturally the dry season was just as bad. The one time quagmire turned into a dust blowing hot desert that covered equipment, weapons, tents and bunkers with a fine film of yellowish-red dirt. It was a constant hassle keeping our eight-inch howitzer in top condition for firing.

As the Christmas season of 1966 approached there was all kind of scuttlebutt floating around An Hoa that Bob Hope might pay our outpost a visit. Bob was known to unexpectedly drop in on some remote spot during his Christmas tour and I guess who ever started the rumor figured that An Hoa was as about as remote as you could get in Vietnam. No one really believed the bullshit but it did help our sagging moral somewhat just to think about it. After all, we realized that An Hoa was a fire support base and we were constantly fighting the VC and NVA, and no one in their right mind would come to this ass hole of the Nam voluntarily that had an iota of common sense.

Jayne Mansfiels-She was the sexual icon of the 1950s and 1960s. The actress was born in Pennsylvania in 1933 and raised in Texas. Jayne appeared in over 50 films and acted on Broadway and TV. Her most notable movies were, Will Success Spoil Rock Hunter and, It Takes A Thief. She Was killed in a car crash near New Orleans on June 29, 1967, shortly after returning from a Vietnam USO tour.

Evidently the high brass got wind of the BS being passed around about a USO show going to visit An Hoa and how happy the troops were looking forward to this possibility. I don't think any of the Marines pulling duty at An Hoa during Christmas of 1966 will ever figure out how it happened but sure enough official word was passed that a USO troupe would pay an hour visit Christmas Eve day. And to top it off the show coming would include the famous cowboy movie actor Tex

Ritter and the even more famous, big busted, blond haired sexpot actress Jayne Mansfield. Yeah, sure. We snuffies all sort of looked at one another with expressions like "who are they trying to shit!"

But when the Seabees began erecting a stage of sorts at the end of the airstrip even the most doubting Gyrene started thinking maybe it was for real. Like all good Marines we loved watching somebody else work and when not on duty there was always a throng of Jarheads scoping out the Navy construction workers doing their thing. The Seabees did a pretty good job as they normally do and the stage ended up looking real nifty. It had a plywood roof for shade cover built over the actual stage and though rather crude did have a behind the stage area more or less intended to be as dressing rooms. The day before the troupe was supposed to come I was goofing off around the Seabee's handy work and noticed this PFC painting a helmet a bright pink. I asked him what in the hell he was doing and he smiled at me, and said he was making a brassier. "A what?" I asked. He went on to tell me that the senior officer at An Hoa, an artillery major, had ordered him to paint two helmets pink by mixing white paint and red-lead together and then band the chin straps together to make them look like a steel brassier. As a bit of humor, the commanding officer was going to present the pink helmets to Jayne Mansfield and tell her the Marines of An Hoa wanted her to have a special flak jacket to remember them by. Made sense to me!

Christmas Eve day about 500 Marines with a sprinkling of sailors and soldiers waited expectantly for the helicopters to arrive with Jayne Mansfield and Tex Ritter.

It was past noon when the clacking sound of rotor blades was finally heard and a gaggle of choppers swooped low overhead. While the gunships remained on station as protection two large Marine helo's made a gentle landing on the LZ behind the newly constructed stage. As previously planned all of our artillery pieces opened up in a direct fire welcome and also as a deterrent to keep curious gook heads down.

I was one of the lucky ones who was allowed off watch to see the show. The grunts on perimeter duty would have to settle for taking shifts to get a glimpse of the stars. As soon as the sound gear was set up Jayne Mansfield came out from behind the stage and the Marilyn Monroe wantabe waved at the crowd and blew us kisses from her pouted lips as she stood in front of a microphone. She had nothing to worry about as far as her popularity with this group of guys because we went absolutely ape shit just seeing her stand there smiling at us. She was dressed in a low-cut cotton summer print dress with the hem above her knees. White high heel sandals showed off her great legs and with her blond hair and wide ruby lips; in a word she was gorgeous! Jayne had to wait a couple of minutes for the ovation to settle down to a roar. She kept saying "thank you, thank you," then look around at the other people on the stage and shrug her shoulders as if to say, "Is this all they expect out of me?"

When we quieted down enough for her to get a word in she spoke in that husky, sexy voice that would melt any man's heart. "I was really impressed boys by those big loud guns going off when we landed, it made me feel ohoooo sooo safe knowing all you boys have such big guns."

That set the guys off again. Catcalls, whistle and screams drowned her out.

When she finally got our attention and we settled down a bit she threw out another zinger. "I bet you fellows say that to all the girls that drop by." Naturally, we went bonkers again.

To get us settled down this time the major who was the commanding officer of An Hoa got on the microphone and begun his spiel about the special presentation the Marines had for Jayne. "Miss Mansfield, as you know this area is a combat zone. We Marines here call this Indian Country because an attack by the enemy could happen at any time. And I'm sure you've noticed as you've looked around that all of the Marines are wearing heavy protective vest that are called Flak Jackets. We wear these armored vest to protect the vital chest area of our bodies from enemy shrapnel. Well now, we certainly do not want any thing to happen to your vital chest area so the boys here at An Hoa made you your personal Flak Jacket which you may keep in memory of your visit here with us." And two Marines held apart the twin pink painted helmets tied together at the straps. It really did look like a big bra.

Before the troops could start their snickering and make catcalls, I'll be damn if Jayne Mansfield didn't purr into the microphone, "Well boys lets see if my new bra fits." And with a quick motion she lowers the front of her strapless summer dress, showing 500 men she wasn't wearing a real bra. Then she told the two Marines to place her helmet bra over her boobs. To say this brought down the house would be the understatement of the century!

I cannot remember one second what Tex Ritter had to say or did to entertain us but you can believe one thing———he had one hell of a hard act to follow.

40

DON'T COMPLAIN ABOUT THE CHOW
Former Staff Sergeant Howard W. Suttmiller, USMC

After wading the low tide at Tarawa and going through the additional hell of Saipan and Tinian, my outfit, the 8th Marines, 2nd Marine Division, took the idea of hitting the beaches of Okinawa during April of 1945, as one more stepping stone before we'd have to invade Japan. You would probably not be able to understand the relief we all felt when the word was passed on our troop ships that the 2d Marine Division had been designated the "floating reserve" for the Okinawa landing.

From all of our past experiences, those veteran combat Marines, including me, serving in the 8th Regiment, all surmised that the amphibious assault landing would be just like all the rest with heavy causalities on the beaches. Therefore, we were more than surprised when the word was passed early that Easter morning and April Fools Day, that the 1st Marine Division and newly formed 6th Marine Division, landed ashore practically unopposed. The two Army assault divisions had likewise made it ashore with few causalities. The 2d Marine Division aboard troop ships made a diversionary feint at the southeastern side of the island to draw the Japanese defenders away from the main landing beach. Ironically, our division, which never landed, suffered the most casualties that day when kamikazes hit two of our APA's, killing 16 Marines and wounding 37 others.

By April 10th, the threat of Japanese suicide kamikazes working over the anchored fleet offshore caused the high brass to order the 2d Marine Division back to its staging area on Saipan. And that's where the gist of this sea story took place at.

We returned to Saipan, living conditions could not have been worse. Saipan was hot, dusty and downright miserable. About the only thing a person could do was swat fly's, chase land crabs and try to avoid the hundred and one crappy little working parties designed to keep the enlisted men busy. Sure, the members of the 8th Marines weren't getting shot at—at least not too much; you know how it was with "secured" islands, always a sniper or two left behind who didn't get the word to surrender. But just the same down in the enlisted ranks morale was at an all time low and getting worse every day. Most troopers felt they were the forgotten bastards of a war that had passed them by, and that nobody of higher authority gave a damn one way or the other about them or how they had to live.

This poor morale seemed especially bad in the 8th Marines and should have been a warning to the higher ups considering the snappish verbal responses of disrespect taking place along with sullen attitudes. Now Marines are famous for bitching about things that don't suit them, but the wail and cry coming from the 8th Marines was getting damn close to being mutinous. It's been said that disgruntled Marines are happy Marines and not to worry until they become totally moody and quiet. Well, that's exactly what happened with the 8th Marines.

The main complaint the enlisted Marines had was that no one of authority took it serious about the lousy chow being fed them from the field kitchen. Canned B rations are bad enough to start with, but the snuffies felt their mess cooks were a bunch of lazy, don't give a damn types, who served up greasy concoctions never before seen or heard of, let alone being appetizing. So, the 8th Marines went on a food strike. For 10 days over 90% of the regiment's enlisted men refused to eat. Or, they'd go through the chow line and dump what they considered slop on the deck at the end of the line. Our bewildered officers didn't know what to make of our food strike and it finally took the division commanding general, Maj.Gen. Thomas E. Watson to get things settled down. He fired a number of the 8th Marines field cooks and put the fear of God in the new cooks by ordering the chow had best get better quick. It did.

But old General Watson had a good memory when it came to his malcontent 8th Marines troopers. At the end of May our regiment got orders to saddle up because the two Marine divisions still fighting on Okinawa needed some help. You will never be able to convince any Marine differently who served in the 8th at this time that we were sent back to combat because our division commander remembered what outfit went on a food strike! I guess it just proves you shouldn't complain about the chow when you're in the Corps.

==

Howard Suttmiller was recalled as a Marine reserve for the Korean War. Besides wading the low tide at Tarawa he also crunched the snow with the 1st Marine Division during the breakout from the Chosin Reservoir. He is the recipient of the Navy Commendation Medal with "V" device for heroic achievement while on Tarawa. A Widower, Howard is active in the Indianapolis detachment of the Marine Corps League.

41

THE GREAT RAISIN-JACK CAPER
Former Corporal Gene C. Robinson, USMC

In late September 1951, my regiment, the 5th Marines was taken off the lines above Inje, South Korea which was located in the northeast sector of the 1st Marine Division's TAOR (Tactical Area Of Responsibility.) The word was passed that we would be the division reserve for the next month to give us a little "behind the lines" rest and recuperation, better known as R&R.

Much to our surprise the high command really meant it and we were allowed some free time to do as we damn well pleased. A bunch of us guys checked out 12 gauge shotguns from the armory tent and went pheasant hunting up in the many valley fingers separating the various hills and mountains where we were at, while others tried their luck at fishing or played baseball.

The weather was still decent for late September. but here in the mountainous east coast of Korea we knew it could change in a matter of a few hours to blizzard conditions, the same as it had during the Chosin Reservoir campaign fought last year. So, we counted our blessings and made the most out of the leisure time that was given us. In the evenings the special service poggies would show movies on an outdoor screen; most of them John Wayne flicks to keep our asses "Gung Ho" and "Hard-charging!"

My best buddy in Item Company was a huge mountain boy from Lewisburg, West Virginia, PFC Harold K. Harrison. He was a big raw-boned, ruddy-faced lad with sharp, chiseled features. Everyone, including the officers and NCOs called Harrison "H.K." or, "West By God." He liked the West By God the most since it was his trademark he used to emphasize where he hailed from: "West By God Virginia." We were both 19 years old but HK towered over my 5'10", 158-pound body by a good five inches. He carried the base plate and tube for our 60mm mortar and I was his first ammo carrier. Old H.K. was a full-fledged mountaineer and felt right at home up on the hills around us. He was an outstanding shooter and could track game as good as an Indian. I really liked going hunting with him, but hunting wasn't his only skills. Harrison came from a long family line of moon shiners.

One of the other luxuries we enjoyed in the rear was hot chow. A field galley under canvas was located at the site the 5th Marines was bivouacked and the salty professional Marine mess sergeant put out some pretty good chow considering most of it came out of cans.

After eating a reasonable decent beef stew one evening. West By God, along with me and a couple of our other buddies, were taking our time ambling back to our tents. Harrison started talking to us in his soft, slow drawl. "Didja all happen to see those cases of number ten cans off'en to the side of the mess tent under a tarp back thar?"

The three of us answered that we hadn't noticed or paid attention to the mess sergeant's supply stash.

"Well, ah did," answered H.K. "Ah must'ta seen a good couple dozen cases of canned raisins and a goodly amount of sugar to boot. An' since they bake thar own bread, they's got ta be som' pure yeast in th' supply tent locker thar whar the tarps at." Harrison eyed the three of us with a lop-sided sly smile. "Fellers' ah can make us som' gooood shor'nuff shit outta' that stuff."

We immediately saw what he was driving at and being the good teenage Marines we were, the four of us went about planning our next move. The biggest pitfall was what to put the mixture in once the ingredients were procured. Our pal Tom Gideon thought he had the answer. "Why don't we borrow one of those number fifteen size pots the cook uses when we go for the other stuff."

Tom's idea sounded good to us and after the moon dropped behind the mountain peeks, we made a famous Marine Corps maneuver, called, "the midnight survey." Using our best "snoop and poop" tactics, we swept down on the mess hall, swiftly, silent and deadly. At least deadly, if we got caught.

Our mission, a complete success, pot and all, we returned to our area with our plunder and watched H.K. measure and mix the ingredients in the #15 stainless steel pot, complete with pressure lid with its small steam vent. We hid the filled pot temporarily in our tent.

The next morning, we formed another patrol and went about finding a location to hide our concoction for the necessary 15 days H.K. said it would take for fermentation. We also wanted to especially hide our enterprise from those "booze hounds" in the machine-gun squad that would drink anything closely resembling alcohol.

We finally found the perfect hiding place next to a half-collapsed mud constructed Korean hut. Next to the hut was a large clay jug that stood about four feet high the Koreans used to store rice and other dry food in. We knocked the bottom out of the jug and it fit down perfectly over the sealed #15 pot we'd lugged along. Then we packed some cardboard, paper and other trash inside the clay jug on top of the pot to make it look like a trash can. Pleased with our work we strolled back toward our area. Harrison talked to us as we neared the camp. "If'n this weather stays this warm fer fifteen days fellers, I'll guar-ran-tee ya'all, this stuff will knock yer hat in th' creek and yank yer ass in afta it."

Not only did it stay warm, it got down right hot, so to speak, in certain aspects. The mess sergeant went on a rampage trying to find out who stole his #15 pot and raided his food-locker. He came storming though our area with blood in his eyes and a cocked .45 pistol in his hand demanding the low lives give him back his pot. I mean he was really pissed. When he wasn't yelling he kept mumbling something under his breath about, "Fuck 'em, feed 'em fish, fuck the whole bunch of 'em!"

Now anybody that's served more than a few months in the Marine Corps knows you don't want to piss-off the mess sergeant. A mess sergeant is a powerful man in the

Corps and a person not get on the wrong side of, especially in a reserve area. Up on the line, it didn't make any difference since we all had to eat C rats anyhow. But back here, in the rear, look out! This particular mess sergeant was a career Marine who'd cooked and fought his way through the island campaigns of World War II, and there wasn't any doubt in any of our minds the payback he could wrought upon our outfit. What if he started putting salt in the coffee, pepper in the oatmeal, dehydrated eggs half cooked, runny and green; powdered milk warm and lumpy? I mean he good wrack havoc on the entire regiment. We got to thinking about a whole bunch of pissed off Marines going back on the line, and if any of them found out about the four Jarheads who'd screwed up their chow........well, you get my point. To say the four of us started getting real concerned about the mess sergeants mental state, is saying a mouthful, for the simple reason we sure as hell was.

After hashing it over we decided we better return the #15 pot to its rightful owner. It was time for another dangerous "midnight survey." There were a lot of water cans laying around and we figured one of them wouldn't be missed so this time we confiscated one of the five-gallon water cans with a lock down lid. We took the jerry can to our mud hut hideaway and it was a good thing we did. As we approached the clay jar all four of us heard this odd "clicking" noise coming from the jar. Uncovering our cache we found the clicking sound to be the steam vent on the secured lid rattling from the obvious boiling going on inside the pot just as if it was on a burner. H.K, remarked that the brew was "do'en real good." We accomplished the transfer of H.K.'s elixir from the #15 pot to the five-gallon water can and sealed the can tight so it wouldn't "click" like the pot had done. After replacing the fake trash on top of the water can we took the pot to a nearby creek and washed it out. Then we snooped and pooped to get the #15 pot back to the mess tent. This part of the plan seemed to go over real well as there was no more "bear growling" heard from the mess sergeant's tent.

We had some decent warm sunny days for the next several days as we lazed in the rear area. We sat around in groups cleaning our weapons, shooting the shit, writing letters and just screwing-off in general. That is, as long as there wasn't some kind of general military subjects class to attend or a detail to go on. You know the drill, in the Marine Corps wasting time is shit for the birds, and our senior NCOs were always dreaming up little working parties or classes to keep us happy.

Anyhow, we were keeping an eye, or as it were, an ear on our venture. About a week went by when we begin hearing an occasional deep gurgling sound coming from the camouflaged water can. "Blub.....blub, bulb.........BLUB!" Sounded like it was coming from the bowels of hell. But H.K. reassured us, it was doing just fine.

On day 13 the four of us went to the brew hut for our daily inspection tour. H.K. removed the trash from the clay jug, looked down at the water can, then said: "Oh shit fellers...y'all better come look at this heah,"

Now a five-gallon military water can was made pretty sturdy out of rolled steel. They were about 24 inches high and six inches wide and well constructed with hinge locked covers over the opening. But damn if our can hadn't bulged out to around eight inches wide and I swear it was moving. I took one look and said. "That somebitch is 'bout ready to explode!"

Tom Gideon, who had already retreated behind a big rock, asked, "Whut th' hell we gonna do? I ain't about to touch that damn thing!"

The other member of our foursome, PFC Bobby Martinez, spoke up. "We're gonna have to talk to Corporal Fletcher an' let 'em in on what we're doing. I know him and his gun squad has made some hooch outta gook sweet potatoes, an' he'll tell us how to handle it."

Even though we all knew Corporal Ron Fletcher was a pretty cool head, we re-signed ourselves to the fact, that by enlisting his help, we'd have to share our booze with the machine-gun squad.

Fletcher came back to our mud hut and looked the situation over. Shaking his head, he said. "Boys, what we gotta do is get that damn thing out of the area before it blows up. Now go find a long pole and we'll run it through the handles, and with a guy on each side, we'll carefully carry it down to the creek, then open it up to relieve the pressure."

We found a pole quick enough but it took some time to find a Marine brave enough to lift the water can out of the clay jug. I mean, can you imagine the telegram to our next-of-kin: "Your son was killed by the explosion of five gallons of raisin jack." Finally, Corporal Fletcher gingerly lifted out the water can and Tom Gideon and I carried it down to the creek on the long pole we'd found. Our steps were slow due to the fact we kept waiting for the damn thing to blow up at any second.

Since H.K. was experienced with this kind of high explosives, we elected him to flip the handle. The big mountain boy pried up the lid lock with a stick and WHOOSH! It sounded life Old Faithful going off. H.K. stuck his nose down to the opening, took a big whiff, and said. "I'm go'in ta tell ya whut fellers, we got som' gooood shit heah!"

A happy band of Marines trudged there way back to the camp area to fetch their canteens. Naturally, we had to let the machine-gun squad join us, but there was enough raisin jack to go around for everyone. It was a potent brew.

That night the outdoor movie was John Wayne's Sands of Iwo Jima. The original foursome joined the machine-gun boys to watch Sergeant Stricker do his thing. It didn't take us long to get gassed on that brutish elixir. About half way through the movie watching old Duke Wayne in action we were ready for a frontal assault on Moscow. Things went down hill from there.

Our entire gassed up group got so Gung Ho we started harassing a bunch of guys from How Company sitting next to us. We took up a chant: "Red, red, runs the blood of those who defy Fighting Item." That's all it took. Fist started flying and the shit really hit the fan. Some dumb ass had even gave some raisin-jack to a couple of mongrel dogs and damn if they didn't start tearing up each other. The no holds bared melee reached high proportions with our entire company fighting How Company. Swirling dust blocked out the movie screen, fist flew, men yelling, dogs barking. It was a full-fledged Katie-bar-the-door.

I was more interested in my raisin-jack than fighting and was pushing guys out of my way trying to find my half-full canteen when I was caught flush on the jaw by a roundhouse hook that knocked me senseless. I went backward over a log we used as seats and knew right away I had definitely "malfunctioned." But guess what? I found my canteen. I clutched the canteen to my chest as I laid flat on my back looking up at all the legs swirling about me. Another fallen comrade laid a few feet from me and I crawled to him and we both took first aid from my canteen. All of a sudden the area lights went on and officers and older sergeants were everywhere breaking up the brawl. John Wayne's vengeance against the Japs would have to wait.

Captain Diamond, C.O. of Item Company, looked like a satchel charge about to go off when he faced his raggedy ass group of Marines. "There are plenty of Goddamn commies over here for you people to fight without you trying to kill each other. I want you to hear me loud and clear: any injuries resulting from this stupid grab-ass will result in a court-martial! I don't care if your fucking back is broken, when we get ready to move out and if you are not able to perform your duty, you will be sent back to the brig at Inchon pending court-martial!"

The skipper had definitely got my attention and I moved my jaw around to make sure it was still functional.

But the captain wasn't done yet. "And since you clowns have got so much pent up energy then by God I'm ordering a full field dress inspection at oh-seven-hundred tomorrow with no exceptions. If you miss this inspection, you had better be dead! Okay, unit leaders get this grab-ass mob back to the company area."

We were dismissed just in time as far as I was concerned because I didn't feel very good. Everything started getting real weird. Voices echoed in my ears as if from a distance and everyone seemed to be moving in slow motion. When I turned my head it took some time for my eyes to focus. This was about the last thing I remembered.

Later Tom Gideon said that he and one of the machine-gunners had to drag me back to the area where they dumped me next to my pup tent. It rained hard that night and Bobby Martinez told me if he hadn't pulled me into the tent I would have drowned in the three-inch drainage ditch dug around the tent.

The next morning came up gray and colder, very appropriate under the circumstances considering the rude experience we'd went through. Everyone around me was hung over except Nathaniel B. Skates, a big Negro lad from Chattanooga, Tennessee, who was very religious. Nate didn't drink and he just sat there cleaning his rifle for the up-coming inspection, smiling at us with an inner superiority. Then he starts humming the old spiritual song, No Body Knows The Trouble I See.

The way my head was pounding I was ready to puke any second. "Yeah, yeah...I hear ya. Damn it Nate shut up will ya, you've made your point."

Even though we felt bad we paid close attention to our weapons, making sure they were boot camp ready for inspection.

Our company gunny, Gunny Wood came by as we were working on our gear and he gave us some advise that probably saved all our asses. "Now I ain't ask'en any questions but I tell you people what. I'd give some special attention to your canteens if it was me. Empty 'em out and fill 'em up with half sand and half water and shake the shit outta 'em.

After you've scoured 'em good, fill 'em up with fresh water and put in three halizone tablets." He gave us an evil grin and went on his way.

The halizone tablets the Guns was talking about was used for water purification which made the water smell and taste like a combination of bleach and quinine with just one tablet in the canteen. Three would be over-kill but we all followed his advice.

Gunny Woods proved to us that he was a crafty old Marine. The first thing Captain Diamond went for when he conducted his company in formation inspection was our canteens. He opened the screw on lids of every canteen and took a whiff, even going so far as to pour out some of the water for a second smell. He glared at us suspiciously, but Gunny Woods' remedy must have worked. Before dismissing the company from inspection the captain left us with some final words of wisdom. "I want you men to remember we've only got a short time remaining before we go back up on the line. Confine your drinking to your beer rations and leave that wild homegrown shit alone. I know some of you boys are pretty good in making moon-shine, but I want you to knock it off and maybe some of us will get back home alive."

The last few remaining days we spent in the rear before it was time to relieve the 1st Marines were enjoyable and sober.

I do remember the words of H.K. West By God Harrison before we had to shove off though. "I tol yew fellers that would be som goood shit!"

==

Gene "Robbie" Robinson was a wholesale food salesman for 43 years after getting his honorable discharge from the Corps. Presently, he is the Johnson County Indiana Veterans Service Officer and he and his wife Marsha live in Franklin, Indiana. Gene and Marsha have four sons, two daughters and six grandkids. Gene was honored by the State of Indiana by having part of a letter written to his father from Korea inscribed on the Indiana Korean War Memorial.

42

IT'S A SMALL WORLD, ISN'T IT?
Former Corporal George W. Kiser, USMC

I was in the 1st Platoon, "C" Company, 1st Battalion, 9th Marines, 3rd Marine Division in October of 1944 when we were put on out-post duty near the little village of Merizo, Guam. At this time I was a 19-year-old PFC rifleman who was 5' 11" and 150 pounds soaking wet.

The native Chamoros were a friendly people and really quite happy to have a platoon of Marines in their midst. The Japanese occupation of Guam had not been a pleasant one and the Chamoros welcomed us with open arms. They knew there was still plenty of Jap survivors out in the surrounding jungle and that we were there to protect them.

After a few weeks our relationship with the natives was so good that the village mayor called for a Fiesta. Now a Fiesta came from the Spanish influence instilled in the natives from missionaries that came to Guam hundreds of years before to spread their religious beliefs. As a matter of fact, Fiesta is literally translated to a religious ceremony feast. This included processions of gaily-colored costumes and dancing with some pagan heritage rituals thrown in for good measure. In other words, one heck of a big picnic.

We Marines found out that you just don't jump into a Fiesta without a lot of pre-planning and we watched with amusement and wonder at all the activities going on as the Chamoros went about putting their party together.

While all this was going on, it so happened an ocean-going tug pulled into the lagoon fronting on the small town. The skipper of the tug was a salty looking Navy lieutenant commander with an unforgettable face. His features were so weather beaten, especially around his crowfeet eyes, that his face looked like brown parchment paper. He was so ugly, he was what you'd call ruggedly handsome. The commanders' job was to supervise a team of Navy divers who were setting 10 tons of explosives in the shallow coral entrance of the lagoon. They were going to blast out a deep channel so a radar ship could be anchored inside the lagoon.

While the Navy men were completing their work, the head Chamoro that the Fiesta was to begin informed us Marines. Our cook pitched in and helped the natives roast a newly slain cow over an open fire. Other Chamoros cooked special native dishes and baked cakes. After months of a steady diet of Spam and macaroni and cheese we Marines were in heaven with all the fresh food being prepared.

As the sun was setting brightly in the west, the Fiesta was in full swing. Our bellies were full of roast beef and local vegetable dishes. A happy group of Marines. Then all of a sudden BOOM! At least the Navy commander had waited until after the meal was over before he set off the 10 tons of dynamite. After the initial shock, all of the native men raced to their small canoe like boats to pick up the dead fish that certainly would be floating in the lagoon. To their dismay there wasn't any fish because the entire lagoon was covered with eight inches of sandy foam from the explosion.

That wasn't the case the next morning. The tide had cleared out the foam and the beach was littered with hundreds of dead fish that had washed up. You talk about a smelly mess! Boy, what a stink. So what happens? The Marines get the job of picking up all the dead fish and had to bury them in old Jap foxholes above the sand line. Thanks a lot Navy! And great timing to the lieutenant commander.

With Iwo Jima as our next amphibious landing, our great duty with the Chamoros quickly faded to a pleasant memory as did the lieutenant commander busting up our Fiesta, which of course wasn't such a good memory when you think of all those rotten fish we had to bury.

About a year after the war was over, my wife and I were visiting her parents. We were sitting in their living room talking, when a car pulled up out in front of the house. My mother-in-law stood up and went to the window, saying. "I wonder who that could be?" Then she said, "Oh, its Barret Hindes my cousin. How nice. I'm glad he dropped by as I want George to meet him."

When the cousin walked into the room I stood up and we introduced ourselves to one another, shaking hands. I kept staring at him because he looked so familiar to me but I couldn't place where I'd seen him before.

We all sat back down and my mother-in-law said, "George, Barret was in the Navy during the war........"

Whatever else my mother-in-law had intended to say was cut short, because I suddenly recalled where I had seen that face before, and I interrupted her by blurting out. "You SOB I know you! You're the one that blew up that lagoon on Guam! Thanks a lot for all the dead fish I had to pick up and bury."

We all had a good laugh after it was explained to my stunned in-laws the unusual coincidence.

It is indeed, a small world and that's my sea story.

==

George Kiser had a nice story to tell about Iwo Jima that using author's privilege I'll share it with the reader. He said as his troop ship got into position off Iwo in February 1945, the Marines could hardly hear one another talk over the noise of the big ships guns blasting away, aircraft making bombing runs, etc. But when the big flag went up on top of Mt. Suribachi, the bombs and naval gunfire stopped and all of the hundreds of ships laying off the island started honking their horns and blowing their whistles. And all of the Marines waiting to land began cheering like crazy. George said it made everyone feel good about going in. George was severely wounded on Iwo Jima by Japanese mortar shrapnel. He was evacuated to Saipan, where his left leg was cut off below the knee. After being discharged as a corporal on Thanksgiving Day 1945. he entered San Jose

State College, San Jose, California. In 1946 he married his wife Barbara who had just got her R.N. degree. George just recently retired from the real estate business, and he and Barbara enjoy seeing their seven grand-children and three great grand-children. The Kiser's have a son and two daughters and live in Concord, California.

43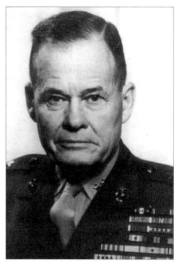

WHY HELLO "CHESTY"
Former Staff Sergeant James G. Smith, USMC

After World War II occupations duties in China I returned to Indianapolis, Indiana, and settled into making a living for my wife and me. I guess I still had that old Marine Corps "Gung Ho" spirit in me and when a couple of pals of mine said they were going to go into the Marine Corps Reserve I said "what the hey" and joined up with them. As it turned out I met a lot of great guys and looked forward to the every Wednesday evening drills with the 16th Infantry Battalion. My best buddy in the outfit was Tom Finch.

When eight North Korean divisions led by Russian T-34 tanks invaded South Korea on June 25, 1950, my wife Hilda took one look at the newspaper, then turned to me and said, "You may as well start packing your gear Jim, there's no way President Truman is going to let them get away with this."

It must be a special intuition wives have since her prediction proved true and in less than a month the 16th Infantry Battalion was activated. We were ordered to get our affairs in order within 30 days. By the end of August 1950 I, and the rest of my reserve outfit was part of the 1st Marine Division and were in the final phase of staging at Camp Pendleton, California.

Once in Korea, me and my buddy Tom Finch got assigned to different outfits. I ended up with the combat engineers and Tom got assigned to the 1st Marines. His regimental commander was the legendary Colonel Lewis B. "Chesty" Puller, who would later be awarded his fifth Navy Cross medal for his gallantry in leading the rear guard out of Koto-ri during the Chosin Reservoir campaign. Like any Marine who served under Chesty, I know Tom was mighty proud to have him as his regimental commanding officer.

LtGen Lewis B. "Chesty" Puller, USMC- Chesty Puller is the Marine Corps' most decorated Marine. Among his many awards for valor are five Navy Cross medals for extraordinary gallantry and the Army Distinguished Service Cross presented to him by General of the Army Douglas MacArthur. He is the author of the book titled MARINE. General Puller died in 1971.

After the Korean War I dropped out of the reserves but did join the Marine Corps League and the 1st Marine Division Association to keep my scarlet and gold juices flowing.

In 1954, I along with a my good pal Tom Finch, who was still in the Marine Corps

Reserve as a Gunnery Sergeant, attended the annual National Convention and reunion of the 1st Marine Division Association being held in Chicago, Illinois. Even though most of the division was still in Korea, keeping an eye on the Chinese during the early truce stage, the Biltmore Hotel off Chicago's famous Loop was filled to capacity with thousands of Marines and former Marines that had served in the division.

This one particular evening Tom and I decided we'd take a break from the convention activities and walk around the downtown area a little and maybe grab a couple of beers. As the two of us was leaving the Biltmore through its big revolving front door, who in all his splendor was coming into the hotel using the same revolving door but Lieutenant General Lewis B, "Chesty" Puller. Tom yelled through his section of the revolving door, "Hey Chesty, I was with you up at the reservoir!"

Chesty Puller glanced at Tom through the glass partition and I'll be damn if he didn't just make a complete circle in the revolving door and came right back out onto the sidewalk where Tom and I was standing. He came right over to Tom and stuck out his hand and with that famous growl he used for a voice, said. "How you doing old boy, what unit was you with?"

Tom said, "I was a BAR man in Item Company, Three/One sir."

"Is that so old bean. well say now that means your company commander is a good friend of mine Captain Bull Fisher. He's a major now, did you know that?"

Tom answered Chesty that he'd heard Captain Fisher had got promoted.

General Puller's aide-de-camp, a young second lieutenant looked at the general with a nervous expression. "Sir, I believe the other generals are awaiting your arrival."

Chesty glanced at his aide and with what might have passed as a smile, then he said. "Son, you run on in there and tell them I'm going to be an hour or so late as I'm out having a couple of beers with one of my men."

With a look of panic the aide replied. "How am I going to find you sir?"

Glancing up and down the street, Chesty then looked back to his aide. "Son, you see that bar down the block there with the big red neon sign. If you run your errand jack rabbit quick you might still find us in there." The Chesty turned to Tom. "Well old bean, are you ready to go have a couple of beers?"

With me looking on with my jaw practically hitting the deck, Tom says, "Aye, aye sir!"

As it turned out we had more than just a couple of beers and I don't know if Chesty ever did meet up with them other generals his aide had referred to.

I never have told this story too many times because I always figured who's gonna believe it if I tell 'em? You know how it is with Chesty stories. If every guy who said he'd been Chesty's driver was telling the truth, then old Chesty must have had a thousand chauffeurs during his career. But on the other hand, since I didn't serve under Chesty and was an eyewitness to this reunion, it doesn't inflate my ego none, so maybe this is one Chesty story that will be believable. Oh, by the way, Chesty's aide-de-camp did find us and the general had to order the young lieutenant to loosen up a little and have a beer with us.

===

Jim lives in Fishers, Indiana with his wife Hilda. He is active in the Marine Corps League and while Department Commandant during the mid-1950's, chartered the leagues only all Women Marine detachment.

44

SLOW BOAT TO OKINAWA
Former Corporal John T. Flack, USMC

I had just turned seventeen when my outfit, 1st Amphibian Tractor Battalion, 1st Marine Division, got the word to saddle up for the Okinawa in invasion. The division had spent the past four months on the island of Pavuvu refitting and filtering replacements into its ranks after the Peleliu campaign. I was one of those replacements. After surviving 12 weeks of Marine boot camp, at San Diego (at age sixteen), and making it through Amphibian School at Del Mar, Camp Pendleton, I didn't think anything else could shock me. I was almost right because prior to hitting the delightful island of Pavuvu, everything had been an adventure. Pavuvu was the pits and I for one, was glad to hear we would be getting off the miserable crab infested, rat infested, hot sand hunk of real estate.

The sergeant in charge of my Amtrak was a big burly Irishman by the name of "Blackie" Jones. He was a no nonsense guy when it came to working, but on the other hand, he enjoyed the close comradeship of being with his three crewman and we all got along real well. Not only was I the junior man on the Amtrak, but I was also the runt of the entire outfit. I only stood five, four inches and weighed all of 135 pounds with sand in my pockets. After being assigned to Blackie's Amtrak, he made me the assistant driver and machine gunner. I couldn't have been more pleased. He also thought it was funnier than hell, when he found out his "new" wet behind the ears replacement, was a cocky little sixteen year older.

I don't know how it came about, but when we staged on Pavuvu's beech to embark upon the LST that would take us to Okinawa, my Amtrak was the first in line. The swabies directing the loading told our driver to back our Amtrak into the port side and go as far back as it would go. He carefully worked the steering levers and backed into the surf and slowly went up the LST's lowered ramp, easing our steel beast, up into the tank deck of the landing ship. Keeping the Amtrak in reverse the driver cautiously backed the amphibious vehicle deeper into the cavernous hull. Two sailors guided us, making sure we got as close to the portside bulkhead as possible. At the end of the tank deck was a large stack of boxes or crates covered with canvas tarpaulins. The sailors directed the Amtrak backwards until the rear end was very near the tarp-covered stack of boxes. Blackie, and I was riding on top of the Amtrak watching curiously as it eased aft. When the order was given for the driver to stop he ended up nudging the huge stack of boxes over our heads which caused an unusual sounding rattle of jostled cans.

One sailor yelled out. "Whoa! Turn it off where you're at."

One of our guys yelled over to the swab. "Hey, what's under the tarp?"

With a growl, the swab replied. "Don't sweat it Gyrene, get your trac tied down."

While the four of us took heavy chains to secure our Amtrak to the deck so it wouldn't shift around once we were underway, the other trac's of our company backed into parking places of their own. The entire well deck of the LST was a beehive of activity as the Marines went about the chore of making sure their trac's were secure. Blackie ordered me to crawl under our trac to check on the chains against the port bulkhead, as he wanted to make sure they were tight. I wasn't overly pleased at having to do this dirty job, since the deck was slimy with water and oil, but had sense enough not to question Blackie. I slithered my way under our trac and elbowed my way along the side, testing the chains as I went. To say it was a hot, cruddy job, would be an understatement. As I got to the rear of the Amtrac I saw that the bottom row of boxes the tarp was covering was about half exposed. Remembering the swabies snotty answer when Jackson had asked what they were, I elbow crawled over to the boxes and pulled back a section of the tarp. No wonder the sailor had told us not to worry about it! The entire stack of boxes was cases of beer! Beer, twenty feet high, five feet deep and twenty feet across! And we had been rationed one can of beer per man, per day, for the last three months! I took out my trusty K-bar knife which I always wore on my belt, and cut into one of the cardboard cases. It must have taken me five minutes to wiggle a can free in the close confines under the Amtrac, but I managed to do it. With no opener I used the K-bar to punch a hole in the can and then tried to figure out how in the hell to drink it since there wasn't enough room to tilt it up over my head. I finally laid sideways and sort of let the beer trickle down the side of my mouth. It was hot of course, but hey, when you're seventeen and just discovered a gold mine, who cared!

I'd started on my second can when Blackie's loud voice startled me. "What the hell didja do under there Flack...fall asleep?"

I replied in a low voice. "Shhhhhhhss, they might hear you."

In a lower tone of voice, Blacke said. "Who's gonna hear me?"

"Give me a minute." I pleaded.

It was a lot easier worming out eight other cans of beer from the case I'd broken into. I placed the beer in the inside cargo pockets of my utility jacket, then wiggled out from under the Amtrac on my back.

Blackie met me as I came out from under the trac. "What the hell was you doing under there?"

Putting a finger to my mouth in a hush like gesture I eased out the top portion of one can. Blackie took one glance at the can of beer and shut up. Inside our Amtrac, the four of us guzzled the beer as I explained what I had discovered was under the tarps.

It was a most happy slow boat ride to Okinawa.

Naturally. being Marines, we couldn't keep our secret from some of our fellow Marines, and feeling sorry for a few dry sailors, we also included them into our small band of brothers that drank all the beer they wanted. With the provision of course, they didn't get loud or boisterous, which on occasion was difficult to curtail. All the same we all made it off Okinawa without having got caught at participating in our little venture.

The finality of this tale has it's riotous aspect of humor. On Easter Sunday and April Fools Day, 1 April 1945, the ramp of our LST was lowered after the large bow doors were opened. Amtrac engines roared to life and one by one the combat landing craft crept off the ramp into the deep water of the sea. Since our Amtrac had been the first aboard, we were the last to leave. As Cpl. Jackson pulled forward in trace behind the next to last Amtrac leaving the LST, a grinding noise was heard behind us. Turning my head sharply around I saw the large stack of tarp covered beer cases tittering precariously. Blackie let out with an "Oh shit!" But there was nothing that was going to stop the obvious avalanche. With a banging crash the entire stack of beer toppled over; many of the top cases onto our trac. An outraged Chief-Master-At-Arms ran alongside our Amtrac, cussing and demanding that we stop. He was so ticked-off he even pounded on the steel side of our trac with his fist. Cpl Jackson naturally didn't stop and Blacke just looked at the Chief-Master-At-Arms with a thin smile and shrug of his shoulders. The last thing I remember as we dropped off the ramp into the water, was the echoing roar of laughter coming from the sailors inside the LST who had witnessed the fall of Mt. Beerisky. It was painfully obvious that my constant runting of the bottom cases of beer had undermined the foundation stability and the only thing that held it up was our Amtrac.

On the other hand, it was more than likely the first time in Marine Corps amphibious combat landings, that the assault troops aboard an Amtrac merrily drank cans of beer before hitting the beech. Not only had we already stocked our Amtrac inside, we kept three cases that had fell onto our trac when the stack went down.

John Flack spent 35 years as an Indianapolis, Indiana police officer. Retiring in 1974 as a lieutenant, John has the distinction of being one of Indiana's most decorated law enforcement officers. He was recalled to active duty during the Korean War. John is also an artist and some of his work can be found at Quantico, Camp Pendleton and on two navy ships. He is active in the Indianapolis Chapter of the 1st Marine Division Association, the Military Order of the Purple Heart, The Chosen Few, and the Marine Corps League. John, and his wife of 50 years Audrey, reside in a suburb of Indianapolis. He holds the Purple Heart for wounds received in action on Okinawa.

45

THAT'S WHAT BUDDIES ARE FOR
Sergeant Vincent Rios, USMC(Ret.)

You know how it is in the Corps; you get to know a guy in the next rack to you and end up buddies for life. This is the way it is with my buddy Lee Moncrief. and me. Lee and I went through boot camp together, ITR together and went to Vietnam together. We got to know one another real good when the two of us were in November Company, 2nd Infantry Training Regiment, San Onofre, California. In January 1965, we were both going through the quaint experience the Marine Corps had of making infantrymen. Of course we weren't alone, and 40 other "boot" Marines, fresh from Marine Corps Recruit Depot, San Diego, shared our Quonset hut living quarters.

It may have been because I was a little too squared away for my own good, but for some reason my Troop Handlers seemed to have quite a bit of faith in me and thought I had what it takes to learn some leadership responsibilities. One day, early in our ITR training, the Senior Troop Handler sent for me to report to him in his office. He rather tersely told me: "Rios, I've decided to make you a Hut Commander."

Naturally, I was too scared to tell my troop handler that the last thing I wanted to be was a Hut Commander, but being a good Marine I snapped out, "Yes sir!" and somehow got out of his hut office without throwing up. The job of a Hut Commander consisted of assigning crappy work details to my peers on a continuing bases. I was sort of an NCOIC without the benefit of stripes to back up my position. It was also a position that automatically singled you out for a ration of crap from your fellow Marines. Right off the bat one of the barrack cliques, that every outfit has, tested my resolve. There was five guys in this clique and it just so happened that leader of the group had the reputation of being the baddest dude in the company that you just didn't want to mess with. For the sake of this story, I'll call him Private Blockhead.

Blockhead let me know right away that he, and his clique wanted the outside detail, which was considered somewhat easier than swabbing decks or cleaning heads. Although I didn't like his surly attitude I just the same immediately assigned all of them to that task, telling myself that they'd volunteered. I guess the clique thought I'd agreed too readily to Blockhead's demand and they plotted to debunk my authority.

It became a war of wills keeping after the five guys to get them to do anything. Every time I ordered one of the clique members to do something he'd look over to Blockhead as if to say, should I do it or not?

The day of reckoning, so to speak, came four days after I'd been named the Hut Commander. On this particular morning Blockhead refused to attend to his outside duties and when I confronted him, to get his attention I slammed his wall locker door shut with a bang, and when doing so, I brushed against him. When it comes to fighting in the lower ranks, the rule of the Corps on deciding who is guilty, is who "hit" who first. I guess Blockhead figured my brushing against him constituted the first "hit." He began to pound on me. My first thought was "He's going to kill me." Even thought the big bruiser out-weighed me and had me a few inches in height, my second thought was, "By God, at least he's going to know I was here!" I pounded him back with all I had until he begged me not to hit him anymore.

What surprised me more than anything was that the other four guys of Blockheads clique hadn't rushed into the hut to help him out. At least I was surprised until I looked around and saw standing by the front hatch, my buddy Lee Moncrief looking at me with a big shit-eating-grin on his face, with an entrenching tool in his hand. He had held off the rest of Blockhead's pals! That's what real buddies are all about.

Vince Rios served with A-1-5, in Vietnam. Rios was severely wounded on 6 February 1969. He lost both legs and his right arm from a land mine. After his medically retirement from the Marine Corps Rios eventually received a masters degree in interdisciplinary social science from San Francisco State University. Rios works for the U. S. Department of Labor as a senior veterans employment advisor. He is the recipient of two Bronze Star Medals with combat "V" and three Purple Hearts. He and his wife Cheryl have five children, the eldest, a graduate of the Naval Academy and presently a Marine naval aviator. Vince, and his buddy Lee Moncrief still pal around together. Vince is active in the 1st Marine Division Association and is currently the Deputy Vice President, Western Area. He is also on the Board of Directors of the Marine Memorial Club in San Francisco.

46

THE TRAIN GUARD
Former Staff Sergeant James G. Smith, USMC

Boot Camp at Parris Island, South Carolina during the fall of 1944 put the fear of God in me by way of a couple of tough drill instructors. Both of my D.I.'s were combat veterans and part of the fear they instilled in the members of my boot platoon was how furious fighters the Japanese soldiers were. The way my D.I.'s put it was that the Japs were as about as sneaky as any combat soldier there is and could slit your throat in a heartbeat.

As it turned out I made it to the South Pacific just in time for the Japanese surrender in August of 1945. Even though I had a stint in the Merchant Marine during World War II at age sixteen, I was still a wet behind the ears, seventeen year old kid as green as they came.

I was assigned to Charlie Company, 1st Battalion, 8th Marines, 2nd Marine Division, which was located at Kagoshima, Japan at the very most southern tip of Honshu Island. Occupation duty as a young replacement and rear rank private meant I got about ever shit detail that came along. Therefore it didn't shock me one bit this particular day when word was passed for me to report to our company first sergeant on the double. I was accustomed of him assigning me to do one thing or the other around the company area. But what my first shirt had for me was a horse of a different color. He told me to get my bedroll, 782 gear and report to the motor transport office for temporary duty.

When I ask him what it was all about, he just said, "You'll find out soon enough Smith."

I knew better than to question him any more so I collected my gear and reported to the Motor Transport Officer. He turned me over to one of his sergeants who gave me a full case of C Rations and issued me a .45 caliber automatic pistol with two clips of ammo. The sergeant then ordered me to get aboard a waiting six-by truck that was waiting for me. I again asked what my duty was and like my first sergeant this NCO said I'd find out soon enough when I reported to the MP shack at the Kagoshima railroad station downtown. The driver of the six-by let me out in front of the Marine MP shack and told me that's were I was to report.

After reporting to this MP sergeant, he said, "Oh yeah, you're the guy from one-eight. Okay ace, here's the scoop. Across the railroad yard there's a Japanese freight train sitting on a siding. The last four cars has war material loaded in them and are being sent to Sasebo. The trips gonna take at least four days, there and back and that's why ya got a case of C'ees. Now listen close. Your job is to guard those four boxcars to their destination. They've all got seals on the doors and you're to make sure that no one tampers with them. You got that private?"

My mind was in a turmoil trying to absorb everything the MP sergeant was telling me but I automatically said, "Yes sir!"

He sort of flinched at the yes sir bit but shaking his head he continued talking to me. "When the train is moving you'll be riding in the caboose, but when it stops, you get your ass out right away and patrol on both sides of those four boxcars. I don't want'ta hear about any of them seals being broken, you understand?"

Once again I yelled "Yes sir!"

He ignored me acting like the boot I was and glancing at his wristwatch, said. "It is now a little past eighteen hundred and the train leaves at twenty hundred. I'll send an MP with you to show you where the boxcars are at and you can relieve the Marine that's been watching them until you showed up.. Okay private that's about it. You got any questions?"

"Where are the other Marines that are part of this detail?" I asked.

For the first time since I walked into the MP shack, the sergeant smiled. "Private, you are the Marine detail. Have a good trip."

Remembering my first General Order of taking charge of my post and all government property in view, I started making my rounds, up one side of the four boxcars, back down to the caboose and up the other side. I kept looking at my wristwatch since I didn't want the train running off without me. There were a lot of Japanese male civilians roaming around all over the train yard, many of them wearing old Japanese army uniforms, and I guess, because of my age and inexperience, I felt all of them were potential saboteurs. I was scared of the Japanese anyway, remembering all the horror stories my two DI's used to tell us. I kept hyper alert because I sure as hell didn't want to end up with a cutthroat.

It was near 1950 by my watch when I figured I'd best get aboard the caboose. I went in and sat on this bench type seat along one wall where I'd tossed my bedroll earlier. In a few minutes, with a jerk, the train began moving. As it started to pick up a little speed the rear door of the caboose was flung open and much to my horror, a Japanese man walked into the car. After giving me a quick glance he sat down at a wood table affixed to the other side of the car. I had no sooner recovered from this shock when the door banged open again, and in walks three more Japanese men wearing old army uniforms who took one look at me and started scowling. These three joined the other man at the table and all of them begun talking in Japanese and looking at me.

I don't think I'll ever be able to convey on paper the emotions I felt at that time but believe me, there was shear terror consuming this seventeen-year old Marine private.

I did not sleep a wink for two days. At every stop I'd jump off the caboose and patrol the outside of the boxcars like I'd been ordered but with my .45 in my right hand, cocked, with a round in the chamber. Sometimes my riding companions would walk past me as I did my patrolling and no doubt saw the drawn .45. And once back in the caboose they'd just sit there and stare at me.

Once we got to Sasebo four Marine MP's and a Japanese policeman met me. I told the MP's of my harrowing experience and they all had a good laugh. The four Japanese trainmen passed by us while I was telling the MP's how scared I'd been and one of them chattered something to the Japanese policeman. After the four railroaders went by the policemen chuckled, then in broken English interpreted what the one man had said. "Don't say boo to that kid. He's wound up tighter than a watch and is so scared he'll shoot you at the drop of a hat."

The MP's got a big charge out of that also. Then, the MP in charge, said. "Hell, Smith, you did such a good job we've got another one for you. On your return trip you can escort two P.A.L.s (Prisoner at Large) back to Kagoshima."

My first thought upon hearing that was, "Well, here we go again!" But much to my surprise, the return trip was uneventful as the prisoners were being punished for minor offenses and cooperated with me fully. All they wanted to do was to get back to 1st Battalion, 8th Marines, as much as I did.

47

A TURKEY OF A STORY
Former Staff Sergeant James G. Smith, USMC

The spring of 1943 I turned sixteen. The kids in my neighborhood, who like me, grew up during the depression of the 1930's, had one major entertainment to look forward to every week and that was the dime movies shown in local theaters. We watched Bill Boyd as Hopalong Cassidy take on the bad guys, along with Pat O'Brien always trying to save James Cagey from a life of crime, and of course there were a few war movies to watch. And like most boys my age I knew exactly what I wanted to be when I grew up. Most of my pals wanted to be cowboys, or policemen, with a goodly percentage wanting to be firemen. But from early childhood I had one goal in mind and that was to be a United States Marine. With World War II going in full swing I was counting the days until I turned seventeen.

One day, a buddy my own age, Bobby Ross, said. "I'm going to write a letter to the Maritime Commission in Chicago and get papers to join the Merchant Marines. I hear they'll let you join at sixteen with your parents consent."

I only heard the word "Marines" and quickly asked for the address so I could write off to get some enlistment papers too.

Being from central Indiana I had absolutely no idea what the Merchant Marines was but reading over the papers sent to me from the Maritime Commission I was able to figure out it had something to do with ships. I knew Marines served aboard ships so thought it had something to do with that. At the same time I knew my mom would have a fit if she thought I'd be sailing the ocean during wartime so Bob and I concocted a story that we would be sailing on the Great Lakes.

It took a lot of pleading to both our moms and dads to get them to sign the parental consist forms but both sets of parents finally gave in and Bob and me sent off our applications.

A couple of weeks went by before Bob and I both received train tickets and orders to report to the Merchant Marine Recruiting Station, Chicago, Illinois. It was an exciting time for two sixteen year old boys to be treated like adults as the both of us went through the physical exams and other induction procedures. As it happened, Bob and I were separated during all the paper work and physicals and when I'd completed everything they had for me to do I was taken to a large room with a bunch of other guys and an officer in a naval uniform swore us into the Merchant Marine. Then we were told to report to this other room and wait for everyone else to be processed. When I walked into the waiting room I spotted Bob, and yelled out. "Hey Bob, I passed with flying colors and got sworn in."

Bob looked at me crestfallen and staring at the floor, said, "I failed the eye test and they won't take me."

"What do you mean they won't take you!" I yelled. "We're in this thing together; if it wasn't for you I wouldn't even thought about joining up!" With a feeling of alarm it suddenly hit me that I was going to be all-alone. What had I got myself into? I wanted my Momma!

The next day found Bob on a train back to Indianapolis, Indiana, and me on a train to the U. S. Maritime Training Station, Sheepshead Bay, Brooklyn, New York.

After twelve weeks of a navy type of boot camp I was assigned to a brand new Liberty Ship, the USS Lighting. Within a short time I was at sea as a member of the Lighting's "Black Gang" (Engine Room oilier.) Our ship was in the middle of a convoy that stretched as far as the eye could see.

To me, the crossing of the Atlantic seemed to take forever. It took twenty-five days to reach the bombed out port of LeHarve, France. We arrived at LeHarve the day Paris fell to the Allies. The docking facilities were in ruins so we had to lay at anchorage to unload. For nineteen days Army DUCKS ferried our cargo to the docks at LeHarve. These DUCKS were amphibious landing vehicles with large rubber tires that looked like a boat. Most of our convoy carried ammunition, tanks, fuel and other need war material. But the USS Lighting was a C2 refrigerated ship. What a surprise it must have been for the army DUCK crews when we hoisted down large cargo nets full of frozen ice cream and frozen turkeys for the coming Thanksgiving and Christmas holidays. There was never a doubt in my mind that a lot of that ice cream probably got eaten before those DUCKS made it to shore. And more than likely, there was some roasted turkey served at private parties before the forthcoming holidays.

I did manage to get several letters off to my folks while in LeHarve as they hadn't heard from me for a long time and had no idea of my whereabouts. In my first letter I fessed up that the Great Lake I was on was a pretty big one.

After returning home, I had a lot to answer to when it came to my mom and dad. But my parents forgave me and my dad gave me a jovial answer: "The Atlantic Ocean is one hell of a Great Lake for a sixteen-year old kid!"

Bless there hearts; they had no inkling what was in store for them. Because I came home after my seventeenth birthday so I could join the United States Marine Corps.

As a side comment, Jim told me it confused the hell out of a lot of Marine NCOs trying to figure out what his three Merchant Marine ribbons stood for.

48

I AIN'T NO BOOT!
Former Staff Sergeant James G. Smith, USMC

The biggest SNAFU that ever happened to me was when my Indianapolis, Indiana reserve outfit, the 16th Infantry Battalion was activated during the onset of the Korean War. (If you don't know what SNAFU stands for, then you were never in the military.)

I had joined the Marine Corps Reserve shortly after my four years of active duty in the Corps that had begun near the end of World War II. Those four years active had been interesting and a good learning experience. I'd spent most of it overseas on occupation duty. After a year in Japan with the 8th Marine, 2nd Marine Division, I was transferred to the 6th Marine Division in China, where I served for almost two years in Tsingtao and Teintsin. I held a combat engineer MOS and was an expert in explosives. When I joined the 16th, the commanding officer, Colonel William T. Smith (no relation) told me during my initial interview that he needed a weapons instructor and with my background I would fill that billet just fine. I held that slot until the outfit was,called to active duty in August 1951, shortly after the Korean War started. I suppose you could say I felt pretty salty and was certainly cocky. After all, I held the permanent rank of sergeant, wore eight combat related ribbons, was a weapons specialist, demolition expert and had a hash mark of service. At least that was what my Service Record Book was supposed to have had in it.

It didn't take long to have the wind taken out of my sails in so far as feeling salty.

The 16th Infantry Battalion arrived at Oceanside, California on a huge troop train late at night. A convoy of Marine six-by trucks awaited on the street near the railroad station to take us to Camp Pendleton which was just a few miles north of Oceanside. Word was passed for all troops to disembark and standby on the platform until you heard your name called, then get aboard a truck which would be pointed out to you. The group of Marines had got pretty small before finally hearing my name called.

Before I got into the six-by I asked this sergeant with a clip board why they just didn't haul the entire outfit to Camp Pendleton all at once instead of calling off every mans name like they'd done. His answer left me confused: "You reservist had to be separated into different categories by your drill points and summer camps so the higher ups can made a decision where to put ya."

The remaining Marines soon joined me and I noticed they were all young teenagers. They must have been fairly new to the unit since I didn't know any of them. I was the only NCO in the group and they kept asking me what the hell was going on. Since I had no idea I told them we'd find out in the morning and not to worry about it.

During the battalion formation the next morning the group I'd came to Pendleton with was told to form up together on the parade deck.

An active duty Marine colonel gave us a welcome aboard and pep talk speech then turned the 16th over to a major before leaving us.

The major gave a little talk about how much we were needed and about training cycles we would be going through before being shipped out to Korea. Then he paused, and said, "Colonel Smith you may dismiss your troops except for the special unit on the left flank."

That's exactly where I was standing.

After the rest of the 16th was marched away the major came over and stood in front of our group of about thirty Marine reserves. He gave us at ease then told us to listen up. "Okay men, I want to inform you what the rules of criteria is before being sent to Korea. If a reservist has completed two summer camps and thirty-six drills, he's considered combat ready and will be assigned to the first overseas draft. Those with one summer camp and eighteen drills will go to tent camp two for further training. You may have noticed that the formation today was made up of three distinct groups. The two larger groups fall into the categories I just mentioned. A review of your Service Record Books reveal that regardless of your rank, none of you meet the criteria I outlined. Therefore, all of you are being transferred to the Marine Corps Recruit Depot, San Diego for boot camp training."

To say that my mouth fell open with my chin hitting the deck would be an understatement. If I'd learned nothing else in four years of active duty, I sure as hell knew how to gripe. To the major's astonishment I broke ranks and went up to the gunny sergeant standing next to him. "You best take another look at my SRB because you are sure as hell not going to send my ass back to boot camp!"

Before the gunny could respond, the major gave me a flinty eye glare, and said. "Just what is your problem Marine?"

I came to formal attention and addressed the major. "Sir, my serial number is 593704; I have the permanent rank of sergeant and I just completed four years of active duty, most of it overseas. I went thorough boot camp at Parris Island in 1945 and you're not about to send me through it again. The reason I don't have all them drill points and summer camps you was talking about is because I haven't been off active duty for a year yet!" I was so pissed it took me a long moment, to add, "Sir!"

Now the majors jaw dropped. It took him a couple of seconds to recover from my outburst but when he regained his composure, he said. "Marine, you come with me and I will get to the bottom of this!"

I waited in an outer office area while the major went into the headquarters office. In about a half-hour this first sergeant came up to me. "Smith, why in the hell didn't you tell someone about this before the major raked my ass over the coals about it."

My dander was still up and I blurted out. "Hell, nobody told me jack-shit till that major said I had to go back through boot camp, and I ain't about to do that!"

I guess the first shirt could tell I was still pissed off, and in a softer tone of voice, he said. "Well, least-ways we've got it squared away now. You're being assigned to Headquarters Company, Second Training Battalion over at Tent Camp Two as a weapons instructors."

It was getting to be a habit but my jaw dropped open again when I digested what he told me. "What the hell's going on now first sergeant? Hells bells, one look at my SRB should tell you I'm more combat ready than about ninety-percent of the Marines you've got slated to go to Korea on the first draft."

The major I'd bitched to before had come out of the headquarters office and over-heard my remark. He said, "Sergeant....(finally admitting that I at least had a rank)...that's why you're staying here for a while. We need people like you to train these kids before they go overseas."

I was crestfallen. In a softer tone of voice I made a last ditch appeal. "Sir, all of my friends are going out on the first draft and I'm gonna feel like a traitor if I'm left behind."

It was to no avail. The major just shook his head and walked away.

Well, at least being a weapons instructor was a hell'uva lot better than going through boot camp again. Just the same I continued to bitch and moan, submitting requests for transfer to a combat unit twice a week. I reckon they got tired of reading my request and hearing me bitch because I eventually joined the third replacement draft to Korea.

49

THE USS MONTROSE – APA 221
Former Staff Sergeant James G. Smith, USMC

It was a pleasant surprise for me when I boarded the APA USS Montrose in the fall of 1951 at Inchon, Korea, to begin my rotation home, and ran into an old buddy of mine, SSgt Thomas L. Finch. Tom had served his Korean tour with the 1st Marines, while I had did my year with Dog Company, 1st Engineer Battalion. We were both happy to see one another and like old comrades do we pounded each others shoulders in celebration of being reunited after having been activated together when our reserve outfit, the 16th Infantry Battalion, was called to active duty during August 1950.

Anyone who had ever been aboard a crowded troopship will remember you only got two meals a day and you stood in long lines to get them. A lot of Marines would eat breakfast, then get back in line for the long wait for the next meal. Heck of a way to spend your time on a ship, but that was the nature of the beast.

The only entertainment we had aboard ship was evening movies. If a person was lucky, after the last meal you'd rush to the compartment the movie was going to be shown in so you could find a good seat. This was hard to do if you if you had not been at the front part of the chow line.

On the other hand, special work details, guards, and other privileged people aboard ship, were issued a round cardboard tag trimmed with a metal band with a hole in it to put a string through that you looped around your neck like your dog tags. A person wearing one of these tags got to go to the head of the chow line.

After two days at sea, Tom Finch sidled up to me where I was staring out at the ocean from the ships rail. Speaking in a low voice, he said. "I got something I want to show you Jim. Follow me."

We strolled casually along the weather deck until Tom grabbed my arm and took me behind a lifeboat. We were out of sight from the other troops but Tom still whispered when he spoke. "Take a look at this." And he raised the tarp covering the life boat, then pointed his finger.

Every item of survival gear in the life boat was tagged with the same round metal framed cardboard that was being used for special chow passes.

Needless to say, from that day on, the two of us were always close to the head of the chow line·and always had good seating locations for the evening movies.

The story doesn't quite end here however, as we did have a big scare.

One day, Tom and I were standing in the chow line (at the front of course) when a chief-master-of-arms, who was controlling access to the mess deck, pointed to Tom, and said. "Sergeant, would you step over here for a minute." I rolled my eyes as I was sure we'd been caught with the phony chow passes. My fears worsened when the CMA looked at Tom, then said. "Sergeant, we've been looking for you for a long time." What he said next left me totally confused. "You've ruined every deck on this ship!"

It turned out that Tom had came into contact with a unit of the British Royal Marines while in Korea, and had traded his boondockers for a pair of hobnailed boots. You can imagine the ass chewing he got from the navy Chief for screwing up all the painted decks on the Montrose by scratching them up. They relieved Tom of his pride and joy combat boots for the duration of the voyage, loaning him a pair of rubber thong shower shoes to wear until we reached San Diego.

The good news of course; was the navy had not caught on to our little scam with the fake chow passes and we continued to stand at the head of the line during the rest of our trip to California.

50

GEE BUT I WANT TO GO HOME
Former Staff Sergeant James G. Smith, USMC

At approximately 1000, on October 23, 1951, the USS Montrose, an APA carrying the first contingent of U. S. Marines to California from the Korean War, edged slowly to a berthing slot at the Navy Base, Pearl Harbor, Hawaii. Over a thousand combat veterans lined the rails, most of them chattering like magpies in excited anticipation of being granted liberty ashore.

To the disappointment of all troops, which shattered their thoughts of hitting the town, an announcement from a navy officer came over the ships loud speaker system: "Now hear this, now hear this! The Montrose will only stay in port long enough to refuel her. As soon as we've refueled we will immediately get under way. Troop commanders, keep your personnel away from the starboard side of the ship and the smoking lamp is out."

While the troop ship tied up at the dock Marine officers begun shooing troops away from the railing on the right side. But this effort came to a sudden halt when many of the Marines noticed a green colored staff car come tearing up the pier and come to a screeching halt in front of the gang way which had just been placed into position. What had caught the eye of the troops was the red flag flying from the fender of the staff car that bore three silver stars. A lieutenant general had come down to meet us?

And sure enough, who should jump out of the staff car but Lieutenant General Lemuel C. Shepherd, who was slated to take over as the Commandant of the Marine Corps on 1 January 1952, with the retirement of General Clifton B. Cates. Old Lemuel C. didn't even take the time to walk up the gang way ladder. Cupping his mouth with both hands he yelled up to a navy lieutenant standing near the top of the gang way. "Tell your captain I have something to say to him son!"

The young lieutenant shouted a "Yes sir!" and with a salute, hastened off toward the bridge.

Less than a minute went by before an older officer with a cheer leaders megaphone to his mouth, bent over the bridge railing, saying. "Sir, I'm Commander Prebble, the captain of the Montrose. What can I do for you general?"

"I am General Shepherd, commander of FMFPac. These are my men you've got aboard and you will give them liberty! Do you understand that Commander Prebble?"

The captain of the Montrose didn't reply for a long moment as he stared down at General Shepherd, who now had both hands on his hips, looking up at him. Finally, the captain said, "Sir, we're only here to take on fuel, that won't give them much liberty time."

General Shepherd was obviously ready for that answer. "I don't care if it's for fifteen minutes. These men are fresh out of Korea and they damn well deserve some liberty."

I feel certain that the entire contingent of Marines held their collective breaths for the few seconds it took for Commander Prebble to answer General Shepherd. "Aye, aye sir, I understand."

The cheer that went up could have probably been heard in Pearl City.

In a couple of minutes the echoing static sound of the loud speaker being turned on was heard. "Now hear this. This is the captain speaking. This vessel will be refueled and ready to make way by sixteen hundred. You are hereby granted liberty and will report back aboard ship not later than fifteen hundred. I repeat, you will be back to the ship by fifteen hundred. That is all."

Another rousing cheer went up, then a thousand Marine rushed to their berthing spaces in the holds to dig out un-pressed khaki uniforms from their sea bags that hadn't been worn for a year. Just seeing those Marines leaving the Montrose was a sight to behold. It was like a swarm of rats leaving a sinking ship!

After enjoying a few hours on land, most of us made it back to the Montrose by 1500. I say most, because some of the troops pushed the time limit to the max. At 1600 crewmen were in the process of raising the gangway when down on the dock a taxi cab came tearing along, with horn honking and headlights flashing. Out jump a bunch of Marines, and the swabies lower the gangway for them. This went on for almost an hour. It was like watching a yo yo. Every time the sailors started raising the ladder another screeching taxi would pull up. We at last got underway and it came as a surprise to no one when word was passed that twenty-three Marines had missed the ship.

After an uneventful five-day cruise we arrived at the port of San Diego. When the USS Montrose swung alongside the navy pier a Marine band started playing California Here I Come, then went into a stirring rendition of the Marines Hymn. There was a small crowd of family and friends of some of the Marines on the pier, along with several dignitaries and newspaper reporters using flash bulbs on their cameras. The welcome back greeters on the pier cheered our arrival home. And standing at parade rest behind the Marine band stood the twenty-three Marines who had missed the ship movement at Pearl Harbor. We learned later they had been flown back to the United States on military aircraft. They all wore big shit-eating grins, and well that they should, because they were all reservist being returned for discharge, and there would be no disciplinary action. Sometimes, it pays to miss a ship.

All the Korean veterans were bussed to the Marine Corps Recruit Depot at San Diego for processing of discharge or transfer to a new duty station. I was among the large group of Marines that were to be released from active duty and sent home. After a short welcome home speech from the MCRD Commanding General, we short-timers then had to go through a couple of bull-shit lectures. We were talked to about how we should rejoin our civilian pursuits with a positive attitude, and carry the proud image of the Corps with us in our daily lives and conduct ourselves accordingly. We also got a reenlistment pitch that had everyone laughing. The final talk had to do with any medical complaints we might have, in that bring them up now, or don't try later to hold the Corps responsible. The carrot on the stick held out to us regarding service connected disabilities, was if you've got a medical problem, it will take another fifteen days to process you. I don't think anybody took advantage of that carrot. The last thing this particular officer who was talking to us had to say sounded something like this: "As you men know, the Koreans use human waste for fertilizer. Most of you have had your share of snooping and pooping through rice paddies filled with that type fertilizer. In addition, just breathing the dust from the roads alongside the rice paddies can cause problems. The very first item of business that you will do, before any other processing is to take place for your release from active duty, will be to provide our medical department with a fecal specimen to determine if you have worms."

As soon as this group meeting broke up each man was given a little cardboard container that reminded me of one of those ice cream cups we used to get as a kid. Matter of fact, the little wooden stick they give us was a dead ringer for the small wood spoons used to get the ice cream out of the little cups. I'm sure you get the idea what we were supposed to do with these two items.

We lined up outside this large troop style community head and a team of navy corpsmen stood by to retrieve the specimen containers and check our names off a roster after we'd done our part of the program.

What a sight that was. Fifty Marines at a time trying to do their business while at the same time a couple of hundred more crowed the head awaiting their turn to get at the unstalled commodes. Many Marines filled their cups, using the little stick spoons without a problem. However, there were many more crying out in desperation: "I can't go!"

In response to those who could not provide an instant "specimen," buddies, or other fellow Marines who just wanted to help out a comrade in distress, would say, "I've got plenty, take some of mine and lets get going."

As soon as we came out of the head we were informed by the corpsmen that our specimen would be tested and in the event worms were shown to be present, those individuals would have to spend an additional four days for medical treatment to clear up the problem.

Later in the day, after all the fecal specimens had been checked, the names of those Marines who were found with worms, were posted on a bulletin board. Have you ever heard Marines cry?

The guys who had "borrowed" their specimen cried the loudest. To a man, they all confessed what they'd done and begged to be tested again. Much to their dismay, the results stood and they stayed behind for the four days of medical treatment.

And what about me? Hell, I had damn near been shitting my pants for the past year every time a communist shell roared over my head, and you can best believe I didn't have any problems taking a crap to put in that little ice cream cup.

51

GRAB ASSING
Former Sergeant William L. Callahan, USMC

My first duty station in the Marine Corps after boot camp at MCRD, San Diego, California, in October 1955, was Marine Barracks, Kodiak, Alaska. Alaska offered great opportunities for an outdoors type of person who enjoyed hunting, fishing and outstanding scenery. Although I was only seventeen years old at the time I did consider myself an outdoor sportsman and really liked the surrounding countryside where I was stationed. But the duty for a boot PFC in a Marine Guard Company on a naval station in Alaska was the pits. Both my older brothers had been Marines during World War II and Korea, and they used to tell me stories of fun filled liberties and all the different places they'd been to and how great it was to be a Marine. Following the family tradition, here I was a Marine, but my brothers sure didn't tell me there was places in the Corps like the naval station at Kodiak. I spent my duty time freezing my ass off walking around huge warehouses out in the middle of nowhere in eight hour duty rotations every other day. And since we were located out in the boonies, the only liberty you got was base liberty which left a lot to be desired.

It got so cold walking sentry duty that two men teams manned all of the outdoor guard post. Each post had a little guard shack with a window and was heated with a small electrical heater. What the sentries would do was to walk post in one hour shifts, with one man in the guard shack keeping warm.

One night I had the duty with PFC Lonny Hayes, who like me, was a seventeen year old Marine fresh out of boot camp. Like most young Marines living in close quarters of a barracks there was always a lot of horse play going on which we called "grab assing." Poor Hayes was the butt of a lot of pranks and practical jokes from his bunk mates because beside being dumber than a box of rocks, he was gullible to a fault. He would believe about anything you told him. Another bad habit Hayes had was that he was a whiner. Nothing suited him and he was always bitching about one thing or the other. On this particular duty night he'd taken the first duty shift and we had already got into a disagreement when after forty-five minutes of walking post he came into the guard shack trying to tell me his first hour was up. I told him he was full of it and shoved him back outside in the cold to walk his other fifteen minutes.

Then, during my first hour of walking around this extremely long warehouse, every time I'd pass by the guard shack, Hayes would give me the finger through the window. So I started thinking about how I could pay him back. You know how it is with immature teenage Marines.

Now the absolutely crazy thing about walking guard duty at this installation was that we were armed with .45 caliber semiautomatic pistols, but we didn't carry any ammo.

The only thing a sentry could do if something did happen on his post was to use a call box to make a report of whatever it was that was going on. But somewhere along the line I had came into possession of a .45 round. I decided to use this bullet to get my little revenge on Hayes for giving me the finger.

The next time I passed the guard shack I went up to the window and showed Hayes the bullet. Then I said, "This is for you." Then I acted like I loaded it in the ammo clip of the .45 and pulled back the receiver which had I really put the shell in the clip it would have armed the weapon for firing. I pointed the pistol at Hayes and took the safety off and cocked the hammer back to full cock. I got my revenge all right. Hayes' eyes got as big and round as saucers and he hit the deck inside the small shack. I rattled the door a couple of times and yelled. "That'll teach you to give me the finger you dumb sonofabitch!" I walked away smiling to myself about what a great stunt I'd pulled.

Hayes didn't say another word to me the remainder of our tour of duty. But when we were in the relief truck riding back to the barracks, he said. "I'm turning your ass in to the Sergeant-of-the-Guard."

I just laughed at him.

After arriving at the barracks I went to my squad bay to sack out. It seemed that I'd no sooner got into my bunk than the Corporal-of-the-Guard came up to me, saying. "Callahan, get dressed, the Officer-of-the-Day wants to see ya."

On my way to the guard room I took the .45 round out of my pocket, opened a window and tossed it out. I figured if there wasn't any evidence then it would be my word against Hayes.

Standing at attention in front of the Officer-of-the-Day, he says. "What's this shit I hear about you pointing a loaded forty-five at PFC Hayes?"

I did my best to put a shocked or surprised expression on my face. "I don't know what you're talking about sir!"

The OD interrogated me for another twenty minutes with me denying the actuations he threw at me. It didn't do me much good though, and I got my first taste of military justice. Fifteen days in the brig————for grab assing!

Bill Callahan eventually was transferred to the 2nd Marine Division at Camp Lejeune and was a part of the 1958 landing in Lebanon. In addition to his Armed Forces Expeditionary Medal, he holds the Combat Action Ribbon, Marine Corps Good Conduct Medal and a Navy Unit Commendation ribbon. Callahan, like his brothers before him, retired from the Indianapolis, Indiana police department. He was the State President for the Fraternal Order of Police and also held several national positions in that organization. After his retirement, he spent several years with the Marion County Sheriffs department. At the present time, he is a special security officer for Eli Lilly and Company. Bill, and his wife Theresa, live in Franklin Township outside Indianapolis, Indiana. They have two grown children, son Bill Jr., who is a Indianapolis firefighter and daughter Lisa, a flight attendant with ATA.

52

I RECOGNIZE THAT FACE
Former Sergeant Hugh O'Brien, USMC

I enlisted into the United States Marine Corps at age seventeen during February 1943. At that time my name was Hugh Krampe.

Just like every Marine that came before me and those that followed, boot camp at Marine Corps Recruit Depot, San Diego, California is firmly etched into my memory. My dad was a retired Marine captain so I knew quite a bit about the Marine Corps. This background made me a rather cocky kid, but it didn't take long before my two drill instructors had put the fear of God in me and convinced me to do things the Marine Corps way.

Hugh O'Brian-

Near the end of my boot platoon's training our DI's gathered all of us around them one day and told us they had something special in store for us. I'm sure we all held our breaths wondering what fate was about to befall us. As it turned out however, our senior DI said that there was going to be some VIP's visiting the recruit depot the next day and we were selected to be one of the platoons to put on a "Field Day" for them. Naturally, this confused us, since what we had learned a field day was had do with cleaning up our huts to white glove perfection for inspection. I know I certainly couldn't figure out why a bunch of big shots would want to watch a group of young recruits clean the decks with a tooth brush. I guess seeing our confused expressions on our faces hit a funny bone with our senior DI because it was the first time I'd ever seen him smile. He went on to tell us that what he was talking about was a different kind of field day than what we were accustomed too.

Our DI went on to explain that we were going to participate in various sporting events and competition of a military nature. There would be a football throwing contest, tag-team relays, seeing who could take apart and put back his rifle the fastest blindfolded, dummy hand grenade tosses at rubber tire targets, and boxing matches. There were other events also, but these are the ones I remember, especially the boxing matches.

The DI went on to say that he needed five boxers for the different weight divisions to represent our platoon. First he asked if any of the guys had any boxing experience and a couple of fellows raised their hands, volunteering they'd fought in the Golden Gloves.

One of the fellows was a heavyweight and the other bantamweight. Since no one else offered they'd been boxers, our DI tried a new tact. In so many words he asked who was the cocky tough guys in the platoon who didn't take any crap off anybody. The platoon members were not shy about pointing fingers at four or five other guys among them. To my absolute surprise and horror, I saw fingers pointed in my direction.

I was a tall, skinny kid, weighing around 135 pounds and six-foot tall. My DI took one look at me, and said. "Krampe, you're my welterweight." Then he went on and gave a pep talk on how the honor of our platoon was at stake and that he expected his "fighters" to make a clean sweep in the ring the next day.

I don't think I slept a wink that night.

John "Duke" Wayne-

The next day we were marched out to the large grinder near the headquarters building. Anyone having been to MCRD, San Diego, will know the location as the sand colored, arched walkway buildings still stands. A total of four platoons was to take part in the fun and games. We were told we could take off our utility blouses and pith helmets and watch the various events until called upon to do our part. Naturally there were a lot of officers and senior NCOs milling around and fawning over the VIPS. To be honest about it I didn't recognize any of the celebrities except for this one rather tall, rugged good looking man who was refereeing the boxing matches, and I couldn't quite place him at first.

The more I looked at this guy refereeing the more I knew I'd seen him before but dang if I could put a name to the face.

It finally came my turn to step into the boxing ring and the referee waved me and the other fellow I was to fight to the middle of the ring to give us instructions. When he started talking in that slow, deep drawl it hit me who he was. It was the famous movie actor John Wayne! The first thing he said to me and the other fellow was, "Do you two want to go by the English rules of boxing, or my rules?" I doubt very seriously if the other fellow knew what John Wayne was asking us: I knew for sure that I didn't! But it didn't make any difference since we weren't about to offend the movie hero. We both said, "Your rules." Well, John Wayne's rules turned out to be that he'd watch us beat the hell out of one another without much interference.

When the bell rang it took only a couple of seconds for me to realize I had a fight on my hands. I found out later my opponent had been a semi-pro welterweight in New York who fought in smokers. He mopped up the deck with me. We were boxing six round matches but with the anything goes style as dictated by the 'Duke', I was in serious trouble. By the forth round I was taking my third knockdown count from John Wayne. He was down on one knee counting and gave me a whispered hiss in my ear between numbers, "Stay down kid."

But like I said before; I was cocky, plus scared of what my DI would do if I let him down so I kept getting back up. When the bell rang ending the final round of the bout there was no doubt who the winner of the match was. The kid from New York won it hands down. After the other Marine came over to me and touched gloves and said a couple of words that I'd given him a good fight, John Wayne came up to me. The Duke put his arms around my shoulder, and said. "That was the gutsiest fight I've ever seen kid."

Even my DI's were proud of me and I didn't catch any wraith for having let the platoon down.

Years later, as I was starting my acting career and before I got to be good friends with the Duke, I was with a group of people at the Brown Derby. My agent was with me and when he spotted John Wayne in the crowd he buttonholed the Duke and steered him over to our table, saying he had someone he wanted the Duke to meet, which was me of course. The Duke was wearing that famous grin of his and gave me a knuckle-breaking handshake. I told him we had met before and answered his questioning cocked eyebrow by telling him about the day he refereed boxing matches for the Marine Corps at San Diego. I went on to tell him that his remark to me that day carried me through my days as a Marine. He gave me a hearty slap on the back, then said in pure Duke Wayne. "I'll be a sonofabitch! Hell yes, I remember you. You wouldn't give up. Pal, let me buy you a drink and I'll give you some advice on how to fight this Hollywood crap!"

Hugh O'Brien has the distinction of being one of the youngest Marine Corps drill instructors ever allowed on the drill field to train recruits. He was eighteen years old. His movie and television career spans fifty years. Hugh is known around the world as TV's Wyatt Earp. He told this writer that his proudest roll was in The Shootist, which was released in 1978; John Wayne's last movie in which everyone knew he was dying of cancer. O'Brien said John Wayne told him that O'Brien would always be remembered by movie buffs as the last bad guy that John Wayne shot. Hugh resides in Beverly Hills, California and is very active in the Hoby Foundation he created to help disadvantaged children.

53

WHAT A WAY TO STAY WARM
Former Sergeant Richard W. Mote, U.S. Army

I was a twenty-year old Sergeant-Technical, (which means I had a block "T" under my three stripes), with A Battery, 456th Field Artillery Battalion,, 505th Parachute Infantry Regiment, 82nd Airborne Division, during the Belgian Ardennes campaign. My job was that of a gun mechanic for my batteries six 105mm howitzers. History buffs will recall that the 82nd Airborne got spread all over hell's half acre during the Normandy invasion, but this story has to do with an unusual event that took place after my outfit earned the title "The battered bastards of Bastogne."

For those of us that fought in the Ardennes, better known, as World War Two's, Battle of the Bulge, all will agree that the weather and conditions created by the weather, were often as bad, and sometimes more perilous than the Germans.

After breaking out of Bastogne, where a German army division had surrounded us, the 82nd headed toward the German border. On a blistering cold January day in early 1945, the six guns of our battery was ordered to be moved to a new location near a crossroads in a small valley of the Ardennes mountains. Now you've got to keep in mind, when I use the term "crossroads" it was more in keeping with the roughest country lane found in America. The road was barely wide enough for a horse drawn farm vehicle let alone our towed 105mm howitzers being pulled by big army trucks. Plus the fact it was freezing with a new blanket of snow covering the ground and trees. We inched along slowly on this path that was supposed to be a road until we came to the junction that was our crossroads. On one side of this location was a small stream trickling under a layer of ice. Tall hedgerows, dense with snow cover lined the other side of the lane. The only place to set up our guns was a small cleared farmers field through the hedgerows. We had to hack our way through the hedgerow to get to the three-fourths acre field. This was a miserable job made worse since it started snowing again. Now, the heavy snow flakes all but blinded the working party trying to get through the hedgerow. One of our guys wielding an axe, said. "Why'n the hell don't they just unlimber a gun and blast our way through?"

Once we got through the hedgerow and onto the small field, I recall thinking how beautiful of a pastoral winter scene this sector was if only one could forget for a moment we were in a war. But that was a fleeting thought, because then we had to dig the guns in and that meant everybody pitched in to help regardless of rank. The only good thing about digging in the guns as much as the frozen earth would allow, was you kept warm while doing the labor. However, the minute you stopped working your sweat turned to instant ice and you shook all over from the bitter cold. By the late afternoon all the guns had been set up and ready for fire missions. With the hazy sun already beginning to set to the west I started looking for a place to stay for the night. The gun crews used their trucks to sleep in and the fire direction control people had tents. We technical types had to fend for ourselves.

A couple of buddies and me nosed around our area looking for anything we could use for shelter since sleeping on the cold ground in pup tents left a lot to be desired. We all three spotted what appeared to be a small farm house about two hundred yards from where the battery was dug in at. The only problem was that we saw smoke curling up from the roof, not the chimney. We surmised the hut had taken a direct hit of some sort. Just the same we walked over to the smoking hut to check it out.

Sure enough, once we went inside the plastered log hut that was about the size of a one-car garage, we saw the log roof ceiling was aglow with brightly smoldering embers. The entire roof and one wall were slowly burning. But damn if it wasn't warm!

The three of us looked at one another with stupid expressions on our faces until I finally voiced an opinion that was probably on my buddies minds too. "You know, with it being ten below zero outside, we could take a chance that the roof won't cave in."

We sort of looked at each other then shrugged our shoulders. What the hell!

It was the warmest night I spent in the Ardennes mountain's, sleeping under the strangest fireplace I'd ever seen then or since. The wind whipping through holes in the walls and roof kept the logs blazing all night but the roof held and never did fall in. Tough logs in that part of the world, huh?

What a way to stay warm!

Richard Mote is a member of the Indianapolis, Indiana World War II Round Table, an organization of veterans from all branches of service. When hearing about this book being put together, he said, "You know, Marines aren't the only ones that's got a tale to tell." Touché!

54

HOW I WON WORLD WAR II
Former Sergeant Art Buchwald, USMC

As time goes on, all of us who have served in different wars come to exaggerate the role we played. Over the years I have developed my part as a Marine in World War II to an art form. Oddly enough, half the people I relate my tongue in cheek deeds of valor to seem to believe me, except Marines of course. At least most Marines. As hard as it is to admit, there are a few Gyrenes floating around out there in the world that are just a tad gullible. On the other hand I must offer this humble appraisal of how I won World War II, which is absolutely the gospel truth. This is a "no shitter" how it happened.

To begin, I will give a little background: I dropped out of high school in Queens, New York at age 17 to enlist in the Marine Corps the summer of 1942. This came about due to a broken heart. I had hitchhiked down to Greensboro, North Carolina, to *Art Buchwald-* see an old flame of the previous summer. When she refused to see me, I went over to the local post office and informed the local Marine recruiting sergeant that I had just seen the films To the Shores of Tripoli and Wake Island, and it was my desire above all else to become a United States Marine. After the recruiting sergeant stopped laughing, it must have occurred to him that he had a recruiting quota to fill and I soon found myself learning the quaint ways of Marine Drill Instructors at Parris Island, South Carolina. I really showed my girl friend, didn't I?

Anyway, after returning to civilian life in the late 1940's, I enrolled in the University of Southern California on the GI Bill.

I suppose it was natural for people to ask me what I did during the war. But since I didn't want to give my life story to every Tom, Dick and Harry and/or Jane, I'd give a flippant answer that I had been a rear gunner on an F4U fighter plane. The jerks were too dumb to know that the gull-winged Corsair was only a one seater. By the 1950's I had broadened my answers to the inquisitive by telling everyone I had shot down 26 Japanese airplanes. By this time, my children were curious, so I decided to up it even more. I said I was commanding general of the 1st Marine Air Wing and was the only one willing to give Pappy Boyington a second chance. Finally, my grandchildren arrived, and I had to do something for them also. So I told them I was the one who dropped the bomb on

Hiroshima.

What did I really do during World War II? I was assigned to the 4th Marine Air Wing when I finished boot camp. This infuriated me so much, because I wanted to see action, that I got up the nerve to question my drill instructor. I said, "When I enlisted in the Marine Corps, they promised me that I would be a paratrooper." He took one look at me and said, "Okay Buchwald, you're a paratrooper, go find a parachute." Then turned on his heels and walked away.

So I ended up being an ordnance man in a fighter squadron. And I wasn't a very good ordnance man. I was once loading a 500-pound bomb on a plane and dropped it. Everyone on the island scrambled for there lives. I pretended my foot was broken so they wouldn't kill me.

The next day, the commanding officer called me in and said, "I'm putting you in for the Navy Cross." I asked why.

He said, "You forgot to fuse the bomb and saved the lives of 500 Marines."

Now I know you're asking yourself what was it I did to win the war. The answer is simple, I got out of the Corps. There are men and women who stayed in after the war and there are those of us who chose to serve our country in civilian life. Had I stayed in and loaded nuclear weapons on our naval ships, no one would be here today.

Art Buchwald, is a famous author and political columnist. After working for the New York Herald Tribune, Buchwald moved to Washington, D.C. and began an inimitable journalistic career that has chronicled the foibles of the nation's political leaders for three decades. His books include I Never Danced at the White House, While Reagan Slept and the acclaimed, "You Can Fool All Of The People All The Time."

55

SIXTEEN ROUNDS OF WP
Gunnery Sergeant Edward J. Herterich, USMC(Ret.)

Over the years as a tanker with that famous "steel coffin" MOS of an1811 it had been drilled into me that the soul purpose of tanks within the U. S. Marine Corps is to support the infantry.

Azimuth Indicators, Elevating Quadrants, Range Cards, Firing Tables, all came together during one incident of combat in Vietnam in 1968.

I was the tank commander of our steel beast on an outpost the Marines had built called C2. This was a rather exposed position between Gio Linh and Con Thein and was supposed to be another link in the so called "McNamara Line." Well, old McNamara may have thought he had a great plan with his idea of small infantry supported fire bases the length of the DMZ; but if C2 was any indicator of his vision, it failed miserably. It was like being fish in the proverbial barrel with the North Vietnamese Army taking pot shots at you any time they felt like it. Of course, being the good Marines we were, we took our lumps and worked on ways to out-fox the fox. It didn't take long for us to figure out that the NVA sometimes got into a rut, so to speak, in the manner they would send in rockets at C2. At least once or twice a week the position would receive enemy rockets that came in from one particular direction.

My platoon of two tanks was supporting 2nd Battalion, 4th Marines, and after a rocket attack this one particular day I went down into the S-3 bunker and had a little chat with the operations officer and his gunny. What I had in mind was for the three-shop to arrange that the Marines standing perimeter watch would all have compasses in there possession and when the rockets began "coming in" to try and shoot an azimuth as close as possible in the direction from which they were being fired. The S-3 immediately agreed to this idea since he instantly saw what I had in mind.

Like clock-work, the next NVA rocket attack we underwent got us a three point intersection to the approximate area the rockets had came from. When we plotted the data on a map which acquired a 1/25,000 triangulation, we saw that the possible source position was behind a small knoll some 2,000 meters from us. With this information two tanks main battery were laid on the target site. We loaded white-phosphorus (WP) rounds in preparation. The tank crews were instructed that when they were on watch and the word "rockets" came over the net, the main gun would instantly fire then continue rapid fire, with adjustments right 50 - three rounds, drop 100, left 50 - for four rounds, then cease fire.

The grunt 03's sound-power telephones were tied into the tanks TI jacks on the rear of our tanks and we were ready to go.

We waited impatiently like a bunch of kids getting ready to go to the circus for the NVA to hit us with their rockets.

Three days later an excited voice was heard coming over the net with the same word repeated four times. "Rockets, rockets, rockets...rockets!"

Our two tanks reacted with precision. Sixteen rounds of WP left the tubes in rapid fire. A great cloud of white, boiling smoke coiled upwards, 2,000 meter away. It was a lovely sight.

The C.O. of 2/4 sent out a patrol into the DMZ to check out the area. What the grunts 03's found was remnants of two NVA rocket carts, puddles of blood and gore with some guts on the deck, and drag marks where bodies had been hauled off.

Suffice to say, we did not get anymore rockets from that area again!

56

TIN CAN DUTY REMEMBERED
Former Seaman 1/C Robert N, Boyd, USN

After high school graduation in Roswell, New Mexico at age 17 in 1944 I, along with a large number of my classmates who like me, had pre-enlisted into the U. S. Navy soon found ourselves undergoing boot training at San Diego, California.

After a whirlwind boot camp my entire company, along with the entire boot battalion, was loaded aboard a Navy transport, which took us to the South Pacific as replacements for the fleet. It took several weeks to sail from San Diego to the Admiralty Island, New Guinea and believe me going to sea for the first time was an experience in its own right. Most all of the newly appointed sailors were sea sick as we learned the age old way of getting our sea legs by going on a long voyage. The compartment I was billeted in held 30 sailors and the smell got so bad I opted to sleep topside on the open deck.

Once at New Guinea the Naval Receiving Station assigned the entire replacement draft to various ships of the line. Many of my shipmates got aircraft carriers and battleships, while others were put aboard destroyer escorts and mine layers. In my case, me and two other fellows I'd went through boot camp with got assigned to the USS Bennett DD-473, a destroyer with a crew of about 450 sailors. The Bennett was a thin-hulled vessel built for speed and like all destroyers was fondly known as a "Tin Can." With its relative small crew the ships company was like a big family where you got to know everyone aboard.

After having reported aboard the Bennett I was surprised to learn that the destroyer had just came out of a years combat action and was returning to San Francisco for an overhaul. So, having sailed all the way across the ocean to the South Pacific, I was now going back to the United States. I was not complaining. On the way back to the states I got to be initiated into that time honored tradition of being accepted to King Neptune's Court after crossing the Equator. Being a Pollywog aboard a destroyer was not a fun time for those being initiated but the salts sure did have a good time at the expense of us new guys. (Have you ever crawled through a tunnel of garbage before and then get your butt paddled when you emerged?)

Upon arriving at Hunters Point in the San Francisco, me and my two boot camp buddies got another surprise. The entire ships company got 30 days free leave for being a returning overseas combat vessel. Boy, I was really learning to like this sailor business! So I got to go home as the conquering hero with less than a year in the Navy wearing two ribbons, the Asiatic-Pacific Campaign and Navy Unit Commendation the ship had earned. All without having heard a shot fired in anger!

It's said that all good things must come to an end and so did my unexpected leave home. With the overhaul of the USS Bennett completed we set sail for Pearl Harbor to join a battle group that was preparing for the invasion of Iwo Jima. At this time I was a radar/sonar operator striker and spent my eight hours on, eight hours off, around the clock, on the bridge of the destroyer. However, being on a small ship did not mean that all of my time off was goof-off time.

On the way to Pearl I was ordered to perform Mess Duty, better known as KP. This meant I used one of my eight hours off working in the ships galley doing menial task for the cook. One funny incident took place during this time, which I always think of as being a mess cook "bad hair day." This one day the menu for the noon meal was fried chicken, mashed potatoes, gravy and corn. Our mess hall was two decks below the galley where the cooking was done and this other sailor and me was taking a large tray of chicken down the ladder to the steam table. The other sailor was backing down the ladder with me holding on to the tray above him and the angle of the tray got too steep and all the chicken fell out on the deck below. We both looked around like we were criminals caught in the act and noting we had not been observed we scooped up the chicken and put it back on the tray and continued on to the steam table as if nothing had happened. The next thing we had to take down was a large pot of gravy. In order to get out of the kitchen area you had to step over a hatch into the spud locker where potatoes were peeled and mashed, then step over another hatch to the main passageway to get to the ladder to go below. The large cast aluminum pot had big carrying handles but it was so full of gravy that when we stepped over the hatch into the spud locker some of the gravy sloshed out on the deck. We continued on to the other hatch, stepping carefully around a big pot of mashed potatoes, not worrying about the spilled gravy. But right behind us another sailor who was carrying a tray of bread to the mess hall slipped on the spilled gravy. He lost his balance and while trying to regain his footing stepped right into the pot of mashed potatoes. The bread went flying as he tried to get his foot out of the mashed potatoes and to add to his dilemma the suction of his foot in the hot potatoes was so great that when he pulled out his foot, his shoe stayed in the potatoes. The head cook saw the entire thing and rushed into the spud locker and reached his hand into the pot and retrieved the sailors shoe and with a large spoon dug out around the fellows footprint which he threw away. Then telling us to keep our mouths shut, he had us pick up the fallen bread and sent the three of us on down to the mess deck. To my knowledge, no one got sick from that meal but it goes to show you never know what may have happened to your chow when you're in the military.

When I had the watch my duty station was in the radar shack near the bridge. During general quarters my combat station was on a 20mm gun located amid-ship on the star-board side. On 19 February 1945 the entire invasion force laid off Iwo Jima and the Marines started their landing operation. Our job was to fire our five-inch guns in support of the Marine landing. Since a destroyer has a low draft this meant we could go in close in offering supporting fire for the Marines and that's exactly what we did. Our fore and aft turrets poured out a steady stream of fire for the Marines' as did other ships of the fleet. But even with all the shells hitting on Iwo the report came to our ship that the first waves of the Marine amphibious landing force was meeting extremely heavy resistance and might have to pull back off the beach. From my close in view from the 20mm gun mount I could see Japanese shells hitting among the landing craft that sent up huge geysers of boiling water. And I also saw the many direct hits that exploded on the troop carrying landing craft. In order to help relieve the pressure on the main landing force word was passed that our ship, along with 75 or so Higgins boats that were circling out of harms way awaiting their turn to go in, would stage a fake landing. We led this group of landing craft toward Iwo's black sand beach about two miles away from the main landing. The ruse worked pretty good as many of the Japanese guns began to focus on the Bennett. By some miracle the hundreds of enemy shells directed our way impacted all around the destroyer but no direct hits.

One of the proudest moments of my life took place on 23 February 1945 when I witnessed U. S. Marines raise Old Glory atop Mount Suribachi. The fleet went wild, blowing ships horns and whistles. Although we had captured the southern end of the island, a lot of fighting remained to be done. At night the main naval force would leave Iwo's coastline and sail out to sea. My destroyer was deployed as part of the picket line out in front of the battleships and carriers to give warning of any attack by Jap subs or approaching aircraft. One bright moonlit night the Bennett was attacked by two Japanese "Betty" bombers. All of our 40mm and 20mm guns let loose with all they had and it will never be known who made the hits but we shot down one of the bombers as it flew directly over our ship on a bombing run. We got the Betty before it dropped its bombs and must have hit it in the open bomb bay as it exploded into a million pieces almost directly over our heads. The other Betty was being used as a torpedo bomber and it launched a torpedo against us that hit our bow but didn't explode. Talk about being lucky! However, at first light while taking soundings in all bilge compartments, which is done daily, it was discovered that the forward bilge was full of water. Looking over the side of the ship as it rolled from side to side, we could see a large hole the Jap torpedo had punched in the bow. Thus ended our Iwo Jima assignment and we were ordered to proceed to Elite Gulf in the Philippines where the Bennett was put into a floating dry dock for repairs.

By the middle of March 1945 our tin can was repaired and after a short shake-down cruise to insure the new plates welded onto our bow was A-Okay we received orders to proceed and join up with a task force heading for Okinawa. The combat landing of Marines from the 1st and 6th Division began on Easter Sunday and April Fools Day, 1 April 1945. This time, instead of providing close in support for the Marines like we had done off Iwo Jima, the Bennett was assigned the mission of picket duty.

There were seven picket stations surrounding the island with American ships positioned in a half arc at each station. The number one picket station was out a hundred miles at sea facing Japan and as usual the mission was that of an early warning system for enemy subs, ships and aircraft. Our patched up destroyer started out at picket station six that was closer to Okinawa than one though five but in the days that followed we soon found ourselves on the number one station. The reason for this was simple enough: As destroyers were sunk or heavily damaged our ship moved up to cover their old position.

Prior to getting the dubious honor of being ordered to the number one picket station we had made many reports of Japanese aircraft heading south to attack our naval forces lying of Okinawa. But being number one in line was a completely different story. From our first day on this station we were attacked by all sorts of Jap airplanes, many of them

Zero bombers. For three days we fought off repeated attempts to sink us from Jap kamikazes. These suicide planes came directly at our ship with the intent of crashing into the Bennett to eliminate her. And for three days our luck held as we either shot the Japs out of the sky or they crashed into the sea without hitting us. On the forth day, our luck ran out.

I was at my general quarters station at a 20mm gun mount on the starboard side when a swarm of kamikazes focused on the Bennett. Two planes came directly at our gun tub and we flamed them both. They crashed in the ocean not more than 15 feet from our mount, which sent up huge plumes of water on us. Another suicide pilot came in at an angel toward our bow and our five inch must have got him because he desegregated in mid-air with parts of his airplane raining down on the forward superstructure. A forth kamikaze came at us from the stern and it too was hit by our heavy barrage of gun-fire and I could clearly see smoke coming from the engine cowling that trailed back in a long, black spiral. The engine was sputtering as it flew low over our 20mm gun mount and so help me I swear I shared a glance with the pilot. I watched the plane as it circled back around our fantail then lost sight of it as it made its way along the port side of the ship. Even though I'd lost sight of the airplane I could still hear the guns on the other side firing like mad. The kamikaze pilot while going down managed to crash his plane onto the port side about mid ship. A bomb went through the side of our ship and exploded in the super saturated boiler sending hot steam and shrapnel throughout the forward engine room. Most of the sailors in the forward engine room were killed outright and all of those not dead were seriously wounded. Our ship was now dead in the water and a sitting duck for any other kamikazes. For reasons I've never understood for over 50 years, no other Jap airplanes attacked us. The Bennett had an aft engine room and the remainder of our black gang was able to get this engine started. We were down by the bow however and it took hours of hard labor to shore up the gaping hole forward and get pumps to get out enough seawater for us to maneuver. At dusk we were able to get underway and began limping our way to Manus Harbor. As it grew darker we found out that the heroic efforts of our damage control parties to plug all the leaks was not all that successful. Seawater came gushing into the forward engine room that flooded it. By daylight we were again down by the bow, this time a good six feet, which meant making headway was about nil. Every portable pump we had was put into action that barely took out the water faster than it was coming in. By the Grace of God we finally made it to Manus Harbor on Okinawa and once there our skipper was told since the forward engine room was now contaminated with salt water the destroyer needed a complete overhaul.

After hasty repairs to make the ship seaworthy we set sail for Pearl Harbor, at a very slow pace. (Our ship got the Navy Commendation ribbon for this campaign also.)

Additional temporary repairs were done at Pearl Harbor and the ship was ordered to the major repair facility, Bremerton, Washington. As before, the ships crew was authorized 30 days leave since it was going to take several months to get the Bennett back in shape. It was great to get to go home and try and forget about kamikazes but I have to admit that it took awhile for me not to automatically duck at the sound of an airplane overhead.

We set sail from Bremerton, Washington, heading to San Diego, California on the newly repaired U.S.S. Bennett in early August 1945. While sailing past San Francisco we got the word the war had ended. What a happy day!

But even with the war over this didn't mean our duty was complete yet. Orders received at San Diego sent us sailing to Dutch Harbor on Kodiak Island, with a stop over at Sitka, Alaska for a few days R&R. What a deal that turned out to be. When we arrived at Dutch Harbor we were met by other ships from our destroyer squadron along with many other ships of the line. All of these other ships had just come out from the war zone and crews being granted liberty was their first liberty in over five months. You can probably imagine what happened. Every bar in Dutch Harbor was crammed full of sailors along with a few seagoing Marines. The liquor stores did a great business also. By 9:00 PM the Shore Patrol could no longer control the rowdy sailors so they asked assistance from the ships anchored in the harbor for more manpower. The bars and liquor stores were closed which started a real riot. Before it was over two sailors had been killed and hundreds of them injured. The next day's liberty party found all the bars and liquor stores nailed shut with Off Limit signs on them. These poor swabs had to content themselves with touring the town and visiting a couple of museums. Have you ever saw a stuffed Kodiak Bear 17 feet tall? I have! I'm sure the old timers still living in Dutch Harbor will remember that September of 1945.

The last mission of the destroyer USS Bennett DD-473, was being an escort for a small convoy, which included a tender carrying U. S. Army Air Force weather personnel and their equipment to Petropavlovsk, Russia on the Kamchatka Peninsula. The flyboys would be staying in the Soviet Union for six months to gather weather data.

The Bennett anchored next to a Russian supply ship and the two vessels were tied together. The Russian's were as fascinated with us as much as we were with them and it didn't take long before we all got to be real friendly with one another. The Russian's loved anything American and it wasn't long before a lot of trading took place with the crews of the two ships. How the Russian supply ship got to be loaded with Japanese war equipment is still a mystery to me but our guys took advantage of the situation to finally get some Japanese war souvenirs. Jap rifles, pistols, helmets, web gear, parts of uniforms were traded for American cigarettes, cigars, candy and cigarette lighters. (I've often wondered what those Russian sailors thought when the lighters ran out of fluid and wouldn't light anymore since they had never seen a cigarette lighter before.)

We also got the chance to visit the port city of Petropavlovsk which was like an old American western town of the 1800's. The streets were mud and sidewalks were made out of wood. It wasn't their fault of course, but the citizens for the most part were very backward. A humorous event took place at the cities openair market. This shipmate of mine was eating an apple and a seed got caught up under his false teeth. Not thinking anything about it he takes out his false teeth to get rid of the irritating apple seed. The Russian people around him stopped in awe staring at this American sailor who just popped his teeth out with no problem. The next thing you know is my buddy has a crowd of people around him and they're giving him rubbles to watch him put his teeth in and out of his mouth. It was like a circus act or a magic act to them, and to us, more than obvious that there wasn't a dentist in Petropavlovsk.

Upon the Bennett's return to San Diego she was decommissioned and put in mothballs. Since I didn't have enough points for discharge, I was transferred to the USS Grant, and a few months later when the Grant was decommissioned in Long Beach, California, I received my honorable discharge.

There were may lonely hours at sea, on watch, staring out at a vast ocean engulfed in thoughts of home and family. I continue to feel a great sense of sorrow for those who gave their lives so that our country would prevail in World War II, and I feel very fortunate that we who survived have a chance to remember them, and all of our military people who gave their lives in all wars, on such hollowed days such as Veterans Day and Memorial Day.

Bob Boyd retired from government service, having worked for the Central Intelligence Agency for better than 25 years. As a photo analyst, Bob was a part of the team that identified soviet missiles in Cuba in 1962. (Prior to the CIA, he was with Army Intelligence for a number of years.) Bob and his wife of 52 years Beatrice, have two daughters, Barbara and Patty. The Boyd's live on Hilton Head Island, South Carolina.

57

A STOLEN PIE
Former Corporal Gilbert E. Belcher, USMC

After enlisting into the U.S. Marine Corps on January 6, 1944 at the ripe old age of eighteen I took my boot at MCRD, San Diego. (I still remember my M-1 rifle number that I was issued and kept the whole time in the Corps: #2121431. How many 73 year olders can say that?)

I was a part of the 62nd replacement draft that left San Diego, California on April 17, 1944 on the APA 124, USS Bland. We zigzagged across the Pacific in a large convoy for seven days until reaching the Hawaiian Islands. The powers that be put our entire replacement draft in a tent camp near Pearl City where we underwent additional training. We got a lot of liberty time but with little money it didn't make much difference, and most of us had to settle for roaming the streets of Pearl City watching the sailors have a good time.

After ten days orders came down that the replacements were to be shipped out on the double. It didn't take any genius to figure out why our replacement draft was needed so fast all of a sudden; it was obvious that one hell of a battle had taken place somewhere and Marines were needed to fill the gaps left by combat causalities. We were loaded on the APA 222 USS Pickaway at Pearl Harbor, and headed toward Guam. Stopping at the Kwajalein Islands for refueling our convoy continued on to complete the two week sailing to Apra Harbor, Guam. Once at Apra we sat on our seabags for four hours until the covered wagons arrived to take us to the Marine Transit Center at the north end of the island.

While awaiting assignments to our new outfits the permanent personnel at the Transit Center had dozens of crappy little work assignments for the replacement Marines to do. The only problem with this was the way us peons got assigned to the various details. In typical Marine Corps fashion, those people with last names starting with the letter A to K caught all of the details. Being I was "Belcher," I was always at the head of the roster!

Most of the work parties dealt with upkeep of the Transit Center. There were ten large mess halls that could feed 1,500 Marines each, and a lot of the guys got duties cleaning them up. All around the mess halls were large areas of pyramid tents with each area having several out-houses and out-door showers. Naturally, these all had to be kept up in ship-shape rear area perfection. I lucked out, if you want to call it lucky, as I got assigned to mess duty. Actually, I ended up getting a pretty cushy job. The Mess Sergeant put me in charge of his food storage room and I worked alone stacking boxes and crates as they came in on trucks.

There was a large Navy bakery on Guam that made bread and pastries that were delivered to the various mess halls by six-by trucks. This one day a truck pulled up from the bakery with a load of pies. Actually, they were more like cobblers since they were baked on large two-foot long, twofoot wide pans. They'd be cut in two-inch squares, which would make about 140 portions per pan. Two small bites for us kids! Anyway, there were nine pans of these cherry pies delivered. The Mess Sergeant had me and two mess men to carry the pies into the back of the Quonset hut mess hall to his galley. This trip went pass a shed that housed a steam boiler that was used for the large steam kettles to cook food. Usually, there was a man inside the steam room at all times to keep an eye on the pressure gauges. As I dutifully made my first trip carrying a large cherry pie into the galley I happened to notice that the boiler room was unmanned. It just so happens that cherry pie is about my most favorite dessert! What would you have done if you were 18 years old and was detailed to carry your favorite dessert into the kitchen? I bolted into the steam room on my second pie carrying trip and placed the big pan under the boiler then stacked a couple of boxes in front of the hiding place.

It was rather comical when the driver of the truck handed the Mess Sergeant the delivery invoice to be signed for nine pies. Since there was only eight pies on a table in the galley the Mess Sergeant refused to sign the receipt. It was like a Keystone Kop movie watching everyone running around trying to locate the ninth pie. Of course, at the time I didn't think it was too funny, and was sweating like mad. The driver finally left muttering to himself since he had to go fetch another cherry pie and the Mess Sergeant was indigent thinking the driver had tried to pull a fast one over on him.

On the other hand, several of my buddies who worked in this screened in hut out in back of the mess hall used for cleaning garbage cans and cutting up boxes, surmised that if a pie was missing, then keep an eye on Belcher.

The rest of the day while I stacked cans in the storeroom I made my plan on how I would go about getting "MY" cherry pie out of the mess hall and to my tent. The Transit Center had this huge outdoor movie theater where all of the troops and camp personnel would go to in the evening to sit on the ground to watch a movie. Since the mess men always worked late in the mess hall as soon as they got done cleaning up the place they'd run to the outdoor movie theater to catch the nights movie. I figured all I had to do was wait for everyone to shag from the mess hall and I could retrieve "MY" pie and get it to my tent without being seen. Boy, my mouth was watering the rest of the day, thinking how I was going to gorge myself on cherry pie.

My simple plan went off without a hitch and all was quiet as I cautiously fitted the big pie filled pan through the flap of my tent. Suddenly, the pan was jerked from my hands! I was stunned to say the least. It was dark in the tent and all I could see was shadowy figures clawing handfuls of pie into their mouths. I cried out in despair. "Stop it! It's my pie!" I barely recognized the muffled voice of my pal Private Earl Beecher, who's mouth was so full of pie he could barely, mumble, "Save some for Belcher, he got it for us." The garbage hut detail had set up an ambush for me and "MY" pie! (I did manage to get a four by eight slab however.)

Gil Belcher spent 36 years in forestry work, retiring as a California Forest Ranger.

He and his wife Virginia have four sons and one daughter, Gil spends his time restoring old cars and to date has restored a 1925 Dodge brothers' touring car, a 1927 Dodge brothers screen side delivery truck, and a 1921 Model T Ford fire truck. He is currently restoring a 1942 Ford jeep that he says will be a mint condition Marine Corps jeep when he completes the work. Gil and his wife live in Oak Run, California.

58

AND THEN I WAS WOUNDED
Former Corporal Gilbert E. Belcher, USMC

As near as I can remember, it was June 26, 1945 at approximately 1230 hours. It was a clear, warm day as I recall and my outfit, Baker Company, 1st Battalion, 1st Marines, 1st Marine Division, was standing down in a reserve status about three miles inland to the north of Naha, Okinawa. We'd seen plenty of action since our April Fools Day and Easter Sunday amphibious landing on the first of April and were enjoying the respite of being in the rear. Although Lieutenant General Geiger had declared Okinawa secure on June 21, someone had forgot to tell the Japanese and fighting continued.

The location B/1/1 was bivouacked at was between a narrow gauge railroad on one side and a fairly large stream flowed gently to our east. A short distance to the west stood a big hill mass that snaked its way around to our southern perimeter that abutted a small dusty road. The road went in an easterly direction, crossing the stream under a small stone bridge. The hill mass had hundreds of burial tombs dug into the side of them and inside many of these tombs fanatical Japanese waited with no intention of surrender. So even though we were "in the rear" we still took incoming potshots from snipers dug into the cave like burial tombs. But this minor inconvenience didn't keep us Marines from enjoying our short rest period that had been afforded us. There was a field kitchen set up under canvas and hot meals were served. It was what was called "B" rations, which meant it came out of cans, but it tasted great to the Marines just to have some warm chow in their bellies. We even had toilets of sorts, slit trenches that you flushed with an entrenching tool of dirt.

I was a BAR man (Browning automatic rifle) and my assistance was Private Earl R. Beecher, Jr. We slept together in a pup tent made from our two shelter halves, and usually where you'd see one of us, you'd see the other. Around 12-noon a runner came to our pup tent from the Company CP. He informed us our company commander wanted the two of us to saddle up and report to the CP by 1300 as we were going to be part of a patrol that was going to go after the snipers dug into the tombs.

As Earl and I walked to the CP after putting on our packs and other equipment, Private Bob Ricks, who had not been a BAR man that long, hailed me, saying he had disassembled his BAR to clean it and couldn't get it back together. Earl took my pack and BAR and went on while I paused to help Ricks. For some reason Ricks also had an M-1 rifle with him and as I dropped on my knees and started to work on his BAR, he hunkered down next to me with the M-1 holding it upright on its butt-plate. It was never fully explained to me what happened but suddenly an explosion took place between Ricks and me. Private Jim Anderson told me later he was the first one to arrive on the scene and found Ricks on his hands and knees with blood squirting out his temple while

I was running around in a small circle holding onto my shattered left arm, my face a bloody mess. Another buddy, Private Harold Medford, told me 29 years later that I did a flip in the air when the explosion took place and landed on my knees with both hands on the ground. I have a clear memory of the ringing in my ears and someone tackling me to pull me down so I could be treated. My left leg was also messed up and a Navy corpsman used his K-Bar knife to cut my utility trousers from belt to ankle so he could get at the injury. My arm, leg and left hip were gushing blood and I cried out for my mother because I knew I was dying. Several Marines held me down while the corpsman applied pressure bandages to my wounds and tried to calm me. Ricks and I were both placed on stretchers and carried to a field ambulance jeep. Someone took our dog tags and this scared me even more. I kept thinking that when I died I'd be listed as "Unknown."

We were taken to the 1st Marine Division Field (Tent) Hospital located at Naha, the capitol city of Okinawa, where I was immediately given three pints of blood. I could see other doctors working on Ricks who lay in the same surgery tent next to me. And I also saw Ricks being carried out of the surgery tent a half-hour later. (It was a year before I found out that he had died in that Field Hospital.)

This Navy surgeon that was working frantically on me must have been very close to a nervous breakdown because he kept yelling at the insanity that the war was being fought with sixteen-year olds. I kept telling him between sobs that I was eighteen but I don't think he believed me. There were several other people attending to me and I can still hear the tinkling of metal hitting metal as shrapnel was dug out of me and put in a stainless steel bowl. I was finally put to sleep and given pain shots.

I awoke sometime at the early dawn the next day and found myself still on the stretcher lying on the ground in this very long tent. The only illumination in the tent came from a small lightbulb flickering on one of the wood tent poles which held the tent up. I felt as if I was in a dark cave. Although barely conscious at first, I could see the long row of stretchers on either side of me running up both sides of the tent. I attempted to raise my upper body for a better look at my surroundings and vomited on an unconscious Marine laying next to me on my left. My left boondockers shoe was gone and I was bandaged from the left ankle to my head; and I couldn't move. Then the pain hit me! I'd never hurt so bad in my life and I never felt so helpless before, or since then. The explosion had also burned me and I could feel the festering sores which was beginning to drive me nuts.

A corpsman with a flashlight saw that I was awake and came over to me. He wiped me off, gave me a shot of morphine after I told him how much I hurt and even covered up my vomit with an entrenching shovel after he cleaned up the other Marine I'd puked on. In a soft voice he asked me where my hometown was at and I told him Corona, California. I'll be dig-gone if he hadn't went through his initial training as a corpsman at the Corona Naval Hospital. I guess he was trying to cheer me up and he did a good job of it, especially when he told me he'd dated several girls in Corona and when I asked him their names, I'll be a son-of-a-gun; I'd went to high school with those girls and knew everyone of them. He told me he'd come back and write a letter to my folks for me so it would beat the official telegram and help ease their anxiety. He did just that.

Many of the Marines around me stayed unconscious during the four days I was in that awful tent. Others cried out for their mothers or hollered out in pain. Generous amounts of pain killing shots were given out to put us to sleep. To this day I can't imagine how those overworked corpsmen handled the misery surrounding them, plus they were constantly working on us. They gave us water to drink and candy bars to eat and sprayed DDT daily to keep the files and mosquitoes at bay. Not much could be done about the smell even though the docs tried to clean up the guys that pissed themselves and crapped in their britches.

On the third day, Earl Beecher and our squad leader found me. During their visit I asked them how Ricks was doing and they sort of sluffed me off, saying he was okay. The two Marines said they'd talked to the chief corpsman about my condition and was glad to say the head doc reported I was going to make it. When I asked them what it was that got me, neither one had a positive answer. But my pal Beecher said that whatever it was not only burned me but also gave me four hundred and fifty holes in my body, from pinhead size to marble size. Their best guess was a sniper round had hit Ricks M-1 causing the ammo in it to explode as the rifle was completely destroyed.

The next day after my buddy Beecher and my squad leader had visited me I was loaded onto a jeep ambulance, along with five other Marines. The jeep had a metal pipe frame work on the hood and rear seat to accommodate six stretchers. I was placed crossways on the hood with another wounded Marine. We drove slowly down to the beach where a DUCK was waiting to take us out to a hospital ship in the bay. A DUCK by the way was a big vehicle with large tires that could also be used as a boat. About a dozen causalities were placed on the deck of the cargo/personnel hold and like a water taxi we were taken to the USS Relief, a Navy hospital ship. When we got alongside the Relief cables were attached to the DUCK and a ships crane hoisted us aboard. It was a beautiful ship; painted white inside and out, shiny brass, and the inside deck was all red linoleum. One of the other things I noticed was the ships intercom played music and offered news reports during the day. I got a top bunk aft on the starboard side and was fortunate that I had a porthole to look out of. The big hospital ship was built to take care of six-hundred bed patients but we had closer to eight-hundred aboard. Some of the fellows had to use stretchers for bunks and were placed in store rooms or other spare room that could be found.. We sailed that night with all lights ablaze and special spot lights on the huge red crosses that adorned both sides of the ship, two to a side. I don't think there was a Marine on that ship that believed the Japanese would honor the Geneva Convention regarding the rule not to fire on a hospital ship. By the 4th of July I had been operated on three times at sea. My bloody dungarees had been taken off me the first day aboard and the only personal items that remained was my wallet with three dollars of invasion currency in it.

One evening I got the urge to take a crap. The ward nurse and corpsman was no-where to be found but I had to go! The crisp cleanliest of my present surroundings prevented me from doing my business in my bunk and I painfully climbed down from the bed and like a mummy slithered the twenty feet to the head. The only problem was that once inside the "John" I couldn't sit down because all the plaster and bandages wouldn't let me bend. Have you ever layed across a commode at a forty-five degree angle and let 'er rip? But, oh my; what a relief! It had been nine days and to say I stunk up that head would be an understatement. Then I was faced with another problem. I couldn't wipe! I know you've heard about Marines taking care of their own. Well let me tell you there was a couple of Marines that came to my rescue that performed duties "Above and Beyond" of taking care of one of their own. My pain had not been that sever getting to the toilet but it took four Marine patients to get me back into my bunk after I'd done my job. Naturally, the nurse and corpsman showed up just as I was being tucked back into bed by my comrades and they got all bent out of shape that I'd got out of the rack. You know how it is with Marines; my heart bled for them being so upset!

Talking about nurses brings up another subject. At night a small light was on over a small desk at the end of the ward-bay where the duty corpsman would do his paper work. My bunk overlooked this desk area which was next to a small treatment room. Late this one night I was awakened by an Army sergeant who was across the narrow aisle from my bunk. In a whispered tone of voice, he said. "Can you see through the vent on the wall over your head? I scooted up in my bunk, lifted my head, and was able to see through the vent into the small treatment room.. I whispered back that I could see inside the room. Like a flash, the Army sergeant was up on my bunk with me while several other patients waited in line. Our duty corpsman was banging a nurse on the treatment table! When they got done the nurse casually strolled through our ward, trying not to pay attention to the pile of wounded men on top of me on my bunk that had been watching her and the corpsman making out. When the duty corpsman came out of the treatment room the catcalls started. He got mad and fussed around trying to get us to quiet down, which didn't do much good. We had his number and he knew it! Whenever he was on duty his face was always red from the "cute" remarks that was fired at him. For the nurse, we had a special game we'd play. When she'd walk down an isle we'd all begin this cadence rhythm in a sing-song voice under our breath: "Ta dum ta dum, dum ta dum....ta dum ta dum, ta dum ta dum." When she'd stop and look around we'd all stop until she started moving again. As red as her face got I do believe she had it figured out why we were playing games with her.

Our hospital ship reached Saipan on July 8, 1945. Army, Navy and Marine bands were on the wharf playing for us. A Marine honor guard was on hand to welcome us back along with a lot of smiling brass. There must have been a couple of hundred Navy WAVES and Army WACS on that wharf all waving and looking pretty. When stretcher bearers brought their loads down to the wharf the WACS and WAVES, along with Red Cross dollies, were on hand to serve us cokes in Red Cross paper cups. News correspondences were having a field day running around taking flash camera pictures of all the gals paying tribute to the wounded warriors.

We wounded were loaded in box like Army ambulances, four to an ambulance with a WAC per vehicle riding with us. The long convoy of ambulances took us to the 148th Army Field Hospital. It was the last time any of us saw a WAC, WAVE or a coke!

59

JAPANESE BATTLE FLAGS
Former Corporal Gilbert E. Belcher, USMC

I was in an Army hospital on Saipan recovering from wounds received on Okinawa when the two atomic bombs were dropped on Japan. The B-29 bomber's Enola Gay and Box Cars that dropped the A-bombs had taken off from the island of Tinian, directly across the channel from Saipan. We patients in the hospital could hear the roar of the B-29s every day before the war ended when they flew off Tinian on their way to Japan.

The official surrender ceremonies held in Tokyo Bay aboard the battleship USS Missouri on September 2, 1945 had already taken place by the time I was transferred to the U. S. Navy Hospital, Guam. By now I was feeling pretty chipper and well on my way to a full recovery. It wasn't long before I was allowed out of the hospital for liberty in Guam's capitol city, Agana. The city was in total ruins having got blown apart during the war but the natives were a friendly sort and were quickly rebuilding. Just the same there wasn't much to do in Agana except walk around and look at the rubble. This didn't keep thousands of army personnel who had been staged on Guam for the ground invasion of Japan to flood the city however. Most of these greenhorns were looking for war souvenirs from the guys that had seen combat so they'd have something to send home to mom and dad or Sally Sue. If you were a Marine they'd button hole you on the street and beg you to sell or trade a war souvenir since the rumor was the Marines were loaded down with them. Unfortunately this wasn't the case and I'm sure I wasn't the only one to realize the market was great if we could only come up with a load of souvenirs. One of the items the dogfaces wanted real badly were the personal little battle flags Japanese soldiers carried as sort of a good luck charm.

It came to pass that I got well enough to be placed in a casual company while I waited reassignment. I had enlisted for four years and didn't have enough points to be rotated back to the states and those in charge of me said I'd probably end up being stationed right here on Guam for awhile once it was decided what to do with me. The first sergeant of the casual barracks figured out real quick what to do with me on a temporary bases and he put me on thirty days mess duty. I'd had mess duty on Guam before and had worked in a supply shed stacking can goods, which turned out to be a sweet job. But this time I ended up in the scullery drying dishes.

The white cotton dishtowels I used were around a foot and a half square. I went through about sixty of them each meal and had to take them out back of the mess hall to dry out on this clothesline that was rigged up for that purpose. This one day after hanging up a supply of wet towels I got to looking at them fluttering on the clothes line and it was like a light going off in my head when it came to me that the things looked just like small flags. I immediately went back to the scullery and opened up a brand new bale of dishtowels. After getting five towels I picked up an empty number ten can then went over to the motor pool and talked to the motor transport corporal and explained the idea I had. I only had to tell him once for him to see what a swell idea I had and he went about getting a gallon of red paint, and some gasoline. I thinned some red paint with the gasoline in the large number ten can. Then I centered one of the white towels over the can and tied it around the edge of the can with string. With a quick move of my hands I upended the can then instantly straightened it back up. The result was a dyed round meatball, looking just like the Japanese naval ensign. But I wasn't done yet. The next step was to get some Japanese writing on the newly made "flag" to make it look more authentic. Anyone having been in the military service will remember the rubber stamps with your name on it and the inkpad with India ink that we used to stamp our clothes. One of the few souvenirs I had was a torn bit of a Japanese newspaper I'd picked up on Okinawa. I have no idea what it was I wrote (or drew) with the trimmed down toothbrush I used when I put those Japanese characters on the towel-flag. But damn if it didn't look real.

I don't remember how much I got for that first flag, but it wasn't long before four of us was spending all our off duty time (and some duty time) manufacturing Japanese battle flags. We were trading them or selling them as fast as the paint would dry. Some of our bartering I do remember. One time we got the use of an Army jeep for a full day and we drove it all over the island on a sightseeing trip. Another time we got a case of eggs and eight steaks from this Army mess sergeant and I remember getting more cases of beer than the four of us could handle.

But all good things must come to an end and my mess sergeant finally took notice that there was a shortage of dish drying towels. By this time I was getting used ones, torn ones, anything I could lay my hands on. I suspect he may have known where his towels were going because one day he got right in my face and let me know that if anymore dish towels came up missing, it would be curtains for me.

So ended a lot of fun and also a lot of loot. I've often wondered what kind of "sea story" those soldiers made up, telling about their battle flags to the folks back home? And I'd bet money that some of those flags could be found to this day in some dusty attic or at a flea market. I'm sure others made flags besides me and the three guys I worked with. But you know what? I bet you I could still recognize the ones we made. They'd be the ones with the Japanese writing that say: Special on rice - ten yen.

60

A SAGA OF A MILITARY POLICEMAN ON GUAM
Former Corporal Gilbert E. Belcher, USMC

When I was a kid growing up there was a saying we kids would use to tease our school chums. It went along the line about hiding behind the door when God passed out brains. In the Marine Corps we had another saying about those fellows who never seemed to get the word or was always up to his ears in something he couldn't handle. We called it "the old ten percenter."

Now you would expect that a Marine who had made it through boot camp and Camp Pendleton, plus having survived combat on Okinawa, would know everything there was to know when it came to military duties. In my case, after convalescing from wounds at the Guam Navy Hospital and spending a long stint at the Marine Transient Center (better known as casual company), it came as a surprise to me that November of 1945, when I was told I was being transferred to the Guam Police Department for duty. Like a lot of Marines I'd had my fair share of guard duty but I didn't have the first clue what an M.P. (Military Police) was supposed to do. So there I was, not quite nineteen years old yet, walking around in Guam's capitol city of Agana in starched khaki's, wearing a pith helmet, red and yellow arm band, a pistol and a badge. Now you've got to keep in mind I'd been given no training and damn little instructions on what I was supposed to do, other than orders to run everybody out of town unless they had a pass. I didn't even know what a pass looked like since no one had shown me one!

I managed to get through my first day as an M.P. by faking it pretty good and was starting to enjoy the power behind the badge so to speak, since no body gave me any lip when I'd stop them and ask if they had a pass. (I'd act like I knew what I was looking at when the soldier, sailor or Marine would hand me his little piece of paper, which I assumed, was a pass.) My second day of duty turned out to be something else however:

Around noon this jeep came bearing down on me like a bat out of hell so I decided to cite the driver for speeding. I raised my hand in a halt signal and the jeep slid to a dusty stop. I noticed a sign below the windshield that read: Provost Marshal. As I approached the driver, and a Marine colonel, I asked myself, what the hell is a provost marshal? I saluted the bird colonel and asked to see his pass. His mouth dropped open for a second and a major sitting next to him began chuckling. As the colonel fiddled in his pocket for his pass he asked me. "Son, do you know who I am?" I replied with a crisp, "No sir!" I scanned the paper handed to me that stated it authorized Colonel R. L. Barraco full access to all native villages at any given hour. It was signed by Colonel R. L. Barraco, Provost Marshal. This confused me since it was the first time I'd ever seen any document signed by the person it was for. I decided to dwell deeper into what was going on. "Pardon me sir," I said. "Just what is a Provost Marshal?" This time, the major sitting next to the colonel laughed out loud. Then the major said. "Private, Colonel Barraco is your boss!" I'm sure great shock was seen on my face. I wanted a trap door to open for me to fall down among the sharks so they could devour me! Colonel Barraco was the "Head Cheese!" the "Top Dog," the "Big Honcho!" The "Big Banana!" There was no doubt about it, not only had I pulled a "ten percent", I was definitely a "behind the door" candidate!

Shakily, I handed back the colonel's pass and stuttered out that all was in order, then did my best to render a snappy military salute. The colonel eyeballed me for a long moment, then almost kindly, asked, "You're one of Lieutenant Anderson's men aren't you?" I swiftly answered, "Yes sir!" He shook his head a couple of times, placed his jeep in gear and peeled out throwing gravel and dust all over me. I could hear the major laughing as they drove away.

The officers had a Officers Mess up on Nimitz Hill and Colonel Barraco told my platoon leader, First Lieutenant Anderson about meeting me. Lieutenant Anderson did not see the humor in it like the good colonel did. You've heard about the snowball that gets bigger as it rolls downhill? Well, it was a steamroller when it got to me! It was determined that I wasn't suitable for town duty and work was found for me out in the boonies.

Northeast of Agana are the villages of Mong Mong and Toto. It came to pass in my duties as an M.P. in the Guam Police Department, that I would patrol these two villages. This was the first time I had a night foot patrol, but I wasn't concerned since I was now a "salt" of two months at being a military policeman. Although it was late January 1946, Guam was still hot and I was wearing my normal starched khaki's, and pith helmet. I was armed with a .30 caliber carbine, a club like nightstick and carried a large Navy flashlight. The corporal-of-the-guard drove me up to Sina Jana, a small village where I would have to walk from to get to my patrol area. Directly across the road from Sina Jana was a two-story house that Ma Bloss ran. She had two daughters and the three of them did a good "red light" business. The corporal pointed to the jungle trail going past Ma Bloss' house and told me to take off. He said he'd pick me up at 2400 and for me to be back down at this location at that time.

Ma Bloss' two daughters waved to me as I walked by and tried to get me to stop for a while, but at least I had sense enough not to be swayed by their invitation and I made my way up the narrow trail. It was a bright moonlit evening and I soon arrived a Mong Mong. The houses in the village were built on post, the floors about four feet off the ground and made out of hand-woven thatch matting. Thick layers of palm tree fronds were roofs and bamboo was used for walls. The only activity at all going on was a native making bread. He had this fifty-gallon barrel he was using as a grill. The barrel sat on rocks and a fire was burning underneath. The bread the man was making was thin like a tortilla. He tore me off a piece for me to eat. It wasn't bad! I spent half an hour with the fellow and watched him fry his bread. Since there wasn't anything going on in Mong Mong to interest an M.P., I bid the man goodbye and headed up the trail to Toto. Toto was a twin of Mong Mong and it too was quiet with not much happening. I was quickly getting bored with my first night duty. This time I came across a man who was straining insects out of cans of Tuba, a local beverage made by and favored by the natives. Tuba was a party drink, the man explained to me. He invited me to sit down and try it. I had been told that to refuse food was an insult and figured Tuba probably came under that same category, so sat down next to him and he poured me a cereal bowl full of the milky looking liquid. I tested it and found it tasted rather bland but not that bad. I sipped at the drink why the man chatted to me. When I got down to the bottom of the bowl I saw a white spot and turned on my flashlight to see what it was. It was a picture of Shirley Temple. The man told me he'd gotten the blue glass bowl, with Shirley Temple's picture on it from a box of cereal that came from the United States before the war. (That bowl would be a collector's item today.)

By my second bowl of Tuba I wasn't feeling bored anymore. The native man and me laughed and talked for two hours, with the man keeping my bowl full.

To this day I don't remember saying goodbye to my newfound friend but I do remember staggering through Mong Mong and that's about the last thing I do remember about my first night patrol.

I woke up early the next morning in my rack at the guard Quonset where I lived. My head felt like it was coming off my shoulders and I was sicker than a dog and barely made it to the head to toss up last nights chow and native bread, along with a white spray of Tuba. Talk about confused! I had no idea how I made it back to the M.P. area. After doing my thing in the head I reeled my way back to my bunk and there stood the corporal-of-the-guard. He was wearing a big shit-eating grin, and said. "So you're alive huh Belcher?" When I asked him how I had made it back since I didn't remember riding with him, he told me the story. He said when he had came to pick me up at 2400 at Sian Jana I was nowhere in sight. After waiting for twenty minutes he strolled up to Ma Bloss' place, thinking maybe I'd taking advantage of the pleasures of the house. A late night patron of Ma Bloss had a weapons carrier with canvas top parked in front of her place. I evidently crawled up in the back of the weapons carrier and laid down on the bench on one side. That's where my corporal had found me and luckily so before the guy in Ma Bloss's had drove back to his base. The corporal, bless his heart, checked in my weapon and poured me into bed. He gave me a real father to son lecture but that was the end of it. Oh—I was very careful about Tuba after that.

To the southeast of Agana was the cities water works that supplied water to the capitol. The water works building was made from poured concrete and it was always locked. The hum of a pump could be heard running inside the building all the time. Even though it would have taken a howitzer to damage the water works it was still a walking sentry post for M.P.s around the clock. I'd never heard of any threat leveled at the Water Works and suspected it was just another "make work" job to keep us busy and out of our beds at night.

One dark night in February 1946, I had the eight to twelve midnight watch and was walking the narrow trail around the Water Works with the aid of my flashlight. It was a jungle-invested path and very spooky with no sound as I made my way around the Water Works. The joke at the time when walking this extremely dark trail was that you had to light a match to see if your flashlight was on. All of a sudden, directly to my left a loud snorting sound let loose. I liked to jumped out of my skin! I clawed at my shoulder holster to get my .45 caliber automatic out and at the same time swung my flashlight toward where the snort had came from. Two gigantic red eyes stared at me not more than six inches from where I stood! I was so frozen with fear I couldn't make my legs move to run. I did manage to scream though! My scream led to another loud snort from the evil wild beast and a stomping sound, but it too, seemed frozen in place. I couldn't breath and my heart beat wildly. Then I noticed the large red eyes were attached to a long black face and large horns curled up around the head in a half circle. It was a caribou!! My flashlight was almost touching the big animal between its eyes. It seemed to take forever but the Mexican standoff finally came to an end when the animal backed away and stomped out of sight. I had came within a fraction of a second of having shot the damn thing. How would I have explained the shooting of a caribou? Especially one that was blinded by my flashlight and was probably as rattled as I had been. When the corporal-of-the-guard picked me up at midnight, nether he or my relief said anything to me about the front of my pants being wet.

Guam's jail, which was run by the Military Government after the war, was located in the southern end of Agana. On one side of the jail compound a shear cliff one hundred feet high overlooked the ocean. A high barbed wire fence enclosed the rest of the jail. At the gate there was a small five by five foot guard hut that was opened on one side and had a pointed roof. This guard hut is where Guamanian policemen and Marine M.P.'s stood watch.

On a very rainy night, I along with two native policemen was standing guard. I was dressed in my M.P. outfit but even wearing a poncho my starched khaki's had wilted. This didn't worry me, as I felt sure there was not going to be anyone dropping by that I had to impress with looking sharp since the four in the morning to eight a.m. tour of guard duty meant nobody was going to see me in the first place. Except of course, the two Guamanian policemen, and they were as miserable looking as me. There is nothing as monotonous as early morning guard duty. After an hour of looking at the heavy rain come down in sheets I became so lulled from weariness to the point I could hardly keep my eyes open. The guard hut did not have any chairs or a bench to sit on but I was so sleepy I just had to get a nap. A wooden ledge that ran around the inside of the hut supported the roof over our head. I told the two policemen I was going to get up on the ledge and take a short nap and to wake me immediately if anyone happened by. Grammarians are pleasant people to be with and there was no problem about me wanting to catch a few winks. It was a tight squeeze but I managed to get up on the narrow ledge and sort of wedge myself in. I covered my head with my poncho and dozed off.

The next damn thing I knew I was thrashing around on the ground all covered up with something and my head hurt like hell. My arms and legs were hemmed in like I was tied up and I had no idea where I was at or what was going on. I never felt so startled or helpless in my life as I frantically rolled around on the ground trying to get myself out of whatever it was that was smothering me. I felt like I'd woke up in a bears den!

Later, the two policemen told me I had fell off the narrow shelf headfirst and landed right on my pith helmet with my poncho wrapped tightly around my chest and head. They further said I went completely nuts and damn near kicked the guard hut apart before rolling out the front opening into the mud and rain. The two policemen said they watched in amazement as I finally got the poncho off me, looked around like I didn't know where I was at, then just sat in the mud for a while with the rain pounding down on me. Naturally I had to listen to their laughter for the rest of the shift. Fortunately my poncho covered up most of my dipped and muddy uniform when I got relieved. Of course this didn't stop the two policemen from telling everyone about the stupid Marine and his nap. The story got better with each telling. Guamanian enjoyed humor and they laughed easily. Like I said before, they were a pleasant people to be around.

61

GET THAT COVER OFF!
Former First Lieutenant Bradford Dillman, USMC

I was a skinny twenty year old when I enlisted into the U. S. Marine Corps in early 1951. Although I was born and raised in San Francisco I went into the Corps after having attended Yale University, and therefore, had the luck of the draw to find out what Parris Island, South Carolina had to offer. Like most Marines I'll never forget my D.I. if I should happen to live to a hundred. The Korean War was in full swing and Marine boot camp had been shortened to twelve weeks to get the grist to the mill as soon as possible. Nevertheless, my senior D.I. Sergeant Betterlich somehow managed to cram sixteen weeks of boot training into those twelve weeks. An unforgettable experience to say the least.

I suppose it was because I jumped instantly at ever command given during boot that caught Sergeant Betterlich's eye because much to my amazement, upon

Bradford Dillman-

graduation, I found that he had recommended that I be selected to go to Officer Candidate School, Quantico, Virginia. Low and behold! After a short boot leave I found myself in boot camp all over again! To this day I can't say for sure which was worse but if I had to absolutely grade one over the other, I'd have to say P.I. inched out OCS by a hair.

The one good thing about having gone through Parris Island first was the fact that I had an edge on the forty or so college grads whose only military experience had been ROTC. In other words I was still jumping at commands instantaneously!

After graduation from Quantico, and commissioned a second lieutenant, I spent some time as an instructor teaching combat vets how to convey their field experience to recruits. Then orders came to report to Camp Pendleton, California for staging prior to being sent overseas as a replacement.

Now at the ripe age of twenty-one, the gold bars of my rank not even tarnished yet, I soon found myself in Camp Pendleton's Tent Camp Two undergoing yet more training.

This one Sunday afternoon heavy with summer heat, the music of meadowlarks ringing in my ears, I stared out of the command post tent at the dry, brown hills that surrounded the valley Tent Camp Two was situated. All of the other tents are deserted except for the one I'm in, because I have the duty as Officer of the Day. I walked back inside the dim tents interior and sat down on a camp chair and picked up the sports section of the L.A. Times. The open tent flaps coax in a breeze from the ocean twenty miles away and I yawn as I scan the newspaper. Across from me at a field desk is my platoon sergeant Staff Sergeant Radburn. He is scowling over fitness reports and pro and con marks for the lower enlisted ranks as only a professional Marine NCO can scowl.

Staff Sergeant Radburn is fifteen years my senior, one cheek disfigured by a knife scar, a broad-shouldered six-four highly decorated Marine veteran of World War II. As a child he may have smiled once and his mother must have slapped him, because he never again repeated the mistake. It also must have taken all of his willpower to control his poorly disguised contempt behind his level gaze regarding his profound despite he held for young second lieutenants. He reminded me a lot of my drill instructor Sergeant Betterlich who also had a mean look about him.

I am thoroughly intimidated by his presence but exercise every right accorded my rank including, this day, an officer's privilege to wear his utility cap indoors since I am under arms with a holstered .45 hooked on my web pistol belt.

My vision blurs over Saturday's box scores, eyes aching for a nap, so I neither see nor hear the entrance of a young private strolling into the tent. Had I noticed him I would have instantly recognized him as just off the bus from boot camp by his buzz haircut. And I would have also noticed he had committed two serious offenses in succession. Rather than knocking on the tent frame and asking permission to enter, he simply wandered inside. Worse, he had forgotten to remove his utility cap.

But my chin is almost on my chest, barely awake, and I did not see the young private.

In a flash I'm jerked to consciousness by the loud voice of Staff Sergeant Radourn. "You stupid asshole! Get that fuckin' cap off 'fore I kick your ass from here to the front gate!"

The response of his screaming order might have been a dead heat between the private and the lieutenant getting their covers off their heads, but the private after all, is a Hollywood Marine, having taken his boot at San Diego. He had never suffered, as I had, the cruelties of a D.I. like Sergeant Bitterlich or the additional boot camp of OCS. Parris Island and Quantico carried the race by a full second. I stand trembling at attention with my cover in my hand.

Staff Sergeant Radburn is astounded by my reflexes and stares at me in wonderment.

I quickly regain a semblance of composure by examining the lining of my cap as if looking for lice or other vermin. Then, scratching my scalp vigorously I utter an order in my best command voice: "Sergeant, make a note, this tent needs to be fumigated."

The versatile actor Bradford Dillman was in the 23rd Replacement Draft for the 1st Marine Division. After release from active duty in 1953 Bradford Dillman gained admittance to the Actors Studio in 1955; among classmates in a very select group was Marilyn Monroe, whom was his good friend until her death. Dillman was cast as a psychotic killer, Artie Strauss, in Compulsion, a film based on the Leopold-Lobe "thrill killing" of 1924. He also played a Marine in In Love and War, but he is best remembered for his outstanding portrayal of the gentle Saint Francis in the film Francis of Assisi. The long time movie star lives in Santa Barbara, California, with his wife Suzy.

62

THE TWITCH-EYED PYGMY
Former Private First Class Jack E. Hoag, USMC

The first time I noticed Private Marvin Holder was when he got off a Marine six-by truck at Camp Elliott, California. He was with a group of other young Marines fresh from San Diego Marine Corps Recruit Depot. In other words "boots!" The reason I happened to notice Holder was because he was so damn short. He stood about five feet four inches with double-soled shoes on. I remember nudging the Marine next to me as the boots got off the truck, "They must be taking pygmies these days."

"These days," were mid-1942 and the boots Holder was a part of were going to help fill the ranks of the 9th Marines, a regiment in the newly formed 3rd Marine Division that would soon be shipping out to the South Pacific.

It happened that Private Holder was assigned to my platoon and some of his background eventually came to light as we continued our training phase. I learned he was sixteen years old from Charlotte, North Carolina. Not only had he lied about his age to the Marine recruiters, he'd also forged his folks name to the enlistment papers and stood on his tiptoes to pass the height requirement. It may have been a case of the recruiters turning their heads the other way since the pressure being put on them to fill huge manpower quotas at the onset of World War II. This seems even more reasonable when I learned Holder's entire boot battalion all came from North Carolina and he was in one of the Tar Heal Platoons from Charlotte who went through boot camp together. Another thing I immediately noticed about the young private was when he talked and got excited his eyes twitched and would blink rapidly. Poor Holder; I don't think half the men in the platoon knew his real name because he became forever known, as the, Twitch-Eyed Pygmy. But he didn't take much crap off anyone because of his size and would fight at the drop of a hat. Plus he was Gung Ho to a fault and on his first liberty in San Diego had a big tattoo of a bulldog put on his right bicep with the words Death Before Dishonor inked under it.

I became better acquainted with the Pygmy during our trip to New Zealand when we sailed across the pond aboard the U.S.S. Mt. Vernon, a converted luxury ship. I was the senior man in our six-man compartment and was put in charge of the other five Marines. We were billeted on what had been a State Room on "E" Deck but six swing down canvas bunks replaced the fancy furniture that no doubt had one time used up the space. It was still pretty good berthing considering the Attack Troop Transports (APA's) we later used. The Pygmy was sea sick for the entire voyage except for the last two days. Since I was in charge of the small detail I felt it my responsibility to stay with the Pygmy and try to nurse him the best I could. Other than forcing him out on deck for some fresh air once in a while he mostly stayed in his bunk and he and I would talk. During these talks I learned his father was a paint contractor back in Charlotte and that he also had an eighteen-year-old sister. He wouldn't tell anyone his sisters name because as he put it, "I ain't gonna have any horny Marines writing my sister." I asked him once why he didn't finish high school before he enlisted and how he was going to miss an important part of his life by not being able to having ever went to a Junior or Senior prom and all the other fun things boys his age should be doing. In his excited manner of blinking his eyes a mile a minute he told me he'd be way ahead of his peers back home when he talked about the war he fought and besides school was kids stuff and he was a man now. Well, for sixteen years old and having made it through boot camp and combat training. I sure as hell wasn't going to argue that point. And he was right about on thing: we sure as hell were going to war. Other than his shortness and baby face I'll have to admit he looked like a miniature man. He had the body build of a weight lifter with a narrow waist and broad shoulders. On working parties he would take off his utility jacket and T-shirt to show off his chest.

While on liberty in Auckland, New Zealand, the Pygmy picked up a large German shepherd. He claimed it was a stray and let it be known that it was his dog. On our last maneuver before we were to be sent to Guadalcanal, the Pygmy took his dog along. The biggest part of this maneuver was a sixty-mile forced march, twenty miles a day carrying full equipment. At the end of the first day the pads of the German shepherd's feet were worn off and the dogs feet were bloody pulps and couldn't walk. Our company commander gave Holder two rounds of live ammo for his carbine and ordered the dog destroyed. Several of the guys, including me, offered to do this for him, but he declined by saying it was his dog and his responsibility to put the animal out of its misery. He disappeared into the bush with the dog limping beside him. Several minutes went by and I guess we all figured he'd lost heart to do his sad duty. Then a single shot rang out. A couple of minutes later Holder was at my pup tent with tears running down his cheeks and he begged me to come with him. I followed him into the bush and found the dog laying on its side with half his lower jaw shot off. Without saying a word Holder handed me his carbine. It wasn't an easy thing for me to do either but I knew the Pygmy was depending on me. After I put the dog out of its misery I promised the little guy that I would never mention the incident to anyone, and I didn't until this writing. From that day on I became the Pygmy's confidant and the only one that he'd talk to about his inside feelings.

I liked the Pygmy and that wasn't always that easy to do with the chip on shoulder because of his slight build and his immaturity that was always putting him in hot water. However, he was always striving to prove himself. One day on Guadalcanal Holder asked me to teach him how to climb a pole with lineman's climbers. I agreed to this and then he requested we do it away from our camp as he didn't want anyone seeing him incase he failed. After several tries he finally made it to five foot off the ground. He was shaking so bad and twitching his eyes that I said to call it a day for this lesson. This is another item I've kept my mouth shut for better than fifty years.

One evening while standing in chow line I happened to notice the Pygmy having a few words with Pop Howard. Now Pop Howard was just the opposite of Holder. He was six foot three and built like Charles Atlas. Even though he was a PFC, Pop was five or six years older than the rest of the teenage Marines and had enlisted so he could be with his little brother. His job in civilian life had been with a distillery in Illinois moving whiskey barrels around all day, so this in itself tells you he was a pretty strong person. In his cocky nasal southern twang Holder tells Pop that, "The bigger they are the harder they fall old man!" Howard reached down and picked up the five foot four inch Holder by the armpits without effort and holding him at arms length shook him like a rag doll. "Listen Pygmy, the smaller they are the farther they fly!" And he tested his theory by tossing Holder a good ten feet in the air. Holder got to his feet and left the chow line. I could see he was embarrassed, but as usual, he'd brought it upon himself.

He was waiting for me in my tent when I returned from chow. It was then that I saw that the boy was more than embarrassed, he was down right broken-hearted. The first thing out of his mouth was asking me if he could move into my tent. "I don't want to be in the same tent with that Big Ox!" He said. My big brother advice to him was short: "I don't know what happened or who's right or who's wrong, but you best make amends with Pop because that Big Ox might just save your ass some day!" The day we got the word that we would be making a landing on Bougainvillea, Holder started hanging around my tent most of the day wanting to talk. Most of the conversations had to do with my talk I'd had with him aboard ship on our way to New Zealand about how he should have stayed in high school. He asked me all kinds of questions about proms and school dances and what was it like to be with a woman. With all his prior bravado about the girls in New Zealand chasing him, he admitted to me he was still a virgin and would probably go home that way. He also talked a lot about his hometown and his family but still didn't mention his sister's name. He also told me how much he missed home. I told him I also missed home and answered all his questions in a serious manner.

On our second day on Bougainvillea, Holder ran to the aid of a wounded Marine during a Japanese air raid and got burned by flaming debris caused by falling bombs. His last words to me were to thank me for being his buddy. I got word several weeks later that he died aboard the destroyer that was to take him to the naval hospital on Guadalcanal and he was buried at sea.

Now fifty-seven years later, I still think of the Twitched-Eyed Pygmy, but it is with fondness and a great deal of sadness.

Jack Hoag was 21 years old when he enlisted into the Corps on June 5, 1942. Returning to his old job as a telephone lineman with Pacific Bell after his discharge in 1945, he ended his career as an electrical engineer with 42 years of service. Jack and his wife will soon celebrate their Golden Anniversary. Their only child, a son, is an Army lieutenant colonel. He is the Historian for the 6th Marine Division Association. The Hoag's live in Santa Ana, California.

63

SHAG McNASTY
Former Private First Class Jack E. Hoag, USMC

My long time Marine buddy and comrade Shag McNasty, alias Thomas J. Dowdalls, left this earthly duty station for a better assignment with the Marine Corps Guard Company, Heaven, at 1300, 9 September 1994.

I first met Shag at Camp Elliot, California, while going through Radio School in 1942. The five six, 130 pound, green eyed, red haired Irishman was always getting himself into capers that usually ended up funnier than hell. At the same time you could get mad as all get out at Shag to the point you'd want to eliminate him, but then, he would look at you with those mischievous Leprechaun eyes, say a word or two with his particular slow drawl, and he'd have you busting a gut laughing.

So how did Shag get the name of Shag McNasty?

This name was coined by Master Technical Sergeant Lou Minor, the senior NCO at Camp Elliot. Master Tech Minor was 28 years old at the time, with eight years in the Corps, four of those years on China duty. He was a big bull of a man, over six foot three with a bellowing, gravely voice that sounded like a foghorn. He was also the youngest and meanest Master Technical Sergeant in the United States Marine Corps.

Tom got assigned to Signal Battalion right out of boot camp San Diego and was given his first liberty, a twelve-hour pass, before he had to report to Radio School the next morning. The happy go lucky Irishman did his best to make up for the long boot camp dry spell by doing more than his fair share in keeping barkeeps busy at several waterfront dives near Camp Elliott. Boy! Did he look a mess the next morning! He was so hung-over he could barley stand at attention, his khaki uniform looked like he slept in it (which he probably had,) he wasn't shaved and he reeked from the cheap booze he'd consumed the night before.

Master Tech Minor called the roll, and one by one those newly assigned to radio school would answer with a "Here Sergeant!" or "Present Sir!" That is until Top Minor called out "Dowdalls?" No answer. The sergeant tried it again: "Private Dowdalls?" Still no response. Private Milton Short who was standing next to Tom Dowdalls, and had went through boot camp with him, gave him a punch in the ribs with his elbow. As if awakened from a dream, Tom said in a weak voice, "Oh...huh..here sir."

Top Minor responded by saying, "Did I hear an answer that time? Raise your hand Dowdalls!"

Tom again had to be punched in the ribs with a whispered reminder that he was supposed to raise his hand.

"Get'cha yer ass up here Dowdalls, I want to take a look at you!" Top Minor invited.

Master Technical Sergeant Minor took one look at Tom, and said in a very loud voice. "By God you look like something the dog done dug up and put on the doorstep! In all my days I've never seen such a nasty looking, shag ass Marine in my life." The sergeant paused but a second before adding, "Boy...from this day on, you're going to be called Shag McNasty, you understand me?"

And from that day on everyone called Shag, Shag.

There are a few dozen stories I could relate about the adventures of Shag McNasty but I'm going to settle on my favorite one to share with you what took place in New Zealand. Liberty spots in Auckland, New Zealand were more or less limited to pubs and movies, or the Red Cross canteen. That is until a few of us got wind of a place called the Peter Pan Club. This club was located at the top of Queen Street and boasted a dance floor with a band. Girls from the local defense plants frequented the club and there were "Sly Grogger's" there to take care of your drink needs. (A Sly Grogger was a bootlegger who sold alcoholic beverages after the 4:00 p.m. wartime pub closure or get booze for you anytime you wanted it.) The band at the Peter Pan Club consisted of a six-string guitar, a sax player, accordion and drum. But it was music and there were girls to dance with. (Number one on the bands hit list was Deep In The Heart of Texas that they played over and over.) The girls wore no make up, had their hair tucked under scarves, and wore gray or black wool skirts with white blouses and heavy Granny Goose shoes. Ah, but they were female! Besides, the way the club was sit up all the booths had curtains you could pull across for a little privacy, and with the dim light and a few drinks, the gals all looked like move stars after a while.

This one night five of us were enjoying ourselves at the Peter Pan Club and we were on our second liter of the local wine that a Sly Grogger had sold us for fifteen American dollars. Directly across from our booth was a booth with six girls by themselves. Shag McNasty decided it was time for him to ask one of the girls to dance. The conversation went something like this:

Shag: "Pardon me miss, would you care to dance?"

Girl: "No thanks Yank, I'm kind of knocked up, you know."

Shag: "Oh I'm sorry, I didn't realize you were in that condition."

Girl: (Smiling): "I don't think you understand Yank. I got screwed today and I'm just kind of knocked up, ya know."

Shag: (Perplexed expression): "And you found out already that you're knocked up?"

Girl: "I still don't think you get it. Yeah, I got screwed today and I'm knocked up; but if you really want to jazz me, let's go ahead and get it over with while the music is playing."

Shag: "Really? Right here with all of these people looking?"

Girl: "Sure. we've got to do it before the band quits playing."

Shag: "Before the band quits playing? Ah..how are we gonna do it?"

The next thing Shag knew he was on the dance floor with the girl not quite knowing what he was supposed to do. He figured he'd really missed out on something when the girl walked off the dance floor after the dance, saying to him. "Keep your pecker up Yank!"

When Shag got back to our booth the four of us were laughing our heads off. Shag didn't take kindly to our humor and with a stern look on his face, said. "I wish you guys would quit laughing. That poor girl has a serious problem!"

We attempted to interpret the girls' conversation with Shag but I don't think he ever did catch on. Here's the translation what the girl was really saying to Shag: She was knocked up. New Zealand slang for being very tired. She got screwed: paid for a day's hard work. Jazzing is dancing and keep your pecker up means keep up your morale.

Shag eventually made sergeant and survived the war. He and I remained life-long pals and always had a good time together at our division reunions. While I'll miss seeing Shag McNasty at our reunions, I'll always have fond memories of him.

64

BY JOVE!
Former Private First Class Jack E. Hoag, USMC

It was the month of September 1943. I was working out of Headquarters, 3d Marine Division that was located in a coconut grove east of Henderson Field on Guadalcanal. At this time I was a radio operator with the 3rd Special Weapons Battalion working with patrols looking for Japanese stragglers left behind when the Nips evacuated the Canal.

Our Ordinance Marine was PFC P. P. Lamb, a tall skinny kid who loved weapons and explosives. Everyone, including officers and NCOs called PFC Lamb "PP." And we also had a mess cook who was a loud mouth Texan who thought he knew everything. Proof of his vast knowledge was to ask him. For this little tale I'll call the mess sergeant Tex.

On a Saturday morning PP asked me If I'd drive him and Tex to the river which was about two miles away as they had some supplies to deliver to a native village. I really didn't want to spend a Saturday with Tex but PP finally conned me into making the trip. We decided that another body was needed to help carry the supplies once at the river and PFC Otha W. Jones was drafted to go with us. The mess cook had his mess man load up the jeep trailer I had hitched to the headquarters jeep. The mess man put into the trailer two twenty pound packages of sugar, a fifty pound bag of flour and a half dozen ten pound cans of salt pork. I was beginning to suspect that our jaunt to the native village had more to do with wanting to barter for souvenirs than a humanitarian gesture of friendship.

During the drive to the Tenaru River the mess cook didn't keep his mouth shut for thirty seconds. He bragged how well he could speak Pigeon English, which meant there would be no problem with communicating with the natives that just happened to be the last tribe of the Solomon Island cannibals. He also talked about how he'd heard that this old cannibal chief at the village had a necklace made of human teeth and maybe he would also have a few shrunken heads he'd trade for the foodstuff we were carrying. My suspicions about the trip being a souvenir expedition was proved true by loud mouth Tex.

After arriving at the river we wadded across with the four of us carrying heavy loads. Tex pointed at a small one-man wide trail that led deep into the jungle and told us it would take us to the village. What he hadn't told us was that the village was a good four miles from the river. Plus the narrow trail went over and under dozens of fallen trees and laced with huge boulders we also had to climb over. We labored for two hours on the treacherous trail and by this time I was having unkind thoughts about my buddy PP and the stupid Texan and his quest for a necklace of human teeth and wanting some shrunken heads. At last we came to a rushing white water stream that was about a hundred feet wide. On the far bank a group of naked native boys who looked to be around ten years old were playing. What they were doing was going upstream a hundred yards or so, jumping into the river and letting the rapids sweep them downstream for a few hundred yards until they'd grab a vine, pull themselves out of the water and do it all over again. All you could see was their little black heads as they rushed by us. At least we knew the village couldn't be to far away.

We got across the stream on a log bridge and not more than fifty yards on up the trail and around a bend we came upon the village. There must have been two-dozen kids, boys and girls, running around naked. Older women with frizzy black hair, topless and wearing white skirts intermingled with half naked younger women and men wearing white sheet like Roman togas. It appeared all the younger women were pregnant or nursing a baby. They were a short people and I don't think anyone was over five feet four.

We were greeted by a handsome young man and Tex immediately went into his so-called language expertise. "Hey fella fella, me gotta good stuff here to give to chief. You fella, fella, go get chief." This was spoken in an extremely loud tone of voice and I suppose Tex thought the louder you talked the better the native would understand him.

The good-looking young native said in an accented English, English. "I am the chief."

This rather confused Tex since he'd heard the chief was an old man. "Ah—chief, me fella, fella looking for old chief fella, fella who got necklace." And he went through hand gestures trying to convey what he meant by a necklace."

"Oh, that would be my father," the young man replied in perfect English. "I'll have someone fetch him."

I don't know if Tex thought he was the best language expert in the world or what, but it didn't phase him or at least he didn't seem to notice that the young native was speaking in pretty damn good English.

"You fella, fella, go send for old chief. Me, fella, fella stay here."

The young man smiled and barked an order in his native tongue.

While PP, Otha Jones and the Texan nosed around the village, looking into all the grass huts, I stayed with the young chief, talking to him. I learned he was twenty-three years old and had three wives and was the father of fourteen children. He had been educated in Australia by Seventh Day Adventist Missionaries and thought Tex was a riot but didn't want to offend the American by pointing out he spoke perfect English. After listening to Simon (His English name) I had to laugh because I too thought it was a riot. Simon then invited me and my group to have afternoon tea with him and his wives. I had no idea what to expect but instantly thanked him and accepted his invitation.

A table under a lean-to was set with white U. S. Navy porcelain mugs and white porcelain plates with boiled yams. We were ushered into the lean-to and assigned places to sit. As we were sitting down an old leather skinned native man ambled into the lean-to. He was naked and one of the young chief's wives quickly got up and tied a loincloth around the old man. It was Simon's father, the elder chief.

Once Tex heard who the old man was he started right in with his "Me fella, fella, you fella, fella" routine and making wild hand gestures to convey to the old man that all of the loot we had brought was for the necklace of human teeth.

The old man just shook his head back and forth and said, "Me Christian."

Tex tried again to no avail and finally the young chief said in perfect English. "Today is our Sabbath and my father will not trade on the Holy Day."

I had to explain to the Texan that Saturday was the Adventist church day and he would have to come back another day if he wanted to trade for the necklace and any shrunken heads the natives might have laying around. I also told Tex that the natives were a lot smarter than he was since they knew we wouldn't cart back the food stuff we'd brought and would leave it here anyway.

The young chief smiled broadly and said. "By Jove, you certainly hit that nail on the head old bean!"

It must have finally hit Tex that the young native was talking in perfect English because his jaw dropped and he just stared at all the smiling faces.

When we departed the natives all started singing Onward Christian Soldier to send us on our way.

I never did let Tex live down the fact that the native could speak better English than he could!

65

THE LIST
Former Private First Class Jack E. Hoag, USMC

You know how it is when you're 10,000 miles away from home on some God for-saken island awaiting orders to mount out for the next island. You end up doing a lot of daydreaming what it's going to be like if you make it back home. By August of 1945 I was a part of the 6th Marine Division that had helped take Okinawa. Now the division was refitting for "the next island:" Japan! We were still on Okinawa when the "List" got started and the more the Marines of my company played with the "List," the larger it got. Now let me explain what this "List" was all about:

During breaks in our training or other free time, we'd set around and shoot the breeze on what the things we wanted most when we got back to the United States. This got so out of hand that we finally made up some rules by saying we would only put on the "List" the ten most important items as voted on. The original "List" looked something like this:

#1.: Get with an American woman (Wives and sweethearts permitted.)

#2.: Get decent bourbon or bonded whiskey at a sit down bar.

#3.: Get ice-cold American beer.

#4.: Get a large lettuce and tomato salad with all the dressing on it you want.

#5.: Get the biggest steak you can find cooked to order.

#6.: Drink all the cold milk you want.

#7.: Eat a large dish of ice cream.

#8.: Sleep all night in a fancy hotel with crisp, clean sheets.

#9.: Buy a pair of comfortable new shoes.

#10.: Visit with family and friends.

Now you've got to realize that this "List" kept changing all the time due to a lot of debating. Values changed with the only constant being finding a girl.

With the dropping of the two Atom Bombs on Japan the reality of making it back home became better than possible. Then the word was passed that there was a bunch of us who were not picked to go to Japan for the surrender and occupation duty. Those of us with over thirty months in a combat zone were authorized by the Secretary of the War Department to be shipped stateside for separation on the first available transportation. I had thirty-two months in the South Pacific! Do you think I was a happy Marine?

Ten enlisted men and four officers boarded the U.S.S. Knudison, a converted four stack destroyer from World War I, used for fast transport. This took place on 11 October 1945 in Guam. Destination? San Diego, California!

Like most Marines aboard a ship the ten enlisted men had nothing to do except sleep, shoot the breeze and wait in chow lines. We spent most of our days on the fantail of the old destroyer discussing what life would be like state side. The tin can stopped at Eniwetok for fuel and stores and no sooner had the Knudison cleared the island than the swabies came up with the scuttlebutt the ship would be putting in at Pearl Harbor, with liberty for all hands, including passengers. At first we Marines thought the swabs were just pulling our legs, trying to put over a fast one on us but damn if the ships skipper didn't pass the word on the PA that the crew and passengers would be allowed six hours ashore when we arrived at Pearl.

Since this would be the only real liberty the ten enlisted Marines had had in over thirty months, and at a civilized port as well, we immediately started working on the "List" again, revising it to make it agreeable by all of us. We were told by crew members that shoes were still rationed in the states but not at Pearl and that there was no shortage of whiskey, fresh vegetables, with milk a plenty. Also, steaks could be found and the government ran a whorehouse on Hotel Street.

It was voted unanimous that we all wanted to see the girls on Hotel Street, have a large steak with a lettuce and tomato salad with gobs of mayonnaise, drink a glass of ice-cold milk, with ice cream for dessert. Then we'd hit a bar and set down like normal human beings and drink stateside whiskey and last but not least we all wanted a pair of dress shoes to replace our scruffy boon dockers.

We dropped anchor at Pearl about 1130 on a Thursday. Liberty Call was set for 1200. With the information about Liberty Call going at noon came the scoop that anyone going on liberty had to be in a full and presentable uniform. This caused instant panic with the Marines! After thirty some odd months the khakis we wore left a little to be desired plus most of us were missing and item or two such as emblems and puss-cutters. But with the help and kindness of the Navy chiefs aboard the tin can and the Marine officers, we all ended up in uniforms of a sort and the ten Marine were in the first liberty boat heading ashore. As soon as we docked we all headed for the main gate.

At the gate we learned from the Marine standing guard that we couldn't leave the Destroyer Base without liberty cards and official Marine Corps I.D. cards. Shocked at this bit of news all ten of us started pleading our case, saying we were damn lucky to have our dog tags, let alone any other form of identification. Besides, after having spent thirty months in combat, base liberty isn't what we had in mind. The Marine gate guard thought it over for a couple of minutes then said the following. "Look fellows, if I let you through and got caught it would be my ass. But, you see that truck with a tarp on it over there by the Officers club?" And he pointed at a Chevy truck with a stick sided flat bed covered with a black tarpaulin. "The driver just delivered some supplies to the O club and is about ready to leave. I'm so used to seeing him come and go in that big truck of his that I never look in the back of it when he leaves the base. Usually, just wave him on through the gate."

Need I say that it didn't take a college graduate to figure that one out? (We never had sense enough to ask the corporal gate guard what his name was. But I'll tell you this; he was one hell of a decent Marine and I never forgot him.)

After the driver found out he had company he was nice enough to drop us off in town in front of a shoe store. The store was closed for the day! Scratch that item of the "List."

We walked down the street to a restaurant that was also closed and didn't open until 1800 which was past our liberty time. So it looked like item two on the "List" was shot.

Huh..but not to worry! On the corner of the next block a garnish neon sign proclaiming an open bar beckoned us. We made a squad rush to the joint and after making our initial frontal beach landing surrounded a large round table, which we secured and occupied. One of the guys asked the female bar hop what kind of whisky they had. She looked at us like we'd just came in from another planet, then said. "How long have you fellows been away from civilization?" She pointed a finger to the back bar and told us to take our pick. There was every brand that was distilled in the states plus from several other countries to boot. Like kids in a candy shop a round was ordered. No one wanted to be a moocher and before we left the bar each of us had bought a round of drinks.

We sort of staggered out of the bar with ten drinks each under our belts and strolled next door where a picture taking concession was located. We asked the lady in charge of the photo booth where Hotel Street was at and with a smirk she told us. Then she said why not get our pictures taken before we went to see the girls and we did. (I still have mine taken with Sam Travis, who like me, was a Pfc.)

With the directions the photo lady had given us we didn't have any problems finding the whorehouse. Actually, you couldn't miss it! There was a line of GI's that extended from the front door down the street a full block and around the corner. But since this was the number one priority on our "List," we queued up at the end of the long line with the early afternoon sun beating down upon us. While inching along we took turns in going to the corner store and returning with ten cold bottles of Primo beer. We'd learned about this was the way to wait your turn from the other guys in line. In other words standard operating procedure.

The other guys in line also told us how the place operated that we were standing in line for. Just outside the front door of the whorehouse stood an MP who would check to see if you were drunk. If declared reasonably sober, you were ushered inside where a Navy corpsman would give you a short arm inspection to make sure you weren't dripping from VD. Once you passed this inspection you could buy a chit for $2.00 and wait your turn. The girls worked in a half dozen rooms. Your chit was good for five minutes. If you couldn't meet the five-minute requirement you were issued a rain check to try it another day. (This was probably one of the better run and more efficient government operations of World War II.)

So we drank our beer, shot the shit, and moved up with the line. By the time we reached the MP it was starting to get dark. It was hard to believe we'd spent that much time in line! The MP takes one look at the ten of us and declared all of us too drunk to go any further. Boy! What a liberty we were having!

We were ordered to go back to our base or face detention till we sobered up. Naturally we all said that we'd head back right away. While walking down the street the biggest, meanest looking Marine among our group started crying. He wailed that he couldn't believe he'd stood in line at a whorehouse, exclaiming what a fool he was when in a few days he would be home with his wife. The other nine of us all felt bad too for the guy (remember, by now we were soused,) and suggested we should help him pick out a gift to take to his wife. This idea straightened out his beer jag and in our drunken, boisterous way we wandered over to the main drag and found a gift shop which we all jammed into. The big guy spotted a necklace with a plastic palm tree with Pearl Harbor embossed upon it. Just the thing for Sally Sue. A small Oriental man pushed through the throng of Marines and seeing Big John holding onto the necklace, said in broken English, "You want to buy?" Suddenly it got real quite and I don't know whom it was, but one of the guys said, "You're not going to buy that thing from a Jap are you?"

The little Oriental store keeper must have dealt with combat Marines in the past and before we knew what was going on he blew on this whistle he had around his neck on a string and it seemed within seconds the store was filled with MP's. None of us ten wanted to miss the boat home by spending time in the brig and to put it mildly, the MP's found they had their hands full. I'm afraid we left the little Oriental mans store a wreck as we "resisted" the MP's and fought our way out the back door. Once out in back was a fence that Sam and I went over which put us in a small back yard of a restaurant. I noticed that not all of our gang was making it as the MP's were hot on our tail picking us off one by one. Sam shouted to me. "Through the restaurant!!" He and I charged through the kitchen and out the front door leaving startled customers watching our hasty departure. We ran across the street and up on a railroad track which we ran along for better than a mile. I was completely spent and telling Sam I had to rest I glanced at my watch. Oh, Dear God! We were late already getting back to the ship. On top of being late neither one of us knew where in the hell we were at. Trudging down the railroad track some more we finally came to a five-foot cyclone wire fence. On the other side of the fence, off in the distance was a bunch of bright lights. Sam said it had to be some kind of a military base. We went over the fence and across a road and sure enough there was a sentry booth with a Marine gate guard. The two of us snuck past the gate guard and seeing the bay at the far end of whatever base we were on we headed that way. We found a dock and walking out on it discovered a liberty boat tied up. Sam asked the coxswain if he'd take us out to our boat. The sailor asked us what was the ships hull number we were off of? Neither Sam or me knew the hull number of the destroyer. We did tell him it was a World War I tin can that had came in around noon and was leaving tonight. The coxswain shook his head and said he was sorry but he was off the cruiser Honolulu and was waiting for his liberty party to show up. The Honolulu? I quickly told the swab that I'd spotted naval gunfire for the Honolulu on Okinawa and that she was also our control ship for most of the battle. (I was telling the truth by the way.) He said, "Well I'll be a son of a bitch! Yeah, I know where your ships at. Hop aboard and I'll take you to her."

Waiting for us aboard the destroyer were our eight buddies. The MP's had turned them over to the shore patrol, who after learning who they were took them off arrest, gave them a ride to the liberty dock and saw to it that they made it out to the destroyer.

Well, that was a pretty fancy "List" we had made up but for our first liberty we only managed to accomplish two items on it and that of course was drink some good American whiskey and a lot of cold beer!

66

CROSS'EN TH' EEQUATER
Former Private First Class Howard M. Pierce, USMC

Now I got to tell ya rite off that a lot of my buddies I served witt in that 22und Marines used ta kind da laugh at me'ans by th' way I talked. But being borne an' reered in back swamp country I doan know any utter way to tell ya dis story.

I an them other Marines from the good old USA hadn't not never been on a shipp on the pasifik oschean befor an' there was lots of tails circulating a'roun on board that big boat named Lurline that would send sum chilles up yer spine, an that's the gospel truth of it!

Som tails those dam saylors scart us with told a bout how some shipps in the past got themselves shipp-recked an' them ravanus sharks was hungrie enuff to evin snappe off yer feet for food, evin if they wuz dirty an smelled reel bad and hadnt not been washed for days at a tyme, even.

I figgered I was'a gettin the strate dope from a' round th' scuttlebuttes where them seastories was being past a' round from them saylors on the Lurline. Afta all we was all Americans an' I knowed thos swabs wouldnt lye to us Marines, who hadnt not never been on any kind of shipp at tall befor ore on any oschean befor either as fer at that goes. We wuz reely green, not jist frum vommitting be'in sea sick an' all, but frum not know'en nothin a bout shipps an' other maratyme stuff.

If'n me an' them other Marines had any sorte of idear what them saylors was a'going to re late two us befor we wen't a board that Lurline, taint know doubt in my mind we'd all put in fer shoredutie sure 'nough, an' never mine 'bout gone'n to sea on any dam shippe! Not never! Boy I shore got to haten shippe board life.

An' I'm heah to tell ya my stumach mussles titened up 'bout th' fust day outta port from Sandy ago, an' when them stormes an' hevie seas begun a'slamming into that shippe Lurline, we was all a'vommiting and a'throeing up all oveh th' place.

Now this shippe was one of them luxrey liners the gov'ment took oveh at th' start of the war so weanes wern't a'liv'en in the holds like we did later on in them thar navy troop shippes they a'called PA's. I was bunk'en up on A Deck in a cabin with eleven other fellows that was called the Gold Room. The reason I knowed this was 'cause the sign was still tacked oveh the door whar I bunked. But that thar sign was 'bout the only fancy thing left an' when we wanted to take a leak or a crap or go get a shower, we had to walk down this long passageway to get to th' head. That re minds me 'bout the time I went an shampued my hare use'n that thar pink coloured Lifebouy soap. They warent no fresh water 'cept fer drink'en so wean'ans had ta shower in salt water. I got all these globs of pink Lifebouy soap glued in my hare and couldn't get it out. I evin tried cuttin it out with my Kaybar Marine knife but that Lifebouy soap jus stuck in my hare all the way to

Samoa. What a gosh awful mess!

As our shippe got near the Eequater som dam fool decided what we needed was som praktise a'goning down them thar rope laddures they called cargoe nets. So they stop the dam shipped rite out in the middle of th' pasifik oschean and tells us to scurry down them thar rope laddures inta this little boat they had oveh the side. We all looked liked a bunch of some kind of skared demented rats clamberring down that dam cargoe net they had a'hangeing off the side of the shippe. Most of us ended up straneing ourselvs in the groinne an' we was som kinda sore aftawards. Then the dam saylors started tell'en us how they heard that most FMF Marines lose thar child maken abilatays from scurryin up and down them cargoe nets and that's why FMF Marines is a dyen breed, 'cause they can't produce a chile after being in the FMF for a year or too. What them swabs tol us was all that clim'en acktivity put two much strayne on yer groine and yer spurms gets reel week and caint swim faste 'nough to catch up with evin the slowest female eggs. This one navie corpsman tol us that it was just as well 'cause if'n we did happen to catch up with any slow eggs with our strayned spurm it would produce som not so bright kids. Then he thought 'bout what he'd tol us an' said that wouldnt be two big of a problem though 'cause they could grow up to be Marines. That didn't set two well with us but at the same time we wurried 'bout it every time weed face that bisiness of climb'en down them things.

Another thing the dum saylors would tell us was we had no choice anyhow 'cept to go down them nets 'cause how else was we supposed to get in them thar landing crafts and amfibulous tracktors and head fer shor whar we'd most likely git shot anyway from the imperiel jap Marines. We Marines didn't take two kindly to that kinda talk an I tol this one swab jus that. So what does he answer me? He says sumpthin stewpid like, "Why yew is out heah to de fend the nashun an if'n we has to ex pend all of yew, then bye golly we'll jus have ta do it!" I had a good noshion to punch him in the face. Heed had it commin, that's fer shur!

Then the swabs a'started tell'en us 'bout cross'en the internashunal dateline called the Eequater. Now I might not have been the smartest Marine on that thar shippe but I shore viewed som of what them saylors had to say with a fare amount of skeptisizm. How'n th' hell culd anyone put a line out in the middle of the pasifik oschean? They talked 'bout somthin they called "keel-haw'len" whar they'd put yew in this chair and drag yew under the shippe from one side to the other an' we better start learn'en to hold our breaths. We was all gonna have to go thru this saramony which wuld make us "Shellbaks" and they told us 'bout goldden draggins and King Nep tune an' a lot of other stuf.

So this wun day we was tol we was getten ready to cross the Eequarter and to stand bye. Now the way I had this Eequarter thing figgered out was that we was a'sail'en down hill and the halfway mark was this line they called the Eequarter. I also figgered that we was a'probably gon'en faster head'en downhill and it was go'en to be a lot slower gettin back home since we'd have to sail uphill. Anyway, I kept look'en fer that Eequarter line an' ta tell ya the truth I never did see the dam thing. That didn't keep the saylors from hav'en thar big saramony on the good ole Lurline when we Marines got made into shellbaks. We had to toe the line for this King Nep tune who was in charge of all the go'ens on and we took sum rediculus abuses which is re quired in order to be a fully flegged shellbak.

They had a Queen Nep tune there two but I doan think it was a reel woman 'cause I don't remember seeing any reel wimmen on the Lurline during the entire trip. Specially one with a mop on her head fer hare. I susspeck it was probily sum dam dum saylor wearin a faked up brassier with a couple of chickens stuffed inside to make it look reel to us. 'Course som of us didnt know for sure if they wuz reet or not. This Queen Nep tune had me go'en all over the ship a'try'en to find a bucket of steam an' just between yew an me I doan think thar is any such thing, 'cause I never could find any! Jus the same I passed the test and was given a sertificate mak'en me a Shellbak.

It seemed to me like every time we Marines somehow got comfortable on that Lurline, that sum dam saylor would find his little whissel and blow it oveh this dam loud speeker. "Whoooooooeeeee! Now Heah this, now heah this. Sweepers man yer brooms! clean sweepdown fore and aft, all decks and laddurs!" It was so loud that I wundered if they ever thought about the fact that them Japs could probbley heah that thar whissel and loud voice a thousand miles away. The fust time I heered it I thought it was a voice from heavin, sumthin like the voice of God booming down out of nowhere and all around us, everwhere! I got so that I hated that whissel so bad I used to go around the shippe a'look'en fer one of those swabs carrying one so I could toss him overboard.

A nother saylor I was ready to toss overboard wuz the one that tol me 'bout the simple an' sanitarie way to dew yer lanudery. He had me tie my dirty dungaree pants to the end of this long rope and drop it oveh the fantail. He said the oschean would clean up my britches better than any wash mashine, What he didnt tell me was how long I wuz supposed to let the dungarees to stay in the oschean a'draggen behind the shippe, so I left em hangin ovehnite to get em good and clean. The next morning I reeled in my line and all that wuz left wuz jist a little bit of a strip from the crotch with a couple of buttons still hangin on. I tell ya: befor we got to Samoa on this mizzerable cruize I had really began to hate sum of them dam saylors!

Howard told me if I messed around too much rewriting his story and editing that he'd come "look'en fer me." Therefore, I left his tale pretty much intact.

67

LIBERTY IN KOBE JAPAN
Name Withheld By Request

During August of 1951 I was up on the line north of Seoul, Korea when word was passed along for me to get my butt to the company CP. Our rifle company command post was little more than a stick in the ground near a fairly large foxhole with sheterhalves over the top of it. The skipper sees me walking up and grins. "Well sergeant, this is indeed your lucky day. Word just came in on the land line you're being rotated back to the States." The captain then shook my hand and told me to shag ass to battalion ASAP to pick up my sea bag I hadn't seen for a year and my orders home.

When I got to battalion I ran into a good buddy of mine who had also got his orders rotating him home and the two of us rode in a jeep together that took us to Inchon where we boarded a troop transport which would take us to the United States. Our sea bags went into the hold, along with the other many hundreds of guys shipping out with us. We all looked pretty cruddy in our dirty and dusty utilities and beat up boon-dockers, with leggings, but you better believe that APA was filled with a bunch of happy Marines.

The troop ship made it to Kobe, Japan the next evening and word was passed it would stay the night and all hands were authorized liberty until 0800 the next morning. Me and my buddy took off as soon as liberty call sounded and like most of the Marines aboard the ship we didn't have any money and looked as about as grungy as you could get. Who cared? We hadn't been let loose on any town or city for better than a year!

We ended up in a Japanese dance hall frequented by American G.I.'s and when the dog faces found out that the reason we looked so crappy was because we'd just arrived from Korea, they treated us like conquering heroes, which was a good thing since I said before we didn't have a dime or one yen between the two of us. The soldiers bought us round after round of Nippon beer and it wasn't too long before the two of us got feeling pretty good.

Somewhere along the line my buddy and I ended up at a Japanese hotel with two baby dolls. (Lets face it, you know that old story; after all we had not seen a decent looking woman in over twelve months.)

Around one o'clock in the morning I heard a loud pounding on the door to the room me and the josan was in. It got my instant attention. Then a shouted order was heard: "Open the door, we know you're in there!" My first thought was it was the hotel proprietor wanting his yen for the evening's entertainment and I padded to the door half naked trying to think up a BS story to tell him why I didn't have any loot. But when I opened the door who should be standing there but two of the biggest looking Army MPs I'd ever seen.

They shoved there way into the room and demanded to see my ID.

I looked at them with a blank stare for a couple of seconds then in a servile tone of voice, just knowing I was in deep shit, said, "Sir, I don't have an ID card and to tell you the truth I damn lucky to have me. I do have my dog tags though." And dangled my brass disc's from the chain around my neck for them to see.

The meanest looking to the two MPs shook his head back and forth in a negitive way, then said. "Marine, every building in his end of town is off limits unless it has a sign on it saying it's on limits. This hotel is off limits! And I don't suppose you've got a liberty pass either do you?"

I could just see me going back to the states in the brig of that APA and kissing ass once again hung my head low and said, "No sir they didn't issue us a pass when they let us off the ship."

The big, mean looking MP who had been staring at me like I was a dangerous criminal, suddenly changed the stern expression on his face. In almost a soft tone of voice, he asked. "Are you one of those Marines off that ship that just came in from Korea?"

"Yes sir, they let us all take off on liberty to grab a few beers, and..well..you know......" I trailed off.

"I tell you what buddy, you finish your business real quick like, then you and your pal down the hall get your asses out of here! We'll be standing outside to make sure, so don't screw up the break I'm giving you."

I must have said "Thank you sir" a dozen times to the Army MP sergeant. (I've always remembered him and I know he remembers me as the Marine that kissed his ass all over the place.)

The two Army MPs solved my no money problem since the girl I was with didn't say a thing when I left without paying her, nor did the man running the hotel. As it turned out it was just as well I didn't have to pay anything since the gal I had been with sure as hell paid me.

Four days later at sea, I told my buddy that had went with me to the hotel that I thought I had the clap. The old salt who'd been in Japan for its surrender and occupation and then spent three years in China, laughed his ass off, and told me I better go kiss the Navy corpsman's ass to keep it off my military record.

I did just that! I told the doc that I'd never even had a case of the crabs before, let alone whatever it was that was causing me to drip like I was now and making my balls look like baloons. The doc ran some test on me and after reviewing the results told me I shouldn't try and catch up in one night what I'd missed out on in the past year. He said I did not have VD but I did have one of the worst strains that he'd ever seen. I was given a jock strap to wear at all times and was told the problem should clear up in a few weeks.

Naturally I told my good pal what the test proved and what the cure was. The big blabbermouth told everyone aboard the damn ship about it and until reaching Treasure Island in San Francisco, I was known as Staff Sergeant Jock Strap.

To this day, when I see my old buddy from time to time, he will still occasionally refer to me as Staff Sergeant Jock Strap.

68

CHINESE ENGINEERS
Former Sergeant Paul G. Martin, USMC

I enlisted into the Marine Corps at age eighteen right out of Bayside High School, Flushing, New York. The date was February 2, 1948, and after my stint at Parris Island I received orders to report to the 2nd Marine Division, Camp Lejeune, North Carolina.

For some reason I was selected to attend a school at Camp Lejeune on Chinese Communist strategy and tactics where I learned many lessons about Mao Tze Tung and his abilities to win victories over the much larger Chinese National forces. It was an interesting course and after successfully completing the sixteen-week school I was transferred to Second Force Recon. What I went through in Recon Company training was almost as bad as boot camp but at least we were treated with a little more dignity with an occasional off base liberty thrown in.

Shortly after the Korean War broke out in June of 1950 I was handpicked by my CO for the 1st Marine Division Recon Company. By this time I was a big bruiser of a corporal and while it may sound flattering to have your commanding officer to select you for an overseas assignment, I wasn't the only one that received orders transferring them to Camp Pendleton, California. If I remember right the Corps was under 85.000 men and took a lot of 2nd Marine Division Marines to fill the empty billets of the under strength 1st Marine Division.

It wasn't long before I, along with a lot of other Marines, was sitting off Inchon, Korea. I had the dubious honor of leading the first recon patrol into Inchon prior to the major landing.

As the war progressed the recon Marines led the way up through central South Korea until reaching Seoul and beyond. When the 1st Marine Division started pushing north recon was again ahead of the infantry using motorized and foot patrols to gather information on the enemy. After the administrative landing at Wonsan, North Korea, where the Marines were greeted by Bob Hope on October 15, 1950, we recon Marines had our work cut out for us. There was a gap of eighty miles between the 8th Army heading toward North Korea's capitol of Pyongyang and the 10th Corps to the east which was inching its way up the peninsula toward the Chosin and Fusen Reservoirs. The mission of the recon Marines was to find out what was going on between this gap. We found more information than we bargained for, especially what we suspected were large organizational units of Chinese troops. There was one thing that was confusing us though. At several locations along this wide river we viewed evidence of enemy activity from our mountain perch using high-powered binoculars. We knew the unbridged river was too deep to ford yet we couldn't figure out how come we could see vehicle tracks and foot prints going right up to the river bank then reappearing on the other side. My platoon sergeant took me aside one late afternoon and said something to me along the following. "Martin, you learned about commie tactics back at Lejeune so how about putting it to use. Take a three man patrol down to the river tonight and find out how they're making it across the thing."

At dusk, me and three other recon Marines made our way down the mountain, being as quiet as we could and carrying no gear except for our carbines which would only be used as a last resort. It was a good three miles to the river but by 2300 we were in position along the riverbank. For the past half-hour we'd heard the singsong chattering of Chinese personnel along with banging and creaking of wood scraping against something. We crept closer to where the noise was coming from and in the dim light of an overcast moon viewed the damndest thing I've ever seen in my life. There not seventy-five yards from us must have been a thousand Chinese soldiers in their quilted coat uniforms lifting a bridge up by hand while standing in pontoon boats on either side of the thing. I couldn't believe my eyes! Then I thought, What in the hell are they placing it on to hold it up? That thought quickly faded from my brain-housing when I told myself, If they're smart enough to figure out how lift a bridge out in the middle of nowhere, then they're sure as hell smart enough to know how to put it on a foundation!

To this day it still amazes me to have seen that sunken bridge and how it was raised. (Later we plotted the coordinates on our battle maps where we saw the various tire tracks and footprints leading down to the river at the different locations. The Air Force and Marine air took care of the sunken bridges. Too bad they couldn't have done it at night; they would have decimated an entire Chinese Engineer Division.)

Paul Martin was honorably discharged from the Marine Corps in February 1952, He is employed with the U.S. Trust Company in New York City and resides in Brooklyn on Marine Avenue. Paul was interviewed on the History channel during September 1999 for the documentary The Korean War: Fire and Ice.

69

A BRIEF TRIP TO THE TWILIGHT ZONE
Former Band Corporal Robert G. Rakestraw, USMC

I was a member of Headquarters Company, 22nd Marines, 6th Marine Division, for the invasion of Okinawa. As a member of the regimental band it would be my job to act as a stretcher barer for wounded and also the grisly job of locating and identifying Marine dead on the battlefield and get the bodies back to graves registration. Not a pleasant mission but something that had to be done. Another thing most people don't know about the various Marine bands in combat was the fact that not only were we the primary defense security for Headquarters Company but also at night we took turns going up to the main line of resistance and fill in overnight, until replacements could be moved up to take the place of infantry casualties.

The 22nd Regimental Band was on board LST 479, traveling alone and not in convoy. This was sort of scary in its own right and the only thing I could think of, was the LST is too slow to keep up with a convoy. Although an LST's hull designation stands for Landing Ship Tank we did not have any tanks aboard the 479. We were filled to capacity however with wooden boxes of various types of ammunition, including tank and artillery shells. Any Marine who's ever been aboard the flat bottomed LST knows there is no space for troops except in the large tank well and this is where the band was at, spread out all over the boxes of ammo.

Around midnight we ran into a storm which created huge swells. The constant slap of the flat bottom of the LST on the ocean waves echoed throughout the tank deck like being inside the world's biggest drum. The steady hammering sound as we beat through the sea had most of the Marine thinking that the LST was going to shake apart. I guess you can't put on paper what it was like with the whole ship rolling, shuddering and creaking as if it would fall apart any minute. All of a sudden, a very loud thumping sound was heard by everyone which instantly startled us even more. The cargo of ammunition boxes were shifting!

With each roll of the ship, the stacks of ammo boxes, which were strapped together, would swing away from the bulkhead, then swing back and crash into the side of the ship. It took members of the band, playing a deadly game at being crushed, an hour to get four by four planks between the shifting cargo and the bulkhead. Was there a big sigh of relief? You bet there was! We onlookers even gave the guys that braved being crushed down on the deck a big applause. As far as I was concerned, they deserved medals of some sort!

Near dawn the storm subsided but swells continued to rock the boat. Since I was feeling a little queasy, I decided to take my blanket and go topside up on deck for some fresh air. I lay down on the deck and fell asleep.

During my sleep I must have dreamed a good dream because when I was awakened by the loud clear sound of chimes playing church hymns, I was so disoriented that I thought I was back home for a moment. I listened to the music half-awake while a warm sun beat down upon me. My next thought filled me with terror: I had died in my sleep and gone to heaven! My eyes snapped open and I saw that I was still aboard the LST. But where was everybody? There was not another soul in sight and I experienced an eerie feeling of dread that I was somehow aboard a ghost ship all-alone. This feeling was reinforced by the continued sound of chimed church music coming to my ears. I jumped up, asking myself, "where is everyone and why is chimes being played?" By now I was intensely curious what was going on and started walking to a side hatch on the super-structure. Suddenly the hatch swung open and two sailors came out on deck and calmly went about their duties. Although it was embarrassing to me, I went up to the two crewmen and asked: "Why are chimes playing church music?"

They both stared at me for a long second, then one of them answered. "Why it's Easter Sunday Marine and the skipper thought you guys would appreciate some peaceful music, considering where you'll be in about an hour."

With my breathing returned to normal I sat back down on the deck and let the warm sun wash over me after my brief trip to the twilight zone. I sat there for quite awhile, enjoying the sunshine, the blue sky, and the Easter music being played over the ship's loudspeaker. The sailor was right. The music was a peaceful and a welcome interlude before the hell of battle.

By mid-afternoon on April 1st, 1945, with the invasion well under way, the LST beached and we disembarked on Okinawa. It was the beginning of the last great battle of World War II, an affair of 82 days of mayhem, death and destruction.

"Rake" as Bob Rakestraw likes to be called, enlisted in the Marine Corps at Rome, Georgia in November 1942 at age 19. Parris Island molded him and Camp Lejeune put on the final touches. He also participated in the Guam and Marshal Islands campaigns. Rake married Roberta Audrey Roberts, a professional dancer in 1946. "Bobbie" (her nickname) eventually opened her own studio and taught dancing until her death in 1998. Rake states his wife installed his love for music, Ballroom and Square dancing which are his hobbies. Robert Rakestraw is a well-known and respected Georgia artist. He lives alone in Rome, the city of his birth.

70

THE BAND'S ALL HERE
Former Corporal John G. "Mac" McCullough, USMC

I was a Marine combat photographer-news correspondent for the 3rd Marine Division in January 1968 during the Tet Offensive launched by the Viet Cong and North Vietnamese Army across South Vietnam. Most of what was written by the press in those hectic days centered narrowly on three major battle situations: Khe Sanh along the DMZ where the 9th and 26th Marines fought four NVA divisions to a standstill; the battle for Hue which involved part of the 1st Marines and all of the 5th Marines; and Saigon, where admittedly, the U.S. Army and ARVN units had their hands full.

A little known and less remembered battle also took place where I just happened to be at when the Tet Offensive commenced. This was the 3rd Marine Division Headquarters (CP), located a few miles north of the port city of Da Nang.

It has been said about the Vietnam War that there was no rear. In the general sense of that statement this was essentially true because of the Viet Cong playing the roll of guerillas. In the same vein, some areas where considered much more secure than others which was the case of the 3rdMarDiv CP. Most of the twenty-one Marine infantry battalions in Vietnam were doing their fighting up and around the DMZ. Therefore, the primary security and defense for the 3rd Marine Division headquarters consisted of a reinforced company of Recon Marines, elements of the 3rd Engineer Battalion, a scattering of ARVN soldiers, and a Seabee outfit, the division Headquarters Company that included the 85 members of 3rd Marine Division band. The division band was designated as a reactionary force in reserve. (For those few who may not know what Recon Marines are, they are considered the elite of the elite, the toughest of the tough, down right lean and mean extraordinary infantrymen; in other words bad asses.)

On Tuesday morning, 30 January 1968, the 3rd Marine Division band marched smartly past the Marine Recon compound and positioned themselves on a graveled area near the huge flagpole in front of the division CP. When a field music blew To The Colors on his bugle, the band struck up the Star Spangled Banner that was the custom when morning colors was raised at the CP. After the American flag was snapping proudly on its staff and the Secure From Colors was sounded, the band marched back along the road past the Recon Marine compound and returned to their living area.

While the 3rd Marine Division band had been playing our national anthem as the flag was being raised, more than 60,000 Viet Cong and NVA troops begun an enormous surprise and coordinated offensive. The enemy attacked every important base and most cities and provincial and district capitals throughout South Vietnam. Most of the ARVN troops who were supposed to be defending these cities was absent on Tet holiday leave.

Obviously, the 3rd Marine Division CP was immediately notified of the enemy onslaught and those units around the command post were placed on one hundred percent alert. Oddly enough, no action took place near the CP during the day, although reports from Da Dang, and other towns and cities close to the CP reported heavy fighting.

That night however, the command post was attacked by what was estimated to be a reinforced regiment of the Viet Cong.

The engineers, Seabees, Headquarters Company personnel and a platoon of ARVN's were holding their own against the determined and vicious enemy attack. This did not seem true with the reinforced company of Recon Marines though. The battle raged throughout the night and four times the Recon Marines radioed for help from the reactionary force, stating they were about to be overran. And four times the 85 members of the band rushed to the Recon Marines position and helped the super Marines stabilize their perimeter. Well, what I said just then is amiss, because by the forth time the 3rd Marine Division band went to assist the Recon Marines, they didn't have 85 men remaining. Combat causalities had decimated the band to over fifty-percent, but the remaining 38 members took pride in the fact that they had helped greatly in making the enemy withdraw from the Recon Marines perimeter. At the same time there was some disgruntled remarks floating around the band area as they licked their wounds. The primary focus the band Marines talked about was the seemingly inability of Recon Marines in holding their own line and having to have the band to come to their rescue four times.

With the attack against the 3rd Marine Division CP broken, bright and early the next morning what was left of the band deployed as usual in front of their living area, unshaven, haggard looking, wearing filthy utilities and completely worn out from the nights fight. But acting as if it was a normal day the band marched past the Recon Marines compound to the parade deck to play the Star Spangled Banner as the colors was hoisted. Considering the fact that the band was now over fifty-percent under strength because of the combat attrition of the night just over, they still managed to do a decent job of sending the American flag up its staff with a stirring rendition of the national anthem. Then, almost ghost like they marched away from the flagpole, so quiet you could barely here their footfall. But when they got abreast of the Recon Marines compound, the Drum Major suddenly gave a crisp couple of orders. "Band halt! Left....face!" Then the Drum Major gave a signal with his tall gold baton and the band members brought their instruments to the ready. With another deft signal the band broke into a slow version of a song made famous my Walt Disney, from his Mouseketeer TV show. I swear you could almost hear the notes spelling out the start of the theme song: 'M....I...C...K...E...Y.............M...O...U....S...E" Then the beat picked up and the band played the entire song again in a lively fashion. And to make sure they were getting their message across to the Recon Marines, the band ended the thing by bringing their instruments down and shouted, "Mickey Mouse!"

They sung the Mickey Mouse song all the way back to their quarters.

It was reported that even Major General Rathvon McC. Tompkins, CG of the 3rd Marine Division, smiled when he heard about his band "in action."

71

THE GENERAL I KNEW
Former Private First Class Jack E. Hoag, USMC

The first time I saw Lemuel C. Shepherd, Jr., he was a full colonel, the commanding officer of the 9th Marines, the regiment I was assigned to. This meeting took place at Camp Elliott, California the summer of 1942 as I rushed back from early noon chow to relieve my pal Private Kennedy, who was standing guard for a top-secret 90mm Ack-Ack gun radar unit. I was puffing on my after lunch pipe as I hastened along, wanting to get my smoke in since we weren't allowed to smoke while standing guard. I spotted three officers coming my way and knew I had to salute them. I guess I wasn't thinking to good, because instead of just putting my pipe in my left hand I jammed it in my mouth and made my snappy salute to the three officers as I walked by. My salute was returned but I didn't get very far past the officers when one of them yelled out, "MARINE! Come back here!"

I did an about face and found myself standing tall in front of the flinty blue eyed bird colonel with silver-gray hair. He looks me straight in the eye, and said. "Son, there is nothing we officers appreciate more than a snappy salute and you gave us a first class one...." (For a newly promoted PFC, fresh out of radio school, my ego soared for a fleeting second.) Then Colonel Shepherd finished what he had to say, "........but the next time you salute an officer TAKE THAT DAMN PIPE OUT OF YOUR MOUTH!"

The next time I saw Colonel Shepherd was during the long walk the 9th Marines did from Camp Elliott to Camp Pendleton along highway 395. The colonel led his regiment walking along at the head of the column with his cane. And when we would stop every hour for a five-minute break Colonel Shepherd spent his time trooping the line checking on his "boys." He must have had an outstanding memory for faces because when he spotted me, he said, "Good to see you again son. How are you doing?"

In early January 1943, the 9th Marines, along with a battalion of the 19th Marines, C Battery, 3rd Special Weapons Battalion, and the 26th Seabees, went aboard the U.S.S. Mt. Vernon. The Mt. Vernon was the largest troop ship on the Pacific Ocean, capable of carrying 2,900 personnel and equipment. Everyday I would observe Colonel Shepherd with a Navy officer, touring the ship, The colonel would pause and talk with the enlisted men, either in groups are just one man. It got that he seemed to stumble into me all the time, even when I was chipping paint. This one day, he paused by me, and said. "Son, every time I turn around I'm running into you. I think it's about time you tell me your name." After I told him who I was he patted me on the shoulder, then walked away.

Once in New Zealand, we walked. And I mean we walked! Everyday it was a five-mile hike which soon turned into ten miles. One Sunday we walked fifteen miles to get us in shape for a twenty miler when we went to the rifle range to sight in our new M-1 rifles. Then, the granddaddy of them all came when we had a field exercise with full packs and equipment, twenty miles a day for three straight days. And just like our march from Elliott to Pendleton, Colonel Shepherd was right there with us, eating the same rations, and trooping the lines during breaks with his now famous cane. And it had become a habit that he always had a word or two for me when he'd see me.

Before we left New Zealand the 3rd Special Weapons Battalion put on a demonstration of our new weapons for the division brass. "A" Battery, with their new 40mm AA guns and directors, "B" Battery, with their new 90mm AA guns and new Marine Corps radar directors, and "C" and "D" Batteries with their half-tracks equipped with 75mm guns. I was stationed 50 yards in rear of the weapons manning radio communications with the base camp and also the airplane that would be pulling targets for the firing display. At my side was a big German shepherd the 1st Platoon of "A" Battery had acquired as a mascot. To get the exercise started, the CG of the 3rd Marine Division, Major General Charles D. Barrett, started giving a little speech. But every time the general opened his mouth the damn German shepherd began to howl. This went on for a couple of minutes until my field radio received an incoming call. When I answered like I always did, "Comm Center, PFC Hoag," the familiar voice of Colonel Shepherd came crackling back at me. "Hoag is that you? Look son, I learned a long time ago that if you want something done go to the man in charge. Keep that damn dog quiet, it's embarrassing the general." After a hasty "Aye, aye Sir!" I took off my belt and muzzled the German shepherd. (This dog later had to be shot when it couldn't walk after the pads of its feet wore off on a 60-mile hike right before we left for Guadalcanal.)

The 3rd Marine Division shipped out to Guadalcanal in July 1943. Colonel Shepherd was promoted to brigadier general and was transferred to the 1st Marine Division.

Although I didn't have the chance to see General Shepherd for quite a while, I did get word that he'd been further transferred to take over the leadership of the 1st Provisional Marine Brigade which was formed on Guadalcanal during April 1944. The brigade consisted of the newly re-formed 4th Marines and the 22nd Marines.

After Bougainvillea, many 3rd Marine Division men helped fill the ranks of the 1st Provisional Marine Brigade that was preparing for an assault landing on occupied Guam. I was among those transferred and got assigned to the 4th Marines. I was back in General Shepherd's outfit.

On May 25, we boarded ships and headed toward Guam. We landed on the 21st of July with the Marines Hymn blaring from ships loudspeakers. On the 29th, I was a part of the honor guard detail when the colors was raised at the site of the old Marine Barracks. General Shepherd gave a speech that day and when he trooped the line of the honor guard he spotted me and stopped. "It's you again Hoag. What are you doing, following me?"

In early August my outfit was dug in along the mesa just north of the airstrip. I had my radios set up and was boiling a can of green tea. I'd "liberated" the tea from a Jap supply depot we'd overran earlier in the day. The brigade chaplain, Chaplain McCorkill, came up to me and asked it I had any spare "bung-fodder." (toilet paper.) He then said, the general had the trots. I handed over a couple of packets of toilet paper and went back to brewing my tea. A short time later General Shepherd walked up to return the part of the toilet paper he hadn't used. I told the general to keep it as I had some more. Thanking me, he said, "What you boiling there Hoag?" I answered him, "Green tea sir, want a cup?" He smiled and answered, "I sure would. I haven't had any decent tea since we left New Zealand." I filled up his canteen cup and gave him half of my brick of green tea. He thanked me again, and said something about green tea being medicinal.

In the middle part of August 1944, the Marine cemetery on Guam was dedicated. I had been assigned the job of setting up the PA system and loud speakers. As I was sitting up this gear the brigade staff, accompanied by Admiral Chester Nimitz, Lieutenant General Holland M. "Howling Mad" Smith, and Major General Roy Geiger, walked up. General Shepherd came over to me, and with the other brass listening in, said, "The green tea did the trick Hoag-took care of my problem. We're waiting for Admiral Spruance. Where's your dog? Don't want him to start up again when we make the dedication." I didn't have the heart to tell him what had become of the German shepherd but the general became distracted seeing Admiral Spruance coming up, although I did hear him mention to the other officers that the comm people had a dog that didn't like officers talking as he wailed ever time an officer opened his mouth.

As anyone knowing anything about the history of the Marine Corps would tell you, after the battle for Guam we re-grouped, and with the inclusion of the last regiment formed in the war, the 29th Marines, we became the 6th Marine Division. Our division, along with the 1st and elements of the 2nd, fought the final battle of World War II, Okinawa. Major General Lemuel C. Shepherd led us through this last campaign. I only saw the general once during the battle for Okinawa before I was wounded and sent back to Guam after a stay on Saipan.

After I was discharged from the Corps in 1945 I returned to my job as a lineman for Pacific Bell in California. I suppose it was because General Shepherd had always seemed to like me that made me keep up with his career after the war. After all, it's not too may PFC's that can say they got their ass chewed out nicely for saluting with a pipe in your mouth and have a general officer remember the incident. Anyway, I was as proud as a peacock when I found out that President Harry Truman had promoted my general who had fought in World War I (where he was wounded three times) to Lieutenant General. And in 1952, when the graduate of the Virginia Military Institute was named as the Commandant of the Marine Corps, I felt as if I'd got a promotion.

I didn't see the general again until 1976, at the 6th Marine Division Association reunion held at San Diego. General Shepherd was sitting in a chair in the meeting hall with a crowd around him and I pushed through to shake his hand. I asked him if he still had the cane that he used when he walked us all over New Zealand. He looked up at me and studied my face for a long moment, then said, "You're PFC Hoag aren't you? Still smoke a pipe?" Then he told me that he'd gave his old cane to the Marine Corps museum at Quantico. Reaching down at the side of his chair he brought up another cane, silver tipped, saying, "But I've got a new one." General Shepherd spent some time talking to me, telling me how come he had to use a cane. He told me about being wounded in France during World War I and how a French doctor wanted to amputate his leg, telling him that a true patriot should be willing to give a limb in the service of his country. And that a German POW doctor had saved his leg through proper field surgery and was the one who had gave him the original cane he carried all through World War II. General

Shepherd really surprised me with his sharp as a tack memory when he asked, ""What ever happened to your dog?" I had to tell him about having to destroy the dog and he shook his head sadly. "What a shame. I always liked that mutt even though it always growled at officers."

During the last four years of the general's life, several of us 6th Marine Division vets would visit him at his La Jolla home. Sometimes two, other times three or four, would stop by on his birthday and the Marine Corps birthday and there were times in between also we'd drop by. We'd always bring him his favorite cake, German chocolate and his favorite drink, scotch. I found out while visiting with him how he had developed a fondness for German chocolate cake and scotch. It was when he was stationed in Coblinz, Germany during occupation duty after World War I, when he was a captain. He was billeted above a bakery and this was where he acquired a love for German chocolate cake. The general joked that the baker, whom he got to know pretty well along with the baker's family, never wanted for coco or flour. He went on to tell an interesting after-math to this story. In 1954, while Commandant of the Marine Corps, General Shepherd made a tour of all the consulates in Europe. Being near Coblinz, Germany, he decided to see if the bakery he had lived above was still standing and directed his driver to the street he thought it to be. There was a bakery and General Shepherd told his driver to stop and he got out of the car to take a closer look. While looking at the bakery a man in his fifties, wearing a white apron, walked across the street and said in broken English, "Captain Shepherd?" The man was the son of the other baker who had been ten years old when "Captain" Shepherd occupied the room above his father's bakery. And why did the general prefer scotch to sour mash whiskey? Being a native of Virginia, the home of American whiskey, he and a fellow cadet drank themselves sick one weekend trying to prove what true, blue Virginians they were and until World War I, just the smell of whis-key made him sick. He was introduced to scotch while in France during the first war and it didn't make him sick.

General Shepherd spoke highly of the German people but not so of the French. His feeling about the Japanese was just a tad bit lower than the French. During one of our visits with the general, a good pal of mine, Len Cotten, told the general he was being pressured to return his war trophy Japanese battle flag to Japan. General Shepherd snorted, then said, "Len, tell 'em to go to hell!"

My son, an Army officer, expressed several times a desire to meet and shake the hand of this general I was always talking about. The occasion presented itself during May 1989. General Shepherd talked to my son for better than twenty minutes, asking where he went to school, when he had been commissioned, what his current duties were, etc. And he related the old story how he'd first met me and my pipe and how he'd squared me away fast like and that I'd turned out to be a pretty good trooper and all. When we got back home my son said, "Pop, no wonder you admire General Shepherd so much. He talked to me like I was a part of his staff. I should have gone Marine instead of Army."

On 10 November 1989, General Shepherd insisted we take the bottle of scotch we'd brought him back with us, saying, "Give the boys in the division a taste of it." We did better than that. It became the 6th Marine Division Association's Last Man's Bottle. We auction it off at every reunion and the proceeds go to the General Lemuel C. Shepherd, Jr., scholarship fund at VMI.

We took the bottle of scotch with its custom built oak protection container to General Shepherd on February 10, 1990, his 94th birthday, to show it to him. He was very pleased with what we had done and what we were doing with the money that came from it.

General Shepherd died soon after this birthday visit. His passing effected me more than the death of my own father which I've questioned myself many times about. His last words to me, on that last birthday, were, "Jack, you remember now, not to salute any officers with your pipe in your mouth." I think this comment is part of the answer why I was so distraught when he died. Although a wide gulf separated our military positions—general, PFC; we were still comrades in arms and fought the same war. We had both heard the sounds of battle, the cries of the wounded, and the silence of death. This made us closer somehow, than a father, son relationship. I will never forget my general!

72

THE HOUSE OF A THOUSAND TITS
First Sergeant Daniel P. Scarborough, USMC(Ret.)

During the Korean War I was the Gunnery Sergeant of the Marine Detachment aboard the U.S.S. Rochester (CA-124). The World War II fast cruiser provided naval gunfire support for our front line troops and we would also make raids in North Korea. Like all seagoing Marine Detachments we manned a couple of five-inch guns when naval gunfire was requested.

Obviously, our duty was one hell of a lot better than our brethren ashore with the 1st Marine Division. We ate hot chow three times a day and sacked out in comfortable bucks with sheets and blankets. Plus we didn't get shot at much. In addition, we did not spend all of our time on station in Korean waters and that is what this story is about.

Shortly after Christmas of 1952, the Rochester received orders from the commander of the U.S. Pacific Fleet that the cruiser would immediately cease its current war mission and proceed directly to French Indo-China for a goodwill tour. This was right in the middle of France's war against the communist Vietnamese Viet Minh. Scuttlebutt around the ship talked about that we were being sent to Indo-China as a show of support and to help boost the morale of the French armed forces there.

We made good time and on New Years eve day, 31 December 1952, the Rochester was making its way up the Saigon river toward the capitol city of Saigon. At that time the Rochester was the largest ship to ever go up river to Saigon. We tied up in time for liberty to be called and sailors and Marines rushed off the ship to celebrate New Years Eve. To insure that Rochester's layover at this port of call would be a "friendly" goodwill visit, I was put in charge of a shore patrol party of Marines and sailors.

I teamed up with a 1st Class Master at Arms and the two of us walked the port streets of Saigon, keeping our eyes on the liberty troops as well as our shore-patrolmen.

While we strolled along the busy streets making our rounds we happened to come across this structure with high wooden walls. It reminded me of an old American western fort with its one sally-port gate and what looked like interspaced guard towers. Curious, I told my sidekick for us to go take a look-see. The gate had two uniformed Vietnamese men standing out front who appeared to be policemen. When me and the 1st Class walked up the two Vietnamese smiled, nodded their heads in a friendly fashion and gave us a greeting of some kind in their language. We returned their greeting and I tried to get across to them that I was wanting to know what the fort like structure was that they were apparently standing gate guard. There was a large sign over the gate which I kept pointing to but the language barrier was too great. About that time a French Foreign Legionnaire came walking out of the gate and I asked, "Hey pal, can you speak English?"

The Legionnaire answered in a thick German accent. "Ja I sprocken a little."

So I asked the fellow what was the scoop with the place and what did the sign over the gate read?

In a serious tone of voice he said the sign roughly translated in English to "A house of a thousand tits." Then he asked us if we wanted to go inside and take a look around. What the soldier had said whetted my curiosity and I told him to lead the way.

Inside the gate on the right was a French police station and on the other side was a bar and dance hall. I would guess that the compound took up two acres and all along the high walls were lean-to's with women in them. Our big Legionnaire spotted a buddy and yelled out to him in rapid French. The other Legionnaire came up, eyeing us curiously. This fellow was also a big brute with a scar running clear across his face from ear to chin. The first Legionnaire conversed with scar face in French for a minute and the guy smiled and uttered an "Ah..yes." Then sticking out his hand to me, he said in perfect English, "My names Smith and Otto here says you gents must be off that American cruiser in the river."

I said that was correct and told him I was a Marine gunnery sergeant, and also introduced the sailor. The English speaking Legionnaire's face lit up, and he said, "Ah Marines...you are almost like the Legion huh?"

I couldn't argue with that except to tell him that the United States Marines were probably better trained and better disciplined. He took that as a good humored dig and said something to the big kraut which had him shaking our hands too and slapping us on our backs, saying the words, "Marines goot!" Damn right! I was happy to hear the French Foreign Legion knew it!

Smith (no doubt in my mind that wasn't his real name and he appeared to be an Englishman.) went on to tell us that there were roughly five hundred women in the compound, thus, the name, the house of a thousand tits. He went on to explain when the French police arrested a woman and she couldn't pay her fine, she was confined to this place until she could earn her release.

The sailor and I shook our heads in amazement, thinking how great this was for the French armed forces to have a ready-made place to go to for fun and games of a sexual nature. It was damn sure the biggest whorehouse I ever saw!

We talked with Smith for another twenty minutes and he told us his father was English and he'd joined the Legion in North Africa right after World War II had ended. With his swarthy looks I suspected he had some Arab blood in his veins also.

Anyway, I assigned a couple of shore patrol teams to patrol the place from the outside. This didn't stop the gals from crowding around the gate and grabbing at my lads in the crotch. Interesting duty to say the least.

The only other significant event that took place this night happened at midnight. It was the first (and only) time I was kissed by a man. As I was making my way through this dance hall this French sailor grabbed me and kissed me on each cheek to celebrate the New Year.

First Sergeant Dan, a native of Casper, Wyoming now calls Roberts, Idaho home. He enlisted into the Corps at age 18 in January 1942. He was wounded on Okinawa in WW II and again in Vietnam. Besides his two Purple Hearts and a slew of other ribbons, he also holds the Distinguished Marksman Badge. After his 1968 Marine retirement Dan became a correctional officer at San Quentin Prison. He says his 20 years there is a sea story in it's own right. He and his wife Donna now take it easy and enjoy their 11 grandchildren their two daughters produced. And also four great-grandchildren.

73

COMBAT'S GRIM HUMOR
Former Corporal William Pierce, USMC

I enlisted into the U.S. Marine Corps in July 1943 while attending Missouri University. Took my "Boot" at San Diego and completed infantry training at Camp Pendleton. Eventually I was aboard a troop ship filled with replacements to fill the depleted ranks of the 3rd Marine Division that was regrouping on Guam after its horrendous campaign there. After being assigned to Baker Company, 1st Battalion, 21st Marines as a rifleman, I spent the next several months on jungle patrols and going through field training for the next battle. Although organized resistance was over we still found plenty of Japanese soldiers and naval personnel to keep us busy.

During these patrols looking for Jap stragglers I observed a combat custom that is probably as old as warfare itself: the souvenir craze. It didn't make any difference what your rank was, it seemed everyone was caught up in wanting a war souvenir to send home. Any enemy soldier, dead or alive, gave up everything equipment wise he may have had on him. Prized finds consisted of personal battle flags, sabers, pistols, rifles, bayonets and binoculars. But the craze also included uniform insignia, caps, other parts of the uniform, and sometimes....a lot more.

It had not taken Marines long to discover that Japanese soldiers had a lot of gold teeth and for some, this became a coveted prize.

One incident gave the members of my platoon a good laugh. We went though a minor skirmish which resulted in no casualties among our outfit but we did kill two Japs. This particular platoon souvenir hound was the first to come across one of the enemy dead. The Jap's mouth was slightly open and there glistened a prominent gold front tooth. The fanatic used the handle of his bayonet to knock out the gold tooth but when it came loose it fell down the dead Jap's throat. So here's this idiot cussing like a mad man shaking the dead soldier upside down trying to dislodge the gold tooth. He never did get the tooth and you could hear him bitching about it for the next week. Naturally we ribbed him and this one Marine said, "Why didn't you just slit his throat open, hell he was already dead and he sure wouldn't have felt it?" In all seriousness, the tooth collector answered, "You know...I didn't think about that!"

We had this other fellow in the platoon named Jack who had been with the outfit through two other campaigns before landing on Guam during the amphibious assault which began on July 21, 1944. Jack could best be described as being just a tad "Asiatic" which meant he had the thousand yard stare of having seen and done to much combat. He was the only guy in our platoon who went on patrol with his bayonet attached to his M-1 rifle; his sunken eyes darting everywhere the entire time and as about as jumpy as a person could get.

One day at our tent camp the word was passed we were going to have an inspection by our battalion commander, with his usual array of staff which included the battalion doctor.

When the inspecting group of officers crowded into our pyramid tent to look around to see how we were living, one of them spotted this gallon glass jar full of brown liquid under Jack's cot. No doubt thinking he had discovered some home made raisin Jack or whiskey of some sort, the major asked in an authoritative tone of voice, "Who's bunk is this?"

Jack spoke up. "That's my rack sir."

The major reached down and picked up the gallon jar and noticed quite a few curled up brownish objects floating around inside it. By now the battalion lieutenant colonel and some of the other officers was staring at the jar also. Looking from the jar to Jack, the major then asked. "What have you got in here, apricots? You making a little home brew are you?"

"Oh, no sir," Jack replied. "Those are my Jap ears."

A hush fell over the inspecting officers.

The battalion doctor stepped forward and took the jug from the major and peered at it. After a few seconds the doctor said, "Yep..those are ears sure as shooting."

The inspecting party quickly left our tent and we could overhear some excited conversation out the front flap, although we couldn't tell what was being said.

After a couple of minutes the Navy doctor came back into the tent and told Jack to pack his gear and come with him.

The next day Jack was shipped out to a rear area to start his trip back to the United States.

We used to laugh at Jack and his stupid jar of ears, but now, instead of laughing, we envied him. He found a way to get home.

The 1st Battalion, 21st Marines tent area on Guam was set up in a coconut grove, surrounded by jungle. We had to maintain a twenty-four hour guard around our perimeter because un-captured Japs would try and slip into camp at night looking for food. For us greenhorns this sentry duty was a very nervous experience. For anyone who has spent time in the jungle you will remember you see and hear a lot of things that may or may not be real.

Even though it was a little scary to be assigned guard duty this one buddy of mine named Ed was always more nervous than the rest of us.

Being a typical teenager I used to play this cruel trick on Ed at night when he would come to relieve me on post. I could hear him and the corporal of the guard coming down the trail a hundred yards away and I knew the corporal of the guard would send Ed on ahead to make the relief. I would get behind a tree and let Ed walk past me, then I'd flip the safety off my M-1, which made a loud, distinct "Click!" I must have done this to Ed a half-dozen times and I got him every time I did it. He would freeze and yell out, "Bill, it's me Ed, your relief!" I wouldn't answer him at first and let him sweat it. When I would step out from behind my tree, Ed's eyes were always as round as saucers and he'd always say, "You promised not to do that again Bill!" And the corporal of the guard usually always had the same thing to say also. "Pierce, he's gonna shoot your ass off one of these nights!" I guess our sense of humor got weird under combat conditions.

While on Guam we were issued two cans of warm beer twice a week if it was available. To maintain control over us in our tent camp area we were not allowed to save more than a weeks allowance. Marines at this time were not famous for saving their beer anyway so the idea of stashing four cans of beer for a mild buzz didn't appeal to anyone that I knew of. Besides, anyone wanting more beer, all they had to do was hitchhike over to one of the U.S. Navy camps on a Saturday and they could buy all the beer they wanted in the swabies slop-chute. (The regulations for the deck-apes and Seabees were glaringly apparent as being quite different than for the Gyrenes.)

One Saturday, several of us from the platoon went to this Navy camp about five miles from the coconut grove to enjoy a few swabies beers. Like everything else the Navy had, their slop-chute met the standards of being a first class operation with some effort put into the place to keep up the sailor's morale. It was in a large Quonset hut with real tables and chairs and even boasted a bar. The five of us bought our brew and sat around a big round table to shoot the bull and watch the half-drunk sailors make asses of themselves stacking beer cans on tables until they toppled over with a loud crash of tin on concrete. At this one table next to us this young seaman had his pet monkey with him he'd acquired in the Philippines. The swab was pouring beer out on the table and the monkey was lapping it up as fast as he poured. It wasn't long before the monkey was drunker than a skunk. It was a wild sight! The monkey staggered all over the table then ran up and down the floor, falling and tripping, clearing cans off tables as it went while baring its teeth in a dumb grin and chattering away the whole time. It was hilarious. Finally the poor animal fell over, passed out. The young seaman retrieved his pet and put it on his table to let the monkey sleep it off. I leaned over and asked the sailor a question. "How long will he be out?"

"Oh, he'll sleep the night through now," the sailor answered. "But no one, including me can get near him in the morning, 'cause he'll have one hell of a hangover and will bite anyone who gets close to him."

Like all good things in life, sooner or later they must come to an end. Our days of mop up patrols and training came to an abrupt end on Guam and we were told to ready ourselves for immediate embarkation.

The 21st Marines loaded up on troop transport ships (APA's) in early February 1945. Destination? Iwo Jima!

We brought along our grim sense of humor with us.

After a couple of island campaigns the average Marine got used to seeing horribly wounded and maimed men and being witness to the equally horrible deaths of so many around them. A certain callous disregard for life seemed to take over in a Marines mind with the exception of seeing a close buddy badly hurt or killed. Enemy dead seldom brought forth any emotion of sadness and to the contrary, many situations created a moment of battlefield humor.

One such incident happened to me and members of my rifle platoon during the battle for Iwo Jima. Members of the platoon spotted a Jap soldier hiding behind a small rock formation he was using for concealment. Since we didn't know if there were other enemy soldiers in this gully behind this Jap, we ruled out a flanking movement and called up the platoon's bazooka man. He got his stovepipe aimed in the right direction and let loose with a round. It was a direct hit as the missile exploded right on the rock formation. Large hunks of rock and coral went flying up in every direction and one of our guys shouted, "Hey, look at that."

Among the rock and coral going up in the air was a Japanese helmet. It flew up a good thirty feet before coming back down with a resounding Thud! We cautiously moved forward to the destroyed position and found the crumpled body of the Jap soldier. The body didn't have a head! For a second we surmised the bazooka man had hit the Jap right in the head with his shot. That is until one of the guys came walking up with a big grin on his face carrying the helmet we had seen flying through the air. The enemy soldiers head was still inside the helmet with the chinstrap tied in place.

The rather short, intense combat common to island hopping battles in World War II can do strange things to the men involved. On Iwo Jima the Marines fought continuously in savage combat for twenty-six straight days and nights. Near the end of the Iwo fighting I had received a field promotion to corporal and during the last two weeks of the campaign I was an acting second lieutenant, having taken over the command of my platoon. About all of our officers up to the rank of major had become causalities, wounded or killed in action. We only had one officer left in B Company, a second lieutenant who was now the company commander.

Most of the guys I had landed with on 21 February when we had been called in from floating reserve to take Airfield #2, were gone. My platoon now was manned mostly by raw recruits, fresh from boot camp, undergoing their baptism of fire. They performed well, but many of them were far beyond that degree of being called nervous. Some were totally scatterbrained!

I had this one kid in my platoon who was just past his seventeenth birthday. During his first firefight I saw him shooting his carbine straight up in the air with his eyes closed! Then, to top this off, a few days later after another fire-fight, he's got powder burns on his throat that are so bad that it has caused black tattooing. No wounds, just the deep imbedded burns. From firing his own carbine! Unbelievable! I asked him what in the hell was he doing, laying his neck across the breech when he fired his weapon? He just stared at me, not comprehending the question. But the stunt that took the cake happened during a night attack several nights later. Under the flickering light of illumination parachute flares I could see him throwing hand grenades one right after the other. The thing that caught my attention was no follow-up explosions. I knew we couldn't have that many dud grenades and went over to him. Sure enough; he was so scared he had forgotten to pull the pins on the grenades. I had a hard time getting a foxhole partner for him after that.

Near the end of the battle for Iwo, my platoon was dug in on line just below a cliff not far from the ocean at the northern tip. This very dark night with no moon or stars shining, it was so quiet you could almost hear your heart beat.

All of a sudden a metallic clanking sound was heard directly in front of our lines. We had no idea what in the hell it was, nor could we see anything. Just this steady, clang, clang. clang. I radioed our mortar section and told them to send up a flare. When the round popped open high in front of us, caught in the white glare was a lone Jap soldier. The flare obviously had startled him because like a deer caught in the beam of a head-light he froze, standing straight up. What a target! Not more than fifty yards from our position and not moving. The entire platoon immediately opened fire on him.

At daylight we moved out and found his body. He had been carrying a dozen water canteens, which like him, was riddled with bullet holes. Now we knew what the odd noise from the night before had been. Apparently the Japanese soldier had volunteered to go through our lines to get water for his unit who were hiding in some nearby caves. Seeing his body laying there gave us time for pause and a reflection that courage was a common virtue on both sides of the lines. In our own crude way we offered this warrior a salute of respect by not laughing at the way he had died.

Bill Pierce returned to his home state of Indiana after the war and finished his education on the GI Bill. He then went to work in his family's lumber and ready mix concrete business for 25 years. After the business was sold Bill became the Assistant Director of the Physical Plant at Valparaiso University and retired from that position. Bill is active with the Marine Corps League and lives in Merrillville, Indiana.

74

LOOK ACE—THEY'RE OURS!
Former Corporal William R. Galati, USMC

The story I'm going to tell I didn't see first hand, but a good pal of mine, whom I'll leave unnamed, swears by the Almighty that the following incident took place in Korea.

As I understand it, the last units of the 1st Marine Division was loading aboard APA's and AKA's at Inchon during February 1954, which would take them back to Camp Pendleton, California via San Francisco and San Diego.

As any Marine will tell you, garrison equipment is precious in the Corps and working parties were making sure that all gear belonging to Marine units were identified so every tent peg would go out on the ships.

It gets dark early at Inchon during February plus a light, wet snow was falling. Just at dusk a convoy of military vehicles pulled onto the dock area and yelling Marines got them staged in groups so they could be lifted aboard this AKA. There were about fifteen six-by trucks, a dozen weapons carriers and ten jeeps.

Even with the light coating of wet snow on the various rolling stock it was very noticeable that all of the vehicles were pretty well beat up, some of them with crushed fenders, others with obvious bullet holes in windows and side paneling. And another thing was also noticeable. Even with the snow covering, the trucks, weapons carriers and jeeps you could plainly decipher they were not the traditional Marine green. Some of them were painted a hasty dirty white, while others bore a sick looking greenish-black tint and none of the paint jobs were done by professional motor transport painters. But the majority of the vehicles had been left with the original color with no effort at disguise, except all of the unit marking had been covered over with slaps of white or black paint and some bore crudely hand painted numbers or symbols over where the old unit markings had be at. The most startling feature all the vehicles shared was white, green or black paint covering a portion of the door panels, along with front and rear panels. Even this attempt to cover up what laid underneath wasn't that successful as the outline of a star could be noticed on most of the military vehicles anyway. And of course, the olive green paint shown like a neon sign. They were all U.S. Army vehicles.

This fact wasn't lost on the major in charge of Army MP's that guarded the port facility.

This Army major, along with a contingent of his MP's effectively put a stop to all the work going on in preparing the vehicles for loading aboard the AKA. In a gruff tone of voice the major, said. "Who's in charge here?"

A raggedy ass looking Marine captain in dirty utilities pushed through the crowd, saying, "I am."

"Those are Army trucks and weapons carriers and jeeps. You can't load those on your ship!" The huffy major retorted.

"They ain't now." Shot back the salty looking captain.

"They ain't now what?" The major asked.

"They ain't Army vehicles no more, they're Marine vehicles."

All but sputtering, the Army major, said, "Whatta ya mean Marine vehicles, you can clearly see the Army markings on them! Your people have stolen these vehicles and you're damn well not going to take them out of Korea!"

"Look ace, I told ya they're ours." The Marine officer said.

Before the Marine captain could fire off another broadside at the snotty major, an Army one star general joined the melee and asked what in the hell was going on.

A hush feel over the group of Marines and Army MP's as the major stuttered through an explanation to the brigadier general. He ended his remarks to the general by saying, "Sir, you can clearly see that those vehicles are Army property."

The general turned to the Marine captain. "Well how about it son. What are the Marines doing with this rag-tag gypsy circus that at one time was obviously U.S. Army?"

"Sir, I'll give it to you straight, with no disrespect intended." The Marine officer replied.

With a nod of his head the general said, "Go ahead son."

"Sir, these vehicles were found abandoned at different locations up around the Chosin and Fusen Reservoir's in late November and early December 1950 by the units of the Fifth and Seventh Marines. Some of 'em had been hit by enemy fire and others driven into ditches, but most of them were just left in the middle of a road and I guess you can sort of say the Marines commandeered them. Got 'em all back in running order and we used them for a while then put 'em under wraps after things got settled down after the pull back from North Korea. We figure they belong to us now."

The Army general was quite for a minute or so, then he looked up at the Marine captain. "Okay son, they're yours, go ahead and load them."

The MP major almost lost it. "But general...they belong to the Army!"

"Yeah, and if the Army really wanted them badly enough, they would have maintained ownership of them at the time, wouldn't they have Major?" And the general turned on his heel and left the smiling Marines who went back to work loading "their" vehicles.

Bill Galati was from Southold, New York. He served in Korea with the 1st Marine Division Recon Company. Prior to his untimely death on 10 June 1999, Bill had been active in the 1st Marine Division Association. He sent in this story two months before he died.

75

FUN IN TJ
Former Sergeant Russell L. Eaglin, USMC

Like a lot of teenage Marines stationed in southern California in the 1960's, I spent a share of liberty time sowing the ole wild oats south of the border in good old Tijuana, Mexico. It was not that Marines were overly fond of TJ, as Tijuana was flippantly called; as matter of fact quite to the contrary. What it boiled down to was the age-old story for young Marines on their way to combat. We were old enough to fight for our country, but not old enough to drink in bars in our country. The various commands in the Marine Corps which were located in southern California frowned on its personnel going to TJ but with the knowledge that you can't keep 'em down on the farm forever, cautioned all hands to never travel south of the border alone and to be damn careful how you conducted yourself because the TJ policia had the reputation of doing its best to separate a gringo serviceman from his gringo dollars.

Most of us had heard the horror stories of Marines getting mugged and worse, getting tossed into the Tijuana jail where an individual sweated out an unpredictable fate.

But like all good Marines, the guys I hung around with just knew they could take care of themselves and getting locked up happened to others, not them.

So, it came to pass, in early 1968, that on one of those lonely weekends where you didn't want to stay aboard the base and think about Vietnam or how homesick you was, that several of us took the San Diego bus south to the border.

After paying our respects to a half dozen of our favorite watering holes half the group decided they wanted some chow but I opted to stay with two buddies who wanted to visit a couple of more clubs. PFC Thomas J. Londe (naturally called "TJ") and PFC Ron Deck, with me tagging along headed to the Boston Club. We had a couple of beers and watched the hourly "entertainment." (Non-Marine reading this don't confuse TJ nightclub entertainment with anything you may have seen in the United States and that includes strip bars. Stag Show voyeurism may be a better phrase.) Anyhow, after watching the Mexican guys and gals do their thing on the small stage the three of us decided to move on to another club around the corner.

When we walked out of the door we paused for a moment to get our bearings and Deck clears his throat and casually spits in the gutter.

This big built Mexican jumps out of the driver's seat of a taxi parked at the curb, runs up to Ron Deck, and yells. "You under arrest!"

Now Deck wasn't a small man and he pushes the Mexican away from him saying, "Who'n the hell do you think you are?"

The Mexican flashes a tin star and says, "Tijuana policia, put your hands on car."

Me and Londe stare dumbfounded as the taxicab cop spread-eagled Ron Deck and frisks him.

Both TJ and I start raising hell. I mouthed off, "How in the hell do we know you're really a cop?"

By now the big Mexican has got Deck handcuffed and he turns to me, pointing a finger. "You find out reel queek if you no shut mouth and mind own business. Say one word and you also go to jail!"

We watched helplessly as our buddy is hauled off to jail in a Tijuana taxicab policia car.

The Tijuana jail was only a few blocks from where we were at so we quickly made our way to the slammer still trying to figure out what Deck had done.

The jail was a peeling stuccoed pukish green painted sprawling building with a large lobby. TJ and I milled around outside the front door trying to get up the nerve to walk into the place but was to scared to do so. We could see Deck sitting in a straight back chair along with about a half-dozen dirty looking Mexicans against this one wall. I guess we waited outside like that for a good forty-five minutes, watching people coming and going, until we noticed that Deck was no longer sitting in the chair. The other Mexicans were gone also.

The fact that we could no longer see our buddy gave us the resolve to enter the lobby area of the jail and talk to the desk sergeant. This fat slob took his sweet time but finally let us know that Ron Deck had been arrested for spitting on the sidewalk and it would take $75. to bail him out.

It might as well been $750., because neither TJ or I had that kind of money; I mean after all, we were both PFC's. (That brings up another point. Besides not being allowed to have a beer as a teenager while wearing a military uniform, our fellow citizens paid their young warriors damn little to defend the country.)

Feeling dejected the two of us sulked back outside. We put our brain housing in full gear and after careful deliberation and good Marine planning, it was decided that TJ would return to base and raise the $75. and that I would stay behind to insure that the Tijuana policia didn't move Deck to "never-never land." TJ immediately headed to the border to catch a bus back to San Diego while I stood guard out in front of the pukish green jail.

After a couple of hours passed I began to get concerned about Deck's welfare. I snooped and pooped around the large jail looking into as many ground floor windows I could find in an effort to locate Ron with no luck. Now I was really worried.

I gazed at the way the jail was built with an intent stare. It sort of reminded me the way school buildings and libraries were built back in my hometown of Brownsburg, Indiana, with the layered bricks and small ledges found at various levels. The more I looked at the jail the more convinced I became that the damn thing could be climbed. So this young Marine decided to climb up the side of the jail and look in the higher windows to find Marine Deck!

I made my way up one side of the building knocking loose stucco off which fell to the alley below me. After peeking into a couple of windows I still hadn't spotted Deck. I inched my way toward a far window near the end of the building on the second floor and it seemed to take me forever to reach it. This time when I peered into the dirty window I saw that I was looking down onto a filthy dirt floor with tall cage like bars surrounding it. It must have been a holding area of some kind since it was filled up with better than a hundred milling people. Most of the men in the pigsty pit were Mexicans but I spotted a few Americans also. And finally, I saw Ron Deck. He was alive and as about as well as could be expected considering all the drunks and whatever else he was herded in with.

Great! I had done my job! Accomplished my mission of having located my pal and ensured he hadn't been carted off to places unknown. To top off my recon mission, and much to Deck's startled amazement, I managed to get his attention, and flash him an Okay sign. He smiled a sickly smile and nodded his head. At least he had the knowledge his buddies hadn't deserted him.

It was at this time that things got real interesting. Just below my second story perch where I was hanging on the side of the jail wall, a real policia car entered the narrow alley. This was not a taxicab cop car but a true blue official looking vehicle with lights, decals and all. The car slowly made its way up the alley and parked right under me. By now, I was having trouble breathing and if there was any lingering intoxication from my previous bar hopping, let me tell you I was stone sober when that Tijuana policia car came to a halt. And the two cops that got out of the car were not dressed like cab drivers either. They almost looked like Mexican bandits with the bandoleers of ammo strapped across their chest, and the shotguns they carried made my eyes grow wide. My short, young Marine life began flashing before my eyes with visions of the policia finding me hanging onto the side of their jail. I knew there would be no time for explanations; they would shoot me on sight! Not a good feeling.

Then of all things the two of them unzipped their pants and began taking a leak on the side of the jail. I must have been shaking like a leaf because a small piece of stucco came floating down between the two of them. One cop said something in Spanish and casually glanced up. How he didn't spot me will remain one of the mysteries of my life. When they finished their job, the two of them got back into the policia car and drove on.

Boy, did those two cops miss the arrest of their careers! I wonder if I could have made a citizens arrest for them pissing on the jail? I can imagine what the fine for that would have been!

TJ returned a few hours later with enough money to bail out Ron Deck. True to the traditions of the Corps, we did not leave one of our own behind. The three of us got on the next bus back to San Diego and we made it in time for muster at MCRD where we were going through Comm School.

Oh, by the way—we decided San Diego liberty was a lot safer from then on, and less costly.

After his honorable discharge from the Marine Corps in June 1970, Russ Eaglin immediately found employment with the Naval Avionics Facility Indianapolis, where his Marine schooling in radar was put to use. NAFI eventually evolved into the Naval Air Warfare Center Indianapolis and Russ retired as a Project Manager in 1996. He is now in real estate. Eaglin is married to Valerie and they have four children, three daughters and one son. Russ enjoys scuba diving and woodworking. He is also the Legislative Officer for the Indianapolis Marine Corps League and devotes much time as a drill instructor with the Central Indiana Young Marines.

76

WAR ZONE RATIONING
Former Sergeant Russell L. Eaglin, USMC

In late 1968, after the Tet Offensive where my outfit, 2nd Battalion, 26th Marines, was part of the Khe Sahn siege, we spent a lot of time at Con Thien on the DMZ. The North Vietnamese Army was still in a pissed off mood because of the ass kicking we'd gave them at Khe Sahn and it seemed to us Marines that the enemy made an extra effort to try and punish us when their intelligence told them where the 26th Marines were located. At least this seemed to be the case that October and November of 1968 when the NVA threw about everything they had at us while we defended Con Thien.

Somewhere along the chain of command it was decided that we'd taken enough lumps after this one particularly ferocious battle and my battalion was ordered back to Dong Ha for rest and refitting, to include replacements to fill our depleted ranks.

The monsoon was upon us and this in itself was enough to drive you nuts. It was still extremely hot at times but with the constant drizzle coupled with full blown cloud burst occasionally which was followed by a chilling wind, we were about as miserable as you could get. There was just no way to get completely dry and this, along with amount of causalities we had taken, had everyone in a foul mood and low morale.

To add to my own low morale, the first few days back at Dong Ha, I had to set in this dank comm tent with the wind howling and help list all the names of our KIAs, MIA's and WIA's from our last encounter with the enemy at Con Thien. It was one of those times where I wanted to go and hide someplace to put it all out of my mind some how but at the same time knew I couldn't do it.

What I really wanted to do was to find a case of beer to at least temporally erase the nightmare I was going through. I don't think I had a cold beer the entire time I was in the Nam but that didn't bother me as by now I was used to drinking it warm. I believe thinking about getting some beer saved my sanity those first few days.

The rule in Nam was if supplies were available a Marine could be issued two beers a day. Well, here we were at the Dong Ha Combat Base, which was also the largest supply base in northern I Corps, and we're told there's no beer to be had.

That was a crock of shit because not more than a click away from our encampment we could see this huge Army beverage dump! At least we assumed it was Army since dogface-armed sentries was guarding the thing. Pallet upon pallet of beer and soft drinks were just sitting there in full view and we Marines being told we couldn't get our beer ration because there wasn't any.

Barbed wire and armed guards at this beverage dump was not much of a challenge for thirsty Marines!

At dusk on our fourth day at Dong Ha, six Marines including me, went out on a night scavenging run. We had planned well and our creeping and crawling through brush and rocky ground brought us to outer edge of the beverage dump. It was darker than the ace of spades but we could make out pallets loaded with cases of beverages not more than five feet from our route of approach. One Marine was assigned the job of keeping the barbwire lifted enough for his buddies to slip under while another Marine was to stay on the outside also to stage the cases as they were brought to the fence. The operation went like clock work. We'd already figured that the most we could carry was three cases each and within a couple of minutes eighteen cases were stacked on the outside of the fence with the four "inside" raiders slithering back under the wire. The only close call came as we slowly made our retrograde movement away from the dump with our clumsy loads. Evidently the noise of our pushing the cases far enough away until we could carry them was heard by one of the Army guards as a high pitched, "Halt, who goes there," was heard. It didn't slow us down an iota and if anything made us move faster.

Back in the single light bulb of the comm tent, the six of us began taking inventory of the cases we had "found." To our dismay we ended up with four cases of beer, five cases of cokes and NINE cases of Club Soda! Damn, damn, damn!! (Or other strong words.)

Huh..but not to worry! Our enterprising Comm Chief somehow got wind that an Army Officers Club near the airstrip was all but out of Club Soda and was willing to do some trading. You betcha! Nine cases of Club Soda as a matter of fact. We got three more cases of beer and a quart of some long sought after hard stuff.

Before the sun set the next day, six very happy Marines had toasted the United States Army many, many times for their wonderful supply system. And for the Marine Corps supply system? War rationing is a bitch isn't it? Long live the innovative Marine!

77

A LIFE-SAVING FLIRTATION

Former Electronics Technician Third Class Robert E. DeGraw, USN

I was stationed aboard the U.S.S. Bon Homme Richard, CVA-31 in 1957. During August of that year we shipped from our homeport at Bremerton, Washington for a six-month Asiatic goodwill tour. After many weeks at sea the aircraft carrier docked at Yokosuka, Japan to take on supplies. All hands not on the duty watch were allowed liberty which was a welcome R&R after the long voyage. We were going to be in port for ten days so that meant the entire crew would get some time off to enjoy the sights of Japan.

On a Sunday morning, the ships chaplain announced over the Bon Homme Richard's PA system, that he was organizing an over-night hike up the famous Mt. Fujiyama. The chaplain invited crewmembers to lay down to his office right after morning chow to sign up for the trip. A full busload of sailors and Marines quickly filled the roster. The chaplain gave the group a briefing on the flight deck prior to our departure and told us about the Pilgrims Trail going up Mt. Fuji. This was a well established trail up the 12,389 feet extinct volcano which had rest stations the Japanese had built every 500 feet of elevation traveled. He also said it wouldn't be necessary to carry a lot of equipment or food since the Japanese had even thought of this for the travelers. There would be large communal huts to stay in overnight plus food venders could be found all up and down the trail. The cost for these facilities would be minimal.

Prior to the chaplains briefing I had challenged the Marine detachment aboard the Bon Homme Richard to a race up Mt. Fuji to see who could make it first, them or my Operation Electronics (OE) Division. Fellow seaman in my division has put me up to this since the primary social activity with the Marines on the trip over from Bremerton, had been total conflict. On most capital ships, Marines usually have the privilege of bunking in officer's country as part of their job is to protect and serve high-ranking officers. But on the Bon Homme Richard, the Marines found themselves bunking amidships while my division was quartered in the more prestigious atmosphere of officers' country. In a nutshell, the Marines were jealous and resorted to a constant series of pranks to vent their frustration. The height of this horseplay took place when several Marines threw a fire hose down into the OEs compartment at 0200 one morning, then turned it on. Have you ever tried to catch a pressure spewing fire hose spraying water as it whipped to and fro, when half asleep? We figured the fire hose stunt was in retaliation for tying their dress uniform shirtsleeves and pants in knots just before Admiral's inspection. Our stunt had been brought on in retaliation for the way the Marines treated one our guys who was given brig time in the ships brig for returning late from leave just before we left Bremerton. Like I said, it had been an on-going battle between the OE Division and the Marine Detachment, and a group of Jarheads jumped at my challenge.

Shortly after morning chow twenty-seven sailors and Marines boarded an old gray Navy bus that awaited us at the bottom of the ladder way. Four of the sailors, including me, were from the OE Division, and there was a half-dozen Marines. The little Japanese bus driver who looked to be in his mid-40's, was well informed about the area we traveled and he offered a running commentary for most of the six-hour trip. Ours was the only bus in sight as we pulled into the rutted cinder gravel parking lot with standing water in the potholes. The bus driver told us that over a million people a year made the pilgrimage up Mt. Fuji since the mountain was considered sacred after its last eruption in 1707. However, he also told us that we were making our pilgrimage near the end of the season and this is the reason we didn't see other busses.

As soon as the trail was pointed out to us everyone took off at a fast pace. The OE guys sprinted past the Marines at a feverish clip and soon left them behind. We never saw anyone from our bus again on our trek up. By the time we reached the seventh level one of our OE guys had dropped out. He was more interested in seeing things rather than making a speed run to the top. Due to our late start on climbing Fuji it was starting to get dark by the time we reached the seventh level and the three of us decided to stay the night at this location. We found the old Japanese man in charge of the overnight hut and paid him our 250 Yen each for the nights lodging. This was a pretty good deal even in 1957 since 360 Yen equaled one US dollar.

The hut we stayed in was unique in it's own right. It stood about five feet high and was constructed with bamboo panels which were covered with a lacquered silk paper. The translucent material let in lots of light. The inside capacity of the hut was about the size of a small living room, maybe eight by ten feet. It was really warm and cozy. What made this travelers hut really unique was the sleeping arrangements. The mat floor was covered with a large quilted material of some sort except for the cooking area near the front entrance, and when the kerosene lantern was extinguished for the night (in other words, "Lights out.") a huge quilt was spread to be used by everyone in the hut. Now this is what you'd really call "communal living."

Prior to lights out we lounged around the hut eating and talking with anyone who spoke English. Suddenly, three gorgeous American women entered the hut which perked us three sailors up immediately. Skip, one of my ship mates, eyes lit up like a Christmas tree and he lost no time going over to the women and introducing himself and flirting up a storm. Chris and I soon joined Skip and the six of us talked about the days hike and how we were off the Bon Homme Richard and our challenge to the Marines. It was sort of difficult to guess at the three very pretty women's age but since I was nineteen, I knew they were older than me. But sailors are going to be sailors regardless, and I too, did my share of flirting. The women, who appeared to be in their 20's said they hadn't seen anyone on their hike up to this elevation who looked like they were Marines. Had the Jarheads gave up already? The short haired blond of the trio, who also looked to be the eldest, mentioned that she and her two companions were going to get up at three o'clock in the morning and continue their hike to the top by following the "wire" up the mountain. The wire she was talking about was a travelers guide staked into the mountainside all the way to the summit for use during fog and other limited visibility. I told the woman that we had been informed not to use the wire at night as sometimes the stakes got knocked down by small landslides. She said she wasn't worried, even though I advised her to wait until first light or let us accompany them since I had brought along a flashlight. But from the way Skip and Chris had so boldly flirted with the girls I suspect my offer was declined because of this.

At lights out, some 20 people had crowded into the hut and we all crawled under the huge quilt. The way it worked was ten people on either side of the longest wall laid stretched out with their toes almost touching in the middle. Skip, true to his nature, kept playing footsy with the girls until a female voice spoke harshly in Japanese. Another Japanese woman who spoke a few words of English offered a translation which basically said to "knock off the bull shit and let us get some sleep."

I was startled awake near three a.m. by Skip shaking my shoulder. He whispered that the three American women had taken off already. Skip was also worried about them trying to climb Fuji in the darkness and said we'd better go after them to insure their safety even though it was obvious they'd taken off early so they could ditch us. Chris Mescher and I reluctantly crawled out of the nice warm spots under the quilt and followed after the girls. The going was absolutely treacherous even using my flashlight. I began to worry also as the only thing the women had to guide them was the wire.

After twenty minutes of steady climbing we heard a female voice screaming in the darkness. "Help!" "Help!" "Up here—come quickly!"

The three of us rushed up hill as fast as we could until we saw in the faint beam of my flashlight the backs of two women bent over a jagged rock ridge tugging on something. I quickly shined my light over the edge of the cliff like ridge and saw the girl dangling below, trying frantically to find a foothold. There was nothing below her but a black abyss. I yelled at Skip and Chris to help me grab hold of the woman as there was no doubt in my mind the other two women were at their last ounce of strength. Once the other two women were out of the way, we lifted the other girl up from her dangerous position to safety. The six of us stood in the darkness hugging each other and exchanged tears of joy from the near fatal mishap.

We re-introduced ourselves and this time the girls told us their names. The girl who was hanging over the cliff was Mary. The three of them took turns in telling us what had happened. They had been doing fine until the wire suddenly turned downward which confused them but they still thought they were following the trail. What the three of them didn't know had happened was the wire had been broken and was hanging over a cliff. Mary walked right off the trail and but for the grace of God would have fallen to the void below had she not grabbed a small bush and hung on until her two companions got her by her wrist.

There was no coyness nor hesitation this time when we invited the three women to join us for the remainder of the upward trek.

Under any other circumstances this would be the end of my "sea story" but the hand of fate wasn't quite finished with the six of us.

At the start of a murky dawn we had made it almost to level nine which was about halfway up Fuji. No sun appeared and a thick fog rolled in making visibility nil. Then it started raining profusely. Between the rain and the fog you couldn't see a person three feet away so we made a daisy chain by holding hands with me leading; although my flashlight offered scant help. The wind picked up and blew the near freezing rain at us without mercy. I was the only one that had brought any kind of rain gear and it was a light nylon jacket and certainly not designed for that kind of rain. Just the same I took it off and insisted Mary put it on. We were dressed for summertime hiking and my two buddies only had cotton wind breakers which didn't do any good either, but they too made the other two girls put them on. With teeth chattering and in a total quandary of what to do the six of us finally voted to try and make it the hundred yards or so to the way station at level nine. As a youngster in my home state of Washington, I had done quiet a bit of climbing and was more accustomed to the inclement weather conditions than my two pals and three women. The only reason I mention this is because I was in a lot better shape than the other five. There was little doubt in my mind that the five people were starting the early signs of hypothermia and I knew I had to find shelter for them quickly. By the time we reached level nine the group was in real trouble as their teeth was chattering uncontrollably.

The level nine hut was managed by two middle-aged Japanese men and though they couldn't speak English they immediately realized the trouble my five companions were suffering. They made hand motions to get inside the hut which was heated by two hibachi pots that we called "botchy" pots. The two men fed some more charcoal into the pots and blew on them to make the fire hotter. Then, with me helping they got the five undressed under the quilt and into warm kimonos. I too stripped down and got into a kimono and joined the huddled group under the community quilt. The Japanese caretakers provided us with warm drinks and took our clothes to their hut to dry.

Once the warmth settled into our bodies we all started laughing and joking about the events of the day and mused with good humor what other bad luck could possible befall us that day. For the three sailors, we would find out before the day was done.

We waited out the rain in the warm confines of the hut and when the two caretakers brought us our dry clothes we dressed as a group under the quilt. Since we had made it this far no one thought about turning back and we continued upwards toward the top of Fuji. Besides, I was gung ho about wanting my "Fuji Stick" branded at every level. The Fuji stick was a long walking cane sold by enterprising Japanese at the pricey cost of 75 Yen. At each level way station for 25 Yen you could have your Fuji Stick branded by the caretaker. Each level had its own brand so a person could prove how far they had made it. What I was really interested in was the special free brand you got if you were the first person of the day to make it to the top.

When we stepped out of the hut it was found the aftermath of the rain storm stayed on as thick fog—thick cold fog! But nothing could stop us now! It took another four hours for the six of us to reach the top of Mt. Fuji. My buddies and the three girls knew of my desire to get the traditional "first person of the day brand" so they let me approach the little Japanese man on the summit to get my walking stick branded. Our big reward for our effort and everything else we had went through was thick fog and a foul odor boiling out of the volcano's crater. The fog kept us from experiencing the full grandeur of viewing the vista below our perch but we did manage to see across the crater, briefly. For some reason your depth perception was screwed up and you had to be careful of your balance. As before, the wind picked up and with the swirling thick fog we again shivered from being cold. With the unpleasant aroma of hydrogen sulfide drifting around us we knocked on several hut doors to find warmth. Most of the ten huts had already closed for the season but we finally found one that was open and went in. Several friendly Japanese men met us and welcomed us to the hibachi pots and began to prepare some food for us. These men were clad like all the other way station level people were dressed: black quilted long sleeved shirts, quilted pants, quilted socks and platform wooden sandals which split their big toe from their other toes. Once more these caretakers saw how miserable we were and made us get under the large quilt blanket and immediately served us hot tea. Skip was back to his flirtatious ways with the three women but they seemed to take his advances with good-humored coyness. But this was when he got the shock of his life. He finally got around to asking the girls what they were doing in Japan and his jaw all but hit the deck when they revealed that all three were Navy nurses stationed at Johnson Air Force Base north of Yokosuka. That meant of course that they were officers and enlisted men aren't supposed to fraternize with officers. With a sickly grin and half-shocked laugh I asked Mary what her rank was. She casually replied, "Commander." The other two women were full lieutenants. Skip's face got real red and it was down right funny how respectful he suddenly became.

After resting for about an hour, Johnson, our fourth party member stumbled into the hut to get warm and told us he too had got caught in the storm and the tough time he had of it.

The three Navy nurses invited us to accompany them back down the mountain and we soon found that going down hill was a lot faster than climbing up. Once we got down below the cloud line that was creating the fog we had been in, the view below us was absolutely magnificent! I don't recall having ever seen anything so beautiful!

Once we got back to the parking lot area all seven of us blanched in dismay. There was no buses or for that matter any vehicle of any sort. I don't know who was more upset, the three Navy nurses are the four enlisted sailors. We hiked a good five miles to the Fujiyama railroad station to try and find transportation back to our ship. It was very frustrating since no one in the village understood English. Here we were, out of money and out of uniform. (We'd been authorized to wear our dungarees for the climb.) The nurses were willing to give us some money but they, like us, had no idea when the next train or bus, or whatever was going to come by. So all we could do was wait.

After a good two hours we heard the rumble of a lot of trucks grinding up the dirt road which turned out to be a convoy of U.S. Army trucks filled with about a hundred soldiers. We tried to wave the trucks down so they'd stop but one by one they passed us by. Finally, at the rear of the truck column came a jeep with two long whip like radio antenna's attached to it. In desperation I stepped out in the middle of the road and waved down what was obviously the command car for the convoy. An army second lieutenant was sitting next to the corporal driver and I asked him politely how we could get back to the Bon Homme Richard docked at Yokosuka. The young Army officer gave me an icy glare, then shaking his head in disgust, picked up his field telephone and barked a few words to whoever was on the other end. "I've found the four AWOL sailors!"

AWOL? I couldn't believe we had been reported Absent Without Leave. That meant we were in BIG trouble.

The nurses heard what this officer had said over his radio and Mary stepped forward, saying, "Pardon me lieutenant, these sailors are not AWOL. They got caught in a storm on Mt. Fuji."

With a sneer, the Army lieutenant rudely said, "You get caught in the storm with them lady?" Then he went on to say it would be best for her to keep her nose out of military matters.

To say that Mary got angry would be putting it mildly. She flipped out her ID card and waved it in the lieutenants face. Even the dumb second lieutenant must have realized a Navy commander was the equivalent rank as an Army lieutenant colonel. And you just don't say things like he had said to a lieutenant colonel. He got all flustered, jumped out of the jeep, stood at attention and saluted Mary. Then he did his best to apologize.

After a few choice words to the lieutenant about Army military courtesy, Commander Mary went on to explain what had happened up on Mt. Fuji and that all of them needed transportation back to Yokosuka. With his new attentive and servile attitude, the lieutenant got back on his radio and told his base to reclassify the sailors from "AWOL" to "Lost in a storm." Our group got a ride back to the Army base were we were fed and put on a "bullet train" back to Yokosuka. The one hundred mile per hour train had us back to our ship in no time.

Back aboard the aircraft carrier they hadn't got the word yet about what had happened and the four of us were ordered to report to the executive officer for a long walk off a short plank. However, the chaplain intervened and got us off the hook.

Later, when I corresponded with Commander Mary, she wrote back to me saying she and the other two nurses were glad that Skip had acted the way he had. It was a flirtation that saved all of their lives.

Incidentally. The Marines never did make it to the top of Fuji. It seems they filled their canteens with beer and never made it pass level seven.

Bob lives in Kirkland, Washington where he runs a hiking business called Hike Masters. He has led excursions in Canada and most of the western U.S. Parks. He is also a writer and a man that fixes almost anything. He has copyrights and patents and several inventions and has also written several books. His dad was a 30-year "Gold Hash Marks" Chief Petty Officer. Bob served eight years in the Navy. He says he's often wondered what ever happened to the three Navy nurses and his shipmates, who's lives he had saved on Fuji.

78

TARAWA AND AFTERWARDS
Former Staff Sergeant Howard W. Suttmiller, Jr., USMC

I enlisted in the Marine Corps at age 19 in my hometown of Indianapolis, Indiana on December 12, 1942.

My folks said good-bye to me when I boarded a Pullman car in Union Station a couple of days later along with 40 other future Marines. We were on our way to San Diego, California.

With cat-calls of "You'll be sorry!" ringing in our ears as our fully loaded bus passed through the front gate of the Marine Corps Recruit Depot on the early morning of December 17, 1942, I begun what was the start of a life time association with the United States Marine Corps.

I survived eight weeks of boot camp that included three weeks at the Camp Mathews Rifle Range where I shot high sharpshooter, missing expert by six points because I adjusted my sights wrong on my Springfield at the 500-yard line. (It took me four shots to figure out my screw up.)

After boot camp training I was sent to Camp Elliott where I spent another six weeks learning to be a heavy, .30 caliber machine gunner. I really learned to love that old water cooled thirty and became pretty good at firing it..

For the next year I worked hard at the art of being an infantryman Marine while at Camp Pendleton, California. The 16th Replacement Battalion boarded the SS Lurline on April 18, 1943, and I was on my way to the South Pacific. This ship carried 5,000 troops at a speed of 28 knots, zigzagging the entire way unescorted through an area called "Torpedo Junction." We made stops at U.S. Samoa, New Caledonia, Sydney and Melbourne, Australia, until finally reaching our destination; Wellington, New Zealand on May 15, 1943. There was a chill in the air upon our arrival because May was winter-time "Down Under." We replacements were put aboard a narrow gauge train that took us 30 miles in an hour and a half, to a little town of 500 people named Packakariki. Just outside of this small town was the base camp of the 2nd Marine Division.

Much to my chagrin I was assigned to a rifle company as a rifleman. I raised hell about this because I was a machine gunner and put in for a transfer to the battalion's weapons company. It didn't take long for my request to be denied with the reason the weapons company TO (Table of Organization) was filled up.

A week later the Section Chief for the Battalion Intelligence Section had me to report to him at Headquarters Company for an interview. He explained he had been reviewing Service Record Books to find someone with an educational background in art and mechanical drawing. A review of my SRB told him I fit the bill for what he was looking for and how would I like to become a draftsman in his section? You betcha! As a member of the 3rd Battalion, 8th Marines Intelligence Section I still went through the rigorous classroom and field training with the rest of the division. It took six months before it was determined the entire division was trained and fit to be classified combat ready Marines.

On October 18, 1943, Landing Team 3/8 went aboard the Coast Guard ship U.S.S. Monrovia and on the 7th of November, we were off the island of Effete, New Hebrides undergoing amphibious landing practice.

After a week of exhaustive ship to shore maneuvers we set sail for open sea. On November 13, 1943 the word was finally passed of where we were heading during a long briefing session held on the topside aft weather deck. Our destination and objective was the island code named "Helen." which we were going to assault. The name of the operation was "Galvanic." None of us had ever heard of Betio Island (rhymes with ratio) which was a part of the Tarawa Atoll in the Gilbert Islands group.

Navy officers told us they were going to "blow the island off the map," and that our landing would be "a breeze." Breeze or not, my intelligence section broke out maps and aerial photos of Betio which was issued to every company in the battalion for review of landing beaches and assigned objectives.

At 0344 on November 20, 1943, our convoy of troopships arrived off the lagoon of Tarawa atoll. Though it was pitch-black most all Marines left their troop compartments to go topside to see what was going on. Battlewagons, cruisers and destroyers lobbed countless red-hot, glowing shells onto Betio but all the Marines could see was billowing smoke and fires. The Japanese let us know they were waiting for us, when at 0600 two high velocity shells hit in the middle of the transport staging area sending up huge plumes of water. This got the attention of our Navy real quick and the troop ships were moved out of the vicinity on the double.

Chow call went of 0430 and all of us assault troops laid below for steak and eggs; the condemned would eat a hardy meal!

After chow all troops were ordered to return to their compartments and "saddle up." Our gear was all ready staged on our racks so all we had to do was put on our haversacks with entrenching tool, buckle up our cartridge belts with two canteens and first aid pouch, drape two extra bandoliers of ammo, across your chest, strap on the two issued hand grenades, pick up our M-1 rifles and put our helmets on. The guys on the lower bunks let their buddies on the higher bucks, some that were tiered seven high, get their gear down first. In addition to my regular load just described, I also carried my map case, a large roll of communication wire and binoculars.

At 0700 the ships PA system blared out the call we had all nervously waited for: "Now hear this, now hear this, all troops lay up to their debarkation stations."

No sooner had Marines begun shuffling toward the hatch to get out of the compartment than an explosion was heard in the adjoining troop compartment. A Marine had jumped down from his bunk three tiers up with his hand grenades hooked to his pack suspenders by the safety pins. One of the safety pins pulled out with the result of five casualties before we even left ship.

At 0800 I took a long, hard look at the island before starting down the landing net to get into the Higgins boat. All I could see was smoke and fire among the stubs of palm trees. Our Higgins boat moved a quarter mile from the ship where we rendezvoused with nine other landing craft and circled with them awaiting the order to head for shore. This went on for better than two hours. The 100-degree temperature coupled with four-foot swells chopping the sea had more than half the Marines in my boat seasick. After what seemed an eternity, the order came at about 1100 for us to form up at the line of departure. It took us an hour to get all the Higgins boats lined up at the LOD. After forming a straight line the command boat signaled for our wave to head for Red Beach #3 at full speed. Red Beach #3 was near the middle of the island five miles away.

The first wave assault troops had hit the beach before 0900 in am tracks to get them across the coral reef into the lagoon. Over half of these caterpillar treaded landing craft had been knocked out by the Japanese. The original plans called for the Higgins boats to stop at the coral reef and the troops would transfer over to the am tracks. But it wasn't going to happen that way for the later waves.

I was going in with the reserve battalion of the 8th Marines and we were being committed for the simple reason we were needed. Causalities had been horrendous and the Japanese Special Naval Landing Force (equivalent to Marine forces) were well dug in with outstanding fields of fire. As we neared Betio enemy anti-boat fire begun firing on us. We had about two miles to go when two of our Higgins boats took directs hits and were destroyed. At about a mile from shore we started getting machine gun fire directed at us and it's a sound a person will never forget. You could clearly hear the bullets smashing into our landing craft.

The long coral reef that encircled the island was around 1,000 yards from the beach. A long pier reached out from the island and near this pier a shipping channel had been blasted through the coral. Our Navy coxswain saw the many landing craft hung up on the reef and yelled down to us he was going to head toward the shipping channel near the pier. I guess this sailor cannot be blamed for being scared with all the murderous machine gun fire coming our way, but what he did next I have never been able to quite forgive him for. He got his boat about ten yards from the end of the pier and dropped the ramp, yelling for everyone to get out. At the same time he put his boat in full reverse. Because I was at the rear of the boat, by the time I came off the ramp into the water, the boat was a good 30 yards from the pier. I remember seeing the heads of fellow Marines bobbing in front of me when I ran off the ramp and thought the men were walking on the bottom. What a surprise I got when I dropped straight down in 10 feet of water!

I fought my way back to the top and tried to swim but the 100 pounds of gear I was carrying sent me straight down to the bottom again. Fortunately, I had been swimming since I was six years old when my uncle threw me in White River in Indianapolis, and said, "Swim." Therefore, the water did not make me panic but I knew I had to get rid of the weight on me or drown. I unhooked my cartridge belt, spread my arms and let my pack drop along with the reel of wire and got the two bandoliers of ammo from around my neck. I suppose I lost my helmet and rifle at the same time as I struggled my way back to the surface. I swam to the pier with machine gun fire chewing up the water around me. The only weapon I had left was a hunting knife on my dungaree trouser web belt.

The pier was built over a stone breakwater which created a lot of hiding places for Jap snipers. Since this location didn't seem any safer than the poor guys out in the middle of the lagoon plodding through the surf wading 800 yards to shore under heavy machine gun fire, I decided to go on in near the pier. I joined up with six other Marines and we started working our way toward the beach while rifle and machine gun fire peppered us. We were in about three and half feet of water and when I stepped on something hard I reached down to see what it was. A helmet! Boy, did I feel a lot better putting that steel pot on my head. Our small group passed one of our wireman from the comm platoon who was laying across some big rocks with his rear end up in the air. He had been wounded and the Navy corpsman who had patched him up had also gave him a good dose of morphine. This guy was as happy as a lark, smiling waving his hands and shouting at everybody that went past him. "Go get 'em boys!" (Later in Hawaii, this fellow didn't even remember a thing about getting wounded,) We continued along the pier until about three-quarters of the way to the beach. To our left, not more than ten yards, was a damaged LCM sitting at an angle in the surf. This looked like a good place to make our final dash to shore from. Making it over to the LCM I started working my way around one side of it when this Marine pushed passed me and headed shoreward. He made it about five yards when a sniper bullet nailed him right between the eyes. Needless to say I went around the other end of the LCM on my hands and knees, with only my newfound helmet sticking out of the water like a sea turtle. I made it the rest of the way in on my hands and knees, thanking God I was still in one piece.

Directly in front of me approximately 20 feet away from the waters edge was a four-foot seawall. The small sandy beach was crammed with wounded Marines laying on ponchos. All type of discarded military equipment littered the area. On the last few feet to the beach I had pushed a dead body out of my way and now I noticed many, many dead bodies of Marines floating to and fro at the waters edge. To my left I saw this big bull bear of a Marine officer chomping on a cigar while he talked on a SCR 300 Field Radio. He was surrounded by other officers and radio operators. It was Colonel David M. Shoup, a fellow Hoosier and commander of the 2nd Marines and also the assault phase commander. In essence, where he stood was the 2nd Marine Division forward command post. Major General Julian C. Smith, Commander of the 2nd Marine Division, and Major General Holland M. "Howlin Mad" Smith, Commander of V Marine Amphibious Corps, were both afloat on command ships. Anyway, Shoup saw a bunch of us gawking at him and he takes the cigar from his mouth, and says. "Find some damn rifles and ammo and get your tails over the seawall and start fighting!"

It wasn't hard to find weapons or ammo. Near the head of the pier the division aid station had been set up and there were piles of discarded gear. I picked up an M-1 and a full cartridge belt with two canteens from a collection stacked three feet high. I test fired the M-1 by aiming it in the water away from my comrades. Other Marines also resupplied themselves and up over the seawall we went.

A dozen of us moved forward better than 40 yards inland through an area of shattered palm trees that offered cover as we went from tree to tree.)

Nearing the Japanese built airfield we spotted this big bomb crater located on a taxiway strip just off the main runway. The crater was a good 15 feet across and about eight feet deep with a couple of feet of water in the bottom of it. It was beginning to get dark and we decided this hole made a good defense position with a clear field of fire across the airstrip. We also figured that by staying at this spot that we were offering protection for the division CP.

At dusk the 12 of us drew straws in the form of palm leaf spines to see who would be the first 50% watch for the night. A Jap machine gun opened up which got our attention and we all peered over the rim of the shell hole to see what was going on. One of our lieutenants from Headquarters Company was running like mad, zigzagging across the airstrip with bullets chewing up the sand all around him. All of us in the crater began yelling, "Over here, over here!" The officer heard us and changed his direction but so did the chattering machine gun. He was about ten feet from our hole when he made a big swan dive. But before he came crashing down among us a bullet hit him through the sole of his right boondockers going clear through his foot. Lucky for the lieutenant, one of our guys was a corpsman and he immediately gave first aid on the damaged foot. We knew we couldn't keep the wounded lieutenant in our crater all night so it was decided that we'd wait for a couple of hours until it got good and dark and then try and move him back to the main aid station on the beach. A couple of the guys made a makeshift stretcher out of a couple of ponchos and what appeared to be some kind of bamboo from a bush. Four guys volunteered to get the lieutenant back to the beach and when they started their journey you could hear them calling out hoarsely, "Wounded coming through, wounded Marine coming through." They made it back to the aid station without any trouble and returned to the shell crater within an hour. What was amazing to all of us was it was quiet that first night. We'd been taught by the old timers that the Japs always fought at night and we expected a Banzai attack to take place that never did. It was a good thing the enemy didn't attack us because the truth of the matter is that we'd have probably got pushed back into the lagoon. (We were told later that all the Japanese communication lines had been knocked out and the Jap leaders could not organize a counter-attack.

At daybreak the entire group went back to the division CP to get assignments on what the brass wanted us to do. A major told us to get water, ammo and rations, and haul these items up to the various front line company CP's. And that's exactly what the 12 of us did for the next two days. The evening of the second day I was making my way to the front lines carrying bandoleers of .30 caliber ammo in clips, and a jerry can of water when something hit me hard on the back of my right shoulder and I went down like a ton of bricks had been dropped on me. It was a large piece of spent shrapnel that had come out of nowhere. The football size hunk of metal was so hot I couldn't hold it in my hand. I could hardly believe my luck that I only ended up with a bruised shoulder and of course scared out of my mind.

On the forth morning Betio was declared secured. The stench of death was all around us from more than a thousand decomposing bodies that were in an advanced state of decay due to the tropical heat. Navy corpsmen had their hands full and were kept busy treating everyone for coral cuts that became instantly infected. The "doc's" also worked on minor wounds of Marines who hadn't sought medical treatment during the heat of battle and also treated countless cases of sun-cracked lips.

What was left of my battalion mustered on the fourth day and we were ordered to head to the long pier so we could get into Higgins boats that would take us off Betio. On the way walking out on the long pier that had saved my neck, we could all see hundreds of bodies of our comrades who had made the supreme sacrifice floating in the water. The tide had finally come in—three days late. The freak low tide the day of our landing had caused most small boats to get hung up on the coral reef and Marines had no choice but to wade better than 800 yards to get ashore in the face of gunfire so tremendous it defies description. I'll never forget the sound the Jap bullets made hissing into the water. When I came in on the 20th the waters edge was 30 feet from the seawall. Now, with high tide it was less than three feet from the wall. At lease the tide brought our dead buddies back to the beach so they could get a decent burial. But you know, it also came to me that we wouldn't have had much of a protective beach if the full tide had been in on the 20th. Our feet would have been sticking out in the water while we laid behind the seawall, the only cover there was. Tarawa was a strange battle.

We went aboard waiting Higgins boats and were taken over to the island Bairnki, which turned out to be a tropical paradise. Rolling surf, large sandy beaches with tall palm trees that had not been shredded by pre-invasion naval gunfire. Lo and behold, much to everyone's surprise, we had been brought to Bairnki for a little rest and recuperation. Hardly anyone believed it! But sure enough, our colonel told us it was time to try and settle down and attempt to get the four days of hell out of our system. We were told to take it easy, swim and relax as we saw fit. Blankets and rations were issued and we took baths and washed clothing to try and get the smell of death off of our bodies and dungarees.

Late the next morning we were ordered to saddle up again and board the waiting Higgins boats that took us out to our old troop ship, the U.S.S. Monrovia. We all must have had the look of death on our faces as the sailors went out of their way to be nice to us. Many of the swabs came down the landing net to take our packs and help us up to the ship. Never had ship's troop chow tasted so good.

I'll share with you an eerie feeling I experienced that first night back aboard ship. The troop compartments were not as full as they had been six days ago and hardly anyone had to take one of the upper five tier high bunks. It was ghostly quiet that first night staring at those empty bunks and I'm sure I wasn't the only one lost in my own thoughts about those vacant bunks and what they represented. It was almost as if you could feel the presence of those missing Marines.

The good news for the Marines aboard the Monrovia was that we were on our way to Hawaii.

Our ship arrived at the big island on December 3, 1943, and we were put in trucks and driven for miles out to the middle of nowhere. We finally went through a gate of sorts with this big overhead sign, reading, CAMP TARAWA. Our location turned out to be part of the famous Parkers Ranch and was situated in a saddle between two active volcanoes with lava flows that became as hard as concrete. There was an abundance of large cactus, sagebrush and sugar cane along with roving herds of cattle right in the middle of our camp. Hawaii? We all felt like we'd been dumped in some parody that represented the middle of Texas! And to top off everything else, clear up until February, ice skims formed on our water buckets. Talk about standard operating procedure for a military camp location. Only the Marine Corps could find a place where you could destroy everything and not hurt anything. And liberty was the pits! The nearest town of any size was Hilo that was a good hour and a half away. And what did Hilo have to offer? The population was 50% Japanese and they didn't want anything to do with the "Jap Killers of Tarawa." At that time, the feeling was more or less mutual.

The division received many replacements and integrated them into the different units until we were up to strength again. A lot of Marines wounded on Tarawa also made it back to the division. Much needed equipment and supplies poured in and we all but worked around the clock getting back to ship shape. Then extensive field and classroom training began and we did this for six months until once again becoming as hard as nails.

When we got the word that our next campaign was another island, this one named Saipan, which we would assault on June 15, 1944, the 2nd Marine Division was once more a top notch-fighting machine.

Tarawa was the bloodiest battle of the war per square yards of ground taken and held. The 2nd Marine Division was awarded the Presidential Unit Citation for its extraordinary gallantry during the four days of Tarawa. This was the first atoll operation of the war and a lot of mistakes were made. But it was also a learning campaign that saved many lives later in the Pacific War.

Of the three Presidential Unit Citations I'm entitled to wear I think the one for Tarawa is the one I'm most proud of.

Before Tarawa, the only thing I knew about war was having seen war movies as a kid. Boy, did I wake up to some of the realities of life. Even with this newfound perception I was still naive in some respects. I figured all amphibious landing operations would be like Tarawa. However, after making four more combat assault-landing operations during World War II, I found out there was only one Tarawa————Thank God!

We have met Howard Suttmiller before. He maintained an affiliation with the Marine Corps after World War II by joining the active reserve. As a member of the Indianapolis based 16th Infantry Battalion, Howard was called to active duty in August 1950 for the Korean War. Not only did he wade the low tide of Tarawa, he also crunched the cold snow with the 1st Marine Division at the Chosin Reservoir and subsequent "Fight to the Sea". Howard is a retired graphic artist. He is active in the Marine Corps League, the 1st Marine Division Association and the World War II Round Table. A widower, he lives in the northeast suburbs of Indianapolis.

79

SHIT DETAIL
First Sergeant Daniel P. Scarborough, USMC(Ret.)

I was a member of the 4th Defense Battalion that had been in Hawaii at the onset of World War II and was quickly moved to Etate in the New Hebrides along with VMF-212. By the time I caught up with the battalion as a young 18-year old PFC, the 900 Marines were part of the defense of New Zealand. After Marines beat the Japanese on Guadalcanal the first part of 1943, my battalion was ordered to prepare for an assault landing and occupation of a small island north of New Georgia in the Solomon's chain, named Vella Lavella.

We used Guadalcanal as a staging area for our forthcoming amphibious operation and landed there in early July 1943. Our camp turned out to be a former Seabee base located near the beach in a coconut grove. The construction sailors knew how to live and all of us Marines were really impressed with our new home that would be ours for the next four weeks. In addition to well-built wood huts, mess hall and other buildings the battalion inherited a magnificent head. A 20 holer with a wood deck and framed with screens and a screen door. There was even a tarp roof on the huge toilet to keep the rain out. This was combat styled throne setting we were not accustomed to.

Every few days our gunny would detail a marine to get some diesel oil to pour in the deep pit and burn out the head. This kept the bugs away and the smell down at the same time.

One day the gunny designated PFC Lockburner for the shit detail. Lockburner was a damned good Marine but a little slow on the uptake, if you get my meaning. He was very conscientious and listened to the gunny very close when the guns gave him his job assignment. The gunny told Lockburner to go down to the motor pool, draw out a five-gallon can of diesel oil and burn out the head.

Lockburner did an excellent job. He poured the five-gallon diesel oil all over the wood deck and wooden seats and torched the head. It burned to the ground.

Lockburner's shit detail got him on the "shit list" with his fellow Marines and to this day he has never lived it down.

We have met First Sergeant Scarborough before with his tale The House of a Thousand Tits. The six foot three, 250-pound Marine served in World War II, the Korean and Vietnam Wars. A part of his interesting career was a tour with the Marine Corps Rifle and Pistol Team.

80

WIA
Former Private First Class William A. Hecht, USMC

I was a rifleman in B Company, 1st Battalion, 22nd Marines in February 1944. Our outfit at this time was a "bastard" meaning that we were an independent regiment under the command of a first rate Marine Colonel John T. Walker. We were born on Samoa where we'd spent 18 months doing boring garrison duty but that all changed from February 1944 on. Although an orphan regiment at the time of this tale, we would eventually become a part of the 1st Provisional Marine Brigade that was the principle outfit that became the 6th Marine Division.

Now what I'm gonna tell ya has to do with one of those stinking little battles that hardly anyone knows about. You'll have ta dig hard in them thar history books about the Corps to find what I'm a'talk'en about. In February 1944 10,000 troops of a combined Army-Marine expedition assaulted several islands that were part of the 40 island atoll named Eniwetok which was part of the Marshall Islands chain.

My outfit, the 22nd Marines would tackle Engebi, a triangular island where the Japanese had built an airfield at the north end of the atoll. The other outfits would go after Eniwetok Island and Parry Island, plus five smaller islets. The Nips the 22nd would face numbered around 1,200 and they were battle-hardened veterans from Manchuria. Okay, that's enough background, so let me tell ya what happened to me.

We landed on the 18th of February on Engebi's lagoon-side beaches and was practically unopposed. What we didn't know right away was that the Japs had concentrated their defense in a large coconut grove inland. It didn't take long when we advanced inland to find out what the Nips were up to. They had hundreds of these interlocking spider holes with tunnels going from one to another. What they'd do was let a Marine pass by their camouflaged spider hole then jump up and shoot a guy in the back.

I found out about this tactic in an unusual manner. As I was walking along I felt something hit me hard from behind and the next thing I knew I felt this wetness going down my leg. Sonofabitch! I'd been shot sure 'nough and that was my blood pouring down my leg. I automatically hit the deck and one of my buddies ran up to me and turned me over. Then he started laughing which I thought was kind of odd since I'd just got shot. "You can get up now Bill," he says. "But you're gonna need a new canteen 'cause yours is shot clean through." Damn, if it hadn't been my water ration I felt dribbling down my leg.

We continued the advance and passed a lot of dead Japs as we went. I managed to get in a little souvenir hunting when I got pinned down behind this Jap corpse. Then, I'll be dang if I didn't stand up from that body to move on when I got shot again! This time right in the head! It knocked my helmet clear off and like the other time I dropped to the deck. My same old buddy come a' running up to me and this time he just shakes his head when he hands me my helmet. The damn thing has a hole in it but I'm not wounded.

You heard the old story 'bout three times being a charm? Well, I sure as hell don't call it any charm but a little later when I felt sumpthin punch me right in the chest that knocked me on my ass I guessed right away it was for real this time. An' shore 'nough it was. I got shot dead straight in the middle of my chest, right over my heart. Got no reason to be alive but I do recall a corpsman shaken sum of that new wonder drug sulfa over the wound.

Stretcher-bearers along with a corpsman carried me to the beach. The doc at the beach takes one look at me and calls the chaplain over. The chaplain gives me the last rites. I was awake enough to make the act of Contrition. And I swear I remember someone asking me if my GI insurance was paid up! (It still is by the way.) So then this other corpsman takes a look at me and sprinkled some more sulfa over the bullet hole. He asked me if the bullet went all the way through me? Hell, I didn't know! He wraps me up with a couple of field bandages and yells to some stretcher-bearers that I might make it out to the LST that was our emergency medical operation ship. They carried me down to a Higgins boat along with som other wounded guys and away we go. Every time we hit a swell I knew it was gonna be my last breath and to this day I don't know how I survived that boat ride.

The swabs lowered one of those wire basket stretcher things and I was hoisted aboard by a crane. While I was being lifted to the main deck I noticed this navy photo guy with a Kodak speed graphic hanging over the rail. I'm a'gonna get my picture took. My dungaree jacket is open and I got those field bandages covering my chest with just a trickle of blood seeping down. My partial plate for my two front teeth are in an envelope in my pocket but I give the navy guy a big toothless grin anyway. Two fangs, like a vampire. I flash him a Churchill V for victory sign. Hey, I already see my mug in Life magazine, like that kid from the 22nd on Kwajalein did with the canteen cup of coffee.

But somthin's wrong with the yo yo swabby. His camera is on the blink! He runs fore to aft on the deck, slapping the back of his Kodak. Out of film? Oh well, I coulda been a star.

Other swabs lift me from the basket to a gurney. I'm wheeled into an operating room of sorts and green smocked surgeons look at me curiously. More sulfa. Same question: "Did the bullet come out the back?" Same answer: "Duh!" They'll operate on me later.

Corpsmen wheel me to a private anti-room off from the operating room. They can't turn the gurney into the room! Am I their first patient? They fart around trying to jerk the gurney into the hatch but the damn thing won't fit. It's only a step away so I get off the gurney on my own accord and step into the room while the two golf balls stare at me. I stand there until they become unglued and they put me into a hospital bed. Snow white sheets and pillow cases. I'm flat on my back staring at the overhead still in my utilities. I reach one hand to my waist where I have a Jap Hari Kari knife hidden in a box in the waistband. Yep, it's still there, no one had discovered it. My little souvenir when I was pinned down behind the dead Jap. I'd wrapped it in cotton and tissue paper. It was about ten inches long and beautiful. Bright emeralds, sapphires and rubies in the handle with a pure gold braid, the blade of pure silver. Magnificent! And probably worth a fortune.

I decide to hide the knife in my pillow. When I roll over slightly to do this my eyes grow wide. I'm laying in a pool of blood! My blood! "Corpsman, corpsman!" As loud as I can scream. One comes a' running like they always do. He sizes up the problem immediately after checking out my back. "You're lucky Marine," he says. The bullet came out the back, you won't need surgery."

A half-dozen guys had checked me out on the beach to see if the bullet had gone clear through me. They either didn't roll me far enough or they rolled me the wrong way! All I needed was more sulfa and a clean bandage.

That was the good news. The bad news was that I had blown my hidden treasure by trying to hide the knife under my pillow. The corpsman insisted we put the Hari Kari knife in the ships safe for safekeeping. Of course I never saw it again. Corpsman tells me later someone stole it. No shit! Oh well, I'd stolen it to hadn't I? From a dead Jap.

The next morning I get transferred from the emergency operating LST to the hospital ship Solace. The Solace takes me to Hawaii and eventually I end up at the Sand Point Naval Hospital, Seattle, Washington.

One last odd thing about this. I was allowed to keep my utilities and I never did find a bullet hole in the utility top. How about that? I must have had my top open half way is the only thing I can think of. All the doctors, nurses and corpsmen stateside where amazed that I'd taken a chest shot like that and lived. It was definitely my million-dollar wound.

Bill Hecht will turn 80 in the year 2000. He lives in Washington State and writes regularly to his buddy Howard Pierce who also contributed to this book. Bill told me that he wrote the story the same way he talks and that I better not do too damn much editing. (I didn't.) He also told me he still wonders what in the hell happened to his jeweled Japanese Hari Kari knife.

81

GETCHA SELF A BEER THERE
Major Jim Dion, USMC(Ret.)

Boy oh boy—Korea look out! Here I am riding in a jeep over a road that is so bumpy I can barely hold my seat. I'm hanging on for dear life while the young PFC driving the jeep seems totally unconcerned about the dust he's raising as he swings around hair-pin corners with no guard rails on the narrow trail that descends down into a valley below. He's taking me to my new home for the next year. I reflect for a moment how the road we're traveling on reminds me of North China in 1946, the last time I served with the 1st Marine Division. That duty was my first with the Corps after Parris Island Boot Camp in 1945. And China, like Korea, was far removed from the cushy embassy duty in London I'd served from 1948 to 1951

It's hotter than blue-blazes this tenth day of July 1952 with the yellow-orange orb over our heads frying us in a heat that you only get in the orient. Neither the PFC nor I have had much to say to one another since he was ordered at battalion headquarters to drive me to my assignment, Dog Company, 2nd Battalion, 1st Marines. It wasn't because that I was trying to be standoffish and I felt certain that the PFC wasn't intimidated by the shiny new gold bars on my collar points. It was more of a case where I was terrified of his driving and was praying I wouldn't become a causality before reporting in to my new company commander.

No doubt the driver was accustomed to seeing brand new second lieutenants fresh out of OCS coming aboard the battalion but what he didn't know about me was that I was not exactly a 90-day wonder. As a former gunnery sergeant I had insight into how an infantry unit functioned, but this was my first time in combat.

Somehow we made it safely to the valley encampment of D/2/1 and I was welcomed aboard by my captain company commander who informed me the company was presently on a five day behind the lines R&R. He told me to take my gear and pointed out where Mister Seuss' hooch was located where I'd be bunking.

Mister Seuss turned out to be one of the saltiest Marine 2nd Lieutenants I'd ever seen. There was no doubt in my mind he was a temporary officer, like me, up from the enlisted ranks. He was a grizzled old salt who obviously already had over 20 years invested in "Our Marine Corps." I walked on into the crude shack living quarters to find him laying naked on his cot seeking some relief from the terrible heat.

He sat up when I walked in and shaking my hand introduced himself to me and we spent a few minutes getting to know one another. Then he said, "How'd you like a beer?"

Not knowing he'd instantly made a life-long friend, I smiled, and said, "You betcha!"

Pointing to the back of the dirt floored hooch he said, "Getcha self a beer outta that ammo box there."

I found the metal mortar ammo box counter-sunk in the floor and lifted the lid. There was a large dead rat floating in the improvised refrigerator that was full of water. Pushing aside the rat I reached down and grabbed a couple of cans of beer. Handing one of the cans to Mister Seuss, he took it then smiled at me.

"You're a Mustang aren't you?" (For those that may not be familiar with the term that means former enlisted.)

I smiled back at him and took the church key he offered to open my can of beer. "Yeah I am, how'd you know that?"

"My two room mates are college boy lieutenants. Since I put the rat in the reefer they've stopped raiding my beer supply."

Born in Gloucester, Mass., Jim Dion now calls Sparks, Nevada home. He retired from the Corps in 1970 with 25 years service. Jim holds the Bronze Star with "V" and the Purple Heart. He again served with the 1stMarDiv when in Vietnam. Jim and his wife Maureen, who is from Tipperary, Ireland, also lived in New Zealand for five years after his retirement. Jim and Maureen are the proud parents of twin sons and a daughter.

82

BLUE SIDE - GREEN SIDE
Former Carpenters Mate 2/C Edgar E. Gage, USN

During World War II I was in the 130th Seabee Battalion. We sailed from Rhode Island the early part of March 1944 on what turned out to be a three-week voyage to Hawaii, by way of the Panama Canal.

Once we got to Hawaii my outfit was stationed at the Marine Corps airfield Ewa, which was four miles west of Pearl Harbor and about 20 miles from Honolulu. Where the Seabee's made camp was inside the same fenced area as Barbers Point with the Naval Air Station three miles away.

The thing that impressed me during my battalion's seven-month stay on Hawaii was the very noticeable effects still seen of the December 7, 1941 Japanese sneak attack. A lot of the training and work we Seabee's did was to clear up and rebuild a lot of the facilities on Ewa and Barbers Point.

A couple of days after New Years 1944 the 130th Seabee Battalion boarded and sailed from Hawaii on the SS President Johnson, a converted ocean liner. Our destination: Saipan.

Our ship was about two days from reaching Saipan when the loud speaker blared out a message from our commanding officer. What he had to say was that volunteers were needed for duty with the Marines. The CO laid it on the line that the duty could be extremely dangerous as it had to do with a forthcoming invasion and he was only interested in talking to single men not older than 21. He ended his talk by saying those interested lay below to the mess deck for interviews.

I was 19 and single and felt it was only right that I volunteer.

As soon as we landed on Saipan the company of volunteers from the Seabee battalion were attached to the 2nd Marine Division. We were broke up into platoons and I ended up with the 2nd Battalion, 8th Marines. You can say that for all intent and purposes we were Marines! We trained with them, lived with them and was a part of them. The only difference was our working uniforms. The Marines wore their green or molted combat utilities while the Seabee's working uniform was light blue cotton shirt and dark blue dungarees.

In late February 1944 the 2nd Battalion, 8th Marines, and their attached units boarded the troop ship U.S.S. Dorthea L. Dix. (The only reason I remember this ships name is because a well-known newspaper columnist of the time was named Dorothy Dix.)

We laid at anchor for better than two weeks and I spent most of my time on an oily canvas hatch cover under a landing craft in an effort to find some shade from the blistering sun. The only problem staying under this landing craft was oil and dirt really messed up my working uniform. By the time the Dix joined the Okinawa invasion convoy my blue dungarees were a wreck. But since this was the only clothing I had with me there was no choice but to wear them. Boy, did I look a mess!

We went to general quarters on 29 March and stayed that way for the next three days. Each morning the Marines of the 2nd battalion would climb down the cargo nets and get into Higgins boats landing craft. Then they'd circle around for a while and after an hour or so head toward the south end of the island like they were going to make an assault landing. But they didn't. The line of landing craft would circle back from the beach and return to the Dix. This feint maneuver was done to draw the Japs to the south end of the island. It must have worked pretty good because on Easter Sunday and April Fools Day, 1 April 1945, the 1st and 6th Marine Divisions hit the beach further up the island almost unopposed.

The 2nd Marine Division stayed offshore for better than two weeks as the floating reserve until it was decided not to take any more chances with Jap Kamikaze aircraft attacks that had already hit one troop ship that caused a lot of causalities. We were ordered back to Saipan.

During the two weeks we laid offshore from Okinawa I'd managed to get a ragged set of Marine green utilities and I'd tossed my filthy and torn blue dungarees over the side.

Aboard the Dix a command decision was made regarding the uniform of the day for our trip back to Saipan. (And to this day I have never been able to figure it out why.) It came over the loud speaker that all Marines would wear khaki and all sailors would wear blue dungarees. The order was emphasized that no one would be allowed topside without the proper attire of khaki's or blue dungarees.

Talk about being out of luck! Boy, was I in a lurch. My blue dungarees were laying someplace on the bottom of the Pacific Ocean! If I couldn't get up on deck then I couldn't get to the mess hall, and if I couldn't get to the mess hall, I couldn't eat!

We were only fed twice a day on the troop ship and taking food from the galley was absolutely forbidden. By the second day on our cruise back to Saipan I was one hungry sailor.

The morning of the third day I was laying in my buck in the hold all alone listening to my growling stomach. Everyone else in the compartment was topside standing in the chow line. I jumped down off my third tier bunk to go to the head. Threading my way through the narrow aisle between the stacked canvas racks I happened to glance across to a bunk in the next aisle. Whoa! What do we have here?

There laid a Marine clad only in his skivvie shorts snoring away, dead asleep. His khaki shirt and khaki pants hung on a wire hook made out of a coat hanger affixed to the chain holding up his bunk. I didn't even slow down. A quick turn at the end of the row of bunks and down the other aisle I went with engines full ahead. A fast pass by the sleeping Marine without missing a step and like a kid grabbing the brass ring at a merry-go-round, the suntans were in my hand.

I made it in time to catch morning chow.

By the 1st of May I was back on Okinawa with my regular Seabee outfit. I never did tell anyone about this little escapade but have wondered over the years if the Marine found some other khaki's so he didn't starve to death. If he's still around and happens to read this please accept a sincere apology from an old construction swab. On the other hand, considering the time I spent with the Marines, I do remember one version of what "Semper Fi Mac" stood for.

Edgar Cage lives in Munising, Michigan near Lake Superior and the Canadian border with his wife of 43 years, Frances. They have ten children, including four they adopted. Edgar is retired from his own plumbing business he ran for over 20 years. He spends his time now gardening, fishing, hunting and trapping.

83

OLD SCHOOL TRADITION
Former Fireman 1/C Jack L. Spencer, USN

This is an after the war Sea Story but certainly fits the criteria and spirit of what Sea Stories are all about.

I was a World War II Tin Can sailor and spent my combat time in the North Atlantic's U-boat war. I'm sure most Jarheads know what a "Tin Can" is, or was, but for those who don't, a Tin Can was a thin hulled destroyer with a low enough draft that we could get in close to the beach. As a matter of fact my ship, the USS Knight DD-633 was converted to a high-speed mine sweeper for the invasion of Japan because we could get in close to the beach. Our hull designation was changed to DMS-40 and we were slated to go ahead of the Marine landings on Kyushu during Operation Olympic. Our mission would have been to clear mines and offer close in gunfire support until sunk. Thank God the Army Air Force blew 'em out of the war with the A bombs before we had to perform our suicide mission. I did end up with the three major battle ribbons however, the American Theatre, European Theatre and the Asian Theatre.

After my discharge in 1946 I used the GI Bill to enroll in Indiana State Teachers College (Eventually named Indiana State University.)

During the war I was a totally immature teenager just like most of the college students attending Indiana State at the time, but now at age twenty I was feeling thirty from having seen too much and done too much. Therefore, I wasn't in the mood to put up with some of the childish customs perpetuated down through the years at the college by upper classmen. At the same time I didn't want to get off on the wrong foot with my classmates while I worked hard to gain a higher education so I did take a little of the crap dished out with a grain of salt. College hazing was a pain in the ass but I tried to cope with it. My six feet, one inch, 190-pound build helped a little from the yo-yos going to far but just the same I was subject to the traditional freshman harassing.

As the new fall semester got underway quite a few other veterans enrolled and like me they were all older than the kids already in school that included the upper classmen. You could always spot a vet a mile away since all of us were in the same boat of not having much money, especially to buy clothes with and we all wore parts of our old uniforms.

I was about three weeks into my freshman year when I walked into the Physical Education building for a class. Me, and a couple of other freshmen were confronted by a large group of sophomores who were all hot to trot to dish out some of the hazing they had went through the previous year. The college had this quaint tradition that all freshmen had to wear this little green beanie while on campus. It was a stupid looking no bill cap, which reminded me of those prayer caps Jewish men, wear. This was the crime me and the two other fellows had been stopped for since none of us was wearing the green beanie.

The sophomores said that we'd have to be punished for not following the rules and our punishment would be getting paddled with these big boards with a handle with holes in it. I was just beginning to put up an argument that I wasn't about to take a paddling when two burly looking fellows came through the PE building door. The dozen or so sophomores spotted them right away as being freshmen and one of the upper classman yelled out an order for these guys to get in line for a paddling since they didn't have on their green bennies either.

I saw right away that the two newcomers were ex-gyrines because they were both wearing dress green uniform blouses. The two Marines eyed the dozen sophomores and one of them said, "You want to paddle my ass pal, come right ahead and try it!"

The sophomores circled the two Marines and I walked over to a bench to watch the show. I wish that I had tickets to sell!

The Marines both had grim grins on their faces as they calmly took off their wide leather belts from around their blouses with the big brass buckles. I don't know how many college boys it takes to whip two Marines, but there wasn't enough that day!

It was all over in less than three minutes. Several sophomores laid sprawled on the deck while others were either limping or running away. This one Marine looked over to me smiling on the bench and asked, "Does that suit you swabby?"

Still grinning, I replied, "It sure as hell does Jarhead!"

As the three of us walked away we strolled through a litter of brown sophomore hats, paddles, books and notebooks and pieces of civilian clothing. These college boys learned something I was told my first week in the Navy——"Don't fight with a Marine, they're nuts!"

Oh...a few days later, the campus newspaper had an article in it written by the Dean of Students. It said that veterans would not be required to wear the green hats. Imagine that!

Jack Spencer spent most of his adult life after college teaching shop classes in both grade and high school. In a personal letter to the author he wrote that the vets looked out for each other during those college years right after the war. He said they didn't try to run the campus because they didn't want to, but they did what they wanted to do regarding dumb rules. Jack offered an example of their unity: One day a professor was at this tavern outside the college checking on college students drinking, which was a no, no. When word of this got to the veterans, hundreds of them went to the bar to buy a drink so the professor could add their names to his list. "Expel one of us, then expel all of us!" Jack lives in Connersville, Indiana.

84

ADMIRAL'S MAST
USMC(Ret.) - Name Withheld by Request

While serving as a platoon sergeant in the 1st Battalion, 9th Marines in Vietnam I got hit pretty bad and had to be med-evaced. I went through the normal routine as a seriously wounded causality. Emergency treatment at a field hospital at Quang Tri, hospital ship out in Da Nang Harbor, C-130 flight to the Navy Hospital Guam and a few months later ending up at the Navy Hospital, Great Lakes Illinois.

Although I hadn't lost a limb I was placed on the seventh floor amputee ward. I suppose it was because of the orthopedic nature of both legs having been wounded, one with a couple of bullets, the other with mortar shrapnel. I also had sustained other wounds that did not require orthopedic treatment.

It turned out that I was the senior NCO on the ward and when there was a problem with a patient or some shit detail that had to be performed, the corpsmen would come to me to take care of whatever needed to be done and to make sure it was taken care of. This was normal at any military hospital. The same thing had taken place at the hospital on Guam so I knew the drill. At least, I thought I did.

Being on an amputee ward presented some leadership problems that a staff NCO doesn't normally run into in the course of a career. There was about a dozen guys like me on the ward that were not amputees but there was over 50 beds filled with teenage Marines that had legs or arms off, some of them multiple amputations. To say there was a morale problem with the disillusioned and bitter kids, is putting it mildly. A few of them were upbeat but for the most part the majority of them were having difficulty coping with the fact that their lives was going to be changed forever. From a professional standpoint I understood where they were coming from and I totally sympathized with their plight. My attitude was, if they wanted to rant and rave and throw a snit fit, then let them do it. They had some major adjustments to make and as far as I was concerned their surly attitude, with little respect for authority, was the beginning of the healing process.

Besides, I was having a few problems trying to cope myself and I don't think my mental health was in the best of shape either. After almost three years of continuous combat from 1966 to 1969, on one long tour, you could say my nerves were on edge. As a professional Marine I felt it was my duty to keep extending my tour to see the job through to the end. And that's just what I did until I finally got carried out of Nam with no hope of ever going back. Even though I was a professional my brain housing was a little screwed up and I too wasn't taking too much shit off anybody either.

One of my biggest problem child amputees was an 18 year old with both legs off above the knee. The corpsmen had learned not to place anything on the moveable over-bed table at this youngster's bed without being right there with him. If left alone for a moment he would clear the table in a heartbeat, regardless of what was on it. More than once I had cleaned up the mess he'd created by shoving his chow tray off onto the deck because a corpsman had turned his back on the kid.

One of the duty Navy nurses on this ward was an old battleaxe lieutenant commander that had more time in the Navy than my 17 years in the Corps. She had to have been in her early 50's and with that much time of service you would think that she'd know how to deal with kids that were combat casualities. She didn't!

She was constantly on the kid's cases, berating them and chewing ass for the multitude of prissy infractions the kids were always doing. And do you think the kids gave a shit? Hell no! They'd sass back at her and it kept the hospital chief-master-at-arms busy on our ward writing out disciplinary reports that was sent to higher authority.

I've got to make one thing clear right now. This broad wasn't chiding these youngsters in an effort to buck them up so they could better face the realities of life. What she was doing had nothing to do with trying to stop them from feeling sorry for themselves or try to instill a better attitude. No, she was simply a witch in ever sense of the word. Matter of fact, she even looked like a witch! She stood about five feet eight, thin as a rail with a hooknose and jutting chin. Her eyes were always wide and darting and her dyed black hair could have almost passed for a crew cut. All she needed was a broom. (Remember the bad witch in the Wizard of Oz? She could have been a stand-in double.)

As the senior patient NCO on the ward I tried to talk to this nurse several times, trying to get across to her that if she had a problem with one of the enlisted men I'd take care of it for her. Her attitude toward me wasn't much different than she held for the kids. I got the feeling she hadn't dealt with too many Marines during her career. And my little chats with her did no good either, even though I kept after her to let me handle problems that arose. No dice. This one day I got so pissed that I went into her little glass cage that was the nurse's station and rather loudly voiced my opinion that she wasn't doing a damn thing to help the morale of her patients. She tried to run me up with the master-of-arms but since there had not been any witnesses to my disrespectfully outburst it was my word against hers, in that she had misunderstood what I'd said. The Chief master-of-arms dropped the matter but told me to cool it.

It wasn't more than three days after that episode that I walked onto the ward to find nurse "Crachet" raising hell with the kid with both legs off. He'd tossed his chow tray again and the nurse was threatening to put him down on the deck on his stumps to clean up the mess. I just flat ass told her to get the hell away from the kid and told her if I ever saw her harassing him again I'd put my boot up her ass and shove her down the ladder well. The shock on her face was well worth the visit I knew I was going to have with the Chief-master-at-arms. She turned on her heels without saying a word and rushed to her glass office where a minute later I saw her on the telephone. It was the first time I'd seen the kid with his legs off smile.

For the next several days everything was real peaceful on the ward with the ogre nurse not bothering the patients, content I suppose that I had been ordered to see a psychiatrist twice a day.

As it turned out the firestorm took place late one night when I came staggering into the ward to hit the rack after a long evening at the chief"s club. Although I was pretty soused my senses picked up a commotion at the far end of the darkened ward. I decided to investigate.

There stood nurse "Crachet" with a towel in her hand flaying away at the double amputee and giving him a lecture ass chewing of some sort. I then noticed her medication tray she carried was on the deck with pills and capsules spilled everywhere. I also saw that the young Marine was crying. I didn't say a word. Instead, I just walked up behind the nurse and gave her a swift kick in her skinny ass. Then I grabbed her by the arm and started pulling her down the corridor. (It was later reported that I was mumbling something along the line that I'd done my level best to deal with her as an NCO and since she wouldn't listen to reason, then by God she could suffer the consequences.) I can't say what I had in my mind at that moment, and it may be that I was actually going to go through with my threat of pushing her out of the ward by way of the ladder well. I do know that she'd lost her footing as I pulled her and remember dragging her down the middle of the ward by one hand while she skidded along on her ass.

The two young Navy corpsmen on night duty came rushing from their cubical to stop me, and rightly so. The only regret I've ever had about this entire situation was that the corpsmen tried to protect their nurse and I decked them both.

By now the entire ward was awake and the noise the patients made from they're hooting and hollering brought in the duty doctor. He was a big black man that I had a lot of respect for because of his compassion toward his patients, and no doubt he instantly took in what was taking place. Nurse "Crachet" had scrambled away from me while I was dealing with her two corpsmen and the doctor quickly walked past her and came up to me. In a calm voice he talked to me, saying that we would sort out "the problems" in the morning and he got close enough to me that he hit me with a needle before I realized what was going on. I don't know what the hell he had in that needle, or how in the hell he happened to come by it, but whatever it was, it knocked me out right then and there.

I awoke later in a private room with a splitting headache and the knowledge I was in a whole heap of trouble.

My first visitor that morning was the black doctor who had this strange smile on his face the entire time he checked me out. Not a word passed between us about our previous encounter and the closest he came to it was when he left the room he looked back at me and shook his head back and forth a couple of times with that odd smile still on his face. My second visitor was the Chief-master-at-arms.

The investigation took a week but in the long run it was a no brainier since the statements from the doctor, Nurse "Crachet", and the two corpsmen were sufficient to hang me with morning colors all by themselves. I was referred, not to Captains Mast, but to Admirals Mast! The commanding officer of the Navy Hospital was a two star admiral. Naturally, I figured this Admirals Mast was just a preliminary routine administrative necessity for better things to come—say a special court-martial.

But an enlisted clerk at the Marine Barracks on Great Lakes Naval Station was either extremely conscientious or had a warped sense of humor. Before sending my Service

Record Book over to the hospital to the admiral's office this office pinky happened to notice that there was a second Bronze Star medal citation in my jacket that had not been presented to me. Now I know that Marines take care of their own, but this clerk who didn't even know me, went above and beyond that standard of duty of looking out for a fellow Marine. He must have went to his adjutant and suggested that wouldn't it be a grand idea, since the British Commandant of the Marine Corps was visiting Great Lakes, to have this Royal Marine present me the Bronze Star Medal with gold star for heroic achievement.

And that's just what took place.

Two days before I was to meet officially with the admiral the British Commandant of the Marine Corps paid a visit to the naval hospital. When the throng of brass accompanying the British commandant came onto the amputee ward; all patients that could walk were at attention in front of their bunks, and those in wheel chairs were likewise in front of their bunks. I think even my double amputee lad was awed by all the brass as he was on his good behavior.

Naturally, Nurse "Crachet" just happened to have the duty that day and she led the commandant, the hospital admiral, and a host of other officers, including the Marine Barracks colonel, along the rows of beds, introducing each patient. The British commandant would shake hands and say a few words to each man, and he gave every patient a small coin with the emblem of the Royal Marines on it that I thought was pretty neat.

When the group got to my bunk I was introduced to the British commandant and the admiral mentioned that I was the sergeant that would be receiving the Bronze Star medal. The commandant was a rather short, thin man with a hairline mustache. He reminded me of the World War II British Field Marshal Bernard Montgomery of Alamein, Africa fame.

A Navy lieutenant jg read the citation and the British commandant pinned on the medal to my green blouse under the five rows of ribbons I already wore. He was very nice and mentioned after viewing my other decorations that I was obviously a good Marine. I could see the eyes rolling from that comment. Then he said, "I say old chap, are you getting along okay?"

I'm sure he was referring about me recovering from combat wounds, but my brain churned in a different direction and for the life of me I have no idea why I blurted out, "Not worth a crap sir, they're getting ready to court-martial me!"

If looks could kill I would have been dead in my tracks from the silted glares I got from the admiral, the colonel and the other brass, including Nurse "Crachet."

I had also stunned the British Commandant. "Oh my, I say. That is very distressing to hear." He fumbled for words for a moment. "The citation that was just read, the medal, how on earth.." He turned toward the admiral. "I say admiral, considering the circumstances, could it be possible that an amnesty of some sort could be issued?"

Tight lipped, the admiral made a terse reply. "I'll take care of it sir."

"Good, very good. Well old chap, you take care." And the British commandant shook my hand again before going to the next bunk.

The kid with both legs off got a Silver Star and his citation paled mine in comparison.

A couple of days later I stood outside the door of the admiral's office on the top deck of the hospital. I had been instructed that when I marched into his office I would see a podium in the middle of the floor and I was to walk up to it and halt a couple of paces directly in front and stand at attention. After cooling my heels for several minutes in the passageway outside the office the Chief-master-of-arms opened the door and ordered me inside.

I spotted the podium and angled directly toward it and came to a halt as ordered, standing at attention.

The admiral's office was huge. I mean it was 50 by 50 feet square at a minimum. There were a number of uniformed people in It too, standing along a side wall. As I stared straight ahead toward wrap around windows overlooking the Navy base it came to me that there must have been a dozen officers and enlisted men in the room with me. Right in my line of vision sat the admiral at his desk a good 30 feet from me. His gigantic desk was located at the corner of the room with windows flanking both sides. He obviously had a great view of the base.

What seemed like a full five minutes went by with me sweating it out at attention while the admiral sat at his desk thumping a pencil staring at me. All of a sudden he abruptly stood up and waving his pencil like a pointer, said. "I want all of you to leave the room except the sergeant."

His order stunned the other officers, but with a shuffling of feet I could hear them all leaving the room. While they were doing this the admiral had sat back down in his big leather swivel chair. After the others had left he continued to let me stand there alone for at least another minute. Then he waved his pencil at me, saying, "C'mon over here and have a seat sergeant."

I'll be damn if the first thing he did was to offer me a cigarette from this fancy silver box. I declined.

Then he looked right at me and said, "We've got a problem here."

I had to bite my tongue to keep from blurting out, "No shit sir!"

He tossed the pencil on his desk and tenting his hands looked at me with hooded eyes. "I understand you've got the entire ward out in the hall there, bed patients and all waiting to testify in your behalf."

"Yes sir." I replied.

"Here what I want you to do. I want you to go to the door and tell the Chief-master-of-arms that you're releasing your witnesses and for him to get them back on the ward. A lot of those boys have no business being up here in the first place. Will you trust me enough to do that for me?"

I stuttered out, "Ye...yes sir."

When I got back to his desk he was leaning on it with his elbows. "I've read a lot of statements and talked with a lot of people the past couple of weeks concerning your bit of stupidity you performed on ward seven." He gave me a second to digest that bit of info, then continued on. "I've also read your psyc reports and evaluations, talked with the chaplain, had a long conversation with the Chief-master-of-arms and the Chief of Nursing. Let me put it to you this way. I believe I have a pretty good picture of what has been taking place on ward seven, and to some degree about you also." He paused again to let me ponder on that tid-bit.

"But the problem we have, is regardless of what may have went on in ward seven, is the fact that you physically laid your hands onto a naval officer. That cannot go unpunished! Plus the fact your were stinking drunk and you abused two enlisted men. On the other hand I have seen your Marine Corps records and know that you are an outstanding field Marine who has shown much courage on the battlefield. The stress of combat is obviously a factor in your situation plus the plea made by our Royal Marine ally has a mitigating influence. What do you suggest I do about this?"

Oh boy! Talk about being over a barrel. But I was starting to see a glimmer that I wasn't going to find myself in the Great Lakes brig and possibly not be a four hash mark private. But how was I to know what he should do to me? It was apparent the admiral was expecting some sort of an answer from me and the only thing I could think of was to be honest with him. "Sir, if you can see your way clear of getting rid of that nurse from being around Marines, then I'll take anything you have to give me."

He actually showed a thin smile. Shaking his head slightly, he said, "Marines. Lord, what would we do without them?" Looking me straight in the eye, he then said, "Son, I'm going to make you a deal. I'm going to take one of your stripes with the stipulation if you can keep your nose clean for the next year, you'll get it back. I don't know how long you have remaining as being a Marine, considering also that you are facing a medical board, but you can assume that even with the restoration of your rank you're going to find it hard to get another stripe, and I think that is punishment enough. And the other item you mentioned has already been taken care of through an immediate recommended retirement." As I digested that bit of information that Nurse "Crachet" was being retired the admiral stood up and I automatically did the same. Reaching his hand out for me to shake it, he said, "If there is ever a next time that you have to take extraordinary measures to look out for the troops, make sure you go up through the chain of command with a request mast, instead of an admiral's mast."

I shook the admiral's hand and said, "Yes sir."

In keeping with the confidentially of this writers request, he did allow the author to mention that the admiral was a man of his word and that he got his rocker back within the year.

85

A PEARL HARBOR TALE
About PFC Albert Gatchel, USMC
as told by
CWO4 Norman H. Hyatt, USMCR(Ret.)

The mighty warship sat anchored in Pearl Harbor that Sunday morning with small waves gently stroking the gray steel hull.

Most of the ships crew was ashore on a liberty weekend but Marine PFC Al Gatchel had the duty. The tall, thin nineteen-year-old was standing the 0400 to 0800 watch as the ships brig guard. There was a little nook with a steel plate for a desk that Gatchel sat at and every half-hour he'd check on the three brig prisoners in his charge, then seeing that the sailors were sleeping peacefully, he'd make a notation in the logbook. That was about all there was to write about in the duty log this 7th day of December 1941.

Bored, Gatchel began reading a Zane Grey western to pass the time. While this practice was frowned upon by his superiors he knew all the brig guards slipped a paperback novel down into the hold on the graveyard shift. The cowboy hero rode across the plains shooting the bad guys and loving the women.

The only sound reaching the bottom of the ship small steel compartment located in the bow section was the occasional slap of a wave against the ships hull. The eerie silence in the brig area made it hard for Gatchel to stay awake and he welcomed the 0530 reveille call for the prisoners so they could get ready for an early morning chow.

After returning the three sailors from the chow hall at 0700, Gatchel secured them back into their cells and noted the event in his duty log. He again propped his feet up on the tiny duty desk to read his western while waiting out his last hour.

As the brigs clock neared 0800 the young Marine was deeply immersed in his western. The hero was in the middle of a showdown and it seemed so real to Gatchel that he actually thought for a moment he'd heard gunfire. And then the sound came again. Suddenly putting the book down he listened closely. He was hearing gunfire!

The sounds of machine guns, explosions and people screaming echoed down into the brig. Gatchel glanced at the brig cells and got up and walked pass them with the three prisoners looking at him curiously. He reached the hatch leading out of the brig then hesitated with the din from above increasing in tempo. The young Marine bent his head and stepped through the oval steel door. Pausing again at the bottom of the ladder way leading topside the PFC did something no Marine should ever do. He left his post.

Gatchel was conscious of the fact he'd left his appointed place of duty, knowing it was a court-martial offense, but two things was on his mind. Where was his relief? And what was going on up there?

He got halfway up the ladder well when an enormous explosion rocked the ship so violently that it knocked the Marine off the stairway, throwing him back down to the bottom deck. The huge blast had also slammed shut the steel hatch to the brig he'd came from. Somehow the explosion had warped the door to a locked position. For several precious minutes Gatchel fought in vain to open the steel door with the prisoners screaming on the other side. More blast rocked the ship. Scared out of his mind, not knowing what was taking place topside, he finally gave up trying to open the stuck hatch. His only thought was to get some help from the Sergeant-of-the-Guard or the Officer-of-the-Day. He realized as he scrambled up the ladder again that he'd have to answer some questions as to why he was out of the brig area when the hatch sealed itself trapping the prisoners. He shrugged off this thought deciding to worry about it later. Besides, he soon found out he had more to worry about anyway when he noticed the ladder he was going up was slanting bow down as if the ship was settling. Gatchel just made it to the topside hatch leading to the foredeck when tons of water began pouring down the ladder well. He had to fight like mad to keep from getting sucked back down from where he'd came.

In a matter of seconds Gatchel found himself swimming in the oily water of Pearl Harbor.

Treading water he saw his ship slowly settle to the harbors bottom, going down bow first. Because of the shallow depth of the harbor the superstructure of the battleship stuck up like a distorted parody of a man-of-war. Other men was in the water with him, some with burns and other injuries and he heard their cries for help. He got a sailor with bad burns onto a floating plank and told him to hold on until better help arrived..

Gatchel also heard the buzz of diving airplanes and looking upward saw swarms of divebombers, fighters and torpedo planes with red meatball markings making passes at other ships. After awhile Gatchel saw small boats and captain's gigs slowly making there way through the debris filled water. One stopped and picked up him and the burned sailor.

Because PFC Albert Gatchel left his post he lived through the date that will live in infamy. But the three prisoners he was in charge of went down with the ship.

Oddly enough, Gatchel never had to answer any inquiries on how he made it off the ship from the brig area. And it was something he did not talk about ever, until he related this story to his nephew, Gunner Norm Hyatt in the late 1950.s.

86

IWO - THE FIRST DAY
Colonel Vern Wanger, USMC(Ret.)

I was a captain company commander of K Company, 3rd Battalion, 23rd Marines, 4th Marine Division that Monday morning, February 19, 1945.

My rifle company was designated the battalion floating reserve for the amphibious assault on Iwo Jima and while the rest of the battalion made the initial landing K Company stood by offshore in Amtrac's prepared for immediate reinforcement when help was needed.

It wasn't long in coming before battalion called me and ordered me to get my reserve company ashore as quick as possible. I ordered our Amtrac to head for the beach and received another message from 3rd Battalion CP to get my company up to Airfield #1 on the double because the battalion could use all the help it could get.

We came in under a curtain of Japanese artillery fire and when my Amtrac rammed onto the beach enemy machine gun fire and mortar fire was raking us. An enemy explosion must have jammed the ramp of our landing craft as it wouldn't lower. I ordered my Marines out over the side. The first man over was hit in the face and shoulder by shrapnel. The rest dropped into waist deep water and struggled on up to the beach through thick sand as withering Japanese small arms fire raked our ranks. Once on the black sand beach it was still a struggle to move and the fire was so intense my men jumped into shell holes while Japanese mortars continued to drop down on us.

The entire area where my company had landed was littered with debris and wounded Marines waiting medical evacuation. I felt sorry for those wounded men but knew I had to get my company off that beach which was like a picture from Dante's inferno.

I no sooner started inland than my radio operator had his walkie-talkie blown out of his hand. Even without communications I knew I had to get my Marines moving forward as there wasn't the slightest doubt in my mind that the 3rd Battalion needed all the help they could get, considering what my company was going through.

A scant 50 yards inland K Company came under devastating machine gun fire and many of my Marines began to fall either dead or wounded. One of my platoon leaders, 2ndLt James Mariedas jumped into a shell hole only to find out a Japanese soldier was already occupying it. In hand to hand combat the Marine lieutenant was able to stab the enemy soldier to death with the soldiers own bayonet.

Ahead, the ground was studded with pillboxes. Many of them were still pouring smoke from the recent effects of Marine satchel explosives and flamethrowers the 3rd Battalion had used to neutralize them. However, no one had told the Japanese they couldn't come back to the semi-ruined fortifications and enemy infiltrators had done just that. My company was again pinned down trying to get up to Airfield #1. K Company Marines flanked this one pillbox and managed to toss in a couple of hand grenades through the rear hatch. The grenades were promptly seen flying out the front gun-slits. So we had to make a dual attack by throwing in grenades both through the front aperture and back door. Once this position was silenced we moved to the next pillbox. After fighting through this maze of pillboxes that were supposed to have already been neutralized, and had caused more casualties in my company, we moved forward again.

My battle map told me I was nearing Airfield #1 and within a couple of hundred yards I saw the battalion dug in facing the airstrip. This is when my company came under direct heavy enemy artillery fire.

I urged my men toward the battalion assault troops not that far away. Even though the battalion was now in sight we found ourselves pinned down once again. The Japanese were using an antiaircraft gun depressed for level firing. I ordered my first platoon commander to send one of his squads to flank the weapon and destroy it. The young lieutenant shook his head sadly, then told me he'd better send two squads since that would make up a twelve man team. I knew we had been taking causalities but my lieutenant's assessment that two of his squads was now down to one squad sobered me. The two squads did in fact eliminate the antiaircraft gun position and we moved on.

My reserve company finally made it to the front lines. Although we had not yet been committed to battle, I had to tell my battalion commander that his reserves had suffered 70% causalities just getting to him. But that's the way it was, that first day on Iwo Jima.

Colonel Vern Wagner was a professor at Indianapolis Marion College for over 30 years. For his gallantry on Iwo Jima he was awarded the Silver Star Medal. He doesn't talk about his wartime's experiences much and this story tends to explain why. Author's humble thanks for sharing it with the reader.

87

THE ROUGHEST LANDING I EVER MADE
Captain Hugh E. Irwin, USMCR(Ret.)

The best Sea Story I ever heard was about the submarine crew in the Philippines that stole an army jeep, then field stripped it to the point where they could get the pieces down the sub hatch for later reassembly at the next port of call. A submarine with its own personal jeep! But that is not my Sea Story.

I got into World War II by way of Guadalcanal as a replacement pilot assigned to VMF-222. My tour with the "Flying Deuces" was a short one but just the same a memorable one. As a boot 2nd lieutenant I was given the job of being my skipper's wingman but I never got to know him personally, even after a dozen missions over Rabaul. The reason has a humorous side to it. Evidently my CO, Major Roy Spurlock, had run afoul of our group commander, LtCol. "Zeb" Hopkins who had put him in hack. For those not knowing military terminology, that meant he was on close restriction, confined to his tent when not on duty. We only saw one another face to face during pre-flight briefings. It was strange not to socialize with the one whose fanny you were expected to protect but by late 1944 the war was moving so swiftly you didn't have time to worry about such trivialities.

In November 1944 I was reassigned to VMF-251 and a month later our squadron was informed that we would be a part of MacArthur's "I shall return" to the Philippines campaign.

We occupied a new airstrip built by Seabees on the southern tip of Samar. For five months we flew close support for army units battling there way from island to island. The F4U Vought Corsair proved its durability during this campaign as conditions could not have been worse for trying to keep fighter planes in the air.

On Sunday, April 8, 1945 while leading a two-plane section doing close support for the Americal Division in retaking of Cebu City, I was unable to release one of the two 500-lb general-purpose bombs carried under the wings of my Corsair. Although the piston driven aircraft was noted for its ruggedness it could hardly be expected to survive the punishment of a hundred missions without some sort of malfunction. So I took it in stride and completed making strafing runs as directed by the Forward Air Control flying below us overlooking the city.

My wingman and I headed for our home strip on Samar and en-route I performed some violent maneuvers over the water to try to shake loose my 500-lb extra cargo dangling under my right wing. This minor acrobatic air show did no good so I radioed the control tower for a straight in approach to avoid an accidental drop in friendly bivouac areas. I proceeded with what I expected to be a normal landing and I had no qualms about the bomb since months earlier I had experienced a similar situation. This took place after a strike on Rabaul when landing on Green Island a stuck 1,000 pounder dropped from my plane as it touched down and rolled harmlessly along the runway.

This would not be the case this time however. As my Corsair glided onto the crushed stone airstrip the 500 pounder jettisoned and in doing so rolled along under my plane. The nose fuse was evidently chewed off as it bounced along; thereby arming the bomb. With one more skip it detonated right under me. My Corsair blew apart all around me as I fought the controls. Within seconds I was in half an airplane with only bits and pieces of a tail section remaining aft of the cockpit and shredded wings and cowling forward. It was the damndest ride I had ever taken in my life! When the hunk of junk finally came to a stand still and realizing I was still in this world, I scrambled from what was left of my Corsair fearing the fire might follow the explosion.

My flight suit was in rags, my parachute was shredded and I could feel the trickle of blood from a dozen lacerations as I fell down in the mud to await help. I heard sirens but no ambulance came my way. (I learned later that none of the ground crew thought that I could have never survived such a blast and medical personnel went to help other Marines who had been struck by some of my bombs shrapnel.)

After fifteen minutes I got up out of my mud puddle and stumbling around in my tattered parachute and flight suit, which was the zipper down the front type, I walked out to the middle of the runway and began yelling. This effort caused my parachute to come undone and there I was dragging that long piece of silk behind me like some lost kid. I guess the white parachute finally aroused some attention from the tower area and an operations jeep sped towards me. So what happens when the two Marines get out of the jeep? Here I am dipped and ripped and those two clowns are so awed by the wrecked Corsair that they don't even pay any attention to me but rather scope out the destroyed airplane. When they at last got done walking around what was left of old number 22 they put me in the jeep and took me to the duty flight surgeon.

The navy doc couldn't believe I had survived the crash either and after stripping my clothes off found that I'd only suffered a couple of dozen cuts most of them not that deep. He gave me a couple of shots and patched up the major bleeding areas before sending me on to the Army Air Force Hospital.

By now the word has spread like wildfire about the Marine pilot who had walked away from a bomb blast while landing his plane. I had to relate my story time and time again and my private hospital room always seemed to have been filled with curious visitors who just wanted to take a look at me. The Air Force doctors remarked it was impossible for someone to have survived that bomb blast with only minor wounds. Praise God they were wrong.

Of the many cuts to my arms and legs and the many small bits of shrapnel imbedded, I only suffered one major laceration to my left shoulder. On April 11th I was released from the hospital after four days.

I was given the choice of returning to the U. .S. or staying with my squadron until fit for duty. I chose the latter for the simple reason that the Marine Corps had spent a lot of time and effort in making me a pilot and I knew where my duty laid. Just the same I enjoyed some "hammock duty" while my buddies continued to help clean up the Philippine liberation. Because my shoulder wound proved slow to heal and was located right where a parachute straps made contact it was two months before I resumed fly-

Captain Irvin's F4U Corsair after his "roughest landing."

ing. By this time my outfit MAG-15, had moved to Okinawa.

A final note: Teenage Filipino girls would come by daily to pick up our laundry at Samar. They were all quite religious and this one girl told me she blamed my accident on the fact I was waging war on a Sunday. I feel instead that the Lord sent a Guardian Angel to look over me that day and that an angel was riding in the cockpit with me during the roughest landing I ever made.

Hugh "Hogi" Irwin lives in Pittsford, New York. After college on the G.I. Bill he went to work for the Kodak Company in Rochester where he eventually retired from. Recalled to active duty during the Korean War he completed his active duty hitch then ended up being placed on a Marine Corps Reserve Volunteer Training Unit assignment of which he also retired from. Among his many military decorations are two Distinguished Flying Crosses and several Air Medals along with the Purple Heart.

88

SWIFT AND IMMEDIATE DISCIPLINARY MEASURES
Master Sergeant Lucian Simmons Jr., USAF(Ret.)

In 1959 after having just completed three years of active duty service in the U.S. Army, I enlisted into the U.S. Navy. I enjoyed the military life but being a ground-pounding infantryman wasn't exactly what I had in mind to improve my education so I decided to give the navy a go.

The navy recruiters said I still had to go through navy boot camp that wasn't a big deal as far as I was concerned and I soon found myself a recruit in Company 019, United States Naval Training Center, San Diego, California.

I was a few years older than the other recruits in my boot training company as the majority of the young men were all in their teens. Our Company Commander was a salty old Chief Petty Officer with 20 years of service. To me he was a fantastic person, even though a task master, very methodical and demanding. His leadership qualities impressed me deeply. He was a big man, over six feet, with sandy hair, ruddy face and 100% navy. After a ten day indoctrination period the chief summoned me to his office.

He told me he'd reviewed my record and noticed my prior service and the fact I had experience as an army drill instructor. (Don't confuse this with Marine DI's, although I did teach drill.) Anyway, he informed me that he was always on the lookout for recruits with former military training such as college ROTC or prior service in their service records. He said he'd been keeping an eye on me and with my military bearing and background he was appointing me a recruit Petty Officer, First Class (AP01.) I was to be the assistant to the Platoon Leader of the 2nd Platoon who was regular navy. My duties would include teaching boots how to drill properly with and without rifles, to make sure they paid attention during classes, keep the squad bay ship shape and insure they obeyed instructions at all times. Chief Stilwell went on to say that he'd back me to the hilt on any decisions I made when it came to administering "swift and immediate disciplinary measures" in the performance of my duty. In other words my job was to "kick ass and take names!"

I wasn't exactly sure of what he meant by swift and immediate disciplinary measures but since he had said he would back me to the hilt on any decisions I made along those lines I developed my own style of justice. Anytime I observed a recruit out of step or goofing off I would walk up behind him and "swiftly" kick him in the ass. Then I'd have a few words to say to the recruit, telling him what his sin had been and that I'd better not catch him doing it again.

Over the eleven week period of boot camp training I literally kicked every man's rear end in my platoon on numerous occasions. My black boot print on their white bell bottoms all but became a 2nd Platoon symbol.

Not that this symbol was taken with any great measure of pride. During this eleven weeks I also had five fistfights, threats of a blanket party from a group of sailors from Texas, and an attempt by one boot to enlist help to kill me. And of course a daily dose of grumbling threats of revenge once boot training was completed. The chief thought I was doing great!

None of this slowed me down from doing my job that had been given me. During drilling I would march next to the real First Class who was calling cadence and giving commands and if I saw someone skylarking, out-of-step or just being stupid, I'd step into the ranks and deliver my "swift" kick. I was also like a hawk during the many classes we were required to take and woe to the recruit I caught napping our goofing off in general.

Naturally the other recruits couldn't figure me out since I was also a navy boot. Who in the hell did this guy think he was? They knew nothing of my background for the simple reason I was a lone wolf without a buddy one, although the First Class Platoon Leader did treat me as an equal to some extent as did Chief Stilwell in a lesser sense. However, the chief was very pleased on how I was handling the task he had assigned me to do.

The 45 boots of the 2nd Platoon finally learned that they better look sharp, stay in step, obey orders and pay attention during instruction or pay the consequences of my deadly foot.

Over the years since my navy boot camp days I've thought about it a lot how I took it to heart in starting a new military career by doing my chief's bidding by being a discipline enforcer and meting out his "swift and immediate" measures. I like to think that my effort had something to do with the fact that the 2nd Platoon won every marching award, swimming award, academic award and had the highest percentage of personnel graduating in our company. Our platoon flag had all the gold stars that were awarded plus a few silver ones. Because of our achievement Company 019 was known as the best in the battalion.

The day we graduated from boot camp everyone in the platoon was promoted to seaman apprentice. I think my boot camp ship mates finally caught on there was something different about me when I came out to that last formation wearing seaman's stripes which was one grade higher than them, and had on my three army ribbons. After the graduation ceremony several of them came up and shook my hand. And during the next four years I ran into several of them around the world and there was no thought of retaliation. They were all proud that we had taken top honors in the battalion and those I met later on remembered that and credited me with helping them to achieve that goal.

And me and the navy? I was assigned to the deck force of a destroyer for four years and of all things suffered from chronic seasickness!

Lucian lives in Oil Trough, Arkansas. He rose to the naval rating of 2nd Class Petty Officer, Gunners mate. Lucian said he really liked the Navy, but as a country boy from

Arkansas could never adapt to the ocean. He said life aboard a ship was not for him and when it came time for him to reenlist he decided he'd better stay on the land, or maybe give the air a try. He enlisted in the U.S. Air Force in 1964 and went on to serve 23 more years in the military of his country.

89

A SAILORS HUMOROUS REFLECTIONS OF WORLD WAR II

Former Radioman 1/C George G. Dawson, USN

When I joined the Navy on my 17th birthday in August 1942 it was my intention to become a gunners mate on a destroyer. I voiced this desire all through boot camp so of course the Navy made me a radioman. After graduating from radio school I was pro-moted to RM 3rd Class and sent to Camp Crowder, Missouri for an advance course through the U.S. Army Signal Corps. Upon completion of this training I received orders to the Navy radio station, Oran, Algeria. So much for being a gunners mate on a de-stroyer.

Before shipping out to North Africa, my shipmates and I were sent to the Navy Receiving Station, Norfolk, Virginia. The citizens and businesses of Norfolk barely tolerated us swabs, and only then to get what money they could pry from our pockets. In the case of me and my four buddies who were going to Algeria with me, money was a premium since our pay records had not caught up with us and we had not been paid for a while.

When the word was passed in our transit barracks that we were getting one last liberty before shipping out, our mood was pretty glum. Here it was our last day in the good old U.S.A. and we couldn't afford to celebrate it. But like all good sailors we weren't going to pass up our last night ashore and we pooled our nickels, dimes, and pennies, and found that we had just enough change for one glass of beer apiece.

The five of us entered this crummy dive near the Navy Base and ordered a beer. The unshaven, brutish looking slob of a bartender was not only unfriendly; he was down right nasty. A two-bit glass of beer didn't mean anything to him and he took his sweet old time pouring it. Even at that he managed to slosh some of our precious brew on the bar when serving the tall glasses to us. He put a cigarette in his mouth while waiting for us to pay and when he reached into his shirt pocket to pull out a book of matches a crumbled up ten-dollar bill fell out and dropped on the bar. He obviously hadn't noticed this as he went on to light up his smoke. We didn't touch the money, nor did we call it to his attention. After he got his cigarette lit he glanced down and saw the bill laying on the bar and he picked it up, went to the cash register, then returned with the change and laid it on the bar in front of us. Ten bucks would buy a goodly amount of beer in those days, and we managed to down a fair amount of suds before returning to the Receiving Station. Did we feel guilty about this bit of petty larceny? Hell no!

I'll never forget my first night in Africa. The Liberty Ship that had brought us to North Africa anchored out in the bay and we Navy men were ordered to go ashore in landing craft. On our way in we had to sail around the mast and upper deck works of many sunken ships. Once ashore we milled around on the beach since no one was there to meet us. It was growing dark and the three dozen of us had no idea what we were supposed to do. Finally, a guard told us that our officers would not be coming until the next morning and that we should find a spot to camp out for the night. We had no idea where we were at so we scouted around in the growing dusk until finding a spot that seemed to be safe, secure, and quiet. We ate K-rations for supper and then using shelter halves and poncho's made two men pup tents to sleep in. A guard roster was made up and we posted armed sentries for security. The next morning we awoke early and checked out more closely where we'd spent the night. To our amazement, we found out that we had settled down right in the middle of a French Navy ammunition depot. There were stacks of huge shells and cases upon cases of gunpowder all around us. Thank God our effort last night to build a fire to ward off the shivering cold African evening climate had failed. We quickly relocated to a different area!

While stationed at the naval base in Oran, a lot of sailors spent there off duty time at a remote beach several miles west of the city to swim and laze in the sun. Since this was an isolated area with no civilians nearby we could change clothes in the open. Eventually, however, some of the guys wanted to bring girl friends to the beach, so a little wooden cabin was built to offer some privacy. A plywood wall separated the guy's changing room from the women's. But sailors will be sailors and it didn't take long for somebody to bore a small peephole in the thin plywood. The guys without female companionship would crowd inside the small changing cubical and take turns kneeling down and peer through the hole to watch the girls undress. We had this one young seaman who was very prudish and he berated the rest of us who took part in our sport. He didn't offend us but he did become the butt of some rude jokes about his manhood and was constantly needled for not taking part in the free show. The needling finally got to him so he breaks down and says he'll take a turn at the peephole. He squatted down and put his eye to the small hole. All of a sudden he jumped back up and his face his beet-red and he looks flustered. "What did you see?" A fellow sailor asked. "Another eye looking in from the other side!" was his classic reply.

One day I was manning the Teletype machine that was a direct line to the French Navy's radio station. I knew all the French communication operators were Navy women whom we called "French Waves," and being that I was lonely and bored, after I completed the official message traffic, I typed in a few friendly words at the end of my transmission. Damn if a friendly reply didn't come shooting back and for the next twenty minutes I shared a conversation with the gal on the other end. She seemed to be very personable and I decided to try my luck in asking her for a date. I typed in a suggestion that we meet somewhere. She agreed to this and a popular bar/restaurant sidewalk cafe in the heart of Oran was selected for our meeting. When the location was determined I typed in, "How will I recognize you?" Her reply clicked over the teletype: "I will wear my uniform and will be sitting at one of the outdoor tables with a magazine in my left hand and holding a glass of white wine in my other hand." Oh boy, I could hardly wait! That evening, I showed up at the sidewalk cafe all spic and span in my Navy whites and raring to go, eager to meet my new friend. But what was this? There sitting at the small tables on the sidewalk were over a dozen French Waves in uniform. Each was holding a magazine in her left hand and each was clutching a glass of white wine in their right hand. It dawned on me real quick that I was a victim of a very clever and well-planned practical joke. Who says the French have no sense of humor?

After Germany surrendered in April 1945 I was sent back to the United States from Oran, given a short home-leave, and then sent to Okinawa where Army, Navy and Marine forces were staging for the invasion of the Japanese homeland. I helped to build a seaplane base on a peninsula that jutted out into the Pacific Ocean from the east side of the island. At first we lived in tents, but then Seabees helped us build Quonset huts and other more stable structures. The only entertainment we had was an occasional movie, and there was little else to do for amusement. But after all our construction was completed there remained some lumber and other building material and we asked permission to use this to build an enlisted men's club house. Our plea was that we'd do the work during our free time and that the club could be used for playing cards, other board games, to have a coke or two and to socialize in a relaxing atmosphere. Permission was granted and we all pitched in and worked our butts off to build our club house. We only got to enjoy our nice recreation room for a few weeks. A couple of guys got into a minor fist fight in the club house and using this incident as an excuse, our officers ousted us from our club and turned it into an officers club. A well-stocked bar was installed with both beer and booze, and seamen were assigned to tend bar for the brass, and to keep the place clean, etc. The enlisted men were furious, but nothing could be done about it. That is, until Mother Nature stepped in.

A fierce typhoon struck Okinawa. I was manning the radio shack, which was located on top of a hill overlooking the seaplane base below. Right in the middle of the storm I received an urgent message that required immediate attention. Leaving my assistant radioman in charge I took off downhill in the howling wind to find the duty officer. Not only couldn't I find the duty officer, I couldn't find any officer anywhere! After checking out the officer's mess, the officer's quarters and various offices, I got to thinking they must be in "their" club. When I walked into the former enlisted club, now officers club, nobody was there except the seaman who served as a bartender. He told me that all the officers had hightailed it inland to ride out the storm at a safer location. Then he smiled, and asked, "How about a drink?" I'm not much of a drinker, but being I was cold and wet I took a couple of snorts that day. The bartender seaman said something about how it took a typhoon for an enlisted man to enjoy club privileges in a club that was his in the first place. I agreed with him and decided to do something about it. The word spread rapidly that there were no officers on the base and they had left "their" club unattended. Sailors quickly braved the storm to converge on the officers' club and went to work on the officers' liquor and beer supply. The strong drinks brought out spiteful thoughts of animosity against the officers' and in a mood of revenge "their" club was trashed. Empty bottles were smashed, tables and chairs broken, wall pictures ripped apart, a total mess.

When the brass returned the next day it took them awhile to figure out how the typhoon managed to enter "their" club, destroy the liquor supply and furnishings, yet leave the building virtually unharmed.

They must have got the point however. After Japan surrendered, the war over, we were in the process of closing down the seaplane base. The officers invited all of us enlisted men to come over to the club and help polish off the remaining liquor supply.

===

George Dawson has led an interesting life. After WW II he went to work for RCA and after using the GI Bill was appointed to the faculty at New York University, teaching history and economics. In 1962, he and his wife Shirley went to Somalia as a part of NYU volunteers in the Peace Corps. George said, "I almost bought it in Somalia when a hunk of shrapnel just missed me." This happened when Somalia and Ethiopia were having a border war. He added, "Wouldn't it have been ironic to survive two wars and get killed in the Peace Corps?" In 1970 George became Director of Research and Editor of The Journal of Economic Education. In 1975 he resigned that position to become Dean of Empire State College. Retired now, George enjoys reading history, writing, gardening and doing carpentry. He and Shirley live in Wantagh, New York.

90

ABOARD THE USS YANCEY - AKA 93 DURING THE KOREAN WAR
Former Radioman 1/c George G. Dawson, USN

I was one of those sailors who took his Honorable Discharge after World War II then got homesick for the Navy and enlisted in the active reserve. The once a week drills were boring at times but the two week summer cruises were great. At the same time I was able to keep up with my skills as a radio operator and maintain a sense of camaraderie with new shipmates. As any old timer will tell you, June of 1950 changed a lot of things real quick for those swabs in the Navy Reserve.

My entire reserve outfit was called to active duty and within a month after the North Koreans invaded South Korea I found myself in Oakland, California awaiting to sail on my newest ship. The USS Yancey was an AKA that means she was an attack cargo ship. We had berthing space for Marines or Army troops but our primary mission during amphibious operations was to get supplies ashore. The need for AKA's was paramount during World War II but during the Korean War we were little more than a floating supply ship for the other ships of the Seventh Fleet. So our mission during the Korean War was making runs back and forth from California to Korea.

Rough seas didn't bother me that much. In nearly nine years in the Navy I had crossed both the Atlantic and Pacific oceans many times in all kind of weather. Furthermore, I grew up on a small island off the northeast coast of the United States and was accustomed to foul weather and had survived several severe storms, including the great hurricane of 1938. But one trip on the Yancey nearly did me in.

We were sailing the northern route between Oakland and Japan on this particular voyage and from the first day at sea the weather was bad. And it got worse every day. Dark skies, fog, coupled with mist and rain made visibility during daylight hours extremely poor. You could barely tell it was daylight anyway with the slate gray sky hiding the sun and the black water of the Pacific slamming against the ship with a steady pounding. The first few days we all got a lot of laughs seeing coffee mugs and chow trays sliding down the mess tables and crashing on the deck. And someone was always slipping and sliding and falling on their ass. At least the deck apes were making out since they couldn't be expected to chip paint and repaint the outer structure.

By the fifth day conditions worsened to the point that the cooks said it was impossible to prepare hot meals safely so they fed us cold cut sandwiches. At least they keep the big coffee urns going which was about the only warmth we got into our bellies. Sleeping was also virtually impossible. Although we strapped ourselves in our racks, the ship was rolling and pitching so violently that we had to hang to the rack supports just to stay in our bunks. We were carrying a large number of acetylene tanks on the deck right above our sleeping quarters. They broke loose and rolled all around the deck, making terrible noise as they crashed into various obstacles. All the guys in our berthing space wondered if the steel plating above our heads would withstand the blast if a spark set off the acetylene tanks. The storm had gotten so fierce that there was no way we could go out on deck to try and batten down the loose cylinders. So we listened to them crash and bang until finally the sea took most of them off the deck.

We were all bleary-eyed from lack of sleep and everyone, including our officers, were getting short-tempered. In a situation like this, even the simplest task becomes a drudgery of labor. I couldn't even keep my seating in the radio room and had to wedge myself against a bulkhead half standing up to give and receive message traffic. Typewriters in the radio shack broke loose from their mountings even though they'd been bolted to steel tables. Our chairs slid from one bulkhead to the other and the only way I could type at all was with one finger poking at the keys while holding onto a stanchion with the other hand.

High waves crashed over the bow of the ship, making it extremely dangerous to try and walk on deck. Sometimes the stern would be entirely out of the water, and the screws would be turning in the air that caused the ship to shake violently. Then the ship would ride up a huge wave that would suddenly pull out from under the ship and the Yancey would slam back into the water like a sledge hammer—SMACK-BANG! It felt like a giant hand had picked up the vessel and was shaking the life out of it. Then the main radio antenna broke loose and was flying around like a buggy whip on the mast.

Someone would have to try to climb up the mast and secure the antenna. As the head radioman I felt that I ought to be the one to cope with it. When I got on the upper deck from the bridge however, I realized it was going to be impossible to do the job. Even if I could have climbed the mast the whipping antenna wire would have cut me to shreds! I climbed back down to the lower bridge deck on the port side and was making my way along by holding onto the rail when the ship rolled sharply to port. I was looking straight down into the black ocean and the strangest feeling swept over me. It was as if the ship was still erect but the sea was coming up towards me. I yelled to the roaring wind. "We are going to capsize!" A flashing thought swept through my mind as a mental picture of my wife in New York came to me. She was about to become a twenty-three year old widow who might never know what had happened to me. Then, a sense of calm came over me and I thought about my shipmates below. If I'm going to die like this, I want to be with them. We live together and work together, so we ought to die together as well. I struggled to pull myself toward a ladder so I could get to a hatch.

The ship slowly started to right itself. The sea seemed to be receding, and for a few seconds I was standing upright instead of being near enough to the waves that I could have almost slapped them. I dashed to the ladder and scrambled down into the wheelhouse on the bridge. The guys in the wheelhouse were as white as ghosts, their eyes glazed and blank, mouths set in tense, grim lines. A long moment went by then one of the quartermasters pointed to the instrument that showed our list. I stared at it dumbfounded. We were one degree past the point of capsizing. No wonder no one was saying anything! Like me, they were all waiting to die!

I was too scared to go below so I stayed in the wheel-house and no one told me to leave. Minutes seemed like hours but the Yancey proved what a tough old babe she was. We rode out the storm and the seas at last gave way to reasonable thirty foot waves. But after what we had gone through, after that, the rest of the cruise seemed like a pleasure trip.

It's always been said that it is supposed to be better to ride out a typhoon at sea rather than sitting in port to let it pound at you. But after this voyage, I seriously had my doubts on that theory.

The entire crew was bruised and battered and much of our equipment had been ruined or damaged. The only good thing to come out of this experience was that we were ordered back to Oakland immediately for repairs.

Once back in Oakland I called my wife and told her to fly out from New York so we could spend some time together because the Yancey was going to be a couple of weeks in port for repairs.

We had a great time together until my wife lost her purse in San Francisco. All our money, plus her return ticket was in that purse! What were we going to do? I had to explain our predicament to the hotel manager because I didn't know how I could pay for our room, let alone how I was going to get my wife back to New York. It just so happened that a San Francisco newspaper reporter was in the lobby and overheard our plight. He ran a story about us with our photos in his paper the next day. A doctor who was vacationing in the bay area with his family had found my wife's purse. How he came about to read that newspaper story while on vacation I'll never know. But now that he knew who owned the purse, he got in touch with the newspaper, and the reporter was able to write another story with photos on how this Good Samaritan returned my wife's purse. Two times in less than a month a guardian angel looked after me. First on the Yancey during the typhoon and now with my wife in San Francisco.

"Nothing is certain but death and taxes," said Benjamin Franklin. Ben could have included "A sailor's duty," in his statement. With the USS Yancey repaired, our supply mission to Korean waters resumed. There is one other certainty that old Ben might have added to his famous line: That sailors will gripe about the chow, no matter how good or bad the food may be. Take a look at the unpleasant names sailors and Marines have dubbed certain foods. Strong coffee is "battery acid." Margarine or butter, is "Axle grease." Creamed chipped beef on toast, is "Shit on a shingle." Bologna, salami, and other cold cuts, are, "Horse cock." And all cooks, are, "Belly robbers." The most comical complaint that I ever heard about food, however, was aboard the USS Yancey off the coast of Korea. This joker got on the bitch box (ship's loudspeaker) and loudly voiced the following: "Now hear this, now hear this. Will the chicken with today's duty lay down to the galley and swim in the soup!"

Any military man will tell you there are good officers and bad officers. Unfortunately, the AKA 93 had a really bad one during the Korean War whom I'll call Lt.(JG) Jerk. From the enlisted men's point of view Lt.(JG) Jerk was an arrogant and overbearing officer who treated his men in the communications division like dirt under his feet. Even after our radio gang had received the highest praise from headquarters for efficiency, he took full credit and gave us poor evaluation ratings. Besides being rude and crude, he had this habit that he always walked very fast, not because there was any need for speed mind you, but rather because he felt it made him look like he was doing something important. If a sailor happened to be in his way as he rushed about the deck or passageways, he would roughly push you aside without so much as saying, "Make a hole." His habit of rushing everywhere also applied to ladders and going in hatches. He'd go up or down a ladder in a flash, not looking up or down to see if anyone else was in his way. The same went when he'd enter a hatchway, he would just burst in full steam ahead. In other words, a complete self-centered asshole! We were always looking for ways to "take care" of Lt.(JG) Jerk, and one of the things I remember was this one day when two of our signalmen on the upper deck saw him dashing along the lower deck heading to the ladder where they were at. The two signalmen picked up this wooden bench next to the railing and placed it over the top of the ladder. Mister Jerk came charging up the ladder like he always did, without looking, and when his head smacked the bench it knocked him clear back down the ladder, where he sprawled on the deck. This "accident" caused him to be laid up for a few days, which just broke everyone's heart. But the classic put down took place a couple of weeks later when we communicators decide to re-paint the ship's radio shack. We all pitched in to help, covering the radios and other equipment with drop cloths, masking tape various areas and making sure there were no rust spots. When we got all of this done, one man remained inside the compartment to do the spray painting while the rest of us vacated the radio shack. As the senior radioman I stood outside the hatch to warn people not to enter it. But good old, Lt.(JG) Jerk came dashing toward me heading to the radio shack. I yelled a warning. "Don't go in their sir!" He glared at me as if to say, "You don't tell me what to do." and pushed past me before I had a chance to explain. He yanked open the hatch and started to enter. It so happened that our painter was doing the inside of the hatch just as Jerk tried to step in. Jerk got a full blast of spray paint all over the front of his officer tans and face. He stood there paralyzed not knowing what in the hell had happened while every enlisted man in sight choked back the strong impulse to laugh out loud. Even our captain thought it was funny. It wasn't long after that before Lt.(JG) Jerk was transferred and replaced by a new communications officer who was a decent guy. Nobody on the Yancey mourned Jerk's departure.

Sailors are fighters. They will fight any enemy of the United States, first and foremost, but if there is no foreign foe to fight, they'll take it upon themselves to find a brawl somewhere. Civilians who dare insult or disparage the Navy are legitimate targets for bare knuckles, as are other U.S. naval service members who consider themselves superior to "swab jockeys." The same goes for other members of the armed forces who ignite the wrath of the men in Navy blue. And when all else fails, sailors will fight among themselves. This was the case one night when the Yancey was in the Japanese port of Sasebo before going back to Korea.

The harbor was full of ships. Most of them were U.S. Navy men-of-war taking a respite from Korea but there was also a goodly number of auxiliary vessels at anchor such as the USS Yancey - AKA 93. A shipmate pal of mine and I were returning from liberty and we were waiting on the dock for our boat from the Yancey to show up to take us back to the ship. Dozens of other sailors from other anchored ships were also awaiting their liberty boats. Many of the guys were pretty soused from enjoying the great Japanese beer and there was a lot of yelling and carrying on going on around me and my pal as we waited for our boat. Two sailors that I recognized as being from our ship approached us. "Aren't you guys from the Yancey?" This one sailor inquired. When we replied that yes we were, the two sailors told us they were being ridiculed by some sailors off a destroyer and would we be willing to help since they were outnumbered. Both me and my pal agreed to stand by our shipmates since it's an unwritten law of Navy men that you stand by shipmates, come hell or high water. We strolled up to the hecklers and asked them what their problem was. As the tin can sailors started telling us what they thought of AKA sailors, which they said were inferior seamen having to serve aboard an auxiliary vessel instead of a ship of the line; I noted quickly that we were badly outnumbered. Now, I was never one to back down from a fight, but I did have some common sense. There was a good dozen tin can swabs to our four. They were all young sailors and obviously did not realize that the Yancey, along with many other auxiliary ships, had served nobly at such places as Iwo Jima, Tarawa and Okinawa, to name a few. It also was obvious to me that a rational argument would have no effect on the surly attitude of these guys by telling them how ships like the Yancey had been torpedoed, bombed and shelled. That many sailors, just like themselves, had lost their lives while keeping the fleet supplied with food, fuel and ammunition.. Our face off had attracted an audience of other sailors awaiting transportation back to their ships and I knew the situation would soon get out of hand. Perhaps a bit of humor would defuse the situation. I looked right at the glaring faces of the tin can sailors and spoke in a serious, dead-pan tone of voice. "Look fellows, the Yancey has just arrived from the states carrying tons of toilet paper. Just think now, if it wasn't for our ship you guys wouldn't be able to wipe your ass after taking a shit." The onlookers cracked up immediately which was soon followed by grins from the tin can swabs that quickly turned into laughs. We ended up shaking hands and returned to our ships with our noses intact and our knuckles un-bruised.

And so went our life aboard the USS Yancey - AKA 93, during the Korean War.

91

PROOF THAT JUSTICE IS TRULY BLIND
Former Corporal Michael L. Hefflin, USMC

In June of 1967 I was a PFC grunt 0311 in the 2nd Platoon, Lima Company, 3rd Battalion, 26th Marines. My outfit had spent the past two months in the bush around the Khe Sanh TAOR near the Laotian border and west of Ca Lu, South Vietnam. Like all Marine infantry companies in Vietnam we were happy when the word was passed that 3/26 was going to stand down from patrol duties and be assigned to perimeter defense of the Khe Sanh Combat Base. To us grunts, this was like a vacation, getting duty on fixed lines instead of snooping and pooping through the jungle and climbing up and down mountains.

Our first day back at the Khe Sanh Combat Base, by buddy PFC Ray "Hawk" Hawkins and I are hungry as hell and the two of us devised a plan to steal some canned fruit from the field mess tent. There was a walking sentry guarding the galley and supply tent so what we did was Hawk distracted the sentry and when his attention was diverted I charged into the supply tent and made off with two big cans of fruit.

Like all good field Marines, what one Marine "finds," everyone in his squad gets to share. We were dividing up are loot with our squad when the Officer of the Day shows up with two MP's and tells me and Hawk we aren't very good thieves since the Mess Sergeant had spotted us stealing his canned fruit and saw where we went.

The OD takes us to our CO, Captain Dick Camp, and the skipper gives us a weeks K.P. duty as punishment. The two of us were led off to the mess tent to meet our new boss for the next week, which of course, was the Mess Sergeant.

When you're a grunt in the field you only eat two meals a day if you're lucky, and these are combat C rations out of a can. In the bush you seldom get any decent sleep as the 50% on duty watches never seem to work out that way and you're up more than half the night. Plus the fact that an infantryman is assigned night ambush duty, daily patrols and a fair amount of time getting shot at. Now this cook figured he was really going to make it rough on us and he kept us busy day in and day out with shitty little details around his mess area. What the cook didn't realize was, that since we worked for him, which was usually only eight hours, that we had more time off than our fellow comrades in arms. Our outfit was out clearing foliage in front of Khe Sahn's lines for fields of fire, and going on perimeter patrols, and building bunkers, and in general working their butts off 16 hours a day, in addition to standing watch. So while our company is out busting their asses, Hawk and I are enjoying Three Hot's and a Cot. We're eating like pigs and sleeping like babies.

The very day the two of us get released from K.P. duty and are heading back to our company, we both smell this delicious aroma whiffing the air. We instantly change our direction of march and begin a search and capture mission. The sweet smell takes us to the officer's mess and there on this outside counter we see cooling off a dozen freshly baked pies. Old Hawk and I glace at one another, then shaking our heads as if to say, "Well, here we go again," we grab four of the pies and run like hell to our squad. We're greeted like returning heroes and given the largest fox hole to hide in so we can cut up the four pies. It didn't take long for the "evidence" to be consumed from me and Hawk's latest caper. But guess who shows up at our little pie eating party? Yep, the same officer who must have been assigned permanent OD.

So its off to our CO again and this time Captain Camp is not in a happy frame of mind. As the two of us stand at attention taking the skipper's ass chewing that he was giving out very loudly, his words hit home with unpleasant thoughts. Was he really going to send us up to the colonel for office hours with a recommendation we be court-martialed? Or, how serious was he about sending us out as a two-man outpost in enemy territory? My only positive thought at this moment was the fact I knew he couldn't shave our heads and send us to Vietnam! When the captain slowed down to a roar he eyed the two of us and with a sarcastic tone to his voice, said. "Since you two clowns seem to like fucking around mess tents so much, I've got the perfect punishment for you! This time two weeks K.P. duty! Dismissed!"

I had to catch myself from busting out with a laugh but managed to salute the captain, take one step backwards, do an about face, and march out of his quarters.

The mess sergeant put Hawk and I right to work.

When our two weeks were up this time however, we were escorted back to our outfit.

A little later scuttlebutt floated around that the cook had passed the word to never send those two Marines from Lima, 3/26 back on K.P. as the mess hall experienced some losses in the supply lockers and he suspected he knew who might have done it. The culprits were never found though.

The end of this little tale took place at the 25th reunion of the 26th Marines that served in Vietnam that gathered in Reno, Nevada. I recounted this experience to my old CO, Captain Dick Camp, and he and every Marine who heard it cracked up. The skipper slapped me on the back, then said, "Heff, that just goes to show you that justice is truly blind at times."

Mike "Heff" Hefflin entered the Corps from his hometown Osage, Iowa. He was originally with Golf Company, 2nd Battalion, 9th Marines, until getting orders to the 26th Marines. Wounded three times in Vietnam, Heff is now retired on permanent disability. Married to Sharon, they have four children. They now call home Huntington Beach, California. Heff has the interesting hobby collecting old vintage movies. He says he may be the only private citizen to own every movie John Wayne ever made. Heff also contributed stories for two other books about the Marine Corps: Ambush Valley and Lima 6.

92

A TOUGH OLD GAL
Former Diver 1/C Jack Starr, USN

When I reflect back on my childhood years after my father was killed in a car wreck in 1930 when I was ten years old, I have to smile because those years would make a Sea Story all by itself. My mom, sister and I lived in a small town outside of Pittsburgh, Pa and as a young kid I hustled for every penny I could make. I sold newspapers and was even a delivery boy for a black man, carrying half-pints of moonshine to customers when I dropped off newspapers. I gave my mom every cent I earned, sometimes $30. or $40. a week, which wasn't bad for a kid in those days, and the money was used to help her pay for our food, rent and clothes. Things were tough but mom insisted I stay in school and to be perfectly honest, she was the best friend I ever had. When I graduated from high school in 1938 jobs were still scarce as the depression dragged on. I enlisted in the U.S. Army and after basic training was sent to Hawaii. The Army assigned me to G Company, 19th Infantry, Schofield Barracks, TH. (The TH stood for Territory of Hawaii since Hawaii wasn't a state back then.) I was a good soldier and by the time I was 21 years old was a corporal. My pay was $21. a month that didn't go far but that didn't stop young American boys from trying to pick up girls for dates. Our favorite pastime was going down to the Aloha Tower in Honolulu when cruise ships came in and try to meet a girl to show her a good time on her vacation. The Matson Line ran most of the cruise ships out of San Francisco in those days and one of the more popular ships was the SS Monterey that my story is all about.

The SS Monterey began sailing 50-day voyages from San Francisco in 1932 and was a class-act steam ship. She could carry over 1,000 passengers in pampered comfort, including the movie actor Clark Cable who was among the Hollywood stars who toured the South Seas from its decks.

Due to my youthful enthusiasm of seeking female companionship I too got the opportunity to walk the Monterey's decks occasionally, although she was tied up at pier side. However, fate had it in store that I would encounter the SS Monterey again, in a more unusual fashion.

On August 3, 1941 I received an honorable discharge from the U.S. Army. I went home to Pennsylvania and was married in November of that year. Seventeen days after my marriage I got a letter from the Army telling me I'd been recalled to active duty. I glumly went to the federal building in Pittsburgh but before I could make it to the Army office I'd been told to report to a Navy recruiter stopped me and started giving me his pitch. I explained to the fellow about the Army already having dibs on me and showed him my letter. Like the good recruiter he was he said, "Why this ain't a problem. I can take care of this for you in no time. Now what would you rather be doing: out there;

digging ditches and marching everywhere or sailing on a nice ship of the line in this mans Navy?" Believe it or not, I thought about the SS Monterey and as it turned out I never got past that Navy recruiters door.

The Navy showed me I had some talents I never knew existed and within six months after Pearl Harbor I was a qualified Navy diver. My ship was the U.S.S. Fulton AS 11, a submarine tender. Before the war was over I had been all over the South Pacific: Australia, Midway, Saipan. Guam, to name a few places. It wasn't a cruise ship but believe me it was certainly interesting duty.

In the meantime, the SS Monterey was pulling some interesting duty of her own. World War II ended her idyllic voyages in the South Pacific. She was pressed into the naval service and converted to carry 3,841 troops, six times her normal passenger capacity. More often the Monterey hauled as many as 6.800 troops, who had to sleep in shifts in her once luxurious compartments. In November of 1943, the Monterey was carrying reinforcements to Italy through the western Mediterranean Sea when two dozen German airplanes attacked her. She survived the attack with only the loss of her radio antenna. Another ship, the troop carrier Santa Elena, wasn't as lucky, and the Monterey's crew hauled aboard all 1,675 Canadian Army troops before that ship went down.

In the summer of 1944, the submarine tender U.S.S. Fulton was working out Milne Bay, New Guinea. One of the islands many volcano's had erupted and day turned into night from the incredible amount of black ash that filled the sky. The Fulton received a radio message that the blinding ash storm had caused a troop ship heading for Guadalcanal to flounder on a reef near Milne Bay. We were ordered to sail at once to see if we could get the ship off the reef. When we arrived at the scene Navy landing craft were ferrying the 4,000 troops off the ship to the nearby shore. I took one look at that big sucker stuck out there on the reef, and said, "Well I'll be a sonofabitch, it's the SS Monterey!"

Me and another diver went down in diving suits and found that the Monterey had sure as hell imbedded herself hard on the reef but the tough old gal had not sustained any hull damage. We started laying plastic explosives in the coral that we figured would help jar the ship from the reef. This job took ten days and we lived aboard the Monterey while doing it. At night, me and my fellow diver drank all the whiskey we found in officers quarters that helped our attitude considerably. When our skipper off the Fulton asked us why laying the charges was taking so long we told him how careful we were being so we wouldn't damage the ship. Absolutely! I told my buddy about my past experience with the Monterey in Hawaii while we shared our nightly libation and he said what were the odds of me ending up helping to save the ship. He couldn't get over that I knew this ship from my days in the U.S. Army.

When we finally blew our charges it didn't free the Monterey but it did loosen the coral enough that two Navy tugs was able to yank the 18,000-ton ship off the reef. When we went back down to check her out we only found two small dents in the hull. Like I said, she was a tough old gal.

━━━━━━━━━━━━━━━━━━━━━━━━━━━━━━━━━━━━

Jack sent along a newspaper item from the Naples (Florida) Daily News, dated Thursday, March 12, 1998, telling about how the 66-year old Monterey (re-named the SS Britannic) was being sold for scrap. He said he has a nostalgic place in his heart about the "old gal" and felt this Sea Story would be a fitting tribute in her memory. Jack resides in Naples, Florida. The 78-year old former soldier/sailor also wrote how he met the actor Lew Ayers who was a Navy medical corpsman during the war, and the actor Louis Haywood, a Marine photographer. Jack said he buddied around with James Jones while in Hawaii who was the author who wrote From Here To Eternity and the Thin Red Line. Jones was a corporal in A Company, 19th Infantry and was wounded on Guadalcanal.

93

THE WORLDS SHORTEST SEA STORY
Master Sergeant Donald D. Wersler, USMC(Ret.)

During my boot camp training at Parris Island, South Carolina during the summer months of July and August 1943, my twin brother and I were among the 11 sets of twins undergoing training in our battalion at the same time.

Don Wersler's comments on the post card he submitted was longer than his "Sea Story." He wrote that the public relations people at PI made a big deal about the "twin" situation and had a group photo taken and sent to all the newspapers across the United States, including the various military branches newspapers. He and his brother served the entire war aboard the USS Vincennes Cl-64 as sea going Marines. There was another set of Marine twins on the cruiser who were both buglers. It was the custom in World War II, after the deaths of the five Sullivan brothers aboard the light cruiser USS Juneau on November 13, 1942 off Guadalcanal, that brothers be separated. The Wersler twins, and the two Marine buglers were exceptions to that rule by getting permission from their parents to stay together. They stayed on the Vincennes until the end of the war but were finally separated when the two reenlisted. Don's brother got orders for the Philadelphia Navy Yard and he was sent to Parris Island. When Don retired from the Corps he was again stationed at, where else, but at Parris Island, where it had all began 23 years previously. He lives with his wife at Beaufort, South Carolina.

94

HOLD THAT CARRIER
Chief Warrant Officer Three Coy S. Hicks, Jr., USN(Ret.)

I was a 21-year old Seaman Apprentice in 1953 and serving aboard the carrier escort USS Point Cruz (CVE 119). The Korean War was growing to a close but still going on and our aircraft carrier provided close air support for Marine ground troops.

We were home-ported in Yokosuka, Japan and when this Sea Story took place and had just completed a 60-day stand-down in port due to the ship having to undergo machinery overhaul, which could not be completed while deployed at sea.

All hands not standing watch got a final liberty on a Thursday night with orders to report back to the Point Cruz not later than 2400. You know how it is with sailors on liberty. Guys were still coming aboard at day break, having undergone too good of a time ashore doing their last fling for a while. The Chief-Master-At-Arms met the late-comers at the gangway to give them their chits for the extra shit details they would be performing for the next 90 days. This tardiness of reporting back to ship was not unusual and the first or second timers being late knew they would be in hack for awhile and those others who made a habit of a little AOL is why the Navy had so many seamen recruits in those days wearing hash marks. Captains Mast usually cost a stripe. However, this minor punishment was nothing in comparison of what would happen to a sailor that missed ships movement. Missing movement was an automatic court-martial offense and punishment could be extremely harsh, especially in wartime, where the possible threat of being shot by a firing squad could be meted out.

The last group of late comers got aboard at 0700 just as the gangway was being lifted. Dock hands in their blue dungarees stood by to lift the ship's lines so the Point Cruz could get underway.

The entire crew not on watch, including officers, were dressed in their dress blue uniforms and mustered topside along the railings as "to quarters" was blown by the chief boatswain mate on his pipe to prepare all hands to take the salute of a deploying man-of-war, which is an old naval custom.

Just as the ship's lines were taken up and the Point Cruz slowly moved away from the dock a small Japanese taxi came speeding down the pier at a frantic pace, blowing its horn. Those sailors in position along the shoreward rail saw this young sailor jump out of the taxi and run down the pier toward the carrier that is now edging out slowly into the channel. The sailor down on the pier gets to the end of the dock and by now the ship is a good 20 yards from its old mooring.

This character was obviously a signalman assigned to the Quartermaster Division. The reason all the crewmen who witnessed this dramatic scene knew the young sailor was a signalman was because he franticly began to move his arms giving semaphore signals to the bridge. No doubt he was trying to get the bridge officer, which was probably the captain, to stop engines so that he could somehow get aboard.

Alas, his great presence of mind to use his skill as a signalman did not work. A Chief Petty Officer on the bridge used the ship's megaphone to seal the kids fate. "Better luck next time dumb ass. Turn yourself in the shore patrol!"

The young sailor, who was wearing his dress blues pointed to the water. Was he going to swim for it? What was he planning on doing?

Then, all of a sudden his face broke out in a grin and he shook his head back and forth in resignation, turned and walked slowly back down the pier.

We all wondered what had happened to make the sailor smile and when call to quarters was secured we found out. A fellow signalman on the bridge followed up the CPO's terse command with a threeletter message to his shipmate using his semaphore flags. SOL. (If this has to be explained to you, then you have no business reading a book about the Navy and Marine Corps.)

So our tardy sailor was not only an AWOL; he had also missed movement. Such a waste of talent right? I mean he could not do very much flag waving from the brig can he?

Well, he didn't! What old lover boy did proved he had a lot more talent than just being a semaphore signalman. Somehow, he conned the Marines at Yokosuka to let him fly to Korea on one of their milk-run flights in a C-30 transport and when the Point Cruz pulled into Inchon, there he was waiting for us. He was still put in hack, but that's a hell of a lot better than getting shot from a court-martial sentence.

Coy enlisted into the Navy from his hometown, Miami, Florida in February 1952. After his honorable discharge from active duty in 1956 he tried the U.S. Air Force four years but decided he liked the naval service better and maintained a reserve status until retiring from the Navy reserve in 1982. He and his wife Brenda have three children, son Robert, daughters, Catherine and Rebecca. Coy worked in the Aerospace industry and also as a civil service cost studies expert for the Army at Ft. Bragg, North Carolina. He and his wife live in Broadway, North Carolina, a small town 40 miles south from Raleigh. Coy says that he spends his free time bowling, playing golf and doing lawn work.

95

"BONNIE DICK"
Former Aviation Machinist Mate 2/C Leonard J. Suligowski, USN

I enlisted into the Navy at age 19 in 1947. After completing almost a three-year tour at the Naval Air Station, Lakehurst, New Jersey, I received orders to Naval Air Station, North Island, San Diego, California. Thanks to the Communist North Koreans the idyllic beginning of duty at a great location suddenly turned to dust.

The World War II Essex class aircraft carrier, the U.S.S. Bon Homme Richard (CV-31) had been decommissioned the year I joined the Navy and had been setting idle in the mothball fleet at Bremerton, Washington. When President Harry Truman committed the United States to the Korean "Police Action" the "Bonnie Dick" as the carrier was affection ally called, was one of the first ships to be reactivated. I was among the crew that 15th day of January 1951 when Admiral Chester Nimitz handed over the Bonnie Dick to her new skipper, Captain Cecil B. Gill, at the re-commissioning ceremonies. By March the 13th, we were on our way to Korean waters.

I was assigned duty to squadron VC-11 that was a Douglas Sky raider squadron. The prop-driven aircraft of our squadron had been redesigned to handle enclosed state-of-the-art radar systems and were used for airborne early warning operations. The model AD4-W was nicknamed "The Guppy" because its silhouette gave the appearance of a pregnant frog with wings. This was due to the fat looking bulbous fiberglass radar compartment attached to the under-carriage of the cockpit near the wheel housing. The Guppy carried a crew of three, the pilot, and two enlisted electronic technicians who worked in very tight and cramped compartments in the rear of the aircraft. The odd feature about the Guppy, other than the way it looked, was it's antenna rotor was housed in a removable tube like enclosure. We would have to take out this large instrument occasionally to readjust the calibrations. I'll never forget the first time we had to take out the antenna rotor to work on it. Our efforts attracted a large number of other ships personnel who gathered around in curiosity to see what the "belly thing" was all about. As we worked on the rotor the ground crew sailors pressed closer and closer until the circle got so tight we barely had room enough to work. One of the technicians who was helping us, who flew in this particular plane, muttered under his breath to us. "Watch me get rid of these guys." He crawled up into the belly of the Guppy and turned on the radar which caused the antenna to turn round and round with an audible hum. As the antenna made its sweeps the microwaves coming from the radar emitted a small burst of heat that for some reason could only be felt in the genital area. This got the attention of the gawking sailors real quick when they felt the heat hitting their private parts. Then the technician crawled out of the AD4-W and announced very loudly. "Hey you guys, this is a warning. Stay well back from the plane with the radar on. Otherwise you could all become sterile!" You never saw 30 or 40 swabs move so fast in your life as within seconds they had all scattered like a bunch of frightened sparrows. During the remaining eight months we were on station for this cruise, we were left alone when we worked on our aircraft.

Another strange thing I witnessed on the Bonnie Dick was when the leader of the first strike of the day was catapulted off the flight deck in his F9F and the jet went right into the sea. The lucky pilot was plucked from the water within minutes from our ever vigilant helicopter and we never did find out what caused him to go straight in like that, although the scuttlebutt was he may have hit the wrong button that caused a flameout.

The funniest thing I remember seeing on this cruise was when we were on our way back to Japan for ship yard maintenance. As customary when standing down, all aircraft were either stowed in the hanger deck or those topside were pushed back to the stern so the steel landing deck could be refurbished. Once this work was accomplished the crew was allowed to use both decks for recreational sports. The hanger deck could handle a dozen basketball, volleyball and badminton games, and for those interested a game of touch football it could be played on the top-side deck. Even the guys from the "Black Gang" who never got to work top-side because of their engine room duties, were allowed to form a football team. This Black Gang swabby went out for a pass and was so intent on keeping his eye on the ball so he could catch it that he didn't notice how close he was to the out-board elevator. Well, he caught the winning touchdown okay, but went right over the railing falling 50 feet into the sea. The "Man Overboard" alarm immediately blared throughout the ship. Our captain ordered "All Stop." As the carrier slowed sailors and Marines were tossing anything that would float over the side. A helicopter was quickly dispatched and plucked the would be football hero from the choppy sea in record time. Hollywood stole this little humorous jewel of stupidity for the opening scene of the movie Hot Shots. What the moviemakers failed to include was a humorous footnote to the incident. Our over zealous pass receiver was given two weeks extra duty by his department head. The reason for this punishment had everyone aboard the Bonnie Dick laughing: The swab was cited for leaving the ship without permission!

Leonard Suligowski returned to Brooklyn, New York after his five years in the Navy. His occupations over the years have included that as a Radio Announcer, Insurance Investigator, Private Investigator and finally the Senior Partner in a law firm. Now retired Leonard does European heraldic research and is well known for his heraldic artistic work He has written an outstanding eleven page essay about the Bon Homme Richard titled Tales From The Bonnie Dick, from which this Sea Story was taken from.

96

ARMED GUARD STUKA ACES
Former Gunners Mate 3/C Stanley A. Hauser, USN

I quite high school in my hometown of Bloomington, Illinois in March of 1942 so that I could join the Navy and do my part to help out during World War II. This was not an unusual happening in those days as a lot of kids put aside their childhood pursuits after Pearl Harbor to answer the call to colors, even seventeen year olds like me.

After twelve weeks of boot camp at Great Lakes I was sent to Chicago to undergo another twelve weeks of training at the Naval School for Armed Guards. What this intensive training consisted of was teaching young sailors like myself how to man every position on a five-inch gun. This training in naval gunnery was not intended for men-of-war but rather as gunners on Merchant Marine Liberty ships that were being built by the hundreds on the east coast. Each Liberty ship carried two five-inch mounts, one forward the other aft. Sixteen sailors who would man the weapons, with a senior petty officer in charge.

When I completed my Armed Guard training a short home leave was authorized since I now had orders to report to the Brooklyn Navy Yard receiving station to await my vessel. It was not a long wait because the Liberty ship SS William Johnson was launched from the Bethlehem-Fairfield shipyard, Baltimore, Maryland in October 1942.

I, along with my new shipmates boarded the SS William Johnson where we met our boss, a crusty old Chief Petty Officer by the name of Carl Cornell. Chief Cornell's welcome aboard speech was short and to the point, which I still remember most of what he had to say to this day. "You guys have one primary job to do. You keep your five inches cleaned and oiled and be ready on a moments notice to use 'em. You'll be doing daily battle station drills until you can operate the five-inch in your sleep. Your mission is to blow out of the water any sonofabitching U-Boat dumb enough to surface and to shoot down any airplane showing a swastika. And you keep out of the way of the Merchant swabies!"

It wasn't long before our shakedown cruise was completed and we were staged to join up with a huge convoy slated for Bone, Algeria, North Africa.

Our crossing the Atlantic Ocean was no picnic. During the entire voyage our convoy was repeatedly attacked by U-Boat wolf packs. More than once I witnessed the terrifying spectacle of seeing torpedo wakes heading right at the SS William Johnson. The Merchant Marine captain must have had an angel riding on his shoulder because he was able to maneuver his ship out of harms way every time, although one time I saw a torpedo pass by our starboard bow a bare few feet. The teenage gun crew's of the Armed Guard contingent found out quickly what it was like to spend twelve to fifteen hours at a stretch at battle stations manning the five inch guns. When we pulled into the wrecked harbor at Bone, Algeria, you could almost hear the sigh of relief from the young sailors. Finally, we were safe! Are so we thought.

Just because the German submarine arm couldn't sink us made no difference to the Nazi Luftwaffe. For nineteen days straight while in port, Stuka dive-bombers attacked us forty-seven times.

The first airplane we shot down came as a complete surprise to the German pilot. He had just pulled up from a bombing dive on another merchant ship and was flying low past the SS William Johnson, not more than a couple of hundred yards in the air. The pilot actually waved at us as he went by and I've often wondered what he must have thought when we opened up on him with our aft five inch I was on and blew him out of the sky. Two more Stuka pilot's met similar fates on their steep dives on our ship as we met them head on with five-inch shells that also blasted them from the sky. On February 5, 1943, a steady stream of five-inch gunfire from our weapons damaged this German Stuka so bad that the pilot bailed out and his aircraft crashed into the bay. (He was taken prisoner by the way.) But our last kill was probably the most dramatic. This Stuka made a head on attack on the SS William Johnson and the bombs hit close to the bow which sent up a high geyser of green-black sea water that damn near drowned the forward Armed Guard gun crew. As the enemy airplane flew the length of the Liberty ship, the aft five-inch gun crew shot our weapon straight up in the air. Damn if we didn't hit the gull winged Sutka right in its belly that cut the aircraft in two. The front portion dived down into the water while the rear section dropped like a rock almost on top of us.

To say we were a pretty happy bunch of young sailors when we painted our fifth Nazi cross on the side of our gun mount tub would be an understatement. Not a bad months work for a bunch of green swabs manning a merchant ship on its maiden voyage.

Our proudest moment came on April the 17th, 1943, back at the Brooklyn Navy Yard. The Chief of Naval Personnel awarded all members of the Armed Guard crew of the SS William Johnson, the Navy Commendation Ribbon with Metal Pendant and combat V for "remarkable bravery and courageous service."

We were the first Armed Guard air aces.

———————————————————————————————

Stan "Hasty" Hauser also participated in the Normandy D-Day landings in June of 1944. Then he shipped out to the Pacific War Theater in time to be a part of the Philippine liberation. Widowed, Stan spends his retirement years hunting and fishing. He now lives in Sneads, Florida. He told this writer that he recently added another military ribbon to his seven he'd already earned for his World War II service of which he is extremely proud of, even it's 50 years overdue: the Combat Action Ribbon.

97

A LITTLE NOOKY
Former Platoon Sergeant John M. Egan, USMC

I enlisted into the Chicago organized Marine Corps Reserve at age 15 in September 1938. Back in those days the other military outfits required a birth certificate but the Marine Corps would "look the other way" if you had a note from your father attesting to your age and birth date. Plus my dad, a wounded World War I vet, had a good friend who was a first lieutenant in the reserve unit I joined. The depression was still going full swing and about the only way you could go on active duty was to do so from the organized reserve and I was in a situation where it was mandatory that I become an active duty Marine. This situation came about thanks to a kindly old juvenile court judge who determined I was suffering from some "social adjustment problems" and flat ass told my dad and me that if I wasn't in the Marines in the next 60 days I would find myself in the infamous St. Charles Reformatory until age 21. My dad's lieutenant buddy was aware of this fact and I attended drills until such time arrangements were made to send me on active duty.

I was ordered to report to the Federal Building Chicago in full uniform on January 11, 1940. The next day at 0600 I left the Dearborn Street Rail Road station on a train to Parris Island, South Carolina. I'll be damn if a hurricane didn't tear up PI so bad that all of us new recruits awaiting a training cycle was sent up to Quantico, Virginia, where we waited in a casual company for a couple of weeks then sent to San Diego to take our 60 days boot camp.

After boot camp I was on orders along with a full infantry company to join the 4th Marines serving in Peking, China to reinforce the garrison there. As it turned out just prior to shipping out I got into a humdinger of a brawl with an old China hand who cleaned the decks with me and we both ended up getting court-martialed. He got busted to buck private and since I was already a private with nothing to get busted to, I spent 30 days in the San Diego brig. When I got out of the brig my outfit I was supposed to have shipped out with had shoved off and I was sent to the Navy Torpedo Station, Keyport, Washington to become a member of the guard company there. (There is some irony in this because all the guys that I was supposed to have shipped out with to China ended up on Corregidor and was either killed, or were POW's during the entire war where many of them died.)

In May of 1940 I was told to pack my seabag as I was being transferred to the U.S.S. San Francisco to bring up the cruisers Marine Detachment to full TO. This surprised the hell out of me and sure enough I was the only enlisted Marine aboard the San Francisco that had never gone to Sea School. I guess the guard company at Keyport wanted to get rid of me real bad.

But I got along real good as a sea going Marine and by December 7, 1941, I was a corporal. The San Francisco took its lumps when the Japs attacked Pearl Harbor but Marine gunners were credited with shooting down five enemy airplanes.

In June 1942 the San Francisco pulled into Pago Pago, Samoa. We had been at sea for almost seven months and hadn't seen a woman the entire time. When the word was passed that five percent of the crew would be allowed a four-hour liberty in Pago Pago, everybody, and I mean everybody went ape shit. Naturally our two officers of the Marine Detachment found the need to go ashore and our first shirt selected himself and the detachment gunny for liberty. By now I was a platoon sergeant. (that was with a rocker that signified "field infantry qualified". The straight bar meant you were a "technician" staff sergeant.) So the first shirt tells me to select the other Marine who would go ashore on liberty. You better believe I chose ME! RHIP, and anyone not knowing what that stands far has no business reading a book about the military but since I'm a nice guy I'll clue those not in the know: Rank Has Its Privileges!

I missed the only motor launch heading to the naval pier so I hailed an out-rigger canoe and paid a native a buck to take me in.

Once ashore I looked up an old buddy of mine I knew who was stationed on Pago Pago as a part of the Marine Defense Battalion. Charlie Perkins and I spent my short liberty time in his "grass shack" where he lived when off duty with an older native woman I wouldn't have touched with a ten foot pole. God she was ugly! But then Charlie had been on Samoa for a long time and knew the law of the snake that I won't go into. (It's a fact though that any gal gets better looking as time goes by if there's not many gals to go around.) Anyway, Charlie gave me his beer ration and had his woman to cook up some kava roots that knocked my socks off. Kava, when boiled, turns into an intoxicating narcotic beverage. Before my time was up he took me to his PX where I bought a melted box of Hershey bars for the guys in the Marine Detachment and got myself a few cans of sardines. He walked me back down to the Navy pier where I caught the liberty launch back to my ship. (I never saw my pal again and heard later that he'd got killed on Iwo Jima.)

Now you've got to admit this wasn't much of a liberty was it? And it sure as hell wasn't one that my Marines who was waiting for me wanted to hear about. I say "my Marines" as our first sergeant and gunny wern't the kind of people that anyone but an undertaker would await their return. But sure as shooting there lining the deck by the ladder way was the entire 37 privates and PFC's that made up the Marine Detachment who couldn't wait to hear all about my "big liberty."

The catcalls started as I climbed up the ladder. "Hey sarge, you made out didn't you?" "Naw, who would want to screw him?" "C'mon, I know the ole sarge got some nooky!" "Damn right he did, didn't ya sarge?"

As my foot hit the well deck and I faced left to salute the colors the voice of the other platoon sergeant blared above all the rest. "Egan you sonsabitch, ya got sum didn't ya?"

Now was I going to disappoint all those smiling faces? The moral of the troops was obviously at stake. So I put on my best Cheshire cat grin and didn't say a word when I pushed through the group of Marines. The more the guys questioned me the more I put on that smug, self-satisfied smile on my face, shaking my head back and forth.

"C'mon, we know ya made out, tell us about it!" Was the common plea as the throng followed me below decks toward the Marine compartment.

By now I knew I had to keep the ruse going so I stopped by the sickbay and disturbed the three corpsmen who were playing Acy-ducy. I asked for the keys to the clap shack. (In these days if you would log in that you'd had sexual intercourse and took the treatment of inserting this tube with a nozzle in your pecker that contained anti-syphilis "Old Joe" and anti gonorrhea "Clap" medication, then you couldn't be court-martialed if you became infected.) One of the corpsmen shouted at me, "Go fuck yourself Egan, you didn't get laid on that fuck'en island!" An indigent chorus behind me yelled out, "He sure as shit did!" I added my two cents worth by saying, "Hey doc, you don't give me the key I'll report to the officer of the deck you didn't allow me the opportunity to protect myself." One of the other corpsman looked up saying, "I'll be a sonofabitch! He did get a piece of ass!" The smart ass doc jumped up and took the key ring from the hook and tossed it to me. "Get your pro kit and get the key back to me right away." The corpsmen were supposed to watch you stick the damn tube up your wang but they were more interested in Acy-ducy. By now the Marine Detachment had grown with a dozen swabs looking on also and the word spread like wild-fire. "A Marine made out on liberty!"

As I knew they would, the guys left me to my privacy to put the medicine in. Yeah, sure I did. I went through the routine of logging my name on the "Clap Board" since I knew it would be looked at by half the crew before we got back to Pearl Harbor. After putting down my name, rank, serial number and job location, I had to fill in the time of my "exposer" and all the details I could remember. I thought the gals name Tania had an exotic sound to it and I made her around 18 years old and that I'd spent a couple of hours with her and "exposed" myself a total of three times. Hey, if you're going to be a stud, go all the way!

By reveille the next morning I was a celebrity! Or to tell what the swabs were saying, "The only crew member to get screwed in Samoa and a fucking Marine at that!"

Even my commanding officer and executive officer winked at me with sly smiles. The first sergeant and gunny just shook their heads every time they saw me. As I stood night watch in the gun tub with the rest of my crew I would have to recount over and over again, in detail, ("Hey sarge go slower!") every moment of my nooky liberty. This went on for days and they never grew tired at hearing the same old shit.

The grand slam of this farce came the third night back at sea. We had this gunnery officer, a Navy commander, who hated Marines with a purple passion. The scuttlebutt had it that a Marine had knocked up his daughter in Norfolk. One thing was for certain: he would go out of his way to catch a Marine goofing off. He'd prowl around the ship at night and sneak up on the Marine gun crews, hoping to find someone napping so he could write them up. The gun tub I was in charge of was located right under the bridge and around 2330 I'm leaning on the gun shield looking out at the dark waters of the ocean when I felt the presence of a person standing next to me. I turned my head, and there stood the Navy commander who hated Marines. He leans on the shield and at first doesn't say a word. I didn't move or say anything because naturally an enlisted slob doesn't say a word to an officer unless addressed first. After a full minute he says, "Nice evening, huh sergeant?"

"Yes sir, it certainly is," I replied.

Then he offers me this big grin and says, "I hear you made out the other day on liberty. How was it?"

On Friday, November the 13th, 1942 Japanese planes attacked the U.S.S. San Francisco off Guadalcanal. Platoon Sergeant John Egan's gun tub took a direct hit. Five of his men of his gun crew was killed and he was seriously wounded. John spent the next year and a half in various naval hospitals. He was discharged from the Marine Corps due to disability in February 1944. In his own words, he writes, "There I was a 19 year old ex-platoon sergeant let loose on the world with no education or job skills except in weaponry. You didn't get retired due to combat disability back then, only officers did. I was honorably discharged as unfit for further duty in the United States Marine Corps. I had to rely upon the Veterans Administration to pick up the slack. I guess the VA did a decent job of it as I graduated from college and retired as a high school principal." The 77-year old former Marine platoon sergeant also taught and was an administrator in England, France, Italy, Spain, and Germany. He and his wife spend their time living in England and Concord, California.

98

THE DAY I MET GOMER PYLE
Chief Petty Officer Donald A. Bowerman, U. S. Coast Guard Reserve

Before enlisting into the Coast Guard in 1983 I served a four-year hitch in the Navy during the Vietnam War. I was a Quartermaster 3rd Class aboard the aircraft carrier U.S.S. Midway (CVA-41) and during the spring and summer of 1971 spent an extended tour in the Tonkin Gulf which we called Yankee Station. An important part of my job as quartermaster was positioning in the navigation sense. In other words where the ship was at which was much the same as land navigation with a compass although a lot more intricate.

On this particular day, I was standing the 1200-1600 watch on the Navigation Bridge and I had relieved my predecessor early due to wanting to prepare the 1200 ships position for the captain. I gathered all the necessary information in the chart house and went onto the bridge to our plotting table that laid the chart we were using that day. Now determining a ship's position is not exactly a piece of cake, even in the modern era of the 1960's and 70's. We were still trained in the use of the age old mariner's sextant to "shoot" stars but our job was made easier by satellite-positioning equipment.

I worked on the chart for a few minutes in the quiet confines of the bridge. The captain was sitting in his sea chair looking out at the absolutely gorgeous day and his Marine orderly, a lance corporal, was standing behind the skipper a few feet at parade rest also gazing out at the cobalt blue water. All of our birds were in the air and the ballet of men and their equipment on the flight deck below me was relatively quiet too. I picked up my sextant and headed out to the wing bridge for a final reading. I walked through the pilot house past the young Marine to the port side hatch that was open. I paused for a long moment before I stepped out of the hatch to survey all that was around me. What a beautiful day at sea, I thought to myself. The ocean was like glass, one of those times when there was not a ripple or swell in sight; as flat as a shimmering mirror. The balmy temperature and other forces of nature had caused seaweed and kelp to rise from the ocean's floor and form row after row of almost straight lines on the sun-sparkled surface of the water. It almost looked as if mothernature had taken a huge ruler and lined up the rows of kelp and seaweed. For a brief moment it seemed to picturesque and serene to be a wartime scenario. The skipper brought me out of my reverie by rustling in his high chair and making a low grunting sound. I quickly took my reading and returned to my chart.

I was busily engaged in transferring the position data I had collected onto the chart when someone tapped me on my shoulder. Looking up, I saw the young Marine lance corporal standing at my side. He was a good looking kid of about six feet and was about picture perfect as a recruiting poster when it came to his uniform appearance. Although

I'd seen him many times I really didn't know him other than having heard scuttlebutt that some of the other sea going Marines called him Gomer, I suppose after the Gomer Pyle TV sitcom. I gave him a questioning look and he said in his thick southern drawl, "I've been a'watch'en yew guys do that chart work stuff fer a long time, and ah was jus a'wander'en how ya'all is able to figure out whar we's at?"

Now in all honesty I've got to say that I've never been into "Marine Bashing" and I'm not generally prone to instantaneous brilliance, but this was too good to pass up. I stood up, and in a serious tone of voice, said, "You see those lines out there on the water." I pointed a finger at the rows of kelp and seaweed. "Now look down here at my chart. See these lines that's on the chart?" (I was referring to the latitude and longitude lines on the chart.) "Now when these lines intersect with those markers you see out there on the ocean, that tells us where we are once I write down all the numbers."

His reply remains engraved in my memory and I knew instantly why his buddies called him Gomer. "Well golly, an' ah thought what ya'all did was really tuff!"

The captain again stirred in his sea chair and I was just able to hear him mumble, "It's time to get a new orderly."

I don't know if my dumb little joke had anything to do with it or not, but I never saw the lance corporal on bridge watch with the skipper after that day.

Don Bowerman also did a two-year hitch with the Army reserve before finally making a military reserve career with the Coast Guard. He is currently a special agent with the Coast Guard Investigative Service and works out of New Orleans. However, he calls home Branson, Missouri. Don retired from the Jackson County, Missouri Sheriff's Department in 1996. Single, he is an active Mason and Shriner and life member of the VFW and American Legion. Don enjoys photography and messing around with small boats. He also collects antiquities and is very active in his church, especially in the area of youth and family camping.

99

MY ENTIRE ENLISTMENT WAS A SEA STORY
Former PFC Joseph N. DuCanto, USMC

I was orphaned as an infant and spent my childhood in a Utica, New York orphanage for a number of years before being "farmed out" to several foster homes. When I turned 16 on March 18, 1943, I decided it was time for me to strike out on my own and I appeared at the Marine Corps recruiting office, Syracuse, New York with an altered baptismal certificate. The recruiter sort of shook his head at my skinny, short frame, and said, "You know son you've got to be five feet four inches and weigh one-hundred twenty pounds." I knew this already and had been stuffing myself with bread and bananas to help fill out my 113 pounds. Just the same I approached the scales that had a height measurement attachment with some trepidation. The Navy corpsman stared at me a long moment and he too shook his head. Telling me to get up on the scales I watched the corpsman fiddle with the counterweights that kept balancing at the 115 mark. He looked at me again, then measured my height as I stood on my toes. It took the corpsman a long moment and he again shook his head then whispered to me, "Step down son." In a louder tone of voice he shouted out, "One-hundred twenty pounds and five feet four inches." In retrospect I suppose that corpsman was not only being merciful to a wannabe, but also figured I hadn't grown to my fullness and would probably gain an inch or two in the maturation process. I joke about it now that the humping of a heavy pack and equipment, sometimes exceeding my entire body weight, has kept my height forever below 5' 4".

I arrived at Parris Island, South Carolina boot camp with a cacophony of orders harshly conveyed to all of us "puke" civilians like me who dared enter the domain of real Marines. It was at this time that I was also introduced to my first of many living legends of the Corps: Master Gunnery Sergeant Leland "Lou" Diamond. Lou Diamond entered the Corps in the first decade of the 20th Century and had served continuously for 40 years by the time I saw him. He was a legendary member of the First Marine Division Weapons Company on Guadalcanal and was a spectacular mortar man, reputedly being able to place an 81mm mortar straight down a Japanese stack of a ship at better than a 1,000 yards. He was in charge of the delousing plant at PI and there he stood, with his gray goatee, dressed in starched khaki, bedecked in fruit salad from World War I, the Banana Wars, China duty and "The Canal," looking straight at me and glowering in a booming voice. "Move it boot, or I'll hit you in the ass with a crowbar!"

Our senior DI was Sergeant Peterson, who was an old salt. The two junior DI's, both PFC's, were products of "the new Corps" and didn't look much older than some of the boots. I suspect the boot camp experience my platoon went through was better than most during that period because we happened to have a boot by the name of Frank Knox with us. Frank was the nephew of his namesake who was then the Secretary of the Navy, Frank Knox, who just happened to be a close personal friend and confidant of President

Franklin D. Roosevelt. The only serious confrontation I had with Sergeant Peterson was when he had me standing tall in his office wanting to know why I didn't sign up for the $10,000 G.I. life insurance, which the Corps took $3.60 a month from our merger monthly pay to keep in force. After I explained to the senior DI that I was an orphan and did not have anyone in particular that I wished to benefit one cent from my possible demise, he had a quick answer for me that I've always remembered. "Do you know what a point-man is DeCanto?" Not waiting for me to answer he went on. "A point-man is sent out of twenty or thirty yards or more ahead of a rifle platoon to seek out possible enemy contact and/or ambush. When the shooting starts, he is usually among the first to get it! Let me tell ya how we designate a point-man boot. He's the guy without G.I. insurance!" Suffice to say, that I quickly signed the authorization card.

Following a ten day leave after boot camp I reported to Camp Lejeune, North Carolina for advanced infantry training which turned out to be a very short ten day course in becoming familiar with light infantry weapons, such as the BAR, 30 caliber machine gun, flame thrower, grenade launchers and booby traps. Then, herded onto rail cars for a lengthy journey across our great nation to Camp Pendleton, California. It was in the little burg of Oceanside just outside of Pendleton that I met and shook hands with another legend of the Marine Corps, Gunnery Sergeant John "Manila John" Basilone. Manila John Basilone was the first World War II Marine enlisted man to be awarded the Medal of Honor. His amazing display of courage on Guadalcanal where he all but single handed stopped Japanese units with his heavy machine guns from taking Henderson Field not only got him the Medal of Honor, it also demanded that he be brought back to the United States to help with the War Bond drive. Basilone hated this assignment and later managed to overcome strong opposition by getting himself assigned to the Fifth Marine Division that was being formed at Camp Pendleton, when I met him. John was posthumously awarded the Navy Cross for his courage on Iwo Jima. His widow, former Woman Marine Sergeant Lena Basilone, recently died at age 86. Lena was once asked why she had not remarried. Her simple reply said it all: "Once you had the best, you can't settle for less." The twenty minutes I spent with Manila John Basilone is remembered as vividly this day as it was 55 years ago.

I, along with 2,000 Marines and 500 Naval corpsmen sailed from San Diego on the HMS Blumfontain, a converted Dutch merchant vessel taken over by the British. Our Marine contingent was designated as "First Replacement Draft." This clearly spelled out to me that we were being sent to "replace" someone who was not or would no longer be there when we arrived. My temporary platoon leader turned out to be a national football hero from Notre Dame, Angelo Bertelli, who was the sensational 1943 Heisman Trophy winner. Lieutenant Bertelli was a very amiable guy who smoked those wavy Italian cigars which are dipped in some exotic elixir that I'm sure could be mistaken today as a Mexican laughing weed. He did his job with panache and was well liked by his fellow officers and members of his platoon. However, there was one incident that took place that still cracks me up every time I think about it. Lieutenant Bertelli decided to hold a rifle inspection between the hatches and gunnels of the ship. Our rifles were in terrible shape and our "nice guy" platoon leader was reaming out every Marine, one by one, as he inspected their M-1's. When he got to this young Marine standing near the railing and looked at his rifle, the lieutenant went ballistic, and rightfully so. This kids rifle was encrusted with rust and it was a newly issued weapon. Lieutenant Bertelli screamed at the kid as he shoved the rifle back to him, "If I had a rifle that looked like that piece of shit, I'd throw it overboard!" The kid shrugged, then tossed his rifle in the ocean! As the next man in formation I had trouble getting my rifle to inspection arms since I was about to bend over to keep from laughing a belly laugh. I'll never forget the expression on Lieutenant Bertelli's face if I live to be a hundred and ten. The lieutenant halted the inspection and called for the officer of the deck who took the kid away somewhere. We never saw him again.

I was making my way up a ships ladder one day when Lieutenant Bertelli braced me and told me he'd heard that there was an underage Marine in his platoon. Because of my youthful appearance when demanded to know if it was me. By this time I was a "legal" 17 and in no danger of being discharged, so I told him the truth that it wasn't me. What I did not tell the lieutenant was that I knew who he was looking for. This 15 year old was a throwaway kid of the depression years, meaning he'd been on his own since age 12. He was a hulk of a guy, over six feet and being unusually large for his age had successfully enlisted in the merchant marine at age 12 and survived two round trips between New York City and Mermansk, Russia. Enlisting into the Marine Corps at 14 his intention was to make a career of it. After Iwo Jima I went looking for him at his new unit and was told he did not make it. Boy soldiers, as Colonel David H. Hackworth, a well-known military commentator constantly emphasized, are the best in battle, since they fear nothing, have no concept of the future, and lack the judgmental concerns that older warriors exercise.

Our arrival at Guam occurred at the commencement of the rainy season. I soon learned that difference between the "dry season" and the "rainy season" was that during the dry season it only rained once a day. Organized resistance on Guam had supposed to have ended on August 10, 1944. However, no one had told the Japanese hold-outs this and the Third Marine Division continued to mount patrols to dig them out of the jungle. Many of the guys I had came across with were assigned to the First Marine Provisional Brigade that was then forming into the Sixth Marine Division. In my case I found myself standing in front of an officious NCO who was scanning my Service Record Book to decide where to put me. He spotted something in my SRB and looked up. He turned and yelled over his shoulder, "Hey, Jake, here's a kid from your home town!"

Jake turned out to be an "old man" of 29 years of age wearing the stripes of a Tech Sergeant. I soon learned that he had graduated from Syracuse University, had turned down a commission, and had married a girl from my hometown whose family I knew. He was the Headquarters Company Gunny of the Pioneer-Engineer Battalion, Third Marine Division, and he told the clerk corporal to assign me to his outfit. Assignment to the Pioneer-Engineers was eminently more safe for a raw green replacement like me than straight infantry duty, but it was not all hearts and flowers. Even though Guam was supposed to have been secure we still sit up nightly ambushes on trails and watering spots. My first few weeks of manning a light 30-caliber machine gun in the jungle every night, with all the various noises was very unnerving. On my second night out on ambush I heard approaching footsteps crashing through the brush that led me to believe a frontal attack was taking place. I opened up with my air-cooled machine gun that was met with the most unearthly screams I'd ever heard. Complete silence prevailed after the other green-horns in the ambush, along with me, was ordered to cease fire. We were all basket cases and not about to venture out into the jungle to find out what had made those hideous screams. As the morning sun began to show through the thick canopy of vegetation, we saw spread before us not more than ten feet a huge water buffalo lying on its back with all four legs pointed straight up. But my faux pas did not end in a chewing out. Marines are not known to waste anything and we spent the morning hacking up the beast to sizable slugs of rich red meat that had been missing from our diet for a long time. The "Battle of Buffalo Springs" spread throughout the division. A couple of the more humorous aspects during this "lull" took place inside our battalion camp area. On at least four occasions we found Japanese stragglers enjoying our out-door movies with us and twice they were episodes of Japanese soldiers standing in our chow lines to get something to eat. But the classic took place when Betty Hutton, Bob Hope and Betty Grable visited us with their USO show. Caught right in the front row was a Japanese sergeant who spoke perfect English, having been educated in the United States. It was rumored that Bob Hope told the brass to go easy on the nip soldier, alleging saying, "If they like me that much, maybe I can be a secret weapon for you fellows." The punch line to this was the supposed reply from a general officer. "So you don't think his presences had anything to do with the two Betty's?"

Just before we mounted out for Iwo Jima, who in the world joined our outfit than my old DI, now Platoon Sergeant Peterson. I mean what are the odds of this happening? I suppose in some instances this would have been a "boots" dream if he was inclined to seek revenge for past humiliations. Not so, in our case. Sergeant Peterson was genuinely pleased to see me as I was him. Our initial somewhat stiff meeting quickly gave way to comradely acceptance, and we became for a brief time good friends. He was assigned as a platoon sergeant with the 21st Marines and, on Iwo Jima, became by default a platoon leader. Demonstrating to the end what a great Marine he was, Platoon Sergeant Peterson was posthumously awarded the Navy Cross for extraordinary heroism.

No spot on Iwo Jima was ever truly safe so long as one Japanese rifleman or artillery spotter was left alive. The beaches were like a magnet painted with one big bull's-eye. Our most immediate nemesis was Mt. Suribachi, which stood astride of the beach area where my unit, the Pioneers, which was attached to the 21st Marines, was located. You can imagine the sighs of relief and joy when the flag went up at Suribachi, evoking great cheers from the troops on the beach, with ships' whistles and horn blaring throughout the anchorage. For most of us, I believe, the raising of the flag renewed our confidence that despite the cost, we would ultimately conquer the island. The most remarkable thing that happened to me had to do with my fox hole I'd dug in the fine lava sand. (It was digging a hole in a wheat pit.) I had no sooner finished my hole and was standing in it when the Japanese opened up with a furious mortar barrage. Four of my buddies was standing next to this Marine truck when the mortar barrage commenced and they all dove in my hole right on top of me. A mortar round made a direct hit on the truck that sent out even more shrapnel. Every Marine on top of me was seriously wounded and all I got was a terrible blast in the ears.

After Iwo we returned to Guam to stage for the invasion of Japan. The first thing I noticed was how much everyone had changed. My comrades from Iwo all seemed sullen and our new replacements all seemed like a bunch of immature kids. I puzzled about this for several days when it finally hit me. It wasn't the people around me that had changed, it was me! I was no longer a young boy and the near-death experiences I had went through matured me practically overnight. Young boys grow to be old young boys in a hurry in war and it wised me up as no other event in my life has. Being a United States Marine is the greatest thing that ever happened to me.

One last event took place on Guam that I will tell about. In early July 1945, a company runner came looking for me and informed me there was a swabby who was asking for me at the company command post. When I arrived at the CP I found a young man from my home town who's older brother was a good friend of mine. He was off the battle cruiser U.S.S. Indianapolis which was getting ready to depart Guam and he'd taken the time to look me up. The sailor and I spent the day together catching up on what our mutual friends were doing, etc. I never saw him again because unfortunately, my hometown acquaintance was not among those saved when a Japanese submarine torpedoed the U.S.S. Indianapolis.

Joe DuCanto ended up in China with the 6th Marine Division after the 3rd was deactivated. Upon his return to the United States and an honorable discharge, he attended Antioch College and the Law School of the University of Chicago. He has practiced law in Chicago ever since and was selected as one of "the best Lawyers in America" by the American Bar Association. DuCanto has devoted himself to many Marine causes, including membership upon the National Board of the Marine Corps Scholarship Foundation. He divides his time between his law practice and his private detective and security firm, which employs 700 people, operating in five Midwestern states. Ironically, Joe DuCanto, gave a speech, as the guest of honor to Marine Air Control Group 48, Fourth Marine Aircraft Wing's November 1999 Marine Birthday Ball at Highwood, Illinois, in which he titled his talk, "Sea Stories." His contribution to this book are excerpts from that speech.

100

THOSE DARING YOUNG MEN IN THEIR FLYING MACHINES

Former Warrant Officer Two Robert Donald Upchurch, U.S. Army

For reasons that should be obvious (considering the causalities) the United States Army had a crash-course helicopter pilot training program during the sixties and seventies in which kids per se were rushed through a "shake and bake" flight school at Fort Rucker, Alabama. At age 20 I was a product of this required need and no sooner did I have wings pinned on my chest along with gold and red warrant officer one bars that orders were issued sending me to Viet Nam. I was assigned as a "Dust-off" pilot with the 57th Dust Off Squadron supporting the 105th Army Field Hospital, located at Can Tho, in IV Corps, which was about 200 miles south of Saigon. My mission was simple. When me and my crew was on the flight roster and the call came in that causalities required helicopter medevac, I cranked up my old Huey and away we went. The Huey I flew was a beat up old bird almost as old as I was. And during my first six months in the Nam I aged the helicopter a little more by having to fly into some pretty hairy and hot LZ's. Fortunately, I had an outstanding flight chief who was a few years older than me and who damn well showed his age. But Specialist Five Joe Cornell kept our Huey glued together with the help of ground crew mechanics. Even though my bird looked like death warmed over and rattled a little and whistled from patched up gunshot holes when in the air, she was a good ship which handled great and caused me no serious flying problems except when wounded. My favorite enlisted medic was Specialist Five Bob Worley and he too looked older than me and my co-pilot, CWO-1 John Travers. John and I where both baby faces and looked liked we should have been racing soap box derby cars instead of sitting in the flight seats of a Huey. We were both good pilots however and considering this fact, plus the thousands of hours we had flown together in combat situations, we were also both cocky to the nth degree. Although being a Dust-off pilot was stressful to say the least, when you're young and cocky you find ways to ease the tension. Sometimes daring, even by military standards. Like the time I used an unarmed "Bird Dog" observation plane to act like it was making a strafing run against the enemy by firing its marker rockets so I could slip into an impossible LZ to get wounded soldiers. My superiors didn't know whether to court-martial me or give me an award for that little stunt, but it turned out I received the Distinguished Flying Cross.

In early 1970 I had just turned 21 when I came up with a small fun-stunt to help maintain our sanity. I pulled this caper with the assistance of the other guys a half-dozen times and it always cracked us up and kept our morale going.

On the days we were off the flight roster did not mean we could laze around and drink beer or whatever. No, the Army kept us busy with "Milk-run" administrative or logistic flights until we were once again placed on the Dust-off roster. Our usual rotation was four days on and three days off: from Dust Off's that is. (I picked up over 5,000 casualties during my tour, so that tells you right there we were kept busy.) A lot of the admin flights took us to Saigon to pickup new personnel just arriving in-country and transport them back to the hospital and it was during these type flights when we played our little game. I'll tell you about one of them and let you figure out the reaction of the people involved.

This one particular day me and my crew was ordered to Saigon to pick up a couple of nurses and a new doctor who were fresh out of the in processing center at Tan Son Nhut Airfield. FNG's if you know the term. As soon as I landed the Huey the four of us Huey crewmen switched our flight suits. I put on Spec-5 Cornell's uniform and he put on mine. The same went with CWO Travers who donned Doc Worley's flight suit and vice versa. By now the two enlisted men were so accustomed to their roll as acting like warrant officers that there was not the slightest hitch when the doctor major and two female first lieutenant nurses came running out to the pad. Joe and Bob greeted the three officers, shook their hands and welcomed them aboard. To make sure the ruse looked real me and John even loaded up their gear on the Huey, playing the roll of peons. As soon as the three passengers were seated, I offer Joe Cornell a wave of the hand and say, "I'll take her up Mister Upchurch." This always got a head-jerking stare when I'd go pass the officers and climb into the pilots seat, my enlisted rank clearly visible. And it never failed that the officers would look at Bob who was wearing my flight suit with an odd expression, but he'd just smile at them with a silly grin and shrug his shoulders. Of course, the new officers couldn't fail but to notice that the enlisted medic was sitting in the co-pilots seat and the warrants were in the back. The real medic, now acting like CWO-1 John Travers, would casually reassure the newbies that it was okay as him and Upchurch needed some rest and the enlisted men would make the run to the base hospital. "It's only two hundred miles and they can make it in less than two hours."

Naturally the flight home was full of low level tree skimming, river skimming flight with an occasional jump in altitude I called the "Yo Yo" maneuver, and of course one of the "Warrant Officers" in back just had to get in some weapons testing. All for the education and entertainment of the three officers who were experiencing their first time over the wire.

Their pale, terrified facial expressions buoyed our spirits with surpassed amusement.

When we arrived at Can Tho the two nurses and doctor major shakily deplaned and made a bee-line to the hospital commander's office. Colonel La Fave listened to the harrowing rendition of the flight and how his newest replacements narrowly escaped death. I would surmise the three new officers had a problem of comprehension when they saw their new commander start grinning as they told their story of the crazy warrants letting the enlisted men fly the Huey. By the time they had finished telling of this life threatening episode Colonel La Fave was laughing out loud. He waved a hand of the three officers, saying, "They do that all the time, it's okay, welcome to Viet Nam!"

==

Upchurch goes by his middle name Don accumulated two Bronze Star Medals with V and 23 Air Medals in addition to his DFC while in Vietnam. Born in Carthage, Tennessee, Don returned to his place of enlistment, Indianapolis, Indiana, upon his discharge from the Army. He received a master degree in social work and psychology and currently works with homeless veterans in the Marion County area of Indiana. He is married to Janet and they have four children, two daughters and two sons.

101

SOMETIMES MESSING WITH MARINES CAN COME BACK TO HAUNT YOU
Former Quartermaster 1/C George R. Sharrow, U.S.N.

I was serving with a Navy underwater demolition team (UDT) in the mid 1950's when orders came down from ComPhibLant (Commander, Amphibious Forces Atlantic) that my team would support A Navy/Marine Corps mock beach assault exercise in the Caribbean Sea. Marines of the 2nd Marine Division, Camp Lejeune, North Carolina would invade Vieques Island off Puerto Rico.

The UDT team I was assigned to had been through these type exercises before and pretty well knew what to expect.

The amphibious exercise commenced as we knew it would be by a "friendly" naval fleet ships staging a mock invasion feint by appearing just over the horizon about ten miles from Vieques, giving the "enemy" the opportunity to see all the war ships. Then the fleet did a disappearing act by heading out to sea. In a real life situation this was supposed to give a defending enemy the thought that nothing was really going to take place at their particular location and they were being by-passed. I don't know if the battalion of Marines on Vieques which acted the roll of aggressor forces knew this fleet action was a feint action or not. My UDT team did because this was the time for us to go to work. As soon as the fleet faded out of sight an APD (converted destroyer) would come in close and lower a Mike-boat five miles away from the intended landing beach. The Mike-boat was a World War II type of landing craft used by UDT teams. Then the Mike-boat would drop off the six man UDT team a mile or so out and await to pick us up. Our mission was to swim ashore and recon the beach, set our charges on any underwater obstacles, then hide out somewhere in our Mike-boat until the pre-dawn landings scheduled three days later. For five hours the six of us UDT's worked our butts off doing our simulated mission. With our work accomplished it was time to rest and have some fun because we didn't have nothing else to do for the remaining exercise. The Mike-boat coxswain found a secluded and sheltered cove about a mile from the landing beach where we set up camp for our three day wait. The boat had a canvas tarp covering its open deck area to protect us from rain and sun and under the tarp we had folding cots and sleeping bags, plus other little comforts to get us by.

Two hours after dropping anchor a couple of the guys got hungry and went to our food box to get some canned chow. Much to our surprise and dismay some wise guy somewhere had replaced all of our tins of food with gallon size cans of figs. Figs! We couldn't frigging believe it! We were all chowhounds and eating figs for three days isn't exactly what we had in mind. Getting some real food became an immediate priority but we had a small problem to fulfill that need. We were not to be seen or heard by anyone until the exercise was completed.

Like all elite outfits we used the thought process that the difficult we do immediately, the impossible takes a little longer. Luckily for us we had a Chief Boatswains Mate on our team who came up with the solution to do the impossible.

Chief "Red" Allison had spent a lot of time in the Caribbean on APA's that are troop ships used primarily by the Marines. He knew of a small island not far away where the Marines had a tent city set up near a Naval installation known as Roosevelt Rhodes. Chief Red told us the officers even had their own mess tent and sort of a club which was located away from the main encampment. The chief figured there was enough food and beer in this officer's tent to sustain us during our stay. Like the good UDT's we were we quickly devised a raiding plan.

Without going into great detail, we pulled off our raid on that officers mess tent and managed to acquire a canned ham, other canned food stuffs, and three cases of beer. I will say that we did such a good job that no one saw or heard us during this escapade even though United States Marines heavily guarded the area. Once back to our boat we put all the loot into a cargo net and sunk it next to the anchor in fifteen feet of water.

The next day all hell broke loose at the Marine encampment. When the Marine Mess Officer found out about the missing food and beer there was a shake down of every tent on the island. And when that inspection didn't produce the missing items or culprits a massive search was conducted throughout the various small islands. Now you're asking yourself, how did I know this? A simple answer because a squad of Marines who were patrolling the beach line in their own Mike-boat found us. They just knew they'd found the guilty party and came into our cove acting like a bunch of real badasses. I guess they couldn't be faulted for being in a pissed off mood considering all the bull shit their Mess Officer was putting them through. Suffice to say, we sailors played the innocent roll to the hilt and was very indigent when the Jarheads insisted they be allowed to search our boat. Naturally, Chief Red finally gave in and told them to "knock themselves out but you ain't going to find anything." And naturally they didn't since what they were looking for was fifteen under water. After a half-hour all the Marines got back into their boat and returned to their base as very unhappy campers. The remainder of our stay on Vieques was very pleasant, eating good chow and drinking good beer, thanks to the U. S. Marines.

That little incident took place some forty-five years ago when I was a lad of twenty years.

During June 1999, while attending a United States Navy League meeting at the officers club at the Mechanicsburg, Pennsylvania Navy Supply Depot, I was sitting at a table with seven other league members enjoying an after dinner drink and telling sea stories. When it came to my turn, I related the story about raiding the Marine Officers Mess on Roosevelt Rhodes. Everyone at the table got a charge out of my tale——except for this retired Marine colonel who began mumbling to himself. He was visibly upset after having heard my story.

A pal of his asked, "What the hell is wrong with you Steve?"

The retired colonel looked right at me, his face so red I thought for a moment he was having a stroke. "Sharrow's you sonofabitch," he yelled at me. "I was duty Mess Officer and Security Officer when you bastards stole that stuff. I always knew it was you f"ing UDT's but couldn't prove it! You have no idea the crap that came down on me because of that stunt, you SOB."

After a few seconds of stunned silence, the entire table cracked up, except for the colonel and me since I was as amazed at the incredible coincidence as he was pissed off. To soothe the colonel's pissed off mood I bought a round of drinks for everyone at our table and things started chilling down, so I went into greater detail how we carried out the raid. Everyone again had a big laugh at the colonel's expense and he had little choice but to find the humor in it also.

Ironic isn't it? How our past seems to catch up to us! And it also proves, that messing with Marines can sometimes come back to haunt you.

===

George Sharrow enlisted into the Navy in August 1951. Honorabley discharged in August 1955 he attended Millersville University in Lancaster, Pennsylvania and founded Sharrow Janitorial Service in 1973. Retired now, his business continues with his son Jeff at the helm and his wife Joanne as the CEO. George is the author of White Hats of the Navy and he graciously authorized a spin off from one of his stories in that book to be shared here. He has also written several other books and recently formed Sharrow Publications for the publication, sale and marketing of his books.

ABOUT THE AUTHOR

Donald F. Myers was born and raised in Indianapolis, Indiana. On 20 February 1952 at age seventeen he enlisted in the U.S.Marine Corps. His overseas duties include Korea, Japan, Okinawa, the China Sea and over two-years combat duty in Vietnam. He also served at the Naval Mine Depot, Yorktown, Virginia, Camp Elmore, Norfolk, Virginia, Camp Lejeune, North Carolina and Camp Pendleton, California. Myers was a member of the Inspector-Instructor staff, Indianapolis, Indiana for four years prior to his medical retirement from the Corps on 30 April 1973.

A graduate of Arsenal Technical High School of Indianapolis, Myers also attended East Carolina College and successfully completed the College Proficiency Examination Program through the University of the State of New York.

The U. S. Department of Veterans Affairs (VA) employed Myers after leaving the Corps. In 1990, he retired from the VA as a senior counselor. Indiana Governor Evan Bayh awarded Myers Indiana's highest award, the Sagamore of the Wabash upon his retirement from the VA. At retirement after twenty-three years of service with the Indiana Guard Reserve, Colonel Myers was awarded the Indiana Distinguished Service Medal. He is also a Kentucky Colonel and holds the Gold Distinguished Citizen medal.

Besides writing books and articles Don Myers volunteers twenty-five hours a week to the Hoosier Veterans Assistance Foundation that helps homeless veterans. He is active in several veterans organizations and is the National Public Relations Director for the Marine Corps League.

A father of two sons and three daughters Myers resides with his wife Dorothy in Franklin Township, a suburb on the southeast side of Indianapolis.

SEND A BOOK TO A FRIEND

If you enjoyed 101 Sea Stories and would like to share the book with a friend, please send a check or money order made out to ALMAR Books for $22.95 (includes postage and handling) and mail to ALMAR Books, 5342 Elmwood Ave., Suite G, Indianapolis, IN 46203.

Send a note that you want 101 Sea Stories. If you want it sent directly to an individual give name and address and ALMAR will mail it to them along with a personal autograph from the author. Please print or write clearly.

You can also send a friend an autographed copy of Donald F. Myers' YOUR WAR—MY WAR, A Marine In Vietnam. This award-winning book is also $22.95.